THE INTELLECTUAL SITUATION

P.S. 1 Symposium: A Practical Avant-Garde

What We Should Have Known: Two Discussions

What Was the Hipster? A Sociological Investigation

The Trouble Is the Banks: Letters to Wall Street

No Regrets: Three Discussions

Buzz: A Play

Other Russias

Canon/Archive: Studies in Quantitative Formalism

The Earth Dies Streaming: Film Writing, 2002–2018

Missing Time: Essays

THE INTELLECTUAL SITUATION

THE BEST OF N+1'S SECOND DECADE

EDITED BY MARK KROTOV, NIKIL SAVAL, AND DAYNA TORTORICI

n+1 BOOKS

n+1 FOUNDATION   NEW YORK

Published 2024 by n+1 Foundation

37 Greenpoint Avenue #316, Mailbox 18

Brooklyn, New York 11222

www.nplusonemag.com

ISBN 978-1-953813-11-4

Printed by the Sheridan Press

Manufactured in the United States of America

Design by Rachel Ossip

First Printing

The n+1 Foundation's programs are made possible in part by the New York State Council on the Arts with the support of the Office of the Governor and the New York State Legislature, as well as by public funds from the New York City Department of Cultural Affairs, in partnership with the City Council.

"The Feminist" from Rejection *by Tony Tulathimutte. Copyright 2024 by Tony Tulathimutte. Courtesy of HarperCollins Publishers.*

CONTENTS

INTRODUCTION

N+1 WAS FOUNDED IN 2004 AS A LITTLE MAGAZINE WITH BIG AMBI-
tions that would treat literature, culture, and politics as inextricable
concerns. The goal—or at least one of the goals—was to publish a
Partisan Review for the Bush era. The atmosphere of those years was
credulous, quiescent, anti-intellectual: on the political front, liberal
apologists for the Iraq war drowned out the objections of the marginalized left, and on the cultural front, regressive sentimentalism so
dominated American fiction that you couldn't throw a stone without hitting a precocious child narrator. Surely, the founding editors
thought, we can do better than this. *n+1* would be a home for readers
and writers who were tired of being encouraged not to think.

Within a decade, *n+1* had given rise to a new generation of literary intellectuals. ("So many good writers have come tumbling out of
that small journal in the past few years that it's begun to resemble an
intellectual clown car," wrote the *New York Times* book critic Dwight
Garner in 2014.) Essayists, journalists, critics, scholars, and fiction
writers found in the magazine an opportunity to take risks, to treat
their ideas seriously, and to connect their experiences to the broader
social and political environment. Writers like Elif Batuman, Kris-
tin Dombek, and Emily Witt, who got their start in *n+1*, went on to
wider and much deserved literary success. Others who had already

published books—Sheila Heti, Vladimir Sorokin, Siddhartha Deb, and Rebecca Curtis among them—found critical support from the magazine at important moments in their writing lives, and published some of their weirdest and most distinctive work in *n+1*.

Yet despite the magazine's many discoveries, and its gift for cultivating new writers, *n+1* remained best known for the editorial voice of the Intellectual Situation, the opening section of the magazine written by the editors. These short essays marry high theory and street-level observation to examine the defining yet undertheorized features of contemporary life. Early Intellectual Situations thought through climate change and the French sex novel, economic collapse and Gchat, with equal humor and authority, and aimed to write, as it was happening, a history of the present day—an effort that could just as well describe the mission of the magazine as a whole.

That mission held true into *n+1*'s second decade, which is why we chose to call this anthology *The Intellectual Situation*. Each piece included here poses a question that was central to its time, capturing what it was like to be alive and thinking from 2014 to 2024. But there is also some irony to our choice. During this period, the unified voice of the Intellectual Situation began to crack open, often in illuminating and suggestive ways. The personified, editorial "we" from which the section had traditionally been written—often to the irritation of readers, who wondered who exactly this "we" was—gave way to individually authored essays by editors who found more texture and frankness in the first-person singular. (See Dayna Tortorici's "In the Maze," about the culture of male resentment surrounding #MeToo, and Nikil Saval's "Canvassing," his account of knocking on doors for the Bernie Sanders campaign, which prefigured his own successful run for Pennsylvania state senate in 2020.) Not coincidentally, the editorial board was becoming more diverse. Coming up through the ranks at *n+1* was a generation of young editors—us—who shared our predecessors' dry Jewish humor and small-c catholic tastes, but brought with us new perspectives and commitments—particularly feminism, organized labor, and global social movements.

If the writing published under this new generation bears the imprint of the external world more clearly than before, perhaps it's because there was more world to contend with. The decade this anthology spans saw some of the most extraordinary political developments in modern American history. Black Lives Matter, the resurgence of organized labor, the campaigns of Bernie Sanders and the presidency of Donald Trump, the #MeToo movement, the ascent of the far right as a force in the streets and in the courts, the social and economic shockwaves of Covid in the US and around the world, the acceleration of the climate crisis, the housing crisis, and the care crisis, and the horrors and realignments following October 7—inevitably, these events pressed themselves into the work of *n+1*'s writers.

Christina Nichol's "An Account of My Hut" finds bleak comedy and strains of hope as California burns and becomes increasingly unaffordable. Sarah Resnick's "H." follows the author's uncle, an aging man with an opioid addiction, through the crumbling welfare and health-care systems of New York City. Dawn Lundy Martin's "When a Person Goes Missing" reflects on the diverging paths of the author and her brother as she attempts to navigate the byzantine jail system into which he has disappeared. Writing in the spring of 2020 from Italy—the first country to enact a nationwide lockdown—Francesco Pacifico captures the emotional and spatial dislocations of the early pandemic in his "Rome Coronavirus Dispatches." All of these essays are "topical," but to describe them as such risks reducing art to information. Each piece is, first and finally, literature.

The entries in this book range in topic and register, personality and mode, but their shared features point to the essential character of *n+1*. They possess, in no particular order, a critical acuity, an attention to rhythm and style, a strong authorial presence, an appropriate sense of stakes, and an unruly streak—some element of strangeness, ambition, or radicalism that in any other publication would have to be sanded down or contained. This last trait may be what most clearly defines *n+1* and its ethos, if only by negation. The pieces of criticism included here—Jesse McCarthy's "Notes on Trap," Nicolás Medina Mora's "In Praise of the Terrorist," A. S. Hamrah's "Heads Without Bodies," and Gabriel Winant's "Not Every Kid-Bond Matures"—surpass the parameters of a typical review. The essays about organizing and left-wing struggle, like Saval's "Canvassing" and Alyssa Battistoni's "Spadework," depict the work from within without the pieties and false optimism of so much movement writing. The short stories by Bela Shayevich, Tony Tulathimutte, and Christine Smallwood all excavate the abject realities of contemporary sexual politics with great comic panache. Lisa Borst and Mark Krotov's "Why Is Everything So Ugly?"—the most recent Intellectual Situation in *The Intellectual Situation*—incisively asks (and answers) the question on everyone's mind, enabling us to see our built environment anew. Grace Glass and Sasha Tycko's panoramic account of the movement to stop Cop City, which closes this collection, fittingly returns to the "we" established by the magazine's early Intellectual Situations—and finds, in the first-person plural, new potentials for collaboration and solidarity.

Few of these pieces could have appeared in another magazine at their time of publication, and all of them are better for it. But publishing the unpublishable can be lonely work. It is also deeply gratifying, especially when the world recognizes the genius of writers we've championed from the beginning. Tobi Haslett's "Magic Actions" remains the best essay published, anywhere, about the George Floyd rebellion. Anna Wiener's "Uncanny Valley," which drew so much traffic it crashed *n+1*'s website for a week, became the basis for a *New York Times* bestselling memoir. Andrea Long Chu's first published essay, "On Liking Women," launched the "second wave" of trans studies, according to the field's founder, Sandy Stone. (Five years later, Chu won a Pulitzer Prize for criticism for her work in *New York*.) The late and very missed Anthony Veasna So's "Superking Son Scores Again" led, in short order, to *Afterparties*, one of the most celebrated story collections of the decade. At last count, forty-seven books have emerged from *n+1* pieces, or are on their way to doing so.

Anthologies aim for completeness but are necessarily selective. This one is no exception, and it leaves out many of the timely interventions published on the *n+1* website. The magazine's considerable body of writing on and from South Asia, Latin America, and the former Soviet Union is only modestly represented. Reviews of novels, nonfiction books, websites, and other magazines constitute some of the finest work we have published, but here are mostly absent. To that end, *The Intellectual Situation* is best understood as a gateway drug to the vast, heady, and impossibly variegated world of the magazine itself.

Marx wrote in *The Eighteenth Brumaire* that men do not make history under circumstances of their own choosing. So it is with magazines. It has become much harder and more expensive to be an independent magazine that does things its own way—especially since *n+1* has over the past two decades become a more serious enterprise with a staff, an office, and, as of a couple of years ago, running water. But we will always be a place for new and veteran contributors who may not have a home in our era's conservative, dwindling, and increasingly stifled media landscape. We will always aspire to be the outlet where writers do their deepest thinking and most ambitious writing. The magazine came into being not just to reckon with the world, but to reconstitute and remake it in our pages. As long as there is a future to fight for, *n+1* will be a part of the fight.

Mark Krotov, Nikil Saval, and Dayna Tortorici
Brooklyn, New York, May 2024

CANVASSING

NIKIL SAVAL

April 5, 2016

It starts with missed calls from unknown area codes. Text messages: *Hey Nikil! Are you FEELING THE BERN as much as I am? There's a new office in South Philadelphia, and a Political Revolution training going on this Saturday. Can you make it?*

For weeks, I haven't been able to make it. I've gone to the website, indicated my willingness to volunteer, emailed the local organizer to explain my background in labor organizing and why this ought to qualify me for a good volunteer position—but there are *n+1* pieces to edit, plus a work trip to California that I've extended into a visit to my in-laws.

By the pool at their house, which fronts a golf course whose sprinklers turn on every ten minutes during the worst drought in California history, the calls and messages fill me with guilt. I recall the times in fall 2011, during the occupation of Philadelphia's City Hall, when I'd do something frivolous, like browse in a bookstore, and be overcome by the shame that attaches to any private activity undertaken in a moment of public upheaval. Or worse, the feeling that intellectual work, even in the service of politics, is useless—that the only thing to do is to give yourself over entirely to the cause.

When Sanders announced his candidacy, I thought it was fun, a lark, a social democratic road bump for the cavalcade leading to the inevitable Clinton coronation. Then came the rallies, the speeches about *democratic socialism*, the debates in which he hectored opponents and declared the country in crisis. I spent some time looking at the left-wing debates online: It's better for the left to organize outside the campaign than fall into the sickly embrace of the Democratic Party. It's better for the left to use the campaign as a platform for getting its ideas out there. Electoral politics won't solve anything. Electoral politics shouldn't be ceded to the neoliberals and the far right. The endless rehearsals of strategy, the sense that every moment is a fork in the road, every decision critical and indelible—I could go back to 1972 and find the same arguments. No wonder everyone gets burned out: a century spent going over the same ground, trashing one another along the way. Why is the question facing the left always, *Is it good for the left?* What about everyone else?

At afternoon drinks at Melvyn's with the in-laws, Trump's name comes up, and before anyone utters the usual imprecations and prayers, I find myself declaiming that the focus on Trump is misguided—that every Republican candidate seeks to destroy Muslims, and for all the outrage over Ted Cruz's proposal to surveil Muslim communities in the wake of the Brussels attacks, even Obama surveils Muslim communities. In fact, the candidate most likely to take the country to war is Hillary Clinton, and America's endless war has always been against anyone with the slightest tincture of melanin, amirite?! The bartender turns, everyone at the bar turns. Everyone is white, their whiteness suddenly startles me—their skin seems drained, sapped. I've fomented an embarrassed silence. My father-in-law, drawing in his breath, waits out a beat. "I think . . ." he says. "I think that's a little extreme."

Extremism in the defense of liberty, et cetera! But my nervous energy has gotten me nowhere and might be better suited to action. I spend the rest of the afternoon embarrassed. Later in the day I return one of the calls—the Bernie volunteer seems momentarily surprised—and sign up for a canvassing shift.

April 9, 2016

The day of my first canvass shift is cold and clouded over, with a chance of rain and possibly snow. I make an extra pot of coffee to compensate for the dread and the instinctive desire to lie down that confronts me every time I undertake some modicum of real political activity. I think of a line from Dickens's *Our Mutual Friend*: "And yet—like us all, when we swoon—like us all, every day of our lives when we wake—he is instinctively unwilling to be restored to the consciousness of this existence, and would be left dormant, if he could."

I walk down Passyunk, past the endless row of restaurants advertising their strong *Inquirer* reviews. (Philadelphia's "rebirth" is chiefly measured in new restaurants; the urban renaissance will come nestled in a warm kohlrabi puree.) Not a single bookstore, but many vintage furniture stores, a vintage scooter store, a vintage bike-bag store. The office possesses the usual provisional atmosphere of campaign offices: posters, pamphlets, picnic tables, images of Bernie's glasses and halo of white hair everywhere among the pizza boxes. A whiteboard asks why YOU support Bernie. "Because he's for WORKING PEOPLE," et cetera. The office is also empty. There's just one extremely young woman there, who's taken off a semester from college in Chicago to work for the campaign. I tell her I've come to canvass, and that I've done it before—a long time ago, for Obama.

She quickly retrains me: Remember to ring the doorbell and also knock, sometimes the bell doesn't work, try knocking twice; if they don't know who they're voting for, try to persuade them; if they're voting for Hillary, leave them alone (that's between them and their rotten, cynical conscience, she neglects to add); here's the list of Sanders's policies ($15 minimum wage, single-payer health insurance, free higher public education, antifracking, all of it true but not to the point—the point is he's the first candidate in two generations who is not a neoliberal, the first in decades to call himself a socialist, running as a Democrat but, bless him, not one). In the moment, I have trouble recalling *why* I canvassed for Obama, or what I said in his favor. The virtue of the Sanders platform is that I have no trouble articulating what he believes, because much of what he believes, I believe. I can say what I think, for the most part, and it comes out sounding like what Sanders thinks. It occurs to me that I have never felt this way about national electoral politics in my life.

The list of voters she gives me is in deep South Philly, south of Snyder, west of Broad. Dense, hermetic stretches of row-house monotony, where the names largely still rhyme with Yahtzee, Nietzsche. On Saturday afternoon I encounter empty houses, places where people don't answer the door. Nine out of ten times I'm left standing outside, scratching the "Not Home" box with cracked hands, bits of falling ice smudging my marks. Some addresses are impossible to find, and in many places the doorbells don't work. There was a time when these campaigns must have been easier to manage, I think: when people picked up the phone as a matter of course. When regular mail delivery and frequent house visitors meant that having an easily locatable front door and a working doorbell were necessary.

As I walk down one block, a woman not elderly but aged by dire circumstances sucks from a limp cigarette and asks if I'm working for Bernie. I tell her I'm a volunteer, and she asks, her open mouth revealing a stretch of missing teeth, whether Bernie will help. I tell her that he's for working people, that he'll raise the minimum wage. "No," she says, "I need a different kind of help." She tells me she despises Clinton. "I don't think a woman can be President." Gently I suggest that I don't think this is true, but she demurs.

At other doors, I find the fathers of the voters I'm looking for. "She's not home. The rest of us are voting for Trump," one says, "but I hope Bernie wins. I can't stand Clinton." There's something uncanny about facing a Trump voter, someone who presumably wants me expelled from the country, or simply killed by the National Guard, but who nonetheless is the picture of gruff politesse. Or maybe they're just friendly nonracists who vote Republican. I do encounter one genuine racist, whose inner door stands open to the elements as I approach the house. Through the screen door I can see his knees and legs. When I knock he rises slowly, and when he sees me he rushes to the door, swings it open, jabs at the pin I'm wearing. A 75-year-old toothless Italian American with a buzz cut, he sputters, "Vote . . . *for him*! Not in a million years. I'd sooner vote for—for," then he spits it out, "*Sharpton.*" Spent, he lets the door shut. "Now beat it. Scram." I obey.

Another door, vinyl siding: a white woman with several kids racing in and out of the doorway gives me her time. She knows vaguely about the upcoming election, but not who Bernie Sanders is. "There's Trump, but he's just for rich people, right?" He is, I say, but so is Hillary Clinton. I tell her about the speeches to Wall Street, with their significant honoraria, and she raises her eyebrows. I tell her Sanders is for working people like us, and she seems to believe me (though "us" is a questionable concept in this context). I leave some "literature." My last few blocks, I hit a stretch of enthusiastic Sanders supporters: a black woman who has her child tell me the good news, a white woman who actually worked for Sanders in Vermont. One Clinton supporter, the lone professional male in a working-class neighborhood, seems quietly aggrieved by his own choice, mentioning it in a tone of either shame or resignation. When I try to find the door to an apartment above a bodega, a young man in a nearby car asks with palpable suspicion what I'm up to. He relaxes once I explain. "I like Bernie," he says. "Trump's just in it for laughs. I don't think I'm going to vote. Politicians can't do anything. The whole system's rigged anyway."

April 10, 2016

The first sunny day of the year, I get a neighborhood of "turf" (as the campaign calls it) closer to downtown—closer, specifically, to the Whole Foods—and the results speak for themselves. Door after door, Clinton, Clinton, Clinton. "I haven't decided yet, but I'm leaning toward Hillary Clinton." Do you want to discuss why? *No*, as the door slams in my face. Still, most of the houses are empty, or people don't answer the door—somewhere around 80 percent.

In between stretches of unanswered doors, one comes across the full spectrum of weird American habits. At 4 PM: "I'm sorry, we're having dinner." *Wha?* I should have noted how many times I rang the bell, loud barking ensued, and the resident cracked open the door, motioned down at her excited dog, and lifted both arms in a "What can I do?" gesture before shutting the door. Something truly shameful about using the dog as your excuse. "If you ask me they have no business living amongst us!" as Newman said on *Seinfeld*.

At Fitzwater and 9th, the throbbing heart of upper-middle-class row-house Philadelphia, a late-middle-aged woman with closely cropped hair, unfashionable wire-rimmed glasses, and an overall demeanor of skepticism and practiced condescension emerges at the sound of my knocking and engages me in endless street conversation. "To tell you the truth, I don't know," she says, raising her hands questioningly before dramatically shoving them in her jeans pockets. "This week, it got ugly. Sanders showed his grumpy side."

What had happened? Clips of Sanders's discussion with the *New York Daily News* about the banks were released, and led to some hubbub about whether his plans for financial regulation were lucid. Clinton questioned whether Sanders had done "his homework." Sanders said, *I'm not qualified?* She's *not qualified*, followed by indecorous comments about Clinton's support of NAFTA and the war in Iraq. A vapor cloud of horror wafted out from the Clinton camp, *how dare he*, et cetera. I barely followed it—the more I hit the streets, the less I follow the news. I find it unbearable, beside the point, to listen to the debates, even to Sanders himself.

My rough sense is that Sanders was responding to a *Washington Post* headline—"Clinton Questions Whether Sanders Is Qualified to Be President"—rather than to anything she actually said, and I say so. But for this voter, it's a sign of terrible things to come. "I'm worried that you millennials won't vote in the fall if Sanders doesn't get the nomination. Don't you realize that the key thing is to defeat the Republicans?" This is another headline she's quoting. It's amazing, in fact, how often I find that news headlines simply migrate, verbatim and unprocessed, into people's minds and out their mouths; how often I hear people say, "No matter what happens we'll need to *unify the party*," as if they were Democratic Party strategists. I reassure her that "we millennials" understand the nature of the threat from Trump and the rest of the gang, even though I vow to other Sanders supporters that I'll cast my vote for Jill Stein, should it come to that. She voices skepticism about whether Sanders could win a general election (painful memories of the McGovern candidacy), points out that her wife is a staunch Clintonoid and wouldn't even let me in the door. After nearly twenty minutes, she concedes, "Look, I'm going to vote for him."

This conversation feels like a victory and inaugurates a string of houses—closer now to South Philadelphia—where nearly everyone is voting for Sanders. People seem to enjoy keeping me in suspense. "Can I ask if you plan to vote on April 26 in the Democratic primary?" "Yes, you can." "Uh. Are you planning to vote on April 26 in the Democratic primary?" "Yes, I am." "Right. Can I ask who you're voting for?" "Yes, you can." "OK. Who are you voting for?" "BERNIE SANDERS!!!" They shake my hand and send me on my way. I mark box after box: "Strong Sanders."

It seems implausible, entire blocks voting for this weirdo. I can barely believe it, and it occurs to me that I've been thinking of my support for Sanders as a private obsession, a strange fascination unconnected to the preferences and actions of most people. Even the millions of votes cast for him so far seem spectral to me, mere data, unrelated to everyday life. Yet here were strangers who seemed to believe more or less the same insane things I believe, things I usually have trouble uttering, let alone defending, in polite company. The high this gives me is inspiring, and for the first time I begin to fantasize, blithely, about what it would be like for Bernie Sanders, self-described democratic socialist, to become President.

April 14, 2016

Jeff, one of the two lead organizers of the South Philadelphia office, is tall, thin, and stooped; he looks crescent-shaped when standing.* Just 22 years old, he has the manner of a desperately shy child much younger. He wants to meet to talk about what drew me to the campaign. I fear another of those inevitable organizing conversations, the "story of self," in which you're compelled to provide psychological explanations for your political choices. Yes, the personal is political, but it isn't *only* the personal that is political.

At UNITE HERE, the union I spent several years volunteering for, my lead organizers explained how years of poor childhood health or an early growth spurt that left them uncomfortably tall gave them a propensity to feel ill at ease and, consequently, to fight for justice. (But why *this* fight? Why *this* form of action? There was always an intellectual leap.) I could never provide the same explanations. It wasn't that I hadn't suffered deprivations, but I didn't see those deprivations as the primary sources of what I believed. And yet failing to divulge painful secrets made for a very one-sided conversation. It was like failing to rise to the demands of union fraternity: your brother loosed his rich, thick blood and held his wrist to yours, only to watch you pull away. To shirk duty was to invite recrimination.

And so there were subsequent conversations, less forthcoming and more punitive: you were not committed, you lacked the gumption and will to carry the fight to the end. Once I declined to attend a union organizing retreat so I could work on my book, and my lead told me, "Well, you can spend time observing the fight, like a journalist, or you can actually be part of it." I went on the retreat. Another

---

* Names have been changed.

time, when I missed an all-hands meeting so I could represent *n+1* at, of all things, Left Forum, I was told, "You can't flit in and out of the movement. People aren't going to trust you." A friend of mine in the union was practiced at rebuffing these requests to give up his life. "I'm sorry," he would tell his comrades, "it is Sunday evening, and I am not going anywhere. *Thrones* is on. Winter is coming."

After I quit volunteering for the union, I found myself spending afternoons weeping through TV screenings of *Norma Rae*. I missed the commitments I had spent years building. To stand up in the textile factory, to raise the ragged placard with the word *UNION* on it. To stand up to everyone around you. To spend nights and weekends in a kind of exhausted frenzy, making hundreds of phone calls, digging deep into the news archives for a bit of telling data that would help you screw the bosses, driving to one home after another, one workplace after another, pleading with workers, pleading with everyone you knew but, in truth, with yourself, that there was nothing more important, that your work, that laundry and cooking, would all have to wait for this higher cause . . . was there anything greater? I missed it like a limb.

Jeff and I meet at the office around nine in the morning. He and three other organizers are silent, barely awake, craning into the glow of their laptops. We walk to a café down the street; Jeff confesses that he has gone nowhere in the city besides the office and the house he's staying in. He tells me his salary amounts to about $24,000 a year—manageable, in Philadelphia—with free housing, and he lets me pay for his coffee, and for the toast and jam he orders.

Then it begins. Jeff grew up in upstate New York, awkward and weird, in circumstances that were financially uneasy if not grindingly bad. This instilled in him an instinct to fight for those who also felt "left out." He wanted to be a writer, but once he realized he'd leave the University of Chicago with a pile of loans, he got into organizing. Writing fell by the wayside; it no longer meant what it did. Sanders's position on student debt persuaded him to apply for a job with the campaign.

And myself? I give the only story I know to be true. That I grew up a weak liberal, largely unconcerned with politics and more concerned that chain bookstores were displacing my beloved independents. In college I watched from my dormitory as Yamasaki's twin towers, which I had loathed for architectural reasons, fell, and I only became incensed by the war in Afghanistan and Iraq over time. I got a job in publishing and, unhappy with the working conditions, tried and failed to organize a union. At *n+1*, writing about the Atlantic Yards project got me interested in political theory beyond Adorno and Žižek. While in graduate school in California, I began, for reasons that escaped me, to subscribe to *Labor Notes*. I attended panel discussions about the now-arcane fight between SEIU and UNITE HERE in 2009, and found myself impressed by the UNITE HERE crew. I became a regular volunteer until 2013, when I burned out. I wanted to get back into politics, and I found Sanders to be a candidate who held many good positions. I strongly disliked the Clintons, Bill more than Hillary, and was tired of their stranglehold over Democratic politics.

Jeff stares at me mutely the whole time—only stopping me to note that he was 13 or 14 when Obama was first elected—and by the end he doesn't quite respond. Even I recognize something dissatisfying about the story. There is perhaps some part of me that is unwilling to give up the real goods, but in truth I don't even know what they are. All I know is that when Jeff says that he can't write anymore, that organizing has taken over everything, there is something in me that responds.

April 23, 2016

The Sanders people need a "campaign hub" in my neighborhood for the weekend before the primary, and there are no houses or empty offices available. Cautiously I suggest Jeff take a look at my house, a cramped two-and-a-half-story row house that my wife, Shannon, and I rent. He comes over and immediately judges it to be fine. He reminds me that this means hosting volunteers from roughly eight in the morning until nine at night; the day of the actual election, it means starting at seven and working until the polls close, at eight. I would have to train canvassers, another volunteer would enter data from returning canvass packets, another would report totals to the main campaign office in North Philadelphia. I agree to do it.

I get trained in a computer program called Voter Activation Network, or VAN, an extraordinary compendium of voter information and campaign planning software chiefly developed by Obama data nerds. In it, you can look up voters' histories, filter names by demographics and location, use the same methods to target volunteers, look at volunteer histories. What do they do with the data? No one ever explains. But somehow it motivates the entire way the campaign handles canvassing.

The days leading up to the get-out-the-vote are tense. I can think about nothing else, and slowly a poisonous contempt for anyone who can creeps into me. I despise my friends who support Sanders but don't lift a finger to help him. I lament my colleagues, who don't seem to have done anything either. I pick a fight with Shannon, a Sanders supporter who has done no door-to-door work (and who, I decline to remember, is sharing our house with volunteers for four straight days). I can't understand how anyone could be doing anything else, thinking anything else. At the same time, I find it impossible to read election news, or to listen to the simpering voices on NPR. The deeper I get into the campaign, the less I know about it, the less the candidate matters to me, and the more the activity becomes the point. At some point, the success of Sanders's platform forces Clinton to endorse a higher minimum wage. A victory for the campaign—but it barely registers.

Late on Friday, a van pulls up and Jeff unloads several file boxes full of turf packets organized by neighborhood and "ward" (Philadelphia's arcane district system). That night I sleep poorly and wake up early to arrange packets of turf, separating them by ward, stacking them at perpendicular angles. I make a large pot of coffee and drink most of it myself. Andrew, the campaign hub leader, arrives, and we begin to call the volunteers scheduled to arrive at 9 AM. (Part of "following orders" means we don't send text messages, based on some bit of ancient campaign wisdom whose empirical basis is never disclosed. Later in the day we break this rule and achieve much better results.) The calls go to voicemail, and we leave mildly threatening messages asking volunteers to call us back if they can't make their shifts. Andrew gets one guy on the phone and engages him in a lengthy conversation about changing shifts. Overhearing it, I feel the contempt rise in my throat. I corner Andrew in the kitchen and violently whisper, "GET HIM TO COMMIT TO A SHIFT!" Andrew mouths back, "I'M *TRYING*," and it's only then that I recognize what's happening to me.

I have a flashback to the last conversation I had with my union leads, three years ago, when we were in the middle of a campaign to draw attention to budget cuts in the Philadelphia school system. In a drastic escalation, several workers had gone on a weeklong hunger strike. The strike coincided with closing an issue of *n+1*, and I owed the magazine a new draft of an essay. So while workers were starving themselves for justice on Broad Street, I was sitting in a library carrel at the University of Pennsylvania, twenty blocks away, subjecting the phenomenon of visiting professorships by poets from the global south to a quasi-Marxist analysis. I was called to a meeting with my leads in the food court of a shopping mall, where they screamed at me for my apostasy. I screamed back, explaining with a palpable lack of success that I had to write an "Intellectual Situation" on "world literature." I couldn't understand why they were so upset with me. Didn't they realize I had obligations to other people? Finally they said it was impossible to continue this tripartite existence, as writer, editor, and activist; I would have to choose. Only now, as I feel myself trying to undo the choice I made, do I recognize their anger.

The early-morning shift turns out to be a bust—a volunteer or two arrives, we train them and send them off with packets. But it leaves time for one of us to go out, and so I leave Andrew and take a packet in what the campaign has deemed, for reasons again unknown to us, a "high-priority" ward: the fifth, which encompasses some of the richest real estate in the city and some of the most highly touristed areas of "Revolutionary" Philadelphia.

Unfortunately, the area was also subject to an infamous instance of urban renewal, with black residents ejected and their homes razed to make way for high-rise apartments—a history that appears to have some bearing on my ability to contact voters in the area. Many of the addresses are nonexistent in physical reality; the ones that are turn out to be high-rises. Google Maps doesn't help, and I spend hours wandering through parking lots and across modernist expanses of lawn, looking for houses that don't exist. It's as if the voter information hasn't been updated since the 1960s. At other buildings, I spend what feels like an eternity pressing apartment buttons and getting no answer, or dealing with recalcitrant doormen. I mark entire buildings—containing dozens of voters—"inaccessible." I wonder what the Clinton people are doing with areas like these. Can they just count on the luxury dwellers to be theirs?

After walking up and down one block for twenty minutes, I pop into a tourist restaurant, City Tavern, which purports to serve Ben Franklin's own recipe for beer, among other colonial-era delights. I grab a waiter in a tricorn hat, ruffled white shirt, and breeches and ask after the address. He tells me that it doesn't exist and asks what I'm looking for. I explain that I'm part of the Bernie Sanders campaign, and he lights up. "Oh, rock on, brother, we're all feeling the Bern! I'd say 75 percent of us are voting for the guy." He motions to the rest of the waitstaff, a diverse group in 18th-century garb, ferrying plates of squab and flagons of ale.

I get back to my house after this futile exercise, which has taken hours longer than the usual canvassing shift, and discover that, to meet to the campaign's data needs, Andrew has sent a number of volunteers on these high-rise suicide missions. We call up to the deputy field director, who acknowledges that the area is "tough," but

tells us to keep at it, a proposal that is neither reassuring nor compre-
hensible. Then, after some complaining, a plan emerges. Jessie, our
data-entry captain, who is terrified of knocking on doors and making
phone calls and therefore sits on the corner of my couch alternating
between data entry and complaining about the campaign methods,
proposes that we select likely Bernie supporters from apartment
towers, "cut" turf designed specifically for their building, and train
them over the phone to canvass their buildings. This strikes us as a
brilliant idea, and all the more enticing because we have to hide it
from the higher-ups.

Volunteers arrive in waves, in ages and colors that bear no
resemblance to the demographic data constantly used as a cudgel
against Sanders by the media. We train new canvassers in the art
of talking to strangers; we mimic slamming doors in their faces; we
pretend we're on the fence. New Yorkers arrive, bearing the scars
and wisdom of their recent primary. A Danish visitor has traveled
from Aarhus to campaign for Sanders, whom he says would be a
center-right candidate in most of Europe. Nonetheless, he gives
Bernie the Scandinavian stamp of approval. "What Bernie says
about Scandinavia is absolutely true!" he says. "Look, it's not that we
don't have social problems. But at least we have health care, and
we take vacations."

April 26, 2016: Primary Day

After three fourteen-hour days, I've gotten used to the ritual of waking up and arranging packets of turf; of grabbing a slice of cold pizza
from the fridge and all but dipping the crust in my coffee; of looking
up lists of volunteers and texting reminders; of greeting Andrew and
Jessie and making them coffee. My house has become the center
of a Bernie cult on my little block, with its own strange hours and
endless stream of visitors, its piles of paper and "literature." Weird
autodidact campaigners come by: the teenager who made his own list

of Bernie's accomplishments and hands it out at the bodega where he
works; the woman who made sports-themed Bernie buttons (sadly
all Pittsburgh-related, so we can't wear them into the streets without
courting violence).

Happier than I've ever been, I also feel the beginnings of burn-
out. The real staffers are well past this point. Jeff told me days ago
he plans to leave the campaign after the Pennsylvania primary; he
can't keep up the hours and is starting to lose his mind. One day
he comes over to my house, arbitrarily rearranges our turf packets, and then stretches out on my couch and falls asleep for nearly
an hour, even as canvassers filter in and out. Everyone on staff is
chugging coffee and energy drinks, and I'm surprised not to hear of
harder drugs. I'm worried about the out-of-town Bernie staffer we're
hosting, who "sleeps" on a roll-out mattress in my office upstairs. She
arrived in Philadelphia at eleven o'clock Friday and went straight to
the campaign office to work before arriving at our house at 3 AM. At
seven the next morning we heard her coming down the stairs, but
she headed out to work without even stopping to use the bathroom.
All weekend she kept to the same schedule. Yesterday she spent the
night at the office.

Every day, after all the volunteers leave, Andrew, Jessie, and I
enter data, drink beer, and talk about the problems of the candidate
and his campaign. Why aren't there more campaign staffers from
Philadelphia? Why didn't we campaign more heavily in the city's
gay neighborhoods? Why isn't Bernie campaigning for downballot
candidates? Why can't he commit persuasively to Black Lives Matter? We discuss conspiracy theories about Ryan Hughes, the Pennsylvania director for Bernie's campaign, who was apparently taking
money from Hillary's Super PAC. We seem to be preparing for a
loss, even though we're all feeling remarkably bullish about Bernie's
chances. In the midst of one of these bitchfests, we turn on the television to catch the last minute of Sanders being interviewed by Chris
Hayes in Philadelphia, just a mile or two from where we're sitting,
and Sanders's virtuous civics teacher voice, intoning eternal social

democratic truths, makes my eyes mist over. I've grown, despite myself, attached to him as a candidate.

The morning of the primary I go to my polling station and push a button for Bernie Sanders. I also cast a gratified vote for John Fetterman, the lefty mayor of Braddock, PA, who's running for Senate against the Democratic machine candidate Katie McGinty. I stave off the melancholy knowledge that this is all coming to an end by selecting a packet that takes me to the low-rise public housing near my house.

It's Tuesday morning, and not many people are at home. Most of the activity in the neighborhood comes from the bustle of paid-up staff for the machine attorney general candidate, Stephen Zappala. One of them, an older black woman plastering windshields with leaflets, yells at me from across the parking lot. "They're not opening the door for you," she says. "This is Hillary country, *boy!*" putting a nasty emphasis on the last word. I find myself shaken by this outburst of political malice, only managing to smile weakly and chirp, "We'll see!" as I continue to the next house.

I pick up one of the leaflets, which turns out to be a product of the local Democratic political machine. Marked "Official Democratic Ballot," it instructs voters that they should vote for the following names: Hillary Clinton, Stephen Zappala, Katie McGinty. After weeks of willfully ignoring the fact, I come face to face with the reality that we are under the weight of party machinery, or political history. I call back to my house, where there are reports of people—it's not clear who they are—going into the polling booths in the poorest neighborhoods and "helping" voters push buttons for Hillary Clinton. Someone hears through the grapevine that Gloria, a Latina volunteer in Fairhill, a mixed black and Puerto Rican neighborhood with a high percentage of Spanish speakers, has been encountering voters who claim to have voted "for Bill Clinton." On primary day, there are still parts of the city where nobody knows who Bernie Sanders is; many people know only the name Clinton, and are being softly coerced into marking that name, with its long history of varied, unstable meanings. Suddenly the weight of the world begins to fall on me, on all of us. The Bernie bubble is leaking air. It feels like we are up against more than we understand or can handle.

About half the voters I speak to are planning to vote for Hillary. Some laugh when I ask whether they plan to vote for Bernie. Others, predominantly younger, say, "Bernie 2016, brother!" and shake my hand. Near the polling station, I overhear one woman ask another, "Did you vote her in?" and the response, "I voted *him* in!" In the scorched-earth mode of primary-day canvassing, I don't linger to convince Hillary voters or even to tell them their polling place (most already know). I'm not even supposed to waste time with fence-sitters; the point is to get the Bernie supporters to the polls. I try gamely with a woman I spoke to just a few days ago, who seemed impressed with everything I said about Sanders. When I speak to her again, she says she still doesn't know whom she's voting for, and her wary expression lets me know that she's not willing to entertain my attempts to convince her.

At what is nearly my last door, I break the rules one last time to linger with a black woman in her early sixties who's on the fence. "I thought I knew who I was voting for, and now I don't," she says, her rheumy eyes searching. "I've been listening to Bernie on TV just now, the things he says, they give me chills, to hear him say it. But the man has been there for a long time, the man keeping us down, ruining the land. Maybe time for a woman. Where are you from, brother?" India, I say. "You've been there too, you know what I'm talking about, they took everything from you. At the African church, you know they found all those bodies the other day, a burial ground that they didn't even know about? Who knows whose bodies we're walking on? There might be our bodies everywhere, they don't care, black bodies everywhere underneath us, nobody even knows." From here, it's hard to get to the usual topics, but I don't want to get to them, I don't want to leave. Some odd communion is taking place above and beneath the election, something more important, something closer to the limit of what anyone can articulate. She tells me about not going to war anymore, about taking care of her own, and I lightly go over Sanders versus Clinton on these issues, which again seems to miss the point. I leave the door after thanking her for her time—for once really feeling grateful for it—and realize I've spoken to her for half an hour. I still don't know how she's going to vote.

As the day creeps toward zero hour, we find that we've run out of turf. We've covered nearly everything. The South Philadelphia office has run out too. When the main Bernie office hears of it, everyone cheers.

To tamp down my hopes, I give myself turf in Society Hill, one of the wealthiest neighborhoods in Philadelphia, hoping to encounter dozens of Hillary voters and to feel appropriately bad as the polls close. But as I start down roads of tall brick row-house mansions and a summer downpour commences, I find that the tactic doesn't work. The voter lists have been narrowed to the point that I encounter only Bernie supporters. A house of five that voted for Bernie, including one 18-year-old in his first election. A 75-year-old white woman who arrives at the door with her two East Asian grandchildren, whom she asks to let me know who she voted for. "BERNIE SANDERS!" they cry in unison, and mawkishly enough I choke back tears. I suddenly feel as if an era of my life were passing. I leave half my packet unfinished and head back to the house.

Everyone meets at a bar called the Gaslight. As soon as I enter, someone asks, "Did you see?" When I look at the screen, I see the result. Hillary Clinton is standing at a podium next to a giant version of her stolid blue-and-red icon, the H-arrow, somewhere in the Philadelphia Convention Center. It looks like something out of *Citizen Kane*. The campaign staffers are all on their phones, making contingency plans, buying plane tickets. I'm not sure what they're doing. I see Tiffany, my elusive Bernie lodger, and give her a hug. Most people are standing in meek attitudes, stirring their drinks, regarding the TV screen with stoic acknowledgment. We look up wards and districts on our phones. It turns out we won the wards we canvassed, even while Philadelphia as a whole voted almost twice as much for Hillary as for Bernie. Things are somber until the networks call Rhode Island for Bernie, and a modest cheer goes up. A socialist whom I've seen at other primary watch parties does what he always does when Sanders wins a state. He begins to sing an old song:

> For justice thunders condemn-a-a-tion
> A-a bet-ter world's in birth
> No-o more tradi-tion's chains will bind us . . .

Wearily, I mouth the words along with him. "You know this song?" a volunteer friend asks me incredulously.

I find Jeff, who's already handed in his resignation, at the bar and buy him a drink. There, to puncture what might otherwise be one of those ridiculous silences I fall into with him, and in a spirit of sorrowful drunken confession, I retell my "story of self," but I try something different. That I went to a private school on scholarship, where I was one of a few people of color, and felt alienated and unhappy. That I grew up in a wealthy neighborhood and I felt the injustice of a capricious market society keenly. That I took this with me into my writing, but that I wanted to do more. He tells me that this is more convincing than anything I told him before, but I'm not so sure. I tell him that I don't want to be a writer anymore, that I want to give it up, that it seems impossible to do both things—one will always seem false to the other. This, too, seems inadequate, insufficiently "dialectical," but I can't face it any other way.

April 27, 2016

Wake up late. Instead of arranging turf in the morning, I start to pile it up for discard. Still somehow wary, I set aside the turf packets that we printed privately for the apartment towers, which we had not so covertly kept in a folder marked ROGUE OPERATION. Jeff texts me around noon, saying he can come pick it up. He arrives and wordlessly we begin shifting boxes and piles of paper into his station wagon. I open the trunk and find dozens of plastic-wrapped copies of the *London Review of Books*. I wish Jeff good luck. He gives me another one of his mute stares, leavened slightly by the hint of a smile, and heads back to Chicago.

2016

H.

SARAH RESNICK

THERE IS A PHOTO OF YOU STANDING OUTSIDE THE HOUSE IN BOR-
ough Park, grin wide, head back, laughing. Slender in faded blue
jeans against the brick and white stucco, your hair a mass of thick
black curls, a little unkempt. This was you: "the fun one." On our
summer visits to New York, after the long drive south from Ontario,
it is you I want to see most of all.

When your daughter was born, I was 5. As I grew older I envied
her for having you as a father. We rode the F train to Coney Island,
surveying the city through painted windows; ate frankfurters on the
boardwalk.

When I was 12, your mother, my grandmother, passed. We
stopped visiting New York. I didn't see or speak to you for fifteen
years. By the time I went to college, it was apparent that no one knew
where you were.

Suddenly in 2007 you call.

I am living in New York now. You tell your brother, my father,
that you are living at a shelter on the Bowery. He comes to town soon
after, and the three of us go out to dinner. We don't speak much of
the past. You say you are doing well, and we agree to meet again
soon. Your hair is cropped short and you are thin, very thin.

What surprises me most: you have no teeth.

YOU ARE NOT THERE when I stop by after work. The man at the desk gives me this news, not for the first time. I am tired of relying on luck in order to see you. On my next visit I bring you a prepaid cell phone so we can make plans in advance. This makes you happy.

We walk to B&H Dairy, where I order cold borscht and you cherry blintzes. I show you how to use the phone.

My father calls, tells me he has urgent news to share. *I always thought it was cocaine*, he says. *But it was heroin.* He repeats the last word, drawing out the first two syllables. He is wounded, disbelieving. The way his sibling foundered was worse than he had believed. Cocaine is nefarious, sure, but heroin is depraved. He is waiting for me to interrupt—to affirm that I, too, am appalled.

The first time we meet just the two of us, you tell me you have been diagnosed with bipolar disorder. I hardly believe it. You do not conform to any idea I have of a person with bipolar disorder, though the ideas I do have are received, not based on experience. It's just that you seem to me all right, not terribly different from the way I remember you, though your affect is flatter, hollowed. You wear your defeat.

You complain of ceaseless fatigue, a haze in your head. You list your medications: lithium, Topamax, prazosin, Thorazine, lorazepam, also methadone, more I am forgetting, they are always changing. Frankly I am astonished at, worried by, the number of medications you are taking. The lithium concerns me most. I know that it has dangerous side effects. I know that it is used in batteries. Never once does it occur to me that you seem all right because of the meds and not despite them. You are impressionable and take what I say seriously. The only people you talk to are social workers, counselors, medical doctors, psychiatrists, and you do not seek to inform yourself about your own condition. You are not a skeptic. You do not read. You trust what others tell you. The source is of no relevance.

Within weeks—or is it months?—your behavior seems to me more erratic. You are quick to anger. You demand things of me in your text messages. Usually money. I put fifty dollars' worth of minutes on your phone; the next day you've run out, ask for more. Three, four times in a week, you run out of minutes. I tell you it's too expensive to be using the phone in this way, and who are you talking to all of a sudden in any case? You say it is your friend Lenny. He is agoraphobic, you add. He rarely leaves the house. By now you think that I am trying to control you, to do you harm, and you begin making accusations. I get you a better phone plan, and for a few weeks, we do not speak.

Later you explain that you adjusted the dosage of your lithium without first telling your doctor. That was you in a manic phase.

I know better now.

MOSTLY WE TALK ABOUT your daughter, Sophie. She is 21 now and the mother of a boy, 18 months. The father is a young naval officer with whom she has parted ways, but his parents take care of the baby often. You have not seen or spoken to Sophie since long before her son was born. She wants nothing to do with you. You have tried phoning her, you tell me, but she will not take your calls.

You know of her whereabouts, though, because you are in touch with the naval officer's parents. You call them regularly, hear the latest on Sophie and the baby. They must empathize with you, perceive good intentions. One day they allow you to visit when Sophie is not around. You meet your grandson and you are ecstatic. You talk about it for weeks.

Then one day you phone and they say they will no longer take your calls. They ask you not to call again, hang up.

I am optimistic. This phase will pass; Sophie will come to see that you have changed. I think I know you will be reunited.

WE LIKE EATING AT B&H Dairy and return there often. Today I bring you *Tompkins Square Park*, a recent book of black-and-white photographs by Q. Sakamaki. In 1986, Sakamaki moved from Osaka, Japan, to the East Village. Throughout the 1980s and '90s, he documented the park and its surrounding streets, then a gathering place for the city's marginalized and homeless and a stronghold of the antigentrification movement.

We turn the pages, examine the pictures. I ask you what it was like. You tell me about when you loitered outside an abandoned building turned shooting gallery, waiting in line to buy your next fix. Police officers approached you, but you were neither questioned nor arrested. Instead, they emptied your pockets, took your money. They took everyone's money. Then they left.

It is difficult to know whether your memory is reliable, whether you can be relied on. But I have no reason not to believe you.

TODAY IS A GOOD DAY for you. You get new teeth. You are more confident.

JULY 2013. MY EYE LANDS on a headline in the *New York Times*: "Heroin in New England, More Abundant and Deadly." I can't recall the last time I saw heroin in the news. Media coverage of drug use had shifted, or so it seemed to me, to meth.

Officials in Maine, New Hampshire, and Vermont, from "quaint fishing villages" to "the interior of the Great North Woods," are reporting an "alarming comeback" of "one of the most addictive drugs in the world." What's remarkable about the story, according to its authors, is where the comeback is taking place: not in urban centers, but in the smaller cities and rural towns of New England. Experts offer observations. A police captain in Rutland, Vermont, states that heroin is the department's "biggest problem right now." A doctor, an addiction specialist, says, "It's easier to get heroin in some of these places than it is to get a UPS delivery."

Most of the heroin reaching New England originates in Colombia and comes over the US-Mexico border. Between 2005 and 2011, the number of seizures jumped sixfold—presumably in part because of increased border security—but plenty of heroin still got through. In May 2013, six people were arrested in connection with a $3.3 million heroin ring in Springfield and Holyoke, Massachusetts.

The article describes two addicts in particular, both young women. They sell sex for drug money. One overdosed and died after injecting some very pure heroin. The addiction specialist tells us that he is "treating 21-, 22-year-old pregnant women with intravenous heroin addiction." The lone man identified is the companion of one of the women. Beyond his name and age, nothing about him or his circumstances is mentioned. All three are white.

I stop when I read, "Maine is the first state that has limited access to specific medications, including buprenorphine and methadone." I open a new tab, search for what the writers mean by the vague phrase, "has limited access to." Earlier that year, the state enacted legislation to limit how long recovering addicts could stay on methadone, or similar drug-replacement therapies, before they had to start paying out of pocket. Medicaid patients will receive coverage for a maximum of two years.

I know that for some people, like you, this is not enough time.

Moving to the United States from Canada was, for me, eight years earlier, an easy enough transition. Much is shared between the two countries, and the culture shock was minimal. Yet even after all this time, I still find that certain ideas I'd taken for granted throughout adolescence and early adulthood—ideas about what a good society tries to make available for its citizens—are here not to be taken for granted at all.

AT THE BOWERY SHELTER you are a model resident. You participate in group. You see a counselor. You follow the methadone program. You are friendly with others. It is on account of this that you are recommended for Section 8 housing, and before long you are moved into a 200-square-foot studio with a single bed, a private bathroom, a tiny kitchen. The facility, a four-story building, is designated for people living with psychiatric disabilities. Your share of the rent is $260. You are also responsible for your own utilities. These are subsidized based on your income.

For a time you find yourself in a vexing predicament. The state has deemed you "unfit to work." But each of your applications for disability benefits is denied. It is not at all clear how you are meant to survive.

NOVEMBER 2013. The front page of the Saturday paper features a story on buprenorphine under the headline "Addiction Treatment with a Dark Side." Buprenorphine is an opioid used for maintenance therapy like methadone, but is available by prescription. This is new. Since the 1970s, methadone has been distributed through clinics. People participating in methadone programs must go to the clinic at least once a week, and in some cases every day. This is obstructive, even oppressive. A similar drug that can be had by prescription seems like an improvement. But doctors must receive federal certification to be able to prescribe buprenorphine. Federal law limits how many patients a physician can help with the drug at one time. This means that only people with good insurance, or the ability to pay high fees out of pocket, can access it. "The rich man's methadone," the article calls it.

But this—the part that interests me—isn't what the article is about. The article is about how the drug gets "diverted, misused and abused"; how, since 2003, the drug has led to 420 deaths. (By comparison, there are more than 15,500 deaths from opioid overdose each year.) The article is not about the drug's demonstrated efficacy at helping people with opioid dependencies that negatively impact their lives. Or about how restricted access to the drug is likely contributing to its diversion and misuse in the first place. Studies report that at least some people are self-treating their dependencies and withdrawal symptoms. I read elsewhere that medication-assisted treatment with an opioid agonist, such as buprenorphine, is the most effective treatment available for opioid dependencies.

THIS IS WHAT you tell me: From the time you were young, you possessed an antiauthoritarian streak. This disposition did not emerge from any particular maltreatment, by family members, say, or teachers; it was your natural orientation toward the world. You were enthralled by the neighborhood kids who attracted trouble even as you yourself did not act out. You desired proximity to danger and rebelliousness. Unlike your brother, you attempted to differentiate yourself from your family not by transcending your class, but by assuming a posture of nonconformity. You liked drugs because you weren't supposed to like them. For a long time—more than a decade—you were able to manage your use, to keep it, for the most part, recreational.

One time your father found your needle and other supplies for shooting up. He was furious. You wouldn't hear it. When he died years later his heart was still broken.

I have difficulty reconciling all this with what else you have told me of your past. I know that you worked for the police as a 9-1-1 dispatcher. You were good at your job, liked and respected, and soon you found yourself in a supervisory position. You enjoyed the night shift, especially, and for a long stretch the Bronx was your district. The position is notoriously stressful, but you were sharp, capable, levelheaded, and you excelled.

You were fired when your fidelity to heroin was stronger than it was to your job.

YOU LOVE YOUR new apartment, can't believe your good fortune. When I stop to consider it, neither can I.

SOMETIMES I IMAGINE what you will do with your time. I picture you as a volunteer—with other people who use drugs, maybe, or at a food kitchen or shelter. I feel certain that you will want to do this, that you will do something good, in the way that others did good for you. That maybe we will do something good together. Once, when I am volunteering on American Thanksgiving, I invite you to come along. I know that you have nowhere else to go. You tell me you'd prefer to stay home. A few months later, I make the suggestion once more. Again you decline.

Later I come to recognize this as my own bizarre fantasy, a pro-jection of my savior complex, perhaps. I laugh, not for the first time, at the naivete of my younger self.

DECEMBER 2013. Two articles command my attention. The first, a few weeks old, is about a radical clinical trial in Canada comparing the effectiveness of diacetylmorphine—prescription heroin—and the oral painkiller hydromorphone, i.e., Dilaudid, in treating severe heroin dependency in people for whom other therapies have failed. An earlier study in Canada had demonstrated that both diacetylmor-phine and hydromorphone are better than methadone at improving the health and quality of life of longtime opiate users. An unex-pected finding was that many participants couldn't tell the differ-ence between the effects of diacetylmorphine and hydromorphone. But the sample group receiving hydromorphone wasn't large enough to draw scientifically valid conclusions. So the study investigators created a new trial to test this finding.

If hydromorphone were to be found as effective as diacetylmor-phine, it could mean offering people the benefits of prescription heroin without the legal barriers and associated stigma. The study results have yet to be published.

Larry Love, 62, a longtime dependent: "My health and well-being improved vastly" during the trial. Love's doctor applied to Health Can-ada for permission to continue prescribing heroin to Love and twenty other patients after their year in the trial was up. The applications were approved, although renewal was required after ninety days. The federal health minister responded by creating new regulations to pre-vent such approvals. He insisted Ottawa would not "give illicit drugs to drug addicts." Love, four additional patients, and the health-care center that runs the hospital that oversaw the trial are suing the gov-ernment in turn. The doctor who submitted the applications, Scott MacDonald: "As a human being, as a Canadian, as a doctor, I want to be able to offer this treatment to the people who need it. . . . It is effec-tive, it is safe, and it works. . . . I do not know what they are thinking."

The second is an editorial about a Canadian bill that, if passed, would set new guidelines for opening supervised-injection facilities. Like syringe-distribution programs, supervised-injection facilities act as a frontline service for people who use drugs intravenously, giving out sterile needles and other paraphernalia. But they go one step further: users may bring in drugs procured elsewhere and inject them under the watchful eye of trained nurses. Staff members offer instruction on safer technique ("Wash your hands," "Remove the tourniquet before pushing the plunger," "Insert the needle bevel up") and monitor for overdose, which they counteract with naloxone. They do not directly administer injections.

The new law would erect application hurdles so onerous it would effectively prevent the establishment of any new sites. The columnist attacks the government for acting on ideological rather than scientific grounds. "Supervised injection sites are places where horrible things take place." I cringe a little. "The fact is, however, that these activities are even more horrifying when they take place in the streets, and strict prohibition has never been even remotely successful."

There is, I know, only one such facility in all of North America. It's called Insite, and it's in Vancouver.

IT IS A FALL EVENING and we are on our way to a movie. We pass a small group of Chabad men on the street. It is Sukkot and they are trying to identify secular Jews by sight, inviting them to perform the ritual with the date-tree fronds (*lulav*) and lemonlike fruit (*etrog*), shaking them together three times in six different directions. They have a small truck nearby (the Sukkahmobile). You tell me how a Chabad man befriended you once, how you almost became religious. He wanted to help you, and you had no one else. You went to dinners at his house. He would call to ask how you were. You say that he and his family were some of the kindest people you had ever met. But you couldn't stick with it, and one day you stopped responding.

I take you to see *Ballast*, that film of austere, understated realism about a drifter boy and a grieving man in the Mississippi Delta.

It's more about tone than narrative, and I am moved by the beauty and sadness of its barren landscapes. I worry that you are bored, you nod in and out; but afterward you tell me how much you liked it. I decide I will take you to movies often.

WITHIN WEEKS OF Philip Seymour Hoffman's death, a surfeit of reporting:

> Why heroin is spreading in America's suburbs
> How Did Idyllic Vermont Become America's Heroin Capital?
> New England town ripped apart by heroin
> Today's Heroin Addict Is Young, White and Suburban
> Heroin's New Hometown: On Staten Island, Rising Tide of Heroin
>   Takes Hold
> When heroin use hit the suburbs, everything changed
> Heroin in the Suburbs: A Rising Trend in Teens
> Heroin reaching into the suburbs
> Heroin Scourge Overtakes a "Quaint" Vermont Town
> Heroin-gone-wild in Central New York causes jumps in overdoses,
>   deaths
> Actor's heroin death underscores scourge closer to home
> Heroin scourge begs for answers
> New Wisconsin laws fight scourge of heroin
> The scourge of heroin addiction
> Heroin scourge cuts across cultural and economic barriers
> Colombian, Mexican cartels drive LI heroin scourge
> Senate task force hears from Rockland on heroin scourge
> Report shows heroin use reaching epidemic proportions in NH
> America's heroin epidemic: A St. Louis story
> Heroin: Has Virginia Reached an Epidemic?
> United States in the grips of a heroin epidemic
> Cheap, Plentiful, Deadly: Police See Heroin "Epidemic" in Region
> How Staten Island Is Fighting a Raging Heroin and Prescription-Pill
>   Epidemic

A Call to Arms on a Vermont Heroin Epidemic
Fighting Back Against the Heroin Epidemic
Ohio struggles with "epidemic" of heroin overdoses
Cuomo Adds 100 Officers to Units Fighting Heroin
Governors Unite to Fight Heroin in New England
Police Struggle to Fight America's Growing Heroin Epidemic
DuPage officials suggest laws to fight heroin
Taunton Launches Plan to Fight Heroin After Dozens of Overdoses

There are many more I don't write down.

YOUR DISABILITY APPLICATION is finally approved. You will receive monthly Social Security payments of $780. You are also entitled to the disability that has accrued from the time of your first denied application, which, because it was several years ago, now amounts to several thousand dollars.

There is one condition, however. The state has decided that, given your history, you are unfit to oversee your own finances. You will need someone who can demonstrate gainful employment, preferably a family member, to tend to the money on your behalf.

On a winter morning, early, I take the bus from Prospect Heights to the Social Security office in Bushwick. We have an appointment but we wait a long time. I sign where I am asked to. I attest to my reliability. I assume responsibility.

Soon after I set up a bank account where I am your "representative payee." Your money is deposited to it on the first of each month. From this account I pay your rent, your utilities. We meet every week or two, for food, for a movie, but always so that I can provide you with cash for provisions.

This works for a while.

ON THE PHONE ONE DAY you tell me you hurt your arm, a man on the street walked right into you, knocked you down to the ground. When I call a few days later to see how you are feeling, you tell me how strange it is, nearly every guy you pass on the street is eyeing you as if he wants to start a fight. These men, they are always brushing up against you on purpose.

Within a week, maybe two, you begin to ramble about the lock on your door, how it's broken, and how you're sure someone is breaking into your apartment to spy on you. You tell me that one day you came home to find a syringe on the floor. Someone planted it there for a supervisor to find, you're certain of it, other residents want your apartment, they want you gone.

I suggest various ways you might resolve these issues. You have excuses, explanations for why each of my recommendations won't work. I ask a lot of questions. Your paranoia does not involve state secrets, the CIA or FBI, tinfoil hats or aliens, the twin towers or global-government conspiracy theories, but the elevation of small anxieties and fears to delusions of persecution. I try reasoning with you, but sometimes, in order to empathize, I must suspend my desire to be rational and take part in your fantasy world. I learn there is nothing I can do for you; you are autonomous in overseeing your own health care. I encourage you to see your psychiatrist and wait. Once your medication is adjusted, you are no longer afraid.

NOT LONG AFTER your disability payments kick in, the debt collectors send notices to my apartment. One is on behalf of an old landlord who, years ago, sued you for rent payments you never made. It has been more than a decade, but this debt has not been forgotten. I mail a check.

HERE ARE SOME THINGS you might do on a given day: Walk to the methadone clinic to pick up your dose (you are required to go three times a week). Wait in line. Take one bus to the Medicaid office (when your pension kicked in, your monthly benefits went up, pushing you just slightly over the minimum-income requirement). Wait in line. Take one bus to see your psychiatrist (you live in Bushwick; your psychiatrist is in Crown Heights). Wait. Take one bus to the

Supplemental Nutritional Assistance Program office (you lost your EBT card and need to request a new one). Wait in line. Take two trains to see your hepatologist at NYU Langone Medical Center. Wait. Walk to the post office (to pick up the check my father has sent you). Wait in line. Walk to the nearest Western Union (where you would cash checks before you had a bank account). Wait in line. Take the bus and two trains to Maimonides Medical Center in Borough Park (you need a colonoscopy). Wait.

I WRITE DOWN STATISTICS, try to make sense of what I'm reading. In 2012, US physicians wrote 240.9 million prescriptions for painkillers, an increase of 33 percent since 2001. The growth can be attributed to a few related factors: patient-advocacy groups calling for better pain treatment; patients, perhaps influenced by pharmaceutical marketing, requesting drugs from their doctors; doctors, some with questionable ethics, overprescribing drugs.

The US government responded in a predictable way. It introduced more stringent prescription guidelines, authorized DEA investigations and closures of "pill mills." State governments began to use databases to track "doctor shoppers," patients who sought out prescriptions from multiple physicians.

In 2010, Purdue Pharma, the producer and patent holder of OxyContin, introduced an abuse-deterrent version of the drug ostensibly impervious to crushing, breaking, chewing, and dissolving, and therefore more difficult to inhale or inject.

That same year, the number of US drug poisoning deaths involving any opioid analgesic (oxycodone, methadone, or hydrocodone) accounted for 43 percent of the 38,329 drug poisoning deaths, a fourfold increase from 1999, when opioid analgesics were involved in 24 percent of the 16,849 drug poisoning deaths.

Following the government crackdown, supply of pharmaceutical opioids decreased sharply. Demand did not. The street price of prescription painkillers inflated, and many pharmaceutical opioid users opted instead for heroin. A rising supply of heroin kept prices low.

According to one study, more than 81 percent of recent heroin users say they switched after first trying prescription painkillers.

YOU SAY THAT one day, out of the blue, you decided to give it up. Just like that.

YOU CALL AT AROUND ELEVEN on a weeknight to tell me you are going to call an ambulance—you are in pain. Ten days earlier you had surgery on an abdominal hernia. The procedure was supposed to have been minimally invasive, performed with a scope, a few hours all told, and I waited to take you home. But there were complications. They had to cut you open. You were admitted to the hospital, stayed seven nights. Now you are home again but certain that you are not healing properly. When I arrive at your place in Bushwick, the paramedics are helping you into the back of the ambulance. I get in with you. We sit opposite each other. I ask you questions. You are lucid. I expected you to be doubled over, but you are not. The paramedics confirm that your vitals are good. You have no fever. At this point, I am confident that this trip is unnecessary; that there is nothing to worry about except that you are alone, and you understand what that means. But I stay silent as you tell the paramedics to take you to where you want to go.

When we arrive at the emergency room, the triage nurse evaluates you. You tell her about your pain, your recent surgery. Soon you are wearing a bracelet and gown, sound asleep in a bed. It is past midnight. I sit in the vinyl sled-base chair to read, but am more interested in the ER nurses shuffling through the ward, the gurneys wheeling by, bodies and machines, the perverse game of observation and diagnosis. Who among the patients holds the fate worse than all the others? I know that if you're asleep the pain is not as bad as you said it was.

Not far from your bed, just outside the curtain, a young man in a wheelchair, his neck slackened, his chin drooping close to the chest, vomits. It's viscous, like cake batter. It pours out of his mouth and covers the front of his gown. He is unconscious and makes barely any sound. Now is a good time for a walk. I head outside, buy some chips from the gas station.

When I return, the young man has been moved to the center of the ward, where, shuddering now, he continues to vomit. The former contents of his abdomen pool and spread on the floor. A nurse approaches. I point to the man and ask whether something might be done for him. The nurse frowns, tells me that the man is getting what he deserves; he has done this to himself. She walks away. Several nurses pass the gurney, but no one looks at the man.

It is 4 AM by the time the doctor sees you. Everything is fine, he tells us. By now the chaos of the ER has quieted. You slept right through it.

Tomorrow, I will get up early and go into work at an office.

For the first time, I resent you.

THE MORNING I VISIT INSITE I awake to a winter sun, a rare reprieve from Vancouver rain. It is still early when I take the bus downtown. The buildings glimmer gold and red under the warming light.

I decided to come here, to make the long trip to Vancouver, because I wanted to see Insite for myself. I wanted to see the place where people who use drugs intravenously can go to inject more safely, the place where, according even to the supportive editorial I'd read earlier, "horrible things take place." By then I had read enough about supervised injection to know that I thought it less horrible than humane. There is much else for which I would reserve the word *horrible*, including the treatment by law enforcement of people who use drugs.

Between 1992 and 2000, more than 1,200 fatal overdoses were recorded in Vancouver. Many of these took place in the Downtown Eastside, a neighborhood of ten or so square blocks where more than 4,600 people who inject drugs intravenously were known to live. The HIV conversion rate was the highest in the Western world. (This was due in part to the popularity in Vancouver of using cocaine intravenously: cocaine has a very short half-life, and people injecting the drug habitually might do so as many as forty times a day, as compared with heroin, which tends to be injected one to four times a day.) The city, recognizing that American-style prohibition had failed to bring about any improvement, undertook a kind of crash course on drug policy. A succession of public forums, meetings, demonstrations, and conferences with experts from all over the world brought together drug users and their families, service providers, academic researchers, police, and policymakers to examine alternative approaches—heroin-prescription programs, supervised-injection sites, decriminalization.

In 2003, Insite opened as a pilot research program, exempt from the criminal code. It was not the only new service offered in the city, and it was "no silver-bullet solution," a disclaimer Canadian policymakers, activists, and other supporters used often to describe its alternative approaches. But because it seemed to stand at the threshold of what progressive-minded people deemed acceptable—because, for many, it seemed intuitively *wrong*—it received the most attention, and was widely discussed both province- and nationwide. This, too, interested me. Most Vancouver residents initially opposed the facility but came to support it; this took a lot of convincing, and a shift in the way people understand illegal drugs and those who use them. I wanted to know how this had happened.

In 2006, the Conservative Party in Canada won the national election, ousting the Liberals. For the first time since 1993, Canada had a Conservative prime minister; from the start, he began dismantling the country's social programs. Early on, Insite became a battleground for drug policy across the country. The government tried to shut it down, but the Portland Hotel Society (now PHS Community Services Society), the nonprofit group that runs Insite, mounted a human rights case and took it to the Supreme Court. In 2011, Insite won the right to stay open.

Still, I wondered how long it could last. I wanted to know, too, if something like it could ever exist in the United States.

AT 9 AM, FIVE MEN and women sit on the sidewalk on flattened card-board boxes, first in line to enter when the doors open in an hour. Outside I meet Russ Maynard, Insite's program coordinator. He's with several college students from a health-administration program, there on a class visit.

As a group, we walk through the reception area into the injec-tion room. At first glance, it reminds me of a hair salon. The room is wide and bright, lined on one side by mirrors and a row of numbered bays, thirteen in all. Each has a stainless-steel counter, a sink for hand washing, a sharps container, a plastic chair, and an extraction hood to collect smoke and vapors.

A platform with a curvilinear counter, the kind you see in hos-pitals, is raised behind the booths. Lining the countertop are bins that contain all the supplies a person would need to inject drugs—a syringe, a cooker for mixing the drug with water, a sterilized-water capsule for flushing the needle, a tourniquet to tie off a vein. There is, too, a tool for crushing pills.

In the injection room, we arrange our chairs in a loose semi-circle around Russ, who stands. Russ begins his introduction. Insite is operated by Vancouver Coastal Health, the regional health authority, and PHS Community Services Society, a neighborhood nonprofit that focuses on the hard to house. PHS started in 1991, after a residents association converted a hotel into housing for the homeless. Today it provides residences for 1,200 people across six-teen buildings.

PHS also provides a range of community-based programs, including a credit union, a community drop-in center, medical and dental services, a syringe exchange, and an art gallery. Users of Insite can access all this simply by coming in, and to get them to come in is Insite's goal. Making contact is the first step toward connecting people, at their request, to vital services they might need. They call the people who use their services "clients."

Russ presents the group with a moral dilemma. "Imagine you're working at the front desk and a woman walks in and she's eight months pregnant, and she wants to come in and inject. You have to make a quick decision. If the line starts getting backed up, there's going to be an argument, or maybe worse. So what's going to happen?"

The room is silent.

I try to visualize the scenario, but it tests the limits of my open-mindedness. It is difficult to imagine supporting a pregnant woman's injection-drug habit.

"Is she going to leave and the clouds will part and the sunshine will hit her face and she'll see the error of her ways and never use again? Or is she going to take some equipment and go use in an alley or a doorway or a hotel room or something like that? If you do take her in, you can connect her with the nursing staff. You can have her housed by the end of the day. You can connect her with food, with services, all kinds of things. And you forgo all of that if you turn her away."

Someone asks about the mirrors. They are a critical design feature, says Russ. Staff use them to monitor clients while maintaining a respectful distance. Clients use them to ensure a certain amount of caution when injecting—to pay more attention to doing it properly. Russ: "You want it in your veins. Because there's a big wash—imagine a wave coming to hit you—and you won't feel anything for a little while. And if you make a mistake, it means that you have to go back out and perform sex work, or beg, or steal, or whatever it is you do to get the ten dollars you need. And that is stressful."

Since 2007, the staff at Insite has been able to refer visitors to Onsite, a detox center on the building's second floor. There are twelve private rooms, each with its own bathroom. Insite connects between 400 and 450 people each year to detox, which, Russ claims, is more than any other project in Canada.

THE STUDENTS LEAVE. One at a time, men and women, young, old, homeless, ordinary, are called in from the waiting room. As they enter, they announce the drug they will be injecting: "down," "dillies," "crystal" (heroin, Dilaudid, methamphetamine). The reception records their answers in a database, in case of emergency or overdose.

I watch the mirrors from across the room. A stately man in a wool sweater, navy with white snowflakes, drags a fine-tooth comb through his silvery hair, from the top of his forehead back to his nape. He does this twenty or thirty times before tending to his mustache with the same fastidiousness, never breaking focus. Then he pulls a woolen cap over his head and walks out into the sun.

A young nurse examines the arms of a fiftysomething woman. The woman looks afraid. The nurse speaks in soft tones as she runs her hands along the woman's forearms, helps her to locate a vein that isn't damaged, scarred, or collapsed. The nurse ties a tourniquet around her biceps. They both pause. The woman, hand trembling, inserts the needle. The nurse removes the tourniquet. The woman pushes the plunger.

Hours later, I see the same woman on the bus, traveling along Hastings Street. I want to speak to her, consider doing so, even as I know it's not right (privacy). But the woman is with a friend. Instead I watch her, imagine where she's going, how she will spend her time, what her home is like. If anyone awaits her there.

The woman gets off the bus.

I ASK RUSS WHETHER he knows any clients who might be willing to speak with me. He hesitates. Donovan Mahoney is doing well, he says. He puts me in touch. Now I am in Donovan's living room. We sit opposite each other, on separate couches. A series of photographs he has taken hangs on the wall above his head. Today Donovan is a talented photographer. His apartment, the garden level of a house in a middle-class neighborhood, is spacious, with a chef's kitchen and newly laid blond hardwood floors. He wears khaki pants and a gray sweater, slim-fitting with an overlapping V-neck. A baseball cap covers his partially shaved head of thick black hair.

Donovan tells me the story of his twenties: he followed a girl to Vancouver, fell into coke, then rock cocaine, then heroin. He'd always thought heroin was dirty, but after trying it for the first time he felt its reputation was undeserved.

For a while he made money as a dealer. When he wanted to binge, he would go to the Downtown Eastside, stay in an SRO hotel where no one would find him. Then one time he didn't go home. He let his monthly rent payments pass, grew paranoid. He left behind all his belongings, including his car. This was in 2001. He lived on the streets, mostly. He didn't like to feel closed in by walls, especially when he was high. He shoplifted, was caught often, spent many nights in jail.

He was wary of Insite when he first heard about it. On the street, he knew that everyone was working an angle. There's a forthrightness to interactions that doesn't exist elsewhere. He found it freeing. But he couldn't understand what would motivate the staff at Insite.

Now he credits them for helping him to achieve all that he has.

Donovan: "They're inadvertently showing you that there's another way of life. You start to have normal conversations. You say to them, 'What do you do?' They reply, 'I don't know, I'm in a band.' Of course they are. And then they tell you stuff about what they do with their girlfriend. Or how they went away for the weekend and saw their parents. To me, to an addict, they're showing me something. There's a whole other world out there that I don't even understand. They're showing you what it looks like to be a normal human being. Which is incredible, because if I'm shooting dope in an alley, I may bump into somebody who's been through recovery, and they may be able to guide me. But they're not going to be around when you need them.

"Addiction isn't nine to five. It's not like, 'OK, tomorrow at ten o'clock I'm going to go into recovery.' It happens and you don't really see it coming. It's like, *I think right now, if you guys got me in, I think I could go.*"

YOU WANT TO BE in charge of your own money. It is frustrating to have to travel to me every time you run out of cash. Together we visit your social worker, talk about how this could work. He needs to make a recommendation to your psychiatrist, to the state, before this can happen. We review your history. For the first time it is affirmed to me that you are likely to take methadone all your life. The social worker mentions your dose—120 mg—says it's high, that you haven't decreased it since beginning the therapy. You acknowledge as much. Still, it has been stabilizing, and the social worker is not concerned.

I tell the social worker that I will share the bank account with you, monitor your spending. Satisfied, he makes the recommendation. We open a joint account. Your monthly checks will be deposited and you will be responsible for paying your bills, for making sure you have enough to get through the month. I will check on the account through online banking. I keep your savings, a few thousand dollars left over from the disability back payments, in a separate account in your name.

For a year, at least, you manage all right.

I KNOW THAT, in the late '80s and '90s, the rapid spread of HIV through needle sharing galvanized US activists to challenge state laws and distribute hypodermic syringes for free, without a prescription; that the rate of new HIV cases in Vancouver among intravenous drug users persuaded even conservative politicians to consider opening a supervised-injection site; that were it not for the HIV epidemic, many drug-policy reforms in the US and elsewhere might not have occurred.

I find it curious how few articles on the emerging "epidemics"—heroin, opioid—mention the disease. I wonder whether it is because, with antiretrovirals so widely available, HIV is perceived to be less threatening than it once was. I chase the question for a time. I print out medical papers, underline findings. I call an epidemiologist at a prestigious university, who answers my questions patiently. He tells me that some of the best research is being done by an epidemiologist in Kentucky, who has been following a cohort of intravenous drug users since 2008. (Appalachia has disproportionately high rates of nonmedical prescription-opioid use and overdose-related deaths.) No one in the cohort had yet been diagnosed HIV positive, but 70 percent have hepatitis C. I ask why this matters, and he says that rising hepatitis C rates often forecast HIV outbreaks, because the viruses spread through the same behaviors—unprotected sexual intercourse and needle sharing—and both require a certain density of drug users to sustain transmission. But hep C is ten times more infectious, can live outside the body longer, and is extremely difficult to kill; it spreads more easily. A hepatitis C outbreak indicates that all the factors are present for an HIV outbreak.

In many ways, it's a ticking time bomb, the epidemiologist says, especially since, in rural Appalachian communities, knowledge about HIV tends to be minimal; these populations have not previously had to deal with the disease.

I hang up the phone, look up the data set that tracks syringe-distribution programs by state. Kentucky, 0; Tennessee, 0; Georgia, 1; South Carolina, 0; North Carolina, 6; Alabama, 0; Mississippi, 0; Ohio, 2; Virginia, 0; West Virginia, 0; Pennsylvania, 2; New York, 22; Maryland, 1.

YOU ARE WEAK and exhausted, have been for months. Every time we make plans, you cancel. Months pass and I don't see you. When by routine appointment you see your hepatologist, he sends you to the emergency room. You will need a blood transfusion to give you the hemoglobin that you need. By the time I arrive, the blood has been ordered from the bank, is being warmed. We wait for hours. The transfusion itself will take hours, too. I leave you there alone.

Before I go, the doctor tells me that what you are experiencing is a complication from hepatitis C.

WE SIT AT YOUR KITCHEN TABLE beside the four-drawer wooden dresser, its surface lined with pill vials and bottles of methadone.

I tell you about Insite. You appear bewildered, shocked even. "How can that possibly help anyone get off drugs?"

Your first reaction resembles most people's, but it's not what I want you to say. I want you to argue that getting people off drugs need not be the primary goal. I want you to be critical of the status quo—of the morass of law and policy in which you and millions of others are entangled. But you are not. You have only ever been exposed to one idea, one approach: abstinence.

I explain it to you this way: that the most serious harms that arise from drug use—HIV, endocarditis, tetanus, septicemia, thrombosis—come not from the drugs but from external factors. Of all the ways to administer drugs, injecting carries the most risks. The drug solution bypasses the body's natural filtering mechanisms against disease and bacteria. Access to sterile equipment and hygienic injection conditions can mean the difference between living and dying.

I say, thinking you might relate, that policing has an especially devastating effect on people who use drugs intravenously and are entrenched in street life. When they fear the police, they don't stop using, they just move elsewhere—to neighboring areas, where they may create new syringe-sharing networks, or to hidden or indoor locations. In such places, needle sharing is more common, because access to clean needles is cut off. When police are around, users avoid carrying clean needles, for fear of being identified as addicts and harassed. Overdoses increase. Precarious witnesses, fearful that police will follow medical personnel to the scene, fail to seek help.

I have stats at the ready. Nearly 500,000 Americans are incarcerated on drug charges. Another 1.2 million are supervised on probation or parole. Overwhelmingly, those affected are black, and not because they use and sell drugs at higher rates—on the contrary. I say that prison is no place for people who use drugs, help does not await them there. Maintenance therapies using methadone and buprenorphine are not available for people with opioid dependencies. Often an incarcerated person will continue to use drugs throughout a prison stay, and the clandestine nature of his use means that he is now more at risk than he might otherwise have been, using unsterile needles and sharing syringes among multiple inmates. Overdose rates peak in the first few weeks after release from prison, with mortality rates higher than what would be expected in similar demographic groups in the general population.

You begin to understand. You agree none of this is good. But still you are uneasy. You maintain it would be better to encourage people to stop using altogether.

A YEAR HAS PASSED since I spoke with the epidemiologist. I read in the newspaper that more than eighty people in Scott County, Indiana, have tested positive for HIV, most of them from a small town called Austin. The outbreak can be traced to intravenous use of the drug Opana, an opioid analgesic. The transmission rate has been around 80 percent.

Meanwhile a woman in Austin buys a license to carry a handgun because she fears for her young children. The woman takes pictures of "all this stuff going on" and calls the tip line. "I do nothing but," she says. On her lawn is a sign: NO LOITERING OR PROSTITUTING IS ALLOWED IN FRONT OF THESE PREMISES.

YOU RESENT ME NOW. I am trying to help you budget your money. You are spending your entire monthly payment within the first week. When your next deposit comes, I transfer it into the account you cannot access. Every week, I allow you one quarter of your stipend, after deducting your bills and rent. But you won't stop texting me, asking for more money. I try to reason with you, explain why you need the budget. I try putting my foot down, which amounts to ignoring your texts. You say you are buying a lot of $5 bootleg DVDs (Hitchcock is your favorite), but you forget that I know how to do math. And you are not interested in any of the solutions I come up with—a cheap computer, an internet connection, Netflix.

Every time I say no, I know I am passing judgment on you, on the things you desire for yourself (your collection of Adidas sneakers is by now substantial), what you prioritize. I am measuring you against an ethic of responsibility, a conception of the good life, that I do not want to force you to share. I can recognize this, but I can't hew my way out of the irony that accepting your irresponsibility only shifts the burden onto me, and this too seems unjust.

You were lucky once. You and my father sold your childhood home for $300,000. You never risked going to prison to support yourself. But before long, your half was gone, and you started spending my father's share. He cut you off, begged you to stop, but you said no, you had never felt so alive, you were having the time of your life.

WE GO TO THE BANK and close the joint account, transfer your savings. You have total control.

I feel light.

Your savings vanish within a month.

YOU SHOW UP TO an appointment with your psychiatrist, but it is the wrong day. You are confused, delirious. You travel by ambulance to the psychiatric emergency room at a nearby hospital. Your social worker calls to report what has happened. He says you may be showing signs of early-onset dementia. He says you may be abusing your methadone. I tell him about our recent conversation, the one where you told me you were taking Klonopin to sleep at night; the one where you guardedly suggested you may not be taking it as directed.

Two weeks later the social worker calls me again. You have terminated your services with their facility. You are within your rights to do so, and by phoning to let me know, the social worker is breaking protocol. But he is worried, thinks you lied when you said you found a psychiatrist closer to home. He believes you may no longer be fit to take care of yourself. He wants to call Adult Protective Services, would I be all right with that, and might he provide them with my phone number? He says to me, Please, you are the only person H. has.

IT TAKES A FEW DAYS, but I reach you. I come over with pastries from the Doughnut Plant. You seem all right—lucid, lively. You want to know how I know about it all. You are annoyed that someone would call me. You tell me that you like your new facility, that you are happy not to travel to Crown Heights to see your psychiatrist. Getting around the city is hard now. Scoliosis has you bent in two. You are not lying about the existence of this new facility. But when I ask whether you have a new social worker, someone who can help manage your various appointments, who knows what services you are eligible for, who can connect you with the things you need, who you can talk to about your private thoughts, it occurs to you, for the first time, that you do not. I tell you to look into it.

A few weeks later, I hear from my father that you have started traveling to Crown Heights again.

I MET R. THROUGH a dating app. Now I am sitting with him in a wooden booth in a dark bar drinking Campari with soda and lime. We talk, and it's clear he knows a lot of things. He refuses to say much about it, but for years he studied Kabbalah. He also lived in India, studied Buddhism. Now he works as a professor. We share some ideas about politics, enough to make him stand out among the other dates. We seem to be getting along all right.

Recently he has been to Vancouver. I tell him that I've also been there. We talk about the Downtown Eastside, and he tells me he knows and respects the work of Gabor Maté, whom I interviewed on my trip. Maté is a physician and harm-reduction advocate, a proponent of safe injection sites, who worked in the Downtown Eastside for twelve years. He's also a proponent of the healing powers of ayahuasca, which is how R. knows of him. I enjoy this conversation, the overlaps in our knowledge. I tell him about *Da Vinci's Inquest*, the Canadian television program based on Vancouver's chief coroner turned mayor, the same mayor who was in office when Insite opened. R. tells me that he has done, still sometimes does do, heroin. A casual user.

It's like a test. I can recall the many times I have pointed out, in abstract conversations, that heroin's reputation does not align with scientific evidence; that although it can be devastating for some, it is not, in itself, any more dangerous than a lot of other drugs, and people who use heroin are unduly stigmatized. But here it is no longer abstract. Will I hold it against R.?

Later, when I mention this detail to a friend, she frowns. "I like the other guy better."

YOU ARE CURED of your hepatitis after a course of Sovaldi, a new pill that clears the disease in 95 percent of cases. The price of this near-certain cure: $84,000. Each pill costs $1,000. You are fortunate to live in New York, the state where Medicaid coverage of the drug is the most generous. Many states pay for only the sickest patients. You are, relatively speaking, not that sick.

FOR THE FIRST TIME I come across an article in the popular press that challenges the accepted narrative. A professor of psychology and psychiatry named Carl Hart says the heroin public health crisis is a myth. He claims the attorney general is overstating the problem. The commonly cited metrics are insufficient and misleading: the number of people who have tried heroin doesn't tell you how many people have dependency issues.

Weeks later, I underline a sentence in *Drug War Heresies*, a book that attempts to project and evaluate the consequences of various legalization regimes and drug-policy reforms: "One million occasional drug users may pose fewer crime and health problems than 100,000 frequent users."

There are more interviews to transcribe. I've been procrastinating. Today I am listening to my conversation with Gabor Maté. My friends have been trying ayahuasca, going on retreats, and they all seem to know of him, to hold him in high regard.

I know the quote I want, am waiting for him to say it, fast-forward through my own voice.

He says: "Abstinence is just not a model you can force on everybody. There's nothing wrong with it for those for whom it works. But when it comes to drug treatment there's an assumption that one size fits all. And if you're going to wash your hands of people who can't go the abstinence route, then you're giving up."

He says: "Harm reduction means you give out clean needles, you give out sterile water, you resuscitate people if they overdose. You help people inject more safely. You're not treating the addiction. You're not intending to. You're just reducing the harm."

WE DECIDE TO SEE a movie in Williamsburg. In the back of a livery car, you tell me that one thing you really miss, one thing you think you should try to do, is find a female companion. I agree that this would be ideal, but I'm not sure how to help. I say that maybe you should go online. I show you the dating app on my phone and we laugh at its absurdity. I say there must be sites for older people. But you don't have a computer, and you don't have a smartphone. I'm certain you could count the times you've used the internet on one hand.

YOU TELL ME ABOUT the woman in the apartment below you. Whenever you try to shower, she immediately turns on all her faucets and uses up the hot water before you even have time to undress.

I explain the unlikelihood of this—hot-water distribution in a multi-unit building just doesn't work that way. You seem reassured, but the next time we speak, you complain that the problem continues.

Weeks later, you call in a panic. Con Edison is threatening to cut off your service, and you can't afford to pay. The bill is several hundred dollars, despite the subsidy you receive. You tell me you had been running your space heater all day, every day, for weeks—the building had kept the heat on low. You either underestimate my intelligence or the shame is too great.

I call Con Edison, take care of your bill. You haven't sent a payment in six months. When I confront you with this, you insist on your version of the story.

You call a car and ride over to my place because you don't have money to get you through the month. My father says that if I lend it to you, he'll pay me back.

"You know what happened?"

You are sitting at my dining table. You are smiling, and you tell me that when you finally met the hot-water villain, you found her beautiful and fell in love.

You gave her a holiday gift: a note and $30. You stuffed it under her door. She kept the money, of course, but she never acknowledged you.

When you leave I give you extra cash for your car ride home.

A week later, you call to apologize for lying to me about the Con Ed bill. This is a first.

THE CANADIAN GOVERNMENT releases details of a damning audit. The audit alleges that PHS Services, which runs Insite and in 2013 received provincial-government funding worth approximately $18 million, misused corporate credit cards and reimbursed improper expenses:

$8,600 for limousine rides in 2013
almost $900 per night for a stay in a British hotel
more than $2,600 for a stay in a Disneyland resort for two adults
    and two children
$5,832 for a Danube cruise

The article reveals many other missteps.

I wince. I know how hard these people have worked, how much they've done for the hard-to-house in Vancouver. I know this scandal will taint them forever. To open a facility like Insite, to set up crack pipe vending machines (as they have also done)—to challenge the status quo in this way—you can't make mistakes. It's like being a politician. Someone will always want to drag you down.

EVEN AS THE MEDIA NARRATIVE continues to focus on heroin use among middle-class youth in suburban neighborhoods and rural towns, I know that other populations are in need of resources and services. A study by the Centers for Disease Control and Prevention shows that rates of heroin use remain highest among males, 18- to 25-year-olds, people with household incomes below $20,000, people living in urban areas, and people with no health insurance or on Medicaid.

I take the subway up to the Bronx to BOOM!Health, a peer-run harm-reduction organization. With a small grant from the Drug Policy Alliance, BOOM! is trying to open the first legal supervised-injection facility in the US. They've even set up a model site, a single injection booth fashioned after those at Insite. I meet with the organization's president and chief programming officer. He tells me that they want to create a pilot study, much like the one in Vancouver. I know that when advocates in San Francisco tried to set up a facility, the opposition was too great. But BOOM! is optimistic; having Bill de Blasio in the mayor's office presents an opportunity.

I speak with a lawyer specializing in public-health law who argues that a pilot study is not the best strategy. "The people who are moved by evidence are not necessarily legislators. Insite was evaluated every which way. There were so many papers. Most of them are some variation on the theme that it did pretty much what we thought it would do, and it didn't do anything that its detractors thought it might do. Has that proven very persuasive, either in Canada or the US? Not really!"

Framing the facility as an incremental extension of services already available, he suggests, could prove more effective. "Almost do it under the radar." He is not sure that he is correct, but claims that, at least to his knowledge, the federal government never busted a single syringe-exchange program; it was always the local cops and sheriffs.

He adds, hesitantly: "But then the question is: Is that model"—i.e., an unsanctioned facility—"exportable to other cities and states?"

WHEN I BEGAN TO follow the media coverage of the new "heroin scourge," I didn't have strong ideas about "addiction," except that I knew it when I saw it. I believed it was a disease, and that it should be treated as such. But the more I read, the more people I speak with, the more I begin to question this framework. It is clear that no one—no neuroscientist, psychologist, psychiatrist, or physician—can explain what addiction is or account for its contradictions. Tobacco, cocaine, heroin, alcohol, MDMA, amphetamines—are they inherently addictive? Common knowledge suggests they are. But all around me I see exceptions more than the rule, my friends who use, have used, some or all of these drugs, including heroin, casually. I, too, am one of the exceptions.

I conclude that my own point of view is now best represented by the more radical strands of the harm-reduction movement and by legalization; I can argue, morally, intellectually, why these alternatives are better than what we have now.

Following the lead of those in harm-reduction and drug-users' rights groups, I decide to scrub the word *addict* from my vocabulary, to avoid using the term *drug abuser*. The alternatives can be awkward on the page, in a sentence, but it is more important not to reduce a person to this one aspect of her life, not to ascribe all the negative valences carried by these words.

> person with a substance-misuse disorder
> person experiencing a drug problem
> person who uses drugs habitually
> person committed to drug use

I try carrying these over into speech. This, too, is challenging.

I MEET JUDITH in her studio. She is 75, a painter of Indian peafowl, roseate spoonbills, reddish egrets, and other birds of refined plumage and delicate bills. Earlier in the winter, her son, Spencer, died of a methadone overdose. We face each other, seated in chairs, a small table and a glass of water between us. Judith looks the part of a painter. She is poised, like her subjects, and speaks of her son's death with surprising ease.

"Having a son die this way is not the absolute worst thing a mother can experience. I can think of circumstances far worse."

Her stoicism is not an act. Despite countless visits to detox programs and rehab centers, a frightening prison stay, longtime family support, and the benefit of resources unavailable to most, Spencer was unable to stop using drugs in a dangerous way. Judith understands that she's not to blame.

I examine a framed photograph of Spencer that Judith has pulled out on my behalf. He's tall and fit-looking, blue-eyed, sensitive.

Spencer binged. Methadone maintenance never worked for him. Taking anything at all, including methadone, triggered a dangerous cycle. When Spencer overdosed, it was with methadone he received through a program. He had been trying to give up drugs. Judith believes that Spencer was torn between the life he wanted for himself and the life he seemed fated to have. "He had the right to let himself go if he couldn't be happy."

Judith tells me that methadone-maintenance therapy is without a doubt a terrible thing. I want to say: Maybe for some people, like your son, but it has also helped many others. But I can't say it.

Judith says that a person on methadone still has that "all about me" attitude. What she means is that there is a kind of heroin mind, a way of behaving particular to a habitual drug user. The person may prioritize access to heroin above all else, including relationships with loved ones. Lying and stealing are constants in the repertoire of behavior. A person on methadone, Judith is saying, is still in heroin mind.

I make an intellectual case for methadone, say that for some people it can help to stabilize their lives. But Judith stares at me blankly. She is not interested. I want to appeal with a personal example, but I find it hard to come up with one.

She compares those who rely on methadone with those who seek help, and support others, through Narcotics Anonymous, as her son did. The people who commit to these programs, she explains, commit to a life of service. Spencer may have given up on his own life, but he helped save innumerable others. Judith claims the people she met through NA are among the saintliest she knows.

"You should disconnect from your uncle, leave him behind, drop him. He is taking from you without ever giving back."

I feel defensive, uncomfortable, on your behalf and my own. I feel I'm being perceived as weak for deciding that you, while difficult, are still a person worth knowing.

I say I appreciate the advice.

Judith apologizes, tells me what I really need to do is to find a boyfriend who will treat me like a queen.

I AM MISTAKEN. Sophie never does come around. I can't remember the last time you mentioned her name. Two years, maybe more. By now your grandson must be 8 or 9.

With the right login credentials and some basic biographical information—first and last name, an approximate age, a residential state past or present, a relative's given name—there's a lot you can find out about a person, even when Google and Facebook turn up little. When I decide, finally, that I will look for Sophie this way, through databases I can access through my job as a fact-checker, it takes me no more than sixty seconds to locate where she is living.

A trail of email addresses with varying domain names (aol.com, comcast.com, yahoo.com) reveals a few of the websites she's created accounts on: a daily-horoscope generator, a payday-loan provider (cash4thanksgiving.com). Presumably these sites have lax privacy policies. My heart sinks a little when I think of her needing a payday loan; it suggests her life has not been an easy one.

I will write to her, I think.

2016

UNCANNY VALLEY

ANNA WIENER

MORALE IS DOWN. WE ARE MAKING PLENTY OF MONEY, BUT THE office is teeming with salespeople: well-groomed social animals with good posture and dress shoes, men who chuckle and smooth their hair back when they can't connect to our VPN. Their corner of the office is loud; their desks are scattered with freebies from other start-ups, stickers and koozies and flash drives. We escape for drinks and fret about our company culture. "Our culture is dying," we say gravely, apocalyptic prophets all. "What should we do about the culture?"

It's not just the salespeople, of course. It's never just the salespeople. Our culture has been splintering for months. Members of our core team have been shepherded into conference rooms by top-level executives who proceed to question our loyalty. They've noticed the sea change. They've noticed we don't seem as invested. We don't stick around for in-office happy hour anymore; we don't take new hires out for lunch on the company card. We're not hitting our KPIs, we're not serious about the OKRs. People keep using the word *paranoid*. Our primary investor has funded a direct competitor. This is what investors do, but it feels personal: Daddy still loves us, but he loves us less.

We get ourselves out of the office and into a bar. We have more in common than our grievances, but we kick off by speculating about our job security, complaining about the bureaucratic double-downs, casting blame for blocks and poor product decisions. We talk about our IPO like it's the deus ex machina coming down from on high to save us—like it's an inevitability, like our stock options will lift us out of our existential dread, away from the collective anxiety that ebbs and flows. Realistically, we know it could be years before an IPO, if there's an IPO at all; we know in our hearts that money is a salve, not a solution. Still, we are hopeful. We reassure ourselves and one another that this is just a phase; every start-up has its growing pains. Eventually we are drunk enough to change the subject, to remember our more private selves. The people we are on weekends, the people we were for years.

This is a group of secret smokers, and we go in on a communal pack of cigarettes. The problem, we admit between drags, is that we *do* care. We care about one another. We even care about the executives who can make us feel like shit. We want good lives for them, just like we want good lives for ourselves. We care, for fuck's sake, about the company culture. We are among the first twenty employees, and we are making something people want. It feels like ours. Work has wedged its way into our identities, and the only way to maintain sanity is to maintain that we are the company, the company is us. Whenever we see a stranger at the gym wearing a T-shirt with our logo on it, whenever we are mentioned on social media or on a client's blog, whenever we get a positive support ticket, we share it in the company chat room and we're proud, genuinely proud.

But we see now that we've been swimming in the Kool-Aid, and we're coming up for air. We were lucky and in thrall and now we are bureaucrats, punching at our computers, making other people—some *kids*—unfathomably rich. We throw our dead cigarettes on the sidewalk and grind them out under our toes. Phones are opened and taxis summoned; we gulp the dregs of our beers as cartoon cars approach on-screen. We disperse, off to terrorize sleeping roommates and lovers, to answer just one, two more emails before bed. Eight hours later we'll be back in the office, slurping down coffee, running out for congealed breakfast sandwiches, tweaking mediocre scripts and writing halfhearted emails, throwing weary and knowing glances across the table.

I SKIM RECRUITER EMAILS and job listings like horoscopes, skidding down to the perks: competitive salary, dental and vision, 401k, free gym membership, catered lunch, bike storage, ski trips to Tahoe, off-sites to Napa, summits in Vegas, beer on tap, craft beer on tap, kombucha on tap, wine tastings, Whiskey Wednesdays, Open Bar Fridays, massage on-site, yoga on-site, pool table, Ping-Pong table, Ping-Pong robot, ball pit, game night, movie night, go-karts, zip line. Job listings are an excellent place to get sprayed with HR's idea of fun and a 23-year-old's idea of work-life balance. Sometimes I forget I'm not applying to summer camp. *Customized setup: design your ultimate work station with the latest hardware. Change the world around you. Help humanity thrive by enabling*—next! *We work hard, we laugh hard, we give great high-fives. We have engineers in Top-Coder's Top 20. We're not just another social web app. We're not just another project-management tool. We're not just another payment processor.* I get a haircut and start exploring.

Most start-up offices look the same—faux midcentury furniture, brick walls, snack bar, bar cart. Interior designers in Silicon Valley are either brand-conscious or very literal. When tech products are projected into the physical world they become aesthetics unto themselves, as if to insist on their own reality: the office belonging to a home-sharing website is decorated like rooms in its customers' pool houses and pieds-à-terre; the foyer of a hotel-booking start-up has a concierge desk replete with bell (no concierge); the headquarters of a ride-sharing app gleams in the same colors as the app itself, down to the sleek elevator bank. A book-related start-up holds a small and sad library, the shelves half-empty, paperbacks and object-oriented-programming manuals sloping against one another. It reminds me of the people who dressed like Michael Jackson to attend Michael Jackson's funeral.

But this office, of a media app with millions in VC funding but no revenue model, is particularly sexy. This is something that an office shouldn't be, and it jerks my heart rate way, way up. There are views of the city in every direction, fat leather loveseats, electric guitars plugged into amps, teak credenzas with white hardware. It looks like the loft apartment of the famous musician boyfriend I thought I'd have at 22 but somehow never met. I want to take off my dress and my shoes and lie on the voluminous sheepskin rug and eat fistfuls of MDMA, curl my naked body into the Eero Aarnio Ball Chair, never leave.

It's not clear whether I'm here for lunch or an interview, which is normal. I am prepared for both and dressed for neither. My guide leads me through the communal kitchen, which has the trappings of every other start-up pantry: plastic bins of trail mix and Goldfish, bowls of Popchips and miniature candy bars. There's the requisite wholesale box of assorted Clif Bars, and in the fridge are flavored water, string cheese, and single-serving cartons of chocolate milk. It can be hard to tell whether a company is training for a marathon or eating an after-school snack. Once I walked into our kitchen and found two Account Managers pounding Shot Bloks, chewy cubes of glucose marketed to endurance athletes.

Over catered Afghan food, I meet the team, including a billionaire who made his fortune from a website that helps people feel close to celebrities and other strangers they'd hate in real life. He asks where I work, and I tell him. "Oh," he says, not unkindly, snapping a piece of lavash in two, "I know that company. I think I tried to buy you."

I TAKE ANOTHER PERSONAL DAY without giving a reason, an act of defiance that I fear is transparent. I spend the morning drinking coffee and skimming breathless tech press, then creep downtown to spend the afternoon in back-to-back interviews at a peanut-size start-up. All of the interviews are with men, which is fine. I like men. I had a boyfriend; I have a brother. The men ask me questions like, "How would you calculate the number of people who work for the United States Postal Service?" and "How would you describe the internet to a medieval farmer?" and "What is the hardest thing you've ever done?" They tell me to stand in front of the whiteboard and diagram my responses. These questions are self-conscious and infuriating, but it only serves to fuel me. I want to impress; I refuse to be discouraged by their self-importance. Here is a character flaw, my industry origin story: I have always responded positively to negging.

My third interview is with the technical cofounder. He enters the conference room in a crisp blue button-down, looking confidently unprepared. He tells me—apologetically—that he hasn't done many interviews before, and as such he doesn't have a ton of questions to ask me. Nonetheless, the office manager slated an hour for our conversation. This seems OK: I figure we will talk about the company, I will ask routine follow-up questions, and at four they will let me out for the day, like a middle school student, and the city will absorb me and my private errors. Then he tells me that his girlfriend is applying to law school and he's been helping her prep. So instead of a conventional interview, he's just going to have me take a section of the LSAT. I search his face to see if he's kidding.

"If it's cool with you, I'm just going to hang out here and check my email," he says, sliding the test across the table and opening a laptop. He sets a timer.

I finish early, ever the overachiever. I check it twice. The cofounder grades it on the spot. "My mother would be so proud," I joke, feeling brilliant and misplaced and low, lower than low.

HOME IS MY REFUGE, except when it's not. My roommate is turning 30, and to celebrate we are hosting a wine and cheese party at our apartment. Well, she is hosting—I have been invited. Her friends arrive promptly, in business casual. Hundreds of dollars of cheese are represented. "Bi-Rite, obviously," she says, looking elegant in black silk as she smears Humboldt Fog onto a cracker. My roommate works down on the Peninsula, for a website that everyone loathes but no one can stop using. We occupy different spaces: I am in the start-up world, land of perpetual youth, and she is an adult like any other, navigating a corporation, acting the part, negotiating for her place. I admire and do not understand her; it is possible she finds me amusing. Mostly we talk about exercise.

Classical music streams through the house and someone opens a bottle of proper Champagne, which he reassures us is really from France; people clap when the cork pops. My roommate and I are the same age but I feel like a child at my parents' party, and I am immediately envious, homesick. I send myself to my room, lock the door, and change into a very tight dress. I've gained fifteen pounds in trail mix: it never feels like a meal, but there's an aggregate effect. When I reenter the living room, I suck in my stomach and slide between people's backs, looking for a conversation. On the couch, a man in a suit jacket expounds on the cannabis opportunity. Everyone seems very comfortable and nobody talks to me. They tilt their wineglasses at the correct angle; they dust crumbs off their palms with grace. The word I hear the most is *revenue*. No—*strategy*. There's nothing to do but drink and ingratiate myself. I wind up on the roof with a cluster of strangers and find myself missing my mother with a ferocity that carves into my gut. In the distance I can see the tip of the famous Rainbow Flag on Castro Street, whipping.

"Oakland," one of them says. "That's where we want to invest."

"Too dangerous," says another. "My wife would never go for it."

"Of course not," says the first, "but you don't buy to *live* there."

By the time the last guest has filtered out, I am in leggings and a sweatshirt, cleaning ineffectively: scooping up cheese rinds, rinsing plastic glasses, sneaking slices of chocolate cake with my damp hands. My roommate comes to say goodnight, and she is beautiful: tipsy but not toasted, radiant with absorbed goodwill. She repairs to her room with her boyfriend, and I listen from down the hall as they quietly undress, ease into bed, turn over into sleep.

OURS IS A "pickax-during-the-Gold-Rush" product, the kind venture capitalists love to get behind. The product provides a shortcut to database infrastructure, giving people information about their apps and websites that they wouldn't necessarily have on their own. All our customers are other software companies. This is a privileged vantage point from which to observe the tech industry. I would say more, but I signed an NDA.

I am the inaugural customer support rep, or Support Engineer. My job involves looking at strangers' codebases and telling them what they've done wrong in integrating our product with theirs, and how to fix it. There are no unsolvable problems. Perhaps there are not even problems, only mistakes. After nearly three years in book publishing, where I mostly moved on instinct, taste, and feeling, the clarity of this soothes me.

I learn the bare minimum, code-wise, to be able to do my job well—to ask questions only when I'm truly in over my head. Still, I escalate problems all the time. I learn how to talk to our customers about the technology without ever touching the technology itself. I find myself confidently discussing cookies, data mapping, the difference between server-side and client-side integrations. "Just add logic!" I advise cheerfully. This means nothing to me but generally resonates with engineers. It shocks me every time someone nods along.

This is not to confuse confidence with pride. I doubt myself daily. I feel lucky to have this job; I feel desperately out of place. My previous boss—breezy and helpful, earnest in the manner of a man in his early twenties bequeathed $4 million to disrupt libraries—had encouraged me to apply for the role; I had joined his publishing start-up too early and needed something new. "This is the next big company," he had said. "It's a rocket ship." He was right. I had been banking on him being right. Still, there are days when all I want is to disembark, eject myself into space, admit defeat. I pander and apologize and self-deprecate until my manager criticizes me for being a pleaser, at which point it seems most strategic to stop talking.

I convince myself and everyone else that I want to learn how to code, and I'm incentivized to do it: I'm told I will be promoted to

Solutions Architect if I can build a networked, two-player game of checkers in the next few months. One lazy Saturday I give it three hours, then call it a day. I resent the challenge; I resent myself. I tell everyone I can't do it, which is a lesser evil than not wanting to. In this environment, my lack of interest in learning JavaScript feels like a moral failure.

Around here, we nonengineers are pressed to prove our value. The hierarchy is pervasive, ingrained in the industry's dismissal of marketing and its insistence that a good product sells itself; evident in the few "office hours" established for engineers (our scheduled opportunity to approach with questions and bugs); reflected in our salaries and equity allotment, even though it's harder to find a good copywriter than a liberal-arts graduate with a degree in history and twelve weeks' training from an uncredentialed coding dojo. This is a cozy home for believers in bootstrapping and meritocracy, proponents of shallow libertarianism. I am susceptible to it, too. "He just taught himself to code over the summer," I hear myself say one afternoon, with the awe of someone relaying a miracle.

Our soft skills are a necessary inconvenience. We bloat payroll; we dilute conversation; we create process and bureaucracy; we put in requests for yoga classes and Human Resources. We're a dragnet—though we tend to contribute positively to diversity metrics. There is quiet pity for the MBAs.

It's easy for me to dissociate from the inferiority of my job because I've never been particularly proud of my customer-service skills. I'm good at subservience, but it isn't what I would lead with on a first date. I enjoy translating between the software and the customers. I like breaking down information, demystifying technical processes, being one of few with this specific expertise. I like being bossy. People are interesting—unpredictable, emotional—when their expensive software product doesn't behave as expected. Plus, I am almost always permissioned for God Mode.

After a year, my job evolves from support into something the industry calls Customer Success. The new role is more interesting, but the title is so corny and oddly stilted in its pseudosincerity that I cannot bring myself to say it out loud. This turns out to work to my advantage: when I change my email signature to read "Technical Account Manager" instead, it actually elicits a response from previously uncommunicative clients who are—I regret having to buttress stereotypes—always engineers, always founders, and always men.

I visit a friend at his midsize software company and see a woman typing at a treadmill desk. *That's a little on the nose*, I whisper, and he whispers back, *You have no idea—she does Customer Success.*

MY COWORKERS ARE ALL skilled at maneuvering something called a RipStik, a two-wheeled, skateboard-like invention with separated pivoting plates, one for each foot. They glide across the office, twisting and dipping with laptops in hand, taking customer calls on their personal cell phones, shuttling from desk to kitchen to conference room. Mastering the RipStik is a rite of passage, and I cannot do it. After a few weeks of trying, I order a tiny plastic skateboard off eBay, a neon-green Penny board with four wheels that looks coolest when it's not being ridden. I come into the office over the weekend and practice on the Penny, perfecting my balance. It's fast, dangerously so. Mostly I put it under my standing desk and then get onboard, rocking back and forth as I work.

THE BILLBOARDS ALONG the stretch of the 101 that sweeps Silicon Valley have been punchy and declarative lately, advertising apps and other software products that transcend all context and grammatical structure. "We fixed dinner" (meal delivery). "Ask your developer" (cloud-based communications). "How tomorrow works" (file storage). The ads get less dystopian the farther you get from the city: by the airport, they grow international-businessman corporate, and as the land turns over into suburbs you can almost hear the gears shift. A financial-services company—one that's been around for more than a century, a provider of life insurance, investment management, and, in the 1980s, bald-faced fraud—holds a mirror to an audience that perhaps won't want to recognize itself. The ad reads, "Donate to a worthy cause: your retirement."

I attend a networking event at an office whose walls are hung with inspirational posters that quote tech luminaries I've never heard of. The posters say things like "Life is short: build stuff that matters" and "Innovate or die." I am dead. Our interior designer tried hanging posters like these in our office; the front-end engineers relocated them to the bathroom, placed them face to the wall. The event is packed; people roam in clusters, like college freshmen during orientation week. There are a few women, but most of the attendees are young men in start-up twinsets: I pass someone wearing a branded hoodie, unzipped to reveal a shirt with the same logo. I google the company on my cell phone to see what it is, to see if they're hiring. "We have loved mobile since we saw Steve Jobs announce the first iPhone," their website declares, and I close the browser, thinking, *how basic.*

The tenor of these events is usually the same: guilelessly optimistic. People are excited to talk about their start-ups, and all small-talk is a prelude to a pitch. I'm guilty of this, too; I'm proud of my work, and our recruiting bonus is 15 percent of my salary (alignment of company–employee goals and incentives). I talk to two European men who are building a food-delivery app geared toward healthy eaters, like people on the Paleo diet. They're extremely polite and oddly buff. They say they'll invite me to their beta, and I am excited. I like to be on the inside track. I want to help. I tell them that I know a lot of people on the Paleo diet, like the guy in marketing who stores plastic baggies of wet, sautéed meat in the communal refrigerator. I chatter on about Paleo adherents and people who do CrossFit and practice polyamory, and how I admire that they manage to do these things without detrimental physical or emotional consequences. I've learned so much about polyamory and S&M since moving to San Francisco. Ask me anything about *The Ethical Slut*; ask me anything about *Sex at Dawn.* That night, I download the healthy-food app and can't ever imagine using it.

My opinion doesn't matter, of course: a few months later I'll find out that the Europeans raised $30-odd million after pivoting to a new business model and undergoing a radical rebranding, and I'll find this out when our company starts paying them thousands to organize the catering for our in-office meals. The food is served in sturdy tinfoil troughs, and people race to be first in line for self-serve. It is low-carb and delicious, healthier than anything I've ever cooked, well worth someone else's money, and every afternoon I shovel it into my body.

Our own 101 billboard is unveiled on a chilly morning in November, just a few months after I've started. Everyone gets to work early; our office manager orders fresh-squeezed orange juice and pastries, cups of yogurt parfait with granola strata. We've arranged for a company field trip around the corner. We walk in a pack, hands in our pockets, and take a group photograph in front of our ad. I forward it to my parents in New York. In the photograph we've got our arms around one another, smiling and proud. The start-up is still small, just thirty of us or so, but within a year we'll be almost a hundred employees, and shortly thereafter, I'll be gone.

I HAVE LUNCH WITH one of the salespeople, and I like him a lot. He's easy to talk to; he's easy to talk to for a living. We eat large, sloppy sandwiches in the park and gaze out at the tourists.

"So how'd you end up choosing our company?" I ask. Roast turkey drops from my sandwich onto the grass.

"Come on," he says. "I heard there were a bunch of twenty-somethings crushing it in the Valley. How often does that happen?"

I lean in and go to a panel on big data. There are two venture capitalists onstage, dressed identically. They are exceptionally sweaty. Even from the back row, the place feels moist. I've never been in a room with so few women and so much money, and so many people champing at the bit to get a taste. It's like watching two ATMs in conversation. "I want big data on men watching other men talk about data," I whisper to my new friend in sales, who ignores me.

Back at the office, I walk into the bathroom to find a coworker folded over the sink, wiping her face with a paper towel. There aren't many women at this company, and I have encountered almost all of them, at one point or another, crying in the bathroom. "I just hope this is all worth it," she spits in my direction. I know what she means—she's talking about money—but I also know how much equity she has, and I'm confident that even in the best possible scenario, whatever she's experiencing is definitely not. She's out the door and back at her desk before I can conjure up something consoling.

Half of the conversations I overhear these days are about money, but nobody likes to get specific. It behooves everyone to stay theoretical.

A friend's roommate wins a hackathon with corporate sponsorship, and on a rainy Sunday afternoon he is awarded $500,000. (It is actually a million, but who would believe me?) That evening they throw a party at their duplex, which feels like a normal event in the Burning Man off-season—whippits, face paint, high-design vaporizers—except for the oversize foamcore check propped laterally against the bathroom doorframe.

Out by the porch cooler, I run into a friend who works at a company—cloud something—that was recently acquired. I make a joke about this being a billionaire boys' club and he laughs horsily, disproportionate to the humor. I've never seen him like this, but then I've never met anyone who's won the lottery, seen anyone so jazzed on his own good luck. He opens a beer using the edge of his lighter and invites me to drive up to Mendocino in his new convertible. What else do you do after a windfall? "You know who the real winner was, though?" he asks, then immediately names a mutual acquaintance, a brilliant and introverted programmer who was the company's first engineering hire, very likely the linchpin. "Instant multimillionaire," my friend says incredulously, as if hearing his own information for the first time. "At least eight figures."

"Wow," I say, handing my beer to him to open. "What do you think he wants to do?"

My friend deftly pops off the bottle cap, then looks at me and shrugs. "That's a good question," he says, tapping the lighter against the side of his beer. "I don't think he wants to do anything."

AN OLD HIGH SCHOOL FRIEND emails out of the blue to introduce me to his college buddy: a developer, new to the city, "always a great time!" The developer and I agree to meet for drinks. It's not clear whether we're meeting for a date or networking. Not that there's always a difference: I have one friend who found a job by swiping right and know countless others who go to industry conferences just to fuck—nothing gets them hard like a nonsmoking room charged to the company AmEx. The developer is very handsome and stiltedly sweet. He seems like someone who has opinions about fonts, and he does. It's clear from the start that we're there to talk shop. We go to a tiny cocktail bar in the Tenderloin with textured wallpaper and a scrawny bouncer. Photographs are forbidden, which means the place is designed for social media. This city is changing, and I am disgusted by my own complicity.

"There's no menu, so you can't just order, you know, a martini," the developer says, as if I would ever. "You tell the bartender three adjectives, and he'll customize a drink for you accordingly. It's great. It's creative! I've been thinking about my adjectives all day."

What is it like to be fun? What is it like to feel like you've earned this? I try to game the system by asking for something smoky, salty, and angry, crossing my fingers for mezcal; it works. We lean against a wall and sip. The developer tells me about his loft apartment in the Mission, his specialty bikes, how excited he is to go on weeknight camping trips. We talk about cameras and books. We talk about cities we've never visited. I tell him about the personal-shopper service my coworkers all signed up for, how three guys came into work wearing the same sweater; he laughs but looks a little guilty. He's sweet and a little shy about his intelligence, and I know we'll probably never hang out again. Still, I go home that night with the feeling that something, however small, has been lifted.

VENTURE CAPITALISTS have spearheaded massive innovation in the past few decades, not least of which is their incubation of this generation's very worst prose style. The internet is choked with blindly ambitious and professionally inexperienced men giving each other anecdote-based instruction and bullet-point advice. *10 Essential Start-up Lessons You Won't Learn in School. 10 Things Every Successful Entrepreneur Knows. 5 Ways to Stay Humble. Why the Market Always Wins. Why the Customer Is Never Right. How to Deal with Failure. How to Fail Better. How to Fail Up. How to Pivot. How to Pivot Back. 18 Platitudes to Tape Above Your Computer. Raise Your Way to Emotional Acuity. How to Love Something That Doesn't Love You Back.*

Sometimes it feels like everyone is speaking a different language—or the same language, with radically different rules. At our all-hands meeting, we are subjected to a pep talk. Our director looks like he hasn't slept in days, but he straightens up and moves his gaze from face to face, making direct and metered eye contact with everyone around the table. "We are making products," he begins, "that can push the fold of mankind."

A networking-addicted coworker scrolls through a website where people voluntarily post their own résumés. I spy. He clicks through to an engineer who works for an aggressively powerful start-up, one whose rapid expansion, relentless pursuit of domination, and absence of ethical boundaries scare the shit out of me. Under his current company, the engineer has written this job description: "This is a rocket ship, baby. Climb aboard."

I am waiting for the train when I notice the ad: it covers the platform below the escalators. The product is an identity-as-a-service app—it stores passwords—but the company isn't advertising to users; they're advertising their job openings. They're advertising to me. The ad features five people standing in V-formation with their arms crossed. They're all wearing identical blue hoodies. They're also wearing identical rubber unicorn masks; I am standing on one of their heads. The copy reads, "Built by humans, used by unicorns."

We hire an engineer fresh out of a top undergraduate program. She walks confidently into the office, springy and enthusiastic. We've all been looking forward to having a woman on our engineering team. It's a big moment for us. Her onboarding buddy brings her around to make introductions, and as they approach our corner, my coworker leans over and cups his hand around my ear: as though we are colluding, as though we are 5 years old. "I feel sorry," he says, his breath moist against my neck. "Everyone's going to hit on her."

I include this anecdote in an email to my mom. The annual-review cycle is nigh, and I'm on the fence about whether or not to bring up the running list of casual hostilities toward women that add unsolicited spice to the workplace. I tell her about the colleague with the smart-watch app that's just an animated GIF of a woman's breasts bouncing in perpetuity; I tell her about the comments I've fielded about my weight, my lips, my clothing, my sex life; I tell her that the first woman engineer is also the only engineer without SSH access to the servers. I tell her that compared with other women I've met here, I have it good, but the bar is low. It's tricky: I like these coworkers—and I dish it back—but in the parlance of our industry, this behavior is scalable. I don't have any horror stories yet; I'd prefer things stay this way. I expect my mother to respond with words of support and encouragement. I expect her to say, "Yes! You are the change this industry needs." She emails me back almost immediately. "Don't put complaints about sexism in writing," she writes. "Unless, of course, you have a lawyer at the ready."

A MEETING IS DROPPED mysteriously onto our calendars, and at the designated time we shuffle warily into a conference room. The last time this happened, we were given forms that asked us to rate various values on a scale of 1 to 5: our desire to lead a team; the importance of work-life balance. I gave both things a 4 and was told I didn't want it enough.

The conference room has a million-dollar view of downtown San Francisco, but we keep the shades down. Across the street, a bucket drummer bangs out an irregular heartbeat. We sit in a row, backs to the window, laptops open. I look around the room and feel a wave of affection for these men, this small group of misfits who are the only people who understand this new backbone to my life. On the other side of the table, our manager paces back and forth, but he's smiling. He asks us to write down the names of the five smartest people we know, and we dutifully oblige. I look at the list and think about how much I miss my friends back home, how bad I've been at returning phone calls and emails, how bloated I've become with start-up self-importance, how I've stopped making time for what I once held dear. I can feel blood rush to my cheeks.

"OK," my manager says. "Now tell me: why don't they work here?"

MORALE, LIKE ANYTHING, is just another problem to be solved. There is a high premium on break/fix. To solve our problem, management arranges for a team-building exercise. They schedule it on a weeknight evening, and we pretend not to mind. Our team-building begins with beers in the office, and then we travel en masse to a tiny event space at the mouth of the Stockton Tunnel, where two energetic blondes give us sweatbands and shots. The blondes are attractive and athletic, strong limbs wrapped in spandex leggings and tiny shorts, and we are their smudge-edged foils: an army of soft bellies and stiff necks, hands tight with the threat of carpal tunnel. They smear neon face paint across our foreheads and cheeks and tell us we look awesome. The event space warms up as people get drunk and bounce around the room, taking selfies with the CFO, fist-bumping the cofounders without irony, flirting with the new hires who don't yet know any better. We play Skee-Ball. We cluster by the bar and have another round, two.

Eventually, we're dispatched on a scavenger hunt across the city. We pour out of the building and into the street, spreading across rush-hour San Francisco, seeking landmarks; we barrel past tourists and harass taxicab drivers, piss off doormen and stumble into homeless people. We are our own worst representatives, calling apologies over our shoulders. We are sweaty, competitive—maybe happy, really happy.

THE MEETING BEGINS without fanfare. They thought I was an amazing worker at first, working late every night, last out of the office, but now they wonder if the work was just too hard for me to begin with. They need to know: Am I down for the cause? Because if I'm not down for the cause, it's time. They will do this amicably. Of course I'm down, I say, trying not to swivel in my ergonomic chair. I care deeply about the company. I am here for it.

When I say I care deeply, what I mean is I am ready to retire. When I say I'm down, what I mean is I'm scared. I cry twice during the meeting, despite my best efforts. I think about the city I left to come here, the plans I've canceled and the friends I haven't made. I think about how hard I've worked and how demoralizing it is to fail. I think about my values, and I cry even more. It will be months until I call uncle and quit; it will take almost a year to realize I was gaslighting myself, that I was reading from someone else's script.

IT'S CHRISTMASTIME; I'm older, I'm elsewhere. On the train to work, I swipe through social media and hit on a post from the start-up's holiday party, which has its own hashtag. The photograph is of two former teammates, both of them smiling broadly, their teeth as white as I remember. "So grateful to be part of such an amazing team," the caption reads, and I tap through. The hashtag unleashes a stream of photographs featuring people I've never met—beautiful people, the kind of people who look good in athleisure. They look well rested. They look relaxed and happy. They look nothing like me. There's a photograph of what can only be the pre-dinner floor show: an acrobat in a leotard kneeling on a pedestal, her legs contorted, her feet grasping a bow and arrow, poised to release. Her target is a stuffed heart, printed with the company logo. I scroll past animated photo-booth GIFs of strangers, kissing and mugging for the camera, and I recognize their pride, I empathize with their sense of accomplishment—this was one hell of a year, and they have won. I feel gently ill, a callback to the childhood nausea of being left out.

The holiday party my year at the company began with an open bar at 4 PM—the same coworker had shellacked my hair into curls in the office bathroom, both of us excited and exhausted, ready to celebrate. Hours later, we danced against the glass windows of the *Michelin*-starred restaurant our company had bought out for the night, our napkins strewn on the tables, our shoes torn off, our plus-ones shifting in formal wear on the sidelines, the waitstaff studiously withholding visible judgment.

I keep scrolling until I hit a video of this year's after-party, which looks like it was filmed in a club or at a flashy bar mitzvah, save for the company logo projected onto the wall: flashing colored lights illuminate men in stripped-down suits and women in cocktail dresses, all of them bouncing up and down, waving glow sticks and lightsabers to a background of electronic dance music. They've gone pro, I say to myself. "Last night was epic!" someone has commented. Three years have passed since I left. I catch myself searching for my own face anyway.

2016

HEADS WITHOUT BODIES

A. S. HAMRAH

IT RAINED IN BROOKLYN THE DAY AFTER DONALD TRUMP WAS elected. Overnight it had become a damp, drizzly November. The ceiling in the room where I'm writing this developed a leak that morning. Rust-colored water stained the white paint around the light fixture, spreading outward until a steady drip fell off the light bulb into the square glass shade, filling the translucent pan with brown water.

I noticed the leak when the water began to trickle off the corner of the shade nearest my desk. I got a bucket and a stepladder, tipped the shade into the bucket to pour off the dingy water, then unscrewed the shade and removed it. I put the bucket on the floor, looked up, and saw a hole in the ceiling, open to the rain. Here it is, I thought, the first day of the Trump era. I stopped writing, went to the store, bought some cigarettes, and started smoking again.

Late that summer a friend had called from Canada to predict that Trump would win the election, and to invite me, should that happen, to come up and check out the democracy. I lit a cigarette and phoned her. I wanted to be out of the US for Trump's inauguration in January. Could I come up then? I mentioned there was a hole in my ceiling. When we got off the phone I bought a plane ticket to Toronto. It was not expensive. Most people do not travel to Ontario in January if they can help it.

THE CITY OF HAMILTON, where my friend lives, is about forty-five miles southwest of Toronto on Lake Ontario, which, as I found it, was covered in dense fog. Despite the sunlessness, the lake was only part frozen. Hamilton was chilly and gray, a steel town in winter dotted with thrift stores, coffee places huge by New York standards, and record shops selling thrash and grindcore LPs.

My friend does not have television, so we looked for a bar where we could watch the inauguration live on a big flatscreen. I was glad not to be in the US, but I wasn't going to miss the moment a reality-TV con man was sworn in as President of the United States. For some reason I figured Hamilton would have a lot of bars with TVs in them open by 11:30 on a Friday morning. That was not the case. Some bars were open by 11:30 for lunch but had gone gastropub and didn't have televisions anymore.

Our search turned up a place called Fisher's two blocks from the lake, a spot with a long bar, booths, plenty of TVs, and menus in Lucite frames on the tables advertising fishbowls, giant drinks made to share, served in clear globes. Three dozen or so local businessmen, who probably would have gone there to eat anyway, had also gathered to watch the inauguration. Some regulars at the bar cheered when Trump appeared on-screen. The people at the tables looked concerned as Trump was sworn in and surprised when he let go with his "carnage" outburst. The waitress, realizing I was an American, told me she was sorry.

On TV, the Missouri State University Chorale, dressed in black overcoats and burgundy berets, sang "Now We Belong." They sounded as joyless and funereal as they looked in their black coats. It was overcast in Washington DC and the student chorus sang in the rain, which Donald Trump later claimed let up for his address even though it had not.

Behind the new President, Barack Obama looked like he had a migraine. Paul Ryan grinned his new grin, a crazy-looking rictus he had worn since the Republican National Convention. The new Vice President, Mike Pence, appeared serious to the point of menace, as if he had bitten the head off a bald eagle to prove a point and would do it again. George W. Bush, goofy in the kind of transparent rain poncho sold in vending machines in bus stations, showed the world he was a man who had left care behind now that he would not go down as the worst President in American history. Much of the rest of the crowd was made up of *Dick Tracy* villains, rubber masks from a forgotten part of the 20th century, and blondes in the Fox News style. On TV, the helicopter that took away Barack and Michelle Obama rose in silence and slow motion.

After the inauguration, the network cut to a group in the crowd called Bikers for Trump, there from New Jersey. One of them, a man wearing a cap that said Sick Boy on it, complained about the protesters in Washington that day. "I don't have time to protest because I have a job!" he yelled at the camera, even though he was there and not working. Trump declared his inauguration a "national day of patriotic devotion," but it was not a federal holiday. Even as he bellowed about "tombstones across the landscape of our nation" in his crap-weird speech in the rain, postal workers delivered mail in the US and life went on. We ordered another pint as lunch hour ended and the businessmen of Hamilton went back out into the fog.

The next day we went to the Hamilton Women's March, which, with Canadian concern for inclusiveness and safety, had been changed to a Women's Rally because of "accessibility issues." It was held in front of Hamilton's impressive modernist City Hall, a two-tiered, eight-story mini-UN next to the Canadian Football Hall of Fame. Outside, a statue of a receiver reached prayer-like for a football in the sky while a tackler wrapped him around the waist. The two silver athletes looked like toy spacemen from a 1960s version of the future. My Canadian friend pointed out that the tackler also looked like he was giving the receiver a blow job. We stood among the pink-knitted pussy hats dotting the gray weather in the nonmarching crowd and listened to Canadian speeches about what had happened in the US. Nearby, a teenage girl stood on a concrete planter holding a large sign she had drawn in neat serif caps, the first line in mint green, the next in pink, the last in cornflower blue. It read

NO ♀NE

IS AN

ISLAND

The night before the inauguration, we saw a movie at a place where bands play. Doors Pub features an outsize portrait of the heavy-metal singer King Diamond's face in close-up next to the bar, and hosts a 16mm-movie night called Trash Palace. That Thursday, the film was *The Thing with Two Heads*, a cheap American B-grade movie from 1972. It stars Ray Milland as a white surgeon and Rosey Grier as a black convict on death row for killing a cop. Grier is the football player who was standing next to Robert Kennedy when he was assassinated in 1968. The Welsh Milland won an Oscar in 1946 for *The Lost Weekend*, in which he played an alcoholic. By 1972 he was choosing his roles with less care, more daring.

The film's tagline was "They share the same body . . . but hate each other's guts!" I was told that the timing was a coincidence, but even before the film began it was clear that this was a movie about America under Donald Trump. I wasn't prepared, however, for how much Milland would resemble our new President, especially after his head is cut off and grafted onto Grier's left shoulder. Trump and the Ray Milland of 1972 have the same hairstyle and hair color and the same bellicose, insulting demeanor. Their look-alike hair is especially obvious in shots where Milland's head is fake, a mannequin wig-holder for when his decapitated head is carried around independently of its body, or in long-shot chase scenes in which Grier rides a motorcycle with the bewigged paste head attached to him.

Milland's character is terminally ill but has a plan for survival. "I want to transplant my head on a healthy body," he explains. "There is no other way for me to live." The catch is that for a month the two men must share Grier's body while it gets used to the new head.

Then Grier's head will be cut off and the body will be Milland's alone. Grier volunteers for this because he believes he can prove himself innocent while the two men share his body. Milland, already established in the film as a racist who won't work with black doctors, is not told who the only volunteer is.

After the operation, Grier wakes up and sees Milland's Trump-esque head on the operating table next to his own. "Where's the rest of you?" Grier shouts in this new, extra head's face, a reversal of Ronald Reagan's "Where's the rest of me?" from 1942's *Kings Row*. Appalled that he is now attached to a black man, Milland has Grier chloroformed. "The black bastard," he says. "How am I ever going to control him? He could kill me."

The Thing with Two Heads devolves into chase scenes and jokes about racism, but not before making it clear that men like Milland's wealthy surgeon believe experimenting on and killing black men is fine if it allows white men to live, if it gets them closer to living forever. The film is resonant because we know this happened in this country in real life. The story of the Tuskegee syphilis experiment broke in the *New York Times* the same week *The Thing with Two Heads* premiered at drive-ins and in grind houses around the country.

Forty-five years later, little has changed. Jordan Peele's *Get Out*, which premiered a month after the inauguration, updates *The Thing with Two Heads* by eliminating the severed head and making the "coagula" a mind-meld requiring just a touch of brain surgery. In Peele's film, the white man, seeking to extend his life, completely inhabits and controls a younger black man's body, head and all. The body cannot reject the mind that now occupies it, can't argue with it or punch it in the face. The two are fused, and black consciousness stares out from within the film's "sunken place," immobilized and silent. *Get Out*, unlike *The Thing with Two Heads*, decouples *The Defiant Ones* from *The Brain That Wouldn't Die*.

Grier's character in *The Thing with Two Heads*, sitting on death row, was already expendable and doomed. This campy sociopolitical horror film from the Watergate years literalized the conflicts of the civil rights struggle in a grotesque way, asking viewers to take it seriously while inviting them to mock it at the same time. Since then, the film has existed below the level of serious commentary. Yet all of a sudden it speaks to us, because of Trump's head.

Earlier in his career, in 1989, when he was merely a rich gasbag and an annoyance, Trump bought a big ad in the *New York Times* so he could publicly call for the executions of the Central Park Five, young black men accused and convicted of assault and rape. The men were exonerated by DNA evidence in 2002 and released from prison. They sued the City of New York and settled for $41 million. Trump went out of his way last year to let voters know he still believed they were guilty. This is how he thrives. Now he has grafted his head onto our collective body, with his horror-movie hairdo always in our face. Trump's head is struggling to control our actions and responses the same way Milland's head struggled to control Grier's body in this cheap movie. The devil finds work where he can. *The Thing with Two Heads* was too dumb to be noticed by James Baldwin in his book-length essay on race and the movies, and I had to go to Canada to run into it. Now it's the kind of stupid we live with every day.

IN MAY, THE COMEDIAN Kathy Griffin posted a photo on Twitter and Instagram in which she's holding a model of Donald Trump's severed head by the hair, blood dripping from its neck and eyes. The caption she provided referenced Trump's sexist comments about Megyn Kelly, the former Fox News host who moderated a Republican debate during the campaign. "There was blood coming out of his eyes, blood coming out of his . . . wherever," it read, gender-switching Trump's remark about Kelly.

The photo's resemblance to various paintings of Judith holding the severed head of Holofernes, the Assyrian general bent on destroying Judith's city, was noted by some, casting Griffin's stunt as feminist and political beyond the way she had intended. Judith's story, which appears in the Apocrypha, has been a subject for artists since the Renaissance. Caravaggio and Lucas Cranach the Elder

painted Judith with Holofernes's head, as has, more recently, Kehinde
Wiley. Komar and Melamid depicted Holofernes as the stone head of
a statue of Stalin held aloft in a little girl's palm. Women artists have
been understandably drawn to Judith as a subject. Artemisia Gen-
tileschi painted Judith's beheading of Holofernes in the 17th century;
Tina Blondell in 1999. Judith has appeared in movies, too. The year
before he made *The Birth of a Nation*, D. W. Griffith made a film
called *Judith of Bethulia*.

The image of Trump's decapitated head created an uproar.
Griffin was condemned by pretty much everybody, including Trump
himself, who claimed the image upset his youngest son. Everyone
agreed Griffin had crossed a line, and that she was even lamer and
more useless than before, now truly abject. Griffin is not a painter or
a film director. She is a reality-TV star, like Donald Trump, former
host of *The Apprentice,* and, like him, an avid Twitter user. Griffin's
photo was judged to be a stupid, ill-conceived publicity grab, reflecting on her desperation as a self-conscious D-list celebrity—*My Life on
the D-List* was the name of her Bravo reality show. Her social-media
stunt delivered both politics and art history as trash, little more.

Griffin casts her opposition to Trump in a War of the Reality
Stars, using an image of Trump's head, the "big head" of TV close-
ups, disconnected from the rest of its body. More artfully, the
German magazine *Der Spiegel* depicted Trump's head as a flaming
planet hurtling toward Earth, like the planet gone out of its orbit
in Lars von Trier's *Melancholia.* Griffin's apology for her photo, her
botched non–press conference, and her public crying jag all point
to Trumpancholia, a psychological condition now afflicting much
of the planet's population, who have traded the things they used to
enjoy for the constant monitoring of Trump's reality-TV spectacle,
which is broadcast twenty-four hours a day and consumed worldwide. In claiming he wants to make America great again, Trump
promised to bring the country back to the Reagan era, to "morning in America." Instead, we have entered a period of mourning in
America, with Trump not as Ronald Reagan but as another 1980s

character, Max Headroom, a demented TV pitchman, all face and head: an irreal, televised presence in a rubber mask who can pop up anytime because he doesn't sleep.

IN THE AGE OF STREAMING prestige drama, it looked like reality TV was on the wane. But since the Trump retrenchment, the dinosaur broadcast networks have brought back *American Idol* and *Big Brother*. While networks are desperate to get viewers to watch live television in prime time, they have less of a problem in the off-hours. The inauguration, White House press conferences, the Comey hearing—these are examples of reality television unfettered from prime-time scheduling and its half-hour or hour-long formats. As streaming drama can leech onto viewers' lives in the form of binge watching, so can the constant stream of Trumpian reality TV consume viewers' lives in the form of browser-based live bingeing, a back-and-forth between news sources with a heavy thumb on the refresh button. The scheduling of this kind of reality TV is unpredictable, spontaneous, and extends out from live television into social media. It starts and stops according to Donald Trump's whims, while viewers wait for it. It can assemble itself quickly and appear suddenly, going from buffering to full-on catastrophe in a second, with twenty-four-hour news networks trailing behind. Its goals are to monopolize our time and waste our lives as we feed it and keep it alive.

As with competition reality shows in prime time, there are no real winners here besides the producer-host. Any season's winners are discarded and forgotten, and fast. At the time they appear, competitors are main characters, future celebrities, potential stars. In the end, they are all the USA Freedom Kids, those tween girls who performed a Trumpified version of the World War I song "Over There" in patriotic cheerleader costumes at a Florida Trump rally early in the race. Unpaid, the Freedom Kids had to sue the Trump campaign for the money they lost when they were not allowed to sell CDs at their performance.

Where are they today? Nowhere, neither here nor over there. They existed to be televised, briefly. Such acts show up to manipulate our emotions, then disappear. We are appalled by their awkward brainwashed patriotism, or we love it, or both. Like the contestants on *America's Got Talent*—a deaf girl with a beautiful singing voice, or a little blond girl who projects her equally beautiful singing voice without moving her lips, through the puppet mouth of a cartoon rabbit ventriloquist's dummy—they create a momentary disjunction that tugs on the heartstrings, a kitsch mini-catharsis. "America's Got . . . *what is going on?*" becomes our reaction to these convulsive post–Susan Boyle performances, in which ordinary people overcome their disadvantages through televised displays of short-form virtuosity, just to give us one more minute of hope. Humankind cannot bear very much reality, but it can bear a lot of reality TV.

IN CHARLES CHAPLIN'S 1952 movie *Limelight*, a dancer tells Calvero, the character Chaplin plays, that an upcoming benefit might be "the greatest event in theatrical history." "I'm not interested in events," he responds. As Trump news has shoved everything else out of the way this year, the same way Trump pushed aside the prime minister of Montenegro in Brussels, I have begun to feel like Calvero. I'm not interested in events. Or I wish I wasn't.

It has been hard to concentrate on reading books and seeing movies since the election, let alone the kind of blockbusters that begin to appear in early summer, the kind for which critical reception is a selling point. Mild controversy is built into these event movies, a kind of bait for critics, superfans, and trolls. This year, in any case, that has backfired on the studios, who blame the domestic failures of *Alien: Covenant, Pirates of the Caribbean: Dead Men Tell No Tales*, and *The Mummy* on the aggregated critical response at Rotten Tomatoes. When most critics love a movie, as was the case with *Wonder Woman*, the system is working fine. When they don't, critics are destroying the film industry. The studios have the same relationship to the press as Donald Trump. It's love or nothing, and anything less is treason. The studios love an embargo as much as Trump hates leakers, and they depend on China to finance and sell their toxic, low-grade products to an audience they consider even less discerning than the one in the US.

I made it to one failed blockbuster this year, *Baywatch*. It was playing at the Alamo Drafthouse in Brooklyn at the same time as the restored version of Tarkovsky's *Stalker*, "one of the most immersive and rarefied experiences in the history of cinema," as the Drafthouse put it. I could not picture myself sitting in the theater, contemplating ordering an alcoholic milkshake named for a *Big Lebowski* character while rewatching a film the Soviets tried to shut down, a film shot in an irradiated landscape that poisoned people who worked on it. My mistake.

If the people who worked on *Baywatch* were not sickened, they should have been. Ostensibly an opportunity to ogle girls in bathing suits, *Baywatch* is instead wall-to-wall dick jokes and father-figure longing, featuring a corpse-defilement scene in a morgue that is also a dick joke. Who is the audience for watching Zac Efron fondle a dead man's penis? Paramount thinks everyone is. The film ends with Dwayne "The Rock" Johnson, pumped into rage on natural steroids, killing a woman with a bottle rocket. That she is one of the most beautiful women in the world makes it sexy.

Baywatch, like the Trump Administration, was made for the fans, not the critics. As a soft-power exercise in indulging Dwayne Johnson's presidential dreams, the movie works as preview of his future cabinet. His lifeguard character is presented as a natural leader whose battle with drug lords is impeded by a stickler cop. Johnson, a nice-guy strongman, surrounds himself with bimbos played by actresses who went to the Dalton School and Greenwich Academy. The men on his team are Efron, a former Disney star who could someday introduce the candidate at a nominating convention, and an overweight, lovelorn tech nerd, the movie's clumsy fixer and audience stand-in. This mismatched cast made *Baywatch* the only movie I've ever seen that should have come with a chart showing how tall everyone is.

PAMELA ANDERSON'S CAMEO in *Baywatch*, reprising her role from the original TV series, comes at the end of the film. The living Anderson of the present day is pasted into her scene using digital effects, making her appearance seem posthumous. A ghostly presence returned from the 1990s, she is like Laura Palmer in the new *Twin Peaks*. She is dead, yet she lives.

Twin Peaks, a revival from the 1990s like *Baywatch*, is also an event. But *Twin Peaks: The Return* is an event that is an antidote to these other events. It begins with the boredom of staring at a glass box, then demands that we slow down, experience it, think. The sense of dread that the show creates settles in after each episode is over, and the credits roll over some indie band playing a slow song (please bring back Julee Cruise or even Chris Isaak). These interludes provide a contemplative break in this enigmatic anti-cliffhanger's narrative of violence. If it is an exercise in nostalgia and franchise-building, *Twin Peaks* is not an empty spectacle like *Baywatch*, in which a trivial item from the past is resurrected solely for financial reasons, underscoring the growing gap between artistic worth and presumed box-office value. (The show is seven parts in as I write this.)

FBI special agent Dale Cooper resembles James Comey now that Kyle MacLachlan has gotten older. Trapped in the Red Room, seated in a chair in his black suit and dyed black hair, his aging Boy Scout's confusion in the first episode was a preview of the Comey hearing in the Senate. Maybe this is what it was like to be alone with Donald Trump, when Trump nonasked Comey to drop the Flynn investigation. I can hear Trump saying it backward-forward: "I *hhhhope* you can let this *ggoe. Hhheee's* a *ggood gguy.*" Picture Comey at the White House, our new Black Lodge and Trash Palace, reluctantly moving away from the curtain and toward Trump with that awkward smile on his face, waiting to receive the handshake. It's a scene from a David Lynch film, the nice guy pulled toward Frank Booth in *Blue Velvet* or Mr. Eddy in *Lost Highway*. We are pulled in the direction of madness.

And possible decapitation. The severed head has been an image in Lynch's films since *Eraserhead*. Right away, in a bed in an apartment in South Dakota, the new *Twin Peaks* exposes us to a woman's decapi-tated head placed on top of a dead man's headless body. This confusion of heads and bodies points to forces the characters in *Twin Peaks* can't see, which can nevertheless inhabit them and control their lives. *Twin Peaks* foregrounds a kind of American emptiness of the soul that is filled by violence. The show, hopscotching between its original loca-tions and South Dakota, New York, Las Vegas, and Philadelphia, places this evil in the whole country now, not just in a single town.

Dale Cooper slowly wakes up to this new world after twenty-five years in the suspended animation of the long post-Reagan era. The original Gen X viewers of *Twin Peaks* were presented with two possi-ble futures that mirror the lives of the now-fragmented Dale Coopers. One future was to become an amoral criminal; the other, a doddering office worker and domesticated nobody. The "real" Dale Cooper, who confronted esoteric mysteries and searched for answers while flirting with Audrey Horne, has been held in place by evil beyond his control, frozen in the nonspace of the Red Room all this time.

Laura Dern's Diane, Agent Cooper's natural match in Lynch's mystical FBI, has escaped those choices, but is now embittered by the loss of Cooper to a parallel universe. Looking at the evil Cooper through the glass of an interrogation room, she can tell something is wrong but only knows for sure that at some point her world broke with no explanation. Diane is not a murder victim like Laura Palmer, or a housewife like Laura's mother, but she lives bereft, in alcoholism, in alienated rage, and in a helmet wig covering her ears.

"Cheers to the FBI!" Diane snarls as she downs a vodka nip, her belief in the bureau destroyed by years of neglect. We wonder what Cooper and Diane will find when they come back to consciousness amid the random violence and pervasive corruption that has spread from Twin Peaks to the darkest corners of the American nightmare. Longing for resolution, we wait for another head to roll.

2017

LEAGUE OF MEN

ELIZABETH SCHAMBELAN

REREADING THE STORY NOW, THE DETAIL I KEEP RETURNING TO IS the broken coffee table, the shards of glass. It reminds me of the scene in *Heathers* where Heather No. 1 issues her dying croak—*Corn nuts!*—and then falls, smashing her own glass table. The scene opens with a shot of Heather asleep, not lying down but reclining, in a satin-draped bower. The whole movie has that stylized, magical quality. The same is true of Jackie's story, which is why the article caused such an uproar in the first place. It beggared belief. You read it and thought: *Unbelievable!* And in retrospect, the failures of its naturalism seem so clear. The dark chamber, the silhouetted attackers, gathering close . . . But most of all, it's the table, the crystalline pyrotechnics of its shattering. That's the place where the narrative strains hardest against realism, wanting to move into another register altogether. The shards enchant and wound and scintillate, like the Snow Queen's icy darts. A man's body "barrels into her, tripping her backward." Someone, we're told, is kneeling on her hair. We can picture the strands—"long, dark, wavy"—outspread all around her. I wonder if the model here could be Ophelia as rendered by John Everett Millais: a young woman supine, long tresses floating. Has Jackie ever seen the painting? It's a famous work, and a staple of undergrad art-history classes, which is how I first encountered it. I still have the textbook, one of those volumes in Taschen's Basic Genre series, *Pre-Raphaelites*. I was the type of teenager who liked the Pre-Raphaelites, and *Heathers*. Maybe Jackie has similar tastes. But then what was she doing at a frat party, hanging out with a frat guy?

Speculation is pointless when information is so scant. I've been speculating anyway, intermittently, ever since her story was debunked—speculating about why she told the story in the first place. This has been an exercise in intense frustration. Vague suppositions about her personality and its possible disorders are far from satisfactory. What I'm looking for is something resembling an actual rationale, and this is what has proved elusive. There is no biography, no case history, no leaked documents, nothing at all to go on except the story itself—Jackie's story, as told to Sabrina Erdely, who told it to the world in her now-infamous and now-retracted article. And that is why I keep rereading, not *constantly*, but occasionally, when some random prompt, like a Reddit headline about the civil proceedings against *Rolling Stone*, brings the sorry affair to mind.

But it occurs to me that I've been forgetting one of the basic precepts of my education, which is that a story should not be read as a cryptic map of its author's psychic maladies. The author lies beyond diagnosis, because the author, like Ophelia, is dead. I could read her story the way I was taught to read any story—*as* a story, a work of literature. Such a recalibration opens up other lines of inquiry. For instance, if it's literature, what sort of literature is it? When the specimen is perplexing, begin with the question of kind. What is the category, the Basic Genre?

The story would appear to be a dark pulp-fiction potboiler, melodrama in a gothic vein. But it has no structure to speak of, no real arc, and no suspense, no sense that events are hanging in the balance. To the contrary, a certain inexorability seems to drive the action—people make choices, and yet it feels as if something beyond human volition is at work, some kind of dark enchantment that drives the characters toward their violent rendezvous, which is not a climax in the traditional sense because it's not the culmination of anything. And then there's the question of tone, a particular timbre of weirdness or a specific shade of shadow. These impressions hardly constitute an objective opinion, but my opinion on this matter is admittedly not objective. It's a gut feeling I've attempted to justify with only the slightest effort to correct for my confirmation bias. In my defense, I can only say that taxonomy is an inexact science. My classification of this story as a fairy tale is not necessarily more subjective than any other venture into binomial nomenclature.

The fairy-tale genre has its own internal taxonomy, which is governed by the venerable Aarne-Thompson-Uther system. ATU indexes more than two thousand "tale types" from hundreds of cultures, grouping them under a variety of elaborately nested rubrics (Magic Tales, Stories About a Fool, The Truth Comes to Light, et cetera), and assigning each type a unique code. These designations have long been a lingua franca among researchers, the coordinates in a vast nebula of vernacular narrative.

My first thought on consulting this resource was that Jackie's story should be coded ATU 312, The Bluebeard, a tale type in the Magic category, Supernatural Adversaries subcategory. Angela Carter's retelling is titled "The Bloody Chamber." That's what the frat guy's bedroom is, I thought: the bloody chamber, the site of awful truth, incarnadine. But no—Bluebeard's young wife is on a quest. She's taking risks and she knows she's taking them, defying orders, doing exactly the thing she's been forbidden to do. That's not what happens in Jackie's story. As her tale begins, there is a young woman. She's probably not a virgin, but she's definitely not a wife. A maiden, let's say. She might be looking for sex, romance. Or she might just be trying to get from point A to point B. In any case, she's going about her life, and suddenly this seducer appears.

IT'S SUCH A STRANGE STORY, when you think about it. Not the dark forest, the lurking beast—those elements feel familiar enough. It's the act of impersonation that is so bizarre.

I remember a book from my childhood, the wolf on his hind legs in a dress and apron, with a ruffled lady's cap perched between his ears. It wasn't a scary picture. It was comical and kind of cute. At age 4 or 5, I already understood this was a picture of the past. I knew that the dress and the cap and the whole story were *old-fashioned*, safely cordoned from the present.

But whoever invented the story—ATU 333, another Supernatural Adversaries tale—didn't see it that way, because *old-fashioned* is a modern concept, and the people who invented the story didn't have modernity. They didn't have ruffled caps or gingham aprons or a notion of quaintness to which these garments belonged. And they presumably did not have a concept of the wilderness, not the way we do. We think of the wilderness as bounded and finite. For them, it was the matrix in which everything else took place, the default, always ready to reclaim its territory. What did it feel like to tell this story about a wild beast when the wilderness pressed so close? What did it *look* like, in their heads? If you take away the cozy familiarity of that image—a wolf impersonating a grandmother—what are you looking at?

The story is starkly bifurcated: forest, house. The impersonation happens in part two. Part one is considerably more transparent. Intercepting the girl, the wolf engages, charms, inveigles. In *The Uses of Enchantment*, Bruno Bettelheim puts it flatly: "The wolf . . . is the seducer." Bettelheim thinks the girl is attracted to the wolf but also frightened of him because she's not yet sexually mature. His influential reading comports with the interpretations of Sigmund Freud, Carl Jung, and Erich Fromm, who all see the beast as a projection of the girl's sexual confusion.

The wolf is a seducer, or he's a rapist whose modus operandi includes a seduction phase. Beyond the psychoanalytic tradition, the latter interpretation predominates. In Carter's brilliant rendition, "The Company of Wolves," the wolf is a handsome if homicidal lycanthrope, and the sex is consensual. But this is a polemical revision, an implicit endorsement of the idea that the canonical tale is "a parable of rape," as Susan Brownmiller argues in *Against Our Will*. Jack Zipes, a leading scholar of fairy tales, agrees. ATU 333 "is about violation or rape," he commented in the London *Telegraph* in 2009.

In view of the foregoing, I feel confident in my classification. The version of the tale that concerns me—Jackie's version—is a loose variation, with additional beasts entering the picture in the second half, and nary a grandmother in sight. But ATU deals in tale *types*: variations, even dramatic ones, are expected. And when you look at her parable's essential lineaments, there really isn't much ambiguity. Interception, flirtation, change of venue, the transformation of seducer into Supernatural Adversary: ATU 333.

FAIRY-TALE EXPERTS are not often quoted in major dailies. Zipes's remarks in the 2009 *Telegraph* article were occasioned by the work of anthropologist Jamie Tehrani, who had used a method called phylogenetics to analyze thirty-five versions of ATU 333. Phylogenetics was developed to evaluate evolutionary relationships among species, but it is also used to study the evolution of cultural phenomena. As the science correspondent Richard Gray reported, Tehrani's genealogical data-crunching indicated that the thirty-five versions of the tale "shared a common ancestor dating back more than 2,600 years." If this finding is accurate, it doesn't necessarily mean that the tale type came into existence around 2,600 years ago; it only means that the recorded versions began to branch, to evolve along separate tracks, at that point. The original story could theoretically be much older.

Last year, in the Royal Society journal *Open Science*, Tehrani and coauthor Sara Graça da Silva published an analysis of some seventy tale types indicating "with a high degree of confidence" that at least thirty-one were rooted in remote antiquity and another nineteen had a "more than 50 percent likelihood" of being similarly aged. Commenting on these findings in another journal, evolutionary biologist Mark Pagel said: "What really interests me is why these cultural forms exist. . . . Why do these things seem to have such longevity?"

Tehrani offered some general but intriguing speculation on that question in a 2013 *PLOS One* article. "The faithful transmission of narratives over many generations and across cultural and linguistic barriers," he wrote,

> is a rich source of evidence about the kinds of information that we find memorable and [are] motivated to pass on to others. Stories like Little Red Riding Hood . . . would seem to embody several features identified in experimental studies as important cognitive attractors in cultural evolution. These include "minimally counter-intuitive concepts" (e.g. talking animals) [and] "survival-relevant information" (e.g. the danger presented by predators, both literal and metaphorical).

As defined by anthropologist Pascal Boyer, a minimally counter-intuitive concept (MCI) is a concept that meets all but one or two intuitive expectations of a given ontological category. For instance, a wolf that is just like a normal wolf except for the fact that it talks is an MCI. If you keep adding counterintuitive characteristics—the wolf talks, flies, is purple, can turn into water—you will arrive at a maximally counterintuitive concept (MXCI). According to Boyer, an MCI is easier to remember than either a mundane, thoroughly intuitive concept or an MXCI. This memorability is what makes the MCI an important cognitive attractor.

The second type of important cognitive attractor that Tehrani identifies, *survival-relevant information*, needs no explanation. And clearly, ATU 333, aka "Little Red Riding Hood," "Little Red Cap," "Cattarinetta," et cetera, is trying to say something cognitively attractive about predators, literal or metaphoric. The question is what. It tells us to stay away from them, but that is axiomatic where predators are concerned. Other animals don't require a whole cavalcade of concepts to warn them away from creatures that want to eat them (literally or metaphorically), so why should we? There's an issue of economy here, a need to justify the tale's cognitive load. Because human memory is not infinitely capacious, there is a limited amount of space in any oral tradition. If a story, or part of a story, is taking up some of that space, then it's there for a reason.

All the interpreters I've surveyed think ATU 333 works to socialize girls into normative femininity, either by helping them resolve subconscious conflicts (the psychoanalytic model) or by terrorizing them (everybody else's model). Brownmiller argues that the story instills in girls a victim mentality, reinforcing the idea that they are too weak to take risks, and that if they *do* take risks, anything that befalls them is their own fault. By this logic, the moral of the story is not simply *Avoid rapists*; there's an element of preemptive victim blaming as well. Even with this elaboration, however, one detects a mismatch between the simplicity of the message and the convolutions of the plot. *If you stray from the straight and narrow you'll get raped, and your life will be ruined, and we'll all blame you*: there's a short, sharp shock for you, cognitively speaking, especially if you're, like, 5 years old. Threats of violence and draconian sanction tend to stick in the mind all on their own. No need to construct a baroque and bulky narrative edifice.

It's all very murky, like looking at a corroded artifact in a warped, beclouded vitrine. The label says USE UNKNOWN, as museum labels occasionally, hauntingly do. All we can be sure of is that whoever made the thing understood its purpose, and that it *did* have a purpose. At some unknown point in history, ATU 333 made sense—maybe not what we would call sense, rational sense, but sense. Its enchantment had a use, once upon a time.

A BOY IS TRUDGING through the frozen winter steppe. I can picture this vividly. Actually, I don't picture it at all—it's just *there*, a smash cut in a movie in my head. I see it from the point of view of the boy. The icy fur of his hood frames an endless snowscape. The day is very silent, very sunny, very cold. The hood traps a cloud of warmer air, but even within this humid microclimate his face is freezing. His feet crunch through crust then plunge into powder; he sees the crystals of his breath, hears himself breathing, some-one else breathing. There's another boy with him, a kid he's known his whole life. Are they best friends? Have they always hated each other? For some reason, my imagination refuses to hazard an opin-ion on this. Heavy breathing, crunching snow, occasional joking, bickering—two teenage boys, 14, 15—but they're too out of breath to speak much, trudging through the frozen winter steppe. Though they've been psyching themselves up, expressing eagerness to reach their destination, each is secretly consumed by a yearning to turn around and go home.

This is fiction, what I've just written. It might or might not also be history.

IN FEBRUARY 2002, a group of archaeologists working in central France made a startling discovery. Excavating a Gaulish fort known as Gondole, they came upon a grave that contained the skeletons of eight horses and eight men, carefully lined up in two rows. Before burial, the men had been positioned so that each grasped the shoulder of the man in front of him, and the skeletons had stayed that way, perfectly in place. There was no sign of trauma on the bones and no way of knowing how the dead had met their end. But a 2006 report from the archaeological institute Inrap (Institut national de recherches archéologiques préventives) hypothesizes that the men committed suicide. The report quotes Julius Caesar, who in *Bellum Gallicum* wrote about Gaulish warriors called *soldurii*. These *soldurii*, he wrote,

> enjoy all the conveniences of life with those to whose friendship they
> have devoted themselves; if anything calamitous happen to them,
> either they endure the same destiny together with them, or commit
> suicide; nor hitherto, in the memory of men, has there been found
> any [*soldurii*] who, upon his being slain to whose friendship he had
> devoted himself, refused to die.

Archaeologists Dorcas Brown and David Anthony have linked this grave to a tradition they argue was already ancient when Caesar was leading sorties across the Rhine. They draw the connection in their 2012 article "Midwinter Dog Sacrifices and Warrior Initiations in the Late Bronze Age at Krasnosamarskoe." Krasnosamarskoe is a town in western Russia, not too far north of the Kazakh border. About four thousand years ago, it was the site of a peculiar settlement whose inhabitants killed and ate a great many dogs and a number of wolves, first roasting the animals, then chopping them into tiny pieces and consuming them. All of the animals were slaughtered in winter. (This is known from their teeth, which register seasonal variations in diet.)

The culture associated with the site is known as the Srubnaya. Noting that no evidence of canine feasts has been found at any other Srubnaya settlement, the authors suggest that in this society, "eating dogs and wolves was a transgressive act . . . a taboo-violating behavior of a kind often associated with rites of passage. In this case the passage was a transition to a status symbolized by becoming a dog/wolf through the consumption of its flesh." They conjecture that the site "was a central place for the performance of a winter ritual connected to boys' initiations, a place where boys became warriors." The boys must have "trudged through the frozen winter steppe" from miles around to converge there.

Arguing from evidence too complex to summarize here, the authors assert that the Srubnaya people spoke a language that belonged to the Indo-European family, which also includes Farsi, Sanskrit and its descendants, and almost all European tongues. Proceeding from this premise, Brown and Anthony conduct a rapid survey of Indo-European literature, mythology, and material culture, ranging across millennia to track the persistent association of dog or wolf symbolism with "youthful war-bands that operated on the edges of society, and that stayed together for a number of years and then were disbanded when their members reached a certain age." These war-bands "shared several features":

> they were composed of boys . . . who fought together as an age
> set or cohort; they were associated with sexual promiscuity (Latin,
> Vedic, Celtic); they came from the wealthier families (Latin, Vedic);
> their duties centered on fighting and raiding, but could also include
> learning poetry (Celtic, Vedic); they lived "in the wild," apart from
> their families, without possessions (Latin, Vedic, Celtic); and they
> wore animal skins, appeared as if they were wolves or dogs, and bore
> names containing the word wolf or dog.

In Vedic texts dating back some three thousand years, the authors find "midwinter dog sacrifices . . . explicitly linked with ritual specialists described as dog-priests." These priests ministered to "youthful dog-like raiders who divided the year between raiding and learning poetry and verses." Brown and Anthony cite a linguist who showed that "the dog priests . . . and their winter sacrifices represented an extremely archaic aspect of Indic ritual," considerably older than the Rigveda.

The authors point to a wealth of suggestive details in European traditions as well. In ancient Greece, noble youth (*ephebes*) trained for war dressed in animal skins, while in the Roman Lupercalia, "the skin of the dog or wolf was carried or worn by the adolescent sons of the aristocrats, who ran around the walls of Rome, symbolically protecting the community." While the etymology of *Lupercalia* isn't conclusively documented, it is widely presumed to derive from *lupus*, in which case it would mean "Wolf-Fest." In the Volsunga saga, Sigmund dresses his nephew in wolf pelts and instructs him in raiding and combat; in Celtic legend, a great hero is called the Dog of Cullan (Cuchullain); and in Germanic myth, the berserker god Odin goes tearing through the forest on winter nights, his dogs baying at his heels.

As for berserking, the Old Norse *Ynglinga saga* describes warriors who "went without shields, and were made as strong as dogs or wolves. . . . And this is what is called the fury [*wut*] of the berserker."

This quote appears in the essay "Homeric *Lyssa*: Wolfish Rage," by Bruce Lincoln, a professor of religious studies at the University of Chicago. Lincoln considers the contested etymology of the Greek word *lyssa*, "martial fury," arguing that it clearly comes from *lykos*, "wolf." In the *Iliad*, *lyssa* is "a state of wild, uncontrolled rage which is possessed by certain highly gifted warriors." While analogues of this concept are found globally, as in Malay *amok*, such frenzied martial rage is "particularly well documented among the various branches of Indo-European." In addition to Germanic *wut*, there is Celtic *ferg* and Iranian *aesma*.

Lincoln emphasizes the historic depth and geographic breadth of this notion of the lupine warrior:

> Of all the powerful or carnivorous animals . . . the wolf seems to have been the most important for the Indo-European warriors. Reflexes of the old word *wlkwo*, "wolf," are found in literally hundreds of proper names, and [in the names of] numerous peoples, such as the Luvians, Lycians, [et cetera]. . . . Stories of lycanthropy are well known among the Greeks, Romans, Germans, Celts, Anatolians, and Iranians, and these would seem to be traceable to these ancient warrior practices.

In Germanic myth and legend, say Brown and Anthony, these feral war-bands "are called *Männerbünde* . . . a label often applied [by scholars] to all similar Indo-European institutions." *Männerbünde* means "men-league," league of men.

Toward their conclusion, Brown and Anthony speculate on the psychological benefits of a symbolic transformation into a beast of prey. The wolf warriors, they surmise, "would feel no guilt for breaking the taboos of human society because they had not been humans [at the time]."

Finding some way to deal with guilt must have been crucial, not only for individual members of the leagues but for their societies as a whole. This is because membership in the Männerbünde lasted only for a set period. If you were still alive at the end of that time, you had to integrate yourself back into your old community. In order to perform the roles society now needed you to perform—family man, working stiff—you had to shed your tainted and bloody savage identity.

For some, this would have been impossible, no matter what psychological mechanisms were deployed to help. But many others must have managed the reintegration well enough. The rotation back into normalcy is documented in the Vedic texts: "At the end of four years, there was a final sacrifice to transform the dog-warriors into responsible adult men who were ready to return to civil life. They discarded and destroyed their old clothes and dog skins. They became human once again."

THE BOYS TRUDGED *through the frozen winter steppe.* That's an evocative phrase, to me. But does it describe something that actually happened? Bruce Lincoln, for his part, is agnostic. In the preface to his 1991 collection of articles, *Death, War, and Sacrifice* (not a beach read), he addresses the then-raging debate over so-called postmodern relativism and stakes out a kind of soft poststructuralist position with which I am in sympathy. "If myths tell stories about the long ago and far away for purposes of the place and moment in which these stories are told," he writes, "the same may be observed regarding other forms of narrative, scholarship included. . . . This is not to say that scholarship differs in no way from myth, or that research produces only fictions. . . . Still, the books and articles which scholars write and the lectures they give are not just descriptive accounts of something that unproblematically 'is.'"

Something that unproblematically is. Another evocative phrase, especially insofar as it implies its opposite: something that problematically is. We are dealing with ontology, with ontological categories (fact, fantasy, history, fiction) and with things that exceed those categories, pressure them, make them buckle. A supernatural adversary, a werewolf, a psychotic unkillable superwarrior: what is such a creature if not an ontological affront, a thing that should not exist but insists on existing anyway? That seems as good a definition of a monster as any: a being that should not be, but is; a counterintuitive concept with a highly negative valence.

I'm not sure whether one should say that a monster is a minimally counterintuitive concept or a maximally counterintuitive one. MXCI is by far the more charismatic abbreviation, but it's only in fiction that monsters are reliably charismatic. In reality, it really depends on the monster.

"WHEN THE WIND SETS the corn in wave-like motion, the peasants often say, 'The Wolf is going over, or through, the corn,' 'the Rye-wolf is rushing over the field,' 'the Wolf is in the corn.'"

This is Sir James Frazer, writing in *The Golden Bough*. He is using *corn* in the older British sense of the word, as a general term for any type of grain.

The Golden Bough is essentially a real-life version of *The Key to All Mythologies*, the colossal scholarly enterprise that drives the Reverend Casaubon to his grave in *Middlemarch*. Most readers know Frazer's work as a nine-hundred-page book, but this tome, published in 1922, is in fact an abridgment of a twelve-volume series composed over a quarter century (1890–1915). We are informed at the book's outset that Frazer's study grew from his desire to understand a strange Greek ritual involving a sacred grove, its priest king, and the titular tree branch. In order to fathom the nuances of this mystery, the author finds it necessary to canvas world folklore in its entirety, paying particular attention to the relict pagan customs of Europe. As he conducts his tour, Frazer gradually reveals the *unheimlich* occult logic underpinning such *heimlich* festivities as Maypole dancing. (The influence of his studies may be detected in the inestimable 1973 film *The Wicker Man*, among other forays into creepy British-bohemian neo-folklore.)

It turns out that a lot of Europe's relict pagan customs involve wolves. Especially but not only in "France, Germany, and Slavonic countries," the animal is strongly associated with the harvest: the act of cutting the ripe grain is conceptualized as chasing the wolf, or sometimes the dog, out of the fields. As the harvesters work their way through the rows, they gradually eradicate the tall, rustling vegetation in which the wolf conceals himself. Danger lurks as long as there is somewhere for the beast to hide. According to old proverbs, "The wolf sits in the corn, and will tear you to pieces." Children are warned not to stray into the fields, or "the Wolf will eat you."

When the last of the crop is harvested, the dog or wolf is symbolically killed—cause for rejoicing. In many communities, this final sheaf "is called the Wolf," and may be made into an effigy, often clothed like a person. "This indicates a confusion," Frazer observes, or a conflation. The wolf is simultaneously envisioned "as theriomorphic (in animal form) and as anthropomorphic (in human form)."

Confusion is the rule with the wolf. The relationship to society is tense and conflicted. The wolf shouldn't be where he is, in the fields, and yet his transgression is part of the natural order of things, the annual cycle of ritual and agriculture. Sometimes, instead of being killed or in addition to it, the wolf is feted in procession, given gifts. Near Cologne, "it was formerly the custom to give to the last sheaf the shape of a wolf. It was kept in the barn til the corn was threshed. Then it was brought to the farmer, and he had to sprinkle it with beer or brandy."

While the wolf is killed and/or celebrated in autumn, he sometimes shows up at another time of year. "In midwinter," says Frazer, "the Wolf makes his appearance once more. In Poland a man with a wolf's skin thrown over his head is led about at Christmas; or a stuffed wolf is carried about by persons who collect money. There are facts which point to an old custom of leading about a man enveloped in leaves and called the Wolf, while his conductors collected money." This old custom sounds like blackmail, as if the wolf were running a protection racket.

The wolf-racketeer is enveloped in leaves because, of course, he lives in the woods. The fields he haunts so relentlessly are not his habitat. They are the liminal space between village and forest, the place where the wolf pushes his luck—or plays to the edge, to use the alpha-male metaphor favored by former CIA and NSA chief Michael Hayden. In his memoir, *Playing to the Edge*, Hayden explains that his title refers to "playing so close to the line that you get chalk dust on your cleats." What's interesting is the way this assertion about testing boundaries is in fact an admission of crossing them. Hayden is describing an ethos of maximum risk-taking, of doing whatever you suspect you can get away with as a matter of course and a matter of honor. Hesitance is not for wolves but for animals of a feline persuasion. If you and your teammates are all about getting chalk dust on your cleats, then there is no doubt whatsoever that some of you will cross that chalked boundary, from sheer momentum if nothing else.

IT'S A STORY ABOUT violation or rape. Let's assume it was always a story about violation or rape, from the beginning, 2,600 years ago or more. But was it always a story about a wolf? Or was it about a boy—a boy, or rather a man, or rather someone on the cusp between the two—in the skin of a wolf?

We are shown a seemingly deliberate contrast. The wolf is in the forest, his proper domain; the story establishes him there. But then he reappears, having infiltrated the human world. We are looking at this old, old story through an incredibly blurry lens, but that much is clear: the wolf is in the forest and then he's in the house. Not just in the house—the figure of the wolf is now merged with a person. And not just *any* person—a little old lady, a grandmother. This is an especially ludicrous confusion of the theriomorphic and anthropomorphic. It suggests that our wolf possesses a deranged sense of homicidal mischief. "The better to see you with, my dear . . ." It's rather a lark, to him, this escapade of stalking, rape, and murder. Of course, his arch locution is a latter-day fillip. But the way he practically teleports from wilderness to house—*ta da!*—suggests to me that his tricksterish nature was always integral to the tale. Like the theriomorphic-anthropomorphic wolf in the grain, the wolf in this story is a liminal figure, an embodiment of some occult state in which binary conditions are impossibly, gruesomely conflated.

I say gruesomely. Let's suppose that we are talking about an actual historical phenomenon: "youthful war-bands . . . that operated on the edges of society, and that stayed together for a number of years and then were disbanded when their members reached a certain age"; cohorts of young men who were educated in poetry and verses and fighting and raiding, who lived apart from their parents, bonded passionately to one another, perhaps less so to everyone else; boys systematically encouraged not just to fight and to vanquish but to deprecate, to become wild animals, to wreak maximum chaos on their enemies. Once you make that choice, as a society, to create that institution, how do you keep the chaos at bay? How do you make sure it never turns against *you*? The answer is, you don't. Sometimes chaos redounds, refracts, lurks where it doesn't live, shows up at your door. When it does, if you're lucky, it will simply demand its tribute and be on its way. But sometimes, that's not what happens at all.

Why gruesome? Let's further suppose that this story, ATU 333, originated among people who subscribed to a logic whereby a boy in a wolf's skin is a wolf. This is not an impersonation, not a disguise. It's a deformation of ontological categories achieved through what you might call magic. The boy looks nothing like a wolf—he looks like a boy wearing a wolf pelt—but he *is* a wolf. So, if a boy in a wolf's skin is a wolf, wouldn't a wolf in Grandmother's skin be Grandmother? Yes, yes, I'm being morbid, lurid and morbid, but still, might that be the picture the story initially conjured? A boy who has become a wolf transforms himself into yet another thing, obscenely lampooning the ritual that made him what he is, perhaps to make a point (*You expect me to stop being this monster I've become, to suddenly become something else? How's this for something else?*), perhaps just for the fuck of it. Slaying, flaying, grotesque travesty . . . Is that what ATU 333 is asking us to see?

Here is an image of maximum chaos, to be sure, a violent collapsing of binaries that must not collapse if life is to make any sense: male/ female, young/old, outside/inside, bestial/human, slaughtering/ nurturing, profane/sacred. An MXCI, no doubt about it, but not at all difficult to remember, because it achieves its counterintuitive excess through a single operation, this spectacularly sanguinary rupture of oppositions, this ontological carnage. This image—this vision of total, totally malign misrule—would be a powerful cognitive attractor, would it not?

Our contemporary interpretations of ATU 333 are really so patronizing, so presentist. It may be true that, in recent centuries, the story became a tool for cowing girls into sexual docility, but that was not necessarily its original function. With this in mind, how might we reinterpret the tale?

We might at least entertain the possibility that ATU 333 reflects the values of a society with more mettle and less hypocrisy than our own. Perhaps the story was first told by people who understood how grossly contemptible it is to make decisions, *as* a society, and then assiduously deny the consequences of those decisions—deny those consequences with an intensity that looks very much like hysterical blindness. Maybe this unknown ancient society, however grievous its flaws, at least had the guts to confront its own ugly choices. It could have been a parable of rape, yes, of rape and murder and the most extravagant transgression imaginable. But possibly it was less a warning than a ritualized mnemonic. Maybe its function, or one of them, was to ensure that no one could forget or deny the price they had agreed to pay, the price of maintaining a Männerbünde, an institution of wolfishness.

There is no darkly romantic teleology here, no unbroken chain of historical inheritance linking wolf boys to frat boys, just as there is no primordial wellspring of masculine violence that forces wolf boys to kill or frat boys to rape. There are two institutions, two leagues of young men, one belonging to an archaic and semi-mythic past, the other flourishing here and now. Institutions, by definition, are not natural or primal. They are not what just happens when you let boys be boys. They are created and sustained for a reason. They do work.

In order for the Männerbünde to do its work, it was necessary to turn boys into wolves. We don't even know, we cannot and will not name, what we are creating when we somehow transform boys into people who have lost the moral intuition that a woman's body belongs to the woman—who don't suspect that a woman's body is not like a piece of furniture on the curb, not something that belongs to whoever can lift it. We don't know what this means, this absolute objectification that cannot, logically, be just a vile anomaly in an ethical system otherwise egalitarian and humane. We don't know what these crimes mean, these assaults that could not occur so regularly, so predictably, were it not the case that all the players are playing to the edge, not just the small percentage who actually cross the line and rape. We don't know what work this institution performs—this institution of American alpha-bros, of jocks, frat guys, popular dudes, these tight-knit cliques of privileged and socially dominant young men—and we don't know what bargain we have struck, and strike every day, when we permit this institution to exist in a status quo that appears impervious to growing scrutiny and serial outcries and ever-increasing awareness of "incapacitation rape," this so often bloodless and invisible violence. There is, as yet, nothing and no one to make us know it, nothing to make it public knowledge, knowledge that we all share and that we all *acknowledge* that we share. To create that kind of knowledge, you must have more power than whatever forces are working to maintain oblivion. This, too, was a basic precept of my education. Of course, analogous things could be said about so many regimes of disavowed violence—but I'm concerning myself with the one that Jackie concerned *her*self with.

THIS IS THE STORY I've come up with, about the story Jackie told: she did it out of rage. She had no idea she was enraged, but she was. Something had happened, and she wanted to tell other people, so that they would know what happened and know how she felt. But when she tried to tell it—maybe to somebody else, maybe to herself—the story had no power. It didn't sound, in the telling, anything like what it *felt* like in the living. It sounded ordinary, mundane, eminently forgettable, like a million things that had happened to a million other women—but that wasn't what it felt like to her. What it felt like was lurid and strange and violent and violating. I have no idea what *it* was, whether a crime was involved. There's a perfectly legal thing called hogging, where guys deliberately seek out sex partners they find unattractive so they can laugh about it later with their friends. Maybe it was something like that, or maybe it was much milder, an expression of contempt that was avuncular, unthinking, something that transformed her into a thing without even meaning to. Whatever it was, this proximate cause, she didn't know what to do about it. To figure out how to go on from that moment without dying from rage, you need something she didn't have. You need self-insight, or historical insight, or at the very least a certain amount of critical distance, a wry appreciation of the ironies of it all. She didn't have any of that, and that's why she lied, knowingly or unknowingly—or, most likely, both at once.

So she told the story to Sabrina Erdely, who told it to everyone else. Erdely frames the bloody melodrama against a backdrop of dry reportage, to extraordinarily compelling effect. We know she decided to write about campus rape before she knew *which* campus rape she would focus on. She needed to find the right crime, one both exemplary and outrageous, something to create the shock of defamiliarization, to rivet and enrage. I wonder if any journalist in that situation could have resisted the story she found. Imagine interviewing the young woman who had survived a gang rape, and imagine her telling you that one of the rapists had ordered: "Grab its motherfucking leg." If ever there was a fact that was too good to check, it's this one, this amazing line, with its hideous, show-stopping pronoun. And the haunting thing is that Jackie couldn't have come up with that lotion-in-the-basket locution without knowing something true about the way some guys talk and think. That knowledge really is powerfully, memorably distilled in those four bloodcurdling words.

To the extent that Jackie was aware that what she told Sabrina Erdely was not true, it was destructive and wrong, cruel and stupid. If she really was not in command of reality, that would mitigate her culpability, but it wouldn't change the nature of what she did. It was violence. And to me, it was a betrayal—or that's what it felt like. I knew it was irrational to feel that way, but that's how I felt. I want to condemn it, and I *do* condemn it, but I also think I can guess what she was saying, or would have said, which can't be said reasonably. It must be said melodramatically. Something like: Look at this. Don't you fucking dare not look. I'm going to *make* you look. I'm going to *make* you know. You're going to know what we've decided is worth sacrificing, what price we've decided we're willing to pay to maintain this league of men, and this time, you're going to remember.

2017

IN THE MAZE

DAYNA TORTORICI

ONE OF THE PURPOSES OF THIS SECTION* IS TO PROVIDE A TESTI-
mony of a moment—to recognize and record, as C. L. R. James
said—the questions and debates that preoccupy us. But sometimes
life furnishes situations that cannot be approached intellectually.
None of the usual keys fits the lock. An intellectual situation grades
into an emotional situation and becomes untouchable. How do you
write a history of the present, then? Sublimate, sublimate—until that
stops getting you anywhere.

Two years ago, in January 2016, I wrote to my coeditors with
a proposal for an Intellectual Situation about what I felt was an
impending male backlash. One colleague asked, "What backlash?"
Another worried it was too close to the bone. In the end I abandoned the essay because I couldn't find a way in. I couldn't figure
it out.

What was happening was that the men I knew were beginning
to feel persecuted as a class. They remarked on it obliquely, with jokes
that didn't quite sound like jokes, in emails or in offhand remarks
at parties. Irritation and annoyance were souring into something
worse. Men said they felt like they were living in Soviet Russia. The

---

* The Intellectual Situation, which opens each issue of *n+1*.

culture was being hijacked by college students, humorless young people who knew nothing of real life, its paradoxes and disappointments. Soon intellectuals would not be able to sneeze without being sent to the gulag.

Women, too, felt the pressure. "Your generation is so *moral*," a celebrated novelist said to an editor my age. Another friend, a journalist in her fifties, described the heat she got from online feminists for expressing skepticism toward safe spaces. "*I'm* conservative now," she said, meaning to the kids. But the most persistent and least logical complaint came from men—men I knew and men in the media. They could not *speak*. And yet they were speaking. Near the end of 2014, I remember, the right to free speech under the First Amendment had been recast in popular discourse as the right to free speech without consequence, without reaction.

The examples in the press could be innocent and sinister. A Princeton undergraduate, the grandchild of Holocaust survivors, could not argue he was not privileged in *Time* magazine without facing ridicule on Twitter. A tech executive could hardly make a joke without being fired, a young tech executive told me. "Take Mahbod Moghadam," he said. Moghadam was one of the founders of Genius, and had been dismissed for his annotations of the shooter Elliot Rodger's manifesto. ("This is an artful sentence, beautifully written" he wrote. Of Rodger's sister, he added, "Maddy will go on to attend USC and turn into a spoiled hottie.") Once, on my way to work, I heard a story on NPR about a Pennsylvania man named Anthony Elonis who was taking a First Amendment case to the Supreme Court. He was defending his right to make jokes about murdering his ex-wife on Facebook, in the form of non-rhyming, rhythmless rap lyrics. "I'm not going to rest until your body is a mess, / soaked in blood and dying from all the little cuts," he posted. When she filed a restraining order, Elonis posted again. "I've got enough explosives / to take care of the state police and the sheriff's department." Posts about shooting up an elementary school and slitting the throat of a female FBI agent followed. When he was convicted for transmitting intent to injure another person across state lines, via the internet, he argued he was just doing what Eminem did on his albums: joking. Venting, creatively. Under the First Amendment, the government had to prove he had "subjective intent." His initial forty-four-month prison sentence was overturned by the Supreme Court but was ultimately reinstated by an appeals court. I learned later that he had been fired from his job for multiple sexual harassment complaints, just after his wife left him.

How did I feel about all this? Too many ways to say. The aggregate effect of white male resentment across culture disturbed me, as did the confusion of freedom of speech with freedom to ridicule, threaten, harass, and abuse. When it came to the more benign expressions of resentment, in the academy and in the fiefdoms of high culture, I was less sure. On the one hand, I was a person of my generation and generally thought the students to be right. Show me a teenager who isn't a fundamentalist, I thought; what matters is they're pushing for progress. The theorist Sara Ahmed's diagnosis of teachers' reactions to sensitive students as "a moral panic about moral panics" struck me as right. (Her defense of trigger warnings and safe spaces in "Against Students" remains one of the best I know: trigger warnings are "a partial and necessarily inadequate measure to enable some people to stay in the room so that 'difficult issues' can be discussed" and safe spaces, a "technique for dealing with the consequences of histories that are not over. . . . We have safe spaces *so* we can talk about racism not so we can avoid talking about racism!") I also agreed with my colleague Elizabeth Gumport when she observed, speaking to a man in mind but also to me, "It's not that you can't *speak*. It's that other people can *hear* you. And they're telling you what you're saying is crazy."

Still, I had sympathy for what I recognized in some peers as professional anxiety and fear. The way they had learned to live in the world—to write novels, to make art, to teach, to argue about ideas, to conduct themselves in sexual and romantic relationships—no longer fit the time in which they were living. Especially the men.

Their novels, art, teaching methods, ideas, and relationship para-digms were all being condemned as unenlightened or violent. Many of these condemnations issued from social media, where they mul-tiplied and took on the character of a mounting threat: a mob at the gate. But repudiations of the old ways were also turning up in outlets that mattered to them: in reviews, on teaching evaluations, on hir-ing committees. Authors and artists whose work was celebrated as "thoughtful" or "political" not eight years ago were now being singled out as chauvinists and bigots. One might expect this in old age, but to be cast out as a political dinosaur by 52, by 40, by 36? They hadn't even peaked! And with the political right—the actual right—getting away with murder, theft, and exploitation worldwide . . . ? That, at least, was how I gathered they felt. Sometimes I thought they were right. Sometimes I thought they needed to grow up.

The outlet of choice for this cultural moment within my extended circle was Facebook. More and more adults were gather-ing there, particularly academics, and reactions to campus scandals ruled my feed. A mild vertigo attends my memory of this time, which I think of, now, as The Long 2016. It began at least two years prior. There were reactions to Emma Sulkowicz's *Mattress Performance*, to Laura Kipnis's essay in the *Chronicle Review*, to Kenneth Goldsmith's Michael Brown poem, to Joe Scanlan's Donelle Woolford character in the Whitney Biennial, to Caitlyn Jenner's coming out as trans, to Rachel Dolezal's getting outed as white, to the Yale Halloween letter, to Michael Derrick Hudson writing under the name Yi-Fen Chou to get into a *Best American Poetry* anthology, to the phenomenon of Hollywood whitewashing, to sexual abuse allegations against Bill Cosby and Roger Ailes. Meanwhile, in the background, headline after headline about police murders of black people and the upcom-ing presidential election. Many of these Facebook reactions were "bad"—meaning, in my personal shorthand, in bad faith (willful misunderstanding of the issue at hand), a bad look (unflattering to he or she who thought it brave to defend a dominant, conservative belief), or bad politics (reactionary). Yet even the bad takes augured something good. A shift was taking place in the elite institutions. The good that came of it didn't have to trickle down further for me to find value in it. This was my corner of the world. I thought it ought to be better.

The question was at whose expense. It was easy enough to say, "white men," harder to say which ones and how. Class—often the most important dimension—tended to be absent from the calculus. It may once have been a mark of a first-rate intelligence to hold two opposing ideas in mind, but it was now a political necessity to hold three, at least. And what of the difference between the cultural elite and the power elite, the Harold Blooms and the Koch Brothers of the world? While we debated who should be the first to move over, pipe down, or give back, we seemed to understand that the most obvious candidates were beyond our reach. What good would it do, for us, to say that Donald Trump had a bigger "problem" with black voters than Bernie Sanders did, or that Donald Trump would be kinder to Wall Street than Hillary Clinton would? To do so would be to allow a lesser man to set the standard for acceptable behavior. We would tend to our own precincts, hold our own to account.

This may have been bad strategy, in retrospect. Perhaps we lost track of the real enemy. Still, I understand why we pursued it. It's easy to forget how few people anticipated what was coming, and had we not attempted to achieve some kind of equality within our ranks, the finger of blame would have pointed infinitely outward, cueing infinite paralysis. Shouldn't *that* domino, further down the line, be the first to fall? Yes, but we'd played this game before. Women of color couldn't be asked to wait for the white male capitalist class to fall before addressing the blight of racism or sexism on their lives—nor, for that matter, could men of color or white women. It was not solidarity to sweep internal issues under the rug until the real enemy's defeat. Nor was achieving a state of purity before doing politics. But a middle ground was possible. Feminism and antiracism shouldn't have to wait.

Only they would have to wait. By summer 2016, Trump, the echt white-male-resentment and "free-speech" candidate, had proven all kinds of discriminatory speech acceptable by voicing it and nevertheless winning the Republican nomination. A low bar, to be sure, but even his party was horrified when the *Access Hollywood* tape leaked a month before voting day. Trump's remarks crossed a boundary his apologists didn't expect: the GOP's standing benevolent-patriarch attitude toward white women and sex. How depressing it would be, I remember thinking, to muster a win on so pathetic a norm as the purity of white femininity. But I was desperate. I'd take just about anything.

And then, despite the outrage, we didn't win. Although it matters that Trump won the election unfairly, it shouldn't have even been close. Perhaps I'd forgotten what country we lived in, what world. Sexual harassment was by and large accepted as an unfortunate consequence of male biology, and joking or bragging about sexual harassment was a comparably minor offense. Months later, I walked down the street in Manhattan and saw a row of the artist Marilyn Minter's posters wheat-pasted to a wooden construction fence. Gold letters on black read DONALD J. TRUMP above a two-tone image of his smiling face, and across the bottom, THE PRESIDENT OF THE UNITED STATES OF AMERICA. In between was a prose poem of Trump's words captured on the hot mic, iterated across the span of wall:

> I did try and fuck her. She was married.
> I moved on her like a bitch,
> But I couldn't get there.
> And she was married.
> You know I'm automatically attracted to beautiful.
> I just start kissing them. It's like a magnet. Just kiss.
> I don't even wait.
> And when you're a star they let you do it.
> You can do anything . . .
> Grab them by the pussy.
> You can do anything.

YOU CAN DO ANYTHING was the refrain of my childhood. I was a daughter of the Title-IX generation, a lucky girl in a decade when lucky girls of lucky parents were encouraged to play sports, be leaders, wear pants, believe themselves good at math, and aspire to become the first female President of the United States. The culture validated this norm. Politicians and advertisers loved girls. Girls, before they became women, could do anything. (Women were too old to save, an unspoken rule behind all kinds of policy. Need an abortion? Better to keep the kid, who has not yet been ground down by life.) But if girls were taught to be winners, boys were not taught to be losers. On the contrary, to lose was a man's worst fate—especially if he was straight—because winning meant access to sex (a belief held most firmly by the involuntarily celibate). Even then I understood that someone's gain was bound to be perceived as someone else's loss, and over time, I learned not to be too brazen. I maintained a prudent fear of the falling class. Even when men weren't dangerous, they weren't defenseless. Some still had the resources to bring you down, should you be unlucky enough to be crossed by one.

Combine male fragility with white fragility and the perennial fear of falling and you end up with something lethal, potentially. Plenty of men make it through life just fine, but a wealthy white man with a stockpile of arms and a persecution complex is a truly terrifying figure. Elliot Rodger, Stephen Paddock: both these men had money. This is not to say that men punishing women for their pain is a rich thing or a white thing or even a gun thing. It occurs across cultures, eras, and classes, and the experience of being on the receiving end of it varies accordingly. As Houria Bouteldja writes in "We, Indigenous Women":

> In Europe, prisons are brimming with black people and Arabs. Racial profiling almost only concerns men, who are the police's main target. It is in our eyes that they are diminished. And yet they try desperately to reconquer us, often through violence. In a society that is castrating, patriarchal, and racist (or subjected to imperialism), *to*

live is to live with virility. "The cops are killing the men and the men are killing the women. I'm talking about rape. I'm talking about murder," says Audre Lorde. A decolonial feminism must take into account this masculine, indigenous "gender trouble" because the oppression of men reflects directly on us. Yes, we are subjected with full force to the humiliation that is done to them. Male castration, a consequence of racism, is a humiliation for which men make us pay a steep price.

Women pay the price for other humiliations as well. The indignity of downward mobility, real or perceived, is a painful one to suffer, and a man takes it out where he can (Silvia Federici: "The more the man serves and is bossed around, the more he bosses around"). Whatever else it may be, sexual harassment in the "workplace context" is a check on a person's autonomy, a threat to one's means of self-support. It can feel like being put in place, chastised, challenged, or dared. *Sure, you can do anything,* it says. *But don't forget that I can still do this.* The dare comes from winners and losers alike. Either you accept it and pay one price or you don't and pay another. All of it always feels bad.

I imagine that some people feel good about bringing perpetrators to justice, such as it is under the system we have. But I imagine just as many do not want to be responsible for their offender's punishment. They might say: Please don't make it my decision whether you lose your job, are shunned by your peers, or get sent to prison. Prison, unemployment, and social exile are not what I want for men. I'm not here to be the police. I don't want to be responsible for you.

THERE ARE MANY OBSTACLES to honesty in conversations about sexual assault. Loyalty and pity, fear of judgment or retaliation, feelings of complicity or ambivalence—all are good enough reasons not to talk. Alleging sexual misconduct also tends to involve turning one's life upside down and shaking out the contents for public scrutiny. It's rarely done for fun.

When victims do want to talk, however, the litigiousness of men proves an obstacle to honesty. It is not unusual for women who speak too liberally about men to be threatened with legal action. Of all the striking things in Ronan Farrow's *New Yorker* articles about Harvey Weinstein's sex crimes, what struck me most were the allusions to Weinstein's lawyers. "He drags your name through the mud, and he'll come after you hard with his legal team," said one woman who asked not to be named. Another chose to pull her allegation from the record. "I'm so sorry," she told Farrow. "The legal angle is coming at me and I have no recourse."

In the weeks after Jodi Kantor and Megan Twohey first reported the story in the *New York Times*, as colleagues and strangers on the internet moved to identify the Weinsteins within their own industries, I felt uneasy. Behind every brave outing I saw a legal liability. I suppose that's what happens when you know enough men with money. Such men are minor kings among us, men with lawyer-soldiers at their employ who can curtail certain kinds of talk. While I do believe in false allegations, and I do believe that women can be bullies, it's hard, sometimes, not to be cynical about the defense. Some men love free speech almost as much as they love libel lawyers.

"Smart or reckless or both??" I texted my friends when I first saw the Google spreadsheet, titled "Shitty Media Men," that compiled the names, affiliations, and alleged misconduct of men in my field: writers and editors of books, magazines, newspapers, and websites. The document had been started anonymously, and though intended for circulation among women only, it was visible (and editable) to anyone with the link. I saw the names of men I knew and men I didn't, stories I'd heard before and a few I hadn't. "The List," as it came to be called, didn't upset me, but neither did it give me comfort. Mostly I worried about retaliation: the contributors getting sued or worse. "Reckless," a friend texted back. "Not sure how but definitely reckless."

By then I was once again preoccupied by backlash. The day the Weinstein story broke in the *Times* and five days before Farrow's first article, an investigative piece on BuzzFeed had described the range of people who'd sustained an email correspondence with Milo Yiannopoulos, the former Breitbart editor who'd once been the face of the company. In addition to the usual alt-right characters, there were "accomplished people in predominantly liberal industries—entertainment, tech, academia, fashion, and media—who resented what they felt was a censorious coastal cultural orthodoxy." Named among them were two writers I knew, both men, who according to the article had tipped off Milo for stories. One of them was a Facebook friend. He vehemently denied the allegations and said he hadn't written the emails provided by BuzzFeed as proof. The other, as far as I know, said nothing. He was the managing editor of Vice's feminist vertical (he once profiled Ann Coulter) who emailed Yiannopoulos with the request, "Please mock this fat feminist," linking to a story by Lindy West.

The article had made me feel naive. These were the people I'd given the benefit of the doubt, the professional acquaintances who adopted such strong anti-identitarian poses that I often couldn't discern their true sympathies. I figured that like the liberal professionals in the throes of a moral panic about moral panics, they shared the goal of collective liberation but disagreed about how to reach it, and in their disagreement came off as more resistant to change than they were. But what if some of them were not just acting like reactionaries? What if they didn't share the goal?

In the case of Milo's pen pals, their connection to the right was far from abstract: they talked, griped, shared notes. The lesson was that if someone sounds like an enemy and acts like an enemy, he may in fact be an enemy. I wasn't sure what this meant for the men on the List. These were men I'd known to say "woke" in a funny voice, to make intellectual arguments against the redistributive efforts within their control—who they published or how they assigned. They lamented the intrusion of politics on quality art and warned of the perils of hysteria, witch hunts, and sex panics. To prove myself worthy of their confidence I tried not to leap to conclusions. But the allegations against men like this were damning: rape, attempted rape, sexual assault, choking, punching, physical intimidation, and stalking; "verbal intimidation of female colleagues"; "sexual harassment, inappropriate comments and pranks (especially to young women)." Even if half of it was false, I knew at least some of it to be true. At some point it's irresponsible not to connect what a man says with what he does. In the days following the BuzzFeed article, "Who Goes Nazi," Dorothy Thompson's famous *Harper's* piece from 1941, sprang to the collective mind:

> It is an interesting and somewhat macabre parlor game to play at a large gathering of one's acquaintances: to speculate who in a show-down would go Nazi. By now, I think I know. I have gone through the experience many times—in Germany, in Austria, and in France. I have come to know the types: the born Nazis, the Nazis whom democracy itself has created, the certain-to-be fellow-travelers. And I also know those who never, under any conceivable circumstances, would become Nazis.

None of the men I had in mind were Nazis. None resembled the men who'd marched through Charlottesville with tiki torches shouting, "You will not replace us!" But there was another spin on the game, and this was the one that worried me: Who in a showdown would accept the subjugation of women as a necessary political concession? Who would make peace with patriarchy if it meant a nominal win, or defend the accused for the sake of stability? The answer was more men than I'd been prepared to believe. I'd have to work harder not to alienate them, if only to make it harder for them to sell me out.

AND SO I TALKED to men. Men on the List, men not on the List, men secretly half-disappointed that they'd been left off the List, mistaking it for some kind of virility ranking. In the past I'd argued that it shouldn't be women's job to educate men about sexism, and I sympathized with the women who said so now. But reality isn't always how it should be.

Perhaps it was just time for my shift. People take turns in the effort to explain collective pain, and I'd tapped out plenty of times before, pleading exhaustion, depression, and rage. The fact that I had the emotional reserves to discuss harassment at all implied that it was my responsibility to do so. ("It is the responsibility of the oppressed to teach the oppressors their mistakes," Audre Lorde wrote in 1980—"a constant drain of energy.") This is not to say I was good at it: I overestimated the length of my fuse, listening, talking, reasoning, feeling more or less levelheaded—then abruptly shutting down or crying. It was nevertheless more than some friends could muster. From each according to her ability, et cetera.

If my approach was too much about men, my defense is that the situation was about men from the beginning. The shared experience of sexism is not the same thing as feminism, even if the recognition of shared experience is where some people's feminism begins. It was to be expected that the discussion turned to men's fates and feelings. How could guilty men be rehabilitated or justly punished? Under what circumstances could we continue to appreciate their art? As think pieces pondered these questions, other men leapt at the opportunity to make their political enemies' sexual crimes an argument for the superiority of their side. It might have been funny if it weren't so expected, so dark. When a friend and former colleague tweeted about the "male-feminist" journalist who had choked her at the foot of his stairs, right-wing outlets rushed to "amplify" her voice. The pro-Trump website Gateway Pundit quoted her without permission; the Men's Rights activist and alt-right personality Mike Cernovich retweeted the blog post to his 379,000 followers; Breitbart followed up with its own story. "My therapist said that I should sign every tweet with 'also the alt right sucks' so they can't use my tweets in any more articles," she joked.

Leftist men celebrated the fall of liberal male hypocrites, liberals the fall of conservative ones, conservatives and alt-rightists the fall of the liberals and leftists. Happiest were the antisemites, who applauded the feminist takedown of powerful Jewish men. It seemed not to occur to them—or maybe just not to matter?—that any person, any woman, had suffered. Outrage for the victims was just another weapon in an eternal battle between men. I remembered the emergency panel Trump assembled in response to the *Access Hollywood* tape with Juanita Broaddrick, Kathleen Willey, and Paula Jones—women who had accused Bill Clinton of harassment or rape. A fourth woman, Kathy Shelton, had been raped by a man Hillary Clinton defended in court as a young lawyer. As the adage goes: in the game of patriarchy, women aren't the other team, they're the ball.

All this posturing made optimism difficult and clarity imperative. Patiently, my peers and I explained to men that we understood the difference between a touch and a grope, a bad time and rape, and mass online feminist retribution and a right-wing conspiracy (how credulous did they think we were?). Meanwhile, we wrung as much change as we could from this news peg. We called meetings, revised workplace policies, resumed difficult conversations we'd have preferred not to. As we learned during the Long 2016, the self-evident harm of sexual assault is not self-evident at all: no automatic mechanism delivers justice the moment "awareness" is "raised." Donald Trump remains the President. Social media, the staging ground for much of this reckoning, remains easy to manipulate. Our enemies pose as allies, and our allies act like enemies, suspicious that our gain will be their loss.

MUST HISTORY HAVE LOSERS? The record suggests yes. Redistribution is a tricky business. Even simple metaphors for making the world more equitable—leveling a playing field, shifting the balance—can correspond to complex or labor-intensive processes. What freedoms might one have to surrender in order for others to be free? And how to figure it when those freedoms are not symmetrical? A little more power for you might mean a lot less power for me in practice, an exchange that will not feel fair in the short term even if it is in the long term. There is a reason, presumably, that we call it an ethical calculus and not an ethical algebra.

Some things are zero sum—perhaps more things than one cares to admit. To say that feminism is good for boys, that diversity makes a stronger team, or that collective liberation promises a greater, deeper freedom than the individual freedoms we know is comforting and true enough. But just as true, and significantly less consoling, is the guarantee that some will find the world less comfortable in the process of making it habitable for others. It would be easier to give up some privileges if it weren't so traumatic to lose, as it is in our ruthlessly competitive and frequently undemocratic country. Changing the rules of the game might begin with revising what it means to win. I once heard a story about a friend who'd said, offhand at a book group, that he'd throw women under the bus if it meant achieving social democracy in the United States. The story was meant to be chilling—this from a friend?—but it made me laugh. *As if you could do it without us*, I thought, *we who do all the work on the group project*. I wondered what his idea of social democracy was.

As for how men might think about their role in a habitable future—or how anyone might, from a position of having something to lose—a visual metaphor may be useful. Imagine walking through a maze, for years and years, to find that your path has dead-ended near the exit. There's an illusion of proximity, of closeness to the goal: you can see the light through the brush, hear the traffic just outside. It's difficult, in that moment, to accept that you're not in fact close—that you can't jump the hedge, and that to turn around would not be to regress but to proceed. You turn around not because it is morally superior or because it will get you into heaven, but because it is your best and only option. Perhaps redistribution is like that. To attempt it is not to guarantee that the future will be better than the past, only to admit that it can be.

2018

SUPERKING SON SCORES AGAIN

ANTHONY VEASNA SO

SUPERKING SON WAS AN ARTIST LOST IN THE POLITICS OF NORMAL, assimilated life. Sure, his talents were often sidelined, as the store forced him to worry about importing enough spiky-looking fruits every month. (There were only so many Mings he could recruit to carry suitcases filled with jackfruit, bras padded with lychees, and panties stuffed with we-don't-want-to-know through customs.) Sure, he reeked of raw chicken, raw chicken feet, raw cow, raw cow tongue, raw fish, raw squid, raw crab, raw pig, raw pig intestine, and raw—like really raw—pig blood, all jellied, cubed, and stored in buckets before it was thrown into everyone's noodle soup on Sunday mornings. When we walked into the barely air-conditioned store, we pinched our noses to stop from vomiting all over aisle six, which would ruin the only aisle with American products, the one with Cokes and Red Bulls and ten-year-old Lunchables no one ate. (Though the Mas would shove their shopping carts through the vomit without blinking an eye—they've seen much worse.) And sure, Superking Son wasn't nice. He could be cruel, incredibly so. Kevin won't talk to him anymore, and Kevin was our best smasher last season.

Still, even with this in mind (and up our nostrils), even with it creeping through our common sense, and even with our aspirations for something more, we idolized Superking Son. He was a regular

Magic Johnson of badminton, if such a thing could exist; a legend, that is, for the young men of this Cambo hood (a niche fan base, admittedly). The arcs of his lobs, the gentle drifts of his drops, and the lines of his smashes could be thought of, if rendered visible, as the very edge between known and unknown. He could smash a birdie so hard, make it fly so fast, we swore when the birdie zipped by it shattered the force field suffocating us, the one comprising our parents' unreasonable expectations, their paranoia that our world could crumble at a moment's notice and send us back to where we started, starving and poor and subject to a genocidal dictator. Word has it when Superking Son was young, he was an even better player, with a full head of hair.

Yes, to us, Superking Son was our badminton coach, our shuttle-cock king. That's who he would always be. But what was he for everyone else? Well, it's simple—he was the goddamn grocery-store boy.

WE LOOKED TO Superking Son for guidance—on how to deal with our semiracist teachers, who simultaneously thought we were enterprising hoodlums and math nerds that no speak *Engrish* right; on whether wearing tees big enough to cover our asses was as dope as we hoped. And every time we had exciting news, some game-changing gossip we heard from our Mas, like when Gong Sook went crazy from tending to his crop of reefer before he could even sell one bushel, we headed for Superking Grocery Store. So when Kyle informed us about the new transfer kid—Justin—who he spotted smashing birdies and doing insane lunges across the court, being all Kobe Bryant at the local open gym, we dropped our skateboards and rushed to find Superking Son.

We ran from our usual spot, the park where our peddling aunts never set up shop, the one next to the middle school that shut down from gang violence, and we ran because we couldn't skate fast. (Our baggy shirts went down to our knees, covering our asses and compromising our mobility, but who cares about mobility when you look as fly as this?) It was February, and as chilly as a rainless California winter ever got, but we worked up a sweat doing all that running. By the time we found Superking Son in his back storeroom, we dripped beads of salty-ass water from head to toe. We were a crew of yellow-brown boys collapsed onto the floor, exhausted from excitement.

Superking Son greeted us by raising his palm against our faces. "You fools need to shut the fuck up so I can concentrate," he said, even though we hadn't uttered a word. He was talking to Cha Quai Factory Son about how many Khmer donuts he wanted to order that week. Superking Son stared intently at a clipboard, as if he could peer into its soul, his constant pen chewing the only sound we could hear.

"Come on, man, what's taking you so long?" Cha Quai Factory Son grabbed the clipboard away from Superking Son. "Just go with the usual! Why do this song and dance every week?" He pulled out his own unchewed pen and signed the invoice before anyone could let out a whimper about merchandizing fraud. "Stop second-guessing yourself," he continued while shaking his head. "God, I've aged ten years waiting for you to make a decision."

"Stop giving me shit for being a good businessman. You can't do things without thinking," Superking Son said.

"This guy takes one business class at comm and he thinks he's the CEO of Cambo grocery stores. Like he's Steve Jobs and those spoiled Chinese sausages are MacBook Airs," Cha Quai Factory Son joked as he waved the clipboard around. "I was in that class with him, and all we ever learned was that mo' money is better than no money."

Superking Son crossed his arms over his semipudgy chest—over that layer of fat that seemed to have grown at a steady rate since he took over the store. "All right, everyone out of my storeroom. Y'all are sweating all over and I don't want this asswipe smell clinging to my inventory. I sell food people put in their mouths, dammit."

We urged Superking Son to wait, each of us frantic for approval. We raved about Justin, how he could replace Kevin as our team's number-one player, how Kyle swore he was the best player who'd set foot in open gym all year.

"The open gym at the community college?" he said, sarcasm stretching his every syllable into one of those diphthongs we learned about in sophomore English. An entire Shakespearean monologue nestled in the gaps between his words. "That's not saying much. At that open gym, I've seen players smack their doubles partners in the face with their rackets."

We only wanted to make the team better, so Superking Son's reaction disheartened us. Yet it wasn't different from what we had grown to expect from Superking Son. It wasn't worse than that time a pregnant, morning-sick Ming threw up in the frozen tuna bin and ruined a month's worth of fishy profits, which inspired him to assign us two hundred burpees every day for a week. And it was nowhere close to that time his mom, while sweeping, slipped in the produce section and broke her hip, next to the bok choy of all places. (We're pretty sure this was the moment he started balding. By his fifth medical payment, he looked like Bruce Willis in yellow-brown face.) We told ourselves Superking Son was simply stressed out. Everyone, including our own parents, relied on him to supply their food. He needed to restock his shelves for next month or mayhem would commence, we told ourselves, as if the store didn't require restocking every month.

"Bring the kid to conditioning, and we'll see how quickly one of you bastards gets whacked in the head." He stepped over us, grabbed the door, and turned to look down on us. "I'm serious. Get out or I'm locking you guys in here." His biceps flexed, even that small part of his body begging to be bigger than it was.

Cha Quai Factory Son started to leave first, but as he approached the door, he slid behind Superking Son and grabbed him by the shoulders. He massaged him, digging his big, dough-kneading hands into the perpetually tense tissue. We watched as Superking Son's eyebrows furrowed in revolt while his mouth formed silent moans of pleasure. "Okay, let's leave this big boy alone so he can think about BUSINESS," Cha Quai Factory Son said. Then he patted Superking Son on the stomach and jolted out the door.

Superking Son reached out to grab him, almost falling over in the process. He missed, by more than he would admit. And as he leaned forward into the gaping hole of the doorway, watching Cha Quai Factory Son flee from his grasp, we could tell he wanted to scream out some last remark. But he didn't. He probably couldn't decide on anything to say.

THERE ARE STORIES of Superking Son you wouldn't believe. Epic stories, stories that are downright implausible given the laws of physics, gravity, the limitations of the human body. There's the one where Superking Son's doubles partner sprained his ankle during the final match of sectionals. The kid dropped to the ground, right in the middle of the court, and Superking Son fended off the smashes of Edison's two best varsity players by lunging over his partner's injured body. He kept this up for ten minutes, until one of the Edison players also slipped and sprained his ankle, resulting in a historic win for our high school's badminton team. (They later learned the floor had been polished by the janitors, who neglected to tell the badminton coaches. The guys who sprained their ankles sued the school, won a huge settlement, and now both have their own houses in Sacramento. Three bedrooms, two and a half bathrooms, everything you could possibly want.) Then there are the many times he's beaten Cha Quai Factory Son in a singles match, often without letting him score a single point. Once, Superking Son bet Cha Quai Factory Son a hundred dollars he could beat him while eating a Big Mac, one hand gripped around his racket, the other around a juicy burger. Cha Quai Factory Son agreed, but wanted to triple the bet on the stipulation that Superking Son couldn't spill even a shred of lettuce. Halfway through, Superking Son had played so well, he got his friend to throw him another Big Mac, then a box of ten McNuggets. At the end of the match, the gym floor remained spotless. Cha Quai Factory Son refused to eat at McDonald's for ten years.

We didn't believe the stories at first. We thought, Superking Son's talking out of his ass. He wants to talk himself up to kids more than a decade younger than him. That was why he let us practice skating tricks in the parking lot and gave us free Gatorades (albeit the neon-green flavor no one bought, never light blue). Then when we started high school, Superking Son took over as coach of our badminton team. Just as he'd carried the team on his back as a class-ditching player in the '90s, he coached us to two regional championships. (There weren't opportunities to go to state or nationals, no D1 recruiters scouting matches with athletic scholarships in their butt pockets. This was badminton, for god's sake.) Superking Son launched our team to the top of the California Central Valley standings—the first time we called ourselves number one at anything. But more than that, it was from the little gestures—the fluid flair of Superking Son's wrists when demonstrating how to hit, the way he picked up birdies and sent them flying across the gym to any player he chose, the way he tapped into rallies, held his racket with his left hand so as not to annihilate the player he was coaching—that we realized the stories were true.

JUSTIN WAS NOT IMPRESSED. He was the new kid who showed up driving a brand-new Mustang and parked it next to Kyle's minivan, one of those beat-up machines abandoned at the local car shop and then flipped and sold to Cambo ladies like Kyle's mom, who were praying for the day their eldest children could start driving around the youngest. (The Mustang didn't have flames on it, but we could tell from the way Justin spiked his jet-black hair into pointy peaks that he had the clearest intentions to paint red, yellow, and blue flames on its side.) So no, Justin was not impressed with the abandoned parking lots we hung out in, the pop-up restaurants located in Cambo-rented apartments where we ate steaming cups of noodle soup in clean but still roach-infested kitchens, the mall that did so badly Old Navy closed down, and he definitely did not see what we saw in Superking Son.

But Justin, despite the pretensions, was a damn good badminton player. Plus after school he bought us rounds of dollar-menu chicken sandwiches, giving us rides in his Mustang while we inhaled that mystery meat. And we saw where he was coming from, because this year Superking Son was indeed off.

Conditioning was a shit show. Two weeks of Superking Son showing up late, his shirt pits stained with sweat (we hoped it was sweat), fish guts and pig intestines stuck in his hair and stinking up the joint. Two weeks of him never knowing what exercises he wanted us to do, miscounting lunges and crunches and not stopping us from planking until we fell to the ground in pain—he was constantly checking his phone instead of keeping track of what we were doing. And he kept forgetting Kyle's name, Kyle whose dad went into Superking Grocery Store every week to buy lottery tickets and fish-oil pills ("Gotta be healthy for when I'm rich," Kyle's dad often said, kissing both his ticket and pills for good luck), Kyle who Superking Son practically watched grow up, as Superking Son's Ma used to babysit Kyle when he was a baby. (Babysitting for her meant pushing a naked Kyle in a shopping cart through every aisle of the store.)

"What's up with your coach?" Justin asked one day while driving a couple of us home after practice. "I don't mean to be a hater, but I could get better conditioning doing tai chi with the old Asian ladies in the park. Only the left half of my body is getting a workout, man, like if I kept doing this, my muscles will get all imbalanced and I'll topple over."

Not sure of ourselves, we told him there was nothing to worry about because sometimes Superking Son got caught up with the store. Sometimes Superking Son was so stressed out he didn't think straight.

"It's amazing that store makes money looking the way it does. It's such a dump. I hope you guys are right, though. My mom is getting on my case about college applications. She wants me to quit badminton and join Model UN, but I keep telling her that the coach is supposed to be this legend and the team can win a bunch of tournaments. Don't get me wrong, I wanna keep playing badminton, but

. . . I mean, Model UN does have some cute girls . . . girls that wear cute blazers . . . and know stuff about the world . . ."

As Justin trailed off, thinking about all the girls he could woo with his faux diplomacy and political strategy, we saw him slowly slipping away from our world. We saw this college-bound city kid, this Mustang-driving badminton player, how he might be too good for our team, our school, our community of Cambos. Sure, Justin was Cambodian, but he seemed so different. That's what happens when your dad is a pharmacist, we thought, you can just whip out Model UN skills whenever you want.

WE HAD THE MIND to throw an intervention for Superking Son. We needed to do something to keep Justin around. For a week, we met as a team—sans Superking Son—to discuss intervention strategies, talking points, and counterarguments, who would say what and in what order and where each of us would stand to demonstrate the appropriate amount of solidarity. We even made contingency plans, which detailed what to do if Superking Son freaked out and threw produce at our heads to chase us from the premises (it happened more often than not). But when we got to the store, ready for a confrontation, we found Superking Son in the back storeroom surrounded by what looked like a militia, minus the rifles and bulletproof vests. We saw our Hennessy-drenched uncles, the older half-siblings no one talked about, and those cousins who attended our school but never seemed to be present at roll call.

We hid behind the stacked crates and spied on them. Superking Son was in the center of the circle, staring intently at the floor. His hand seemed stuck to his chin. Some ghostly vision played out in front of his eyes, and it shocked the color out of him. Cha Quai Factory Son was there too, his hands on Superking Son's shoulders, like he was both consoling him and holding him back from doing something stupid. A wave of money flashed around the circle, only stopping to be counted and recounted, probably to make sure no one had slipped any bills into his pocket. We spied on them, each of us brainstorming reasons for this meeting that were innocent and harmless, not doomed by the laws of faux-Buddhist karmic retribution. If we're being honest with ourselves, none of us figured out a reason worth a damn.

BADMINTON PRACTICE only got worse. Superking Son coached everyone who wasn't Justin and hardly acknowledged Justin's existence, not even to reprimand him. Yet when we crowded around a Justin match and cheered as he nailed smash after smash, we swore we saw Superking Son in awe of his talent, analyzing Justin's form and failing to find any faults. Sometimes we saw something darker, something seething, within his stares, some envy-fueled plot being calculated in his expression, but then he would break his gaze from Justin. He'd checked his phone for the thousandth time and let anxiety about his father's store overtake, yet again, his love for badminton.

Justin reciprocated Superking Son's snubs. He ignored Superking Son's directions and went through practice entirely on his own agenda. That first week, Superking Son and Justin interacted only through overriding each other's instructions to Ken, Justin's hitting partner. Every practice, Superking Son told Ken to practice drop shots, Justin said smashes, Superking Son yelled at Ken for not doing drop shots, Justin still refused to change drills, Superking Son made Ken do laps around the court for undermining his authority, and so on until Ken bailed on practice, hid in the locker room, and smoked a cigarette for his anxiety. (He stole packs from his dad, who bought them wholesale from Costco. His dad gave them out to relatives in Cambodia like candy, in an effort to pretend he was some hotshot American business tycoon.)

Shit escalated one day when Superking Son was so late that Justin, fed up with waiting, assumed the role of the coach and started practice. We knew that Superking Son would be pissed. We'd seen him fire cashiers for not abiding by his no-double-bagging policy, butchers for using his personal office bathroom and getting pig blood on his fake granite tile. (Of course, he always rehired them because his mom heard from so-and-so's Ming about so-and-so's kids need-ing food on the table and braces to fix their messed-up teeth, because they couldn't eat said food on the table with crooked-ass incisors.) At the same time, we were with Justin. We felt his exasperation. We looked like a gang of little assholes on the floor of the gym, sitting in our butterfly stretches, acting like we were doing something sub-stantial so the janitors wouldn't kick us out and start cleaning.

Justin had charisma, which allowed him to take charge of a group of teens his age without sounding like a douche. For once, practice was going smoothly, no kinks, delays, or conflicting instruc-tions jamming the flow between our hitting drills. We became a well-oiled machine of flying birdies and perfect wrist technique. Not a single one of us smacked another in the head with a racket.

"What the hell is going on here?" Superking Son yelled. He was standing at the double doors, sweating like the pig whose blood had stained the clothes he wore. His phone seemed permanently attached to his hand, he was gripping it so hard. Muffled voices, all sinister and incomprehensible, issued from the speakers.

"You weren't here, so I started everyone on drills," Justin replied, without turning toward Superking Son. He resumed correcting the position of Kyle's legs and arms, while Superking Son stormed across the gym, stepping on birdies. Soon they were standing within inches of each other, their eyes locked. Superking Son's were fiery. Justin's stayed cold.

"You want to repeat that, boy," Superking Son said, straight-ening his posture and locking his shoulders back. He sounded like he was competing in a who-can-breathe-more-heavily contest. We noticed how much taller Justin was than Superking Son.

"We waited for almost an hour. Did you expect us to sit around doing nothing until you got here?" Justin didn't let a whiff of emotion undercut his statements. Superking Son puffed up his chest. He was red in the face, the color rushing to his hairless scalp. We braced our-selves for Superking Son to power up into fire-breathing-angry-uncle mode, for Justin's even-toned facade to disintegrate in the face of decades of pent-up refugee shit and the frustration of premature balding. We thought this was the last of Justin the effective team captain, the stand-in coach, or at least that this confrontation would make practices even more awkward, straight up drive Ken to become a full-blown, black-lungs kind of smoker.

Superking Son sucked in a deep breath, and just when it seemed like he was going to exhale some grade-A-beef insults, hesitation rippled through his expression. Maybe he'd realized it was petty for a business owner to pick fights with a baby-faced high school badminton player. He could've become the levelheaded coach we knew he could be. After all, Superking Son was one of the good Cambo dudes. He didn't belong to that long legacy of guys who spent adulthood sleeping on their moms' couches and eating their moms' cooking. (Kevin's older brother, for instance, literally had a full-time job at the DMV and lived with his mom, paid her jack shit in rent, and never did chores because he was too busy playing video games. One day she snapped, set his PlayStation on fire in the middle of a *Call of Duty* campaign, and switched the TV channel to her favorite show—*Family Feud*.) By taking over the grocery store, Superking Son had done right by his father's life. He had sustained his father's hard work—his empire of raw meat and imported fruits and baked goods baked in random Cambo apartments—and made sure his lifetime of suffering didn't go to waste. We looked up to Superking Son. We wanted to keep it that way.

The hesitation in his face directed his sight to the phone in his hand. A dial tone emitted from the speaker, and its dull beat gradually subdued Superking Son. "Everyone go back to what you were doing," he yelled. We watched him scramble out of the gym. He frantically called back the person he was afraid of snubbing on the phone. He disappeared into the dark hallway. We heard him chant *sorry, sorry, sorry* off into the distance.

THE NEXT WEEK Superking Son posted the roster for our first meet of the season. We crowded around the sheet of paper, excited to see who would play what, ready to be disappointed or excited by our ranking, if we had made JV or varsity or—god help us, humble Buddha bless us—if we'd been cast out into exhibition matches to rot away with the freshmen. We knew Justin would be varsity rank one for singles. We had joked for weeks how he would destroy other rank-one players, even that smug kid from Edison with the thousand-dollar racket (joke's on him, he'd been scammed into buying a counterfeit racket by Kyle's cousin). Justin didn't look at the roster. He just stood behind us with his arms crossed.

"Come on guys, hurry up. I wanna get some food from the gas station before practice," he said. Each of us turned back to look at him. "What's the deal? You know I like my steak-and-cheese taquitos."

The revelation that Justin was not rank one, not rank two, but rank three on the varsity team stunned us. Our mouths dropped to the floor. Ken, who was rank one and unprepared to take on that burden, was breathing so heavily he was basically hyperventilating (the cigarettes didn't help). Justin stood there, silent, staring toward the roster, though there was so much space between him and that sheet of paper, who knows where he was looking.

Justin could have thought of confronting Superking Son. He could raise hell the way his mom did when Mr. White had the gall to give him a B– on his Civil War paper. He could also quit, call it a day, and take his taquitos home to eat. Looking at his face, we couldn't tell exactly what he was thinking. What we did see was not so much anger as pity. It was sad for Superking Son to stoop this low and fuck over a teenager half his age. Maybe we saw in Justin's expression what we all thought ourselves.

THIS TIME WE CONFRONTED Superking Son for real. We found him sitting on a footstool in the aisle at the edge of the building, where customers hardly ever went. Surrounding him were pots and pans, cheap Asian supermarket dishes, and the prayer kits Mas bought to convert their bedrooms into DIY spiritual mausoleums for those who died in the genocide.

We squinted to see him because the store lights didn't reach this aisle, and we looked down on him because he was basically squatting on the ground. You gotta reconsider the team rankings, we said.

"Don't you fools get tired of coming to this shithole?" he asked in a daze. He was looking through us, either at his life or at the spilled rice behind us he would need to sweep sooner or later.

We appealed that we were being serious, that it didn't make sense for Justin to be rank three, not even in terms of stacking our roster against other teams. We would lose all our rank-one and -two matches, we argued. Superking Son sighed, not really registering our words. His face wore that mugshot look our dads got when, instead of getting bowls of noodle soup, we dragged them to eat unlimited salad, soup, and breadsticks at Olive Garden—the look of unresisting contempt.

"Badminton," he said. "It was the only thing I was good at. My body was made for it. Never had to think, make decisions, be all stressed out when I played a match. I just, you know, did it. I used to think something about the hood, the way Cambos like me grew up, made for good badminton. We didn't have it as good as you guys do now. We dealt with a fuckload of bullshit." He spread his arms wide, signaling to us that the store was just that, a fuckload of bullshit. Or maybe he was referring to us, our issue with his decisions as a coach, how we looked up to him, and the pressure of living up to that, as he said, bullshit.

He continued talking, and a couple of us peeled off to grab Gatorades and snacks. We needed sustenance to keep listening to Superking Son's tirade on the ethics of badminton. "You motherfuckers will never really get what we went through, just like how fuckers my age will never understand all that Pol Pot crap."

Stuffing Funyuns wrapped in dry seaweed into our mouths, we asked him what this had to do with Justin's ranking.

"How many times do I have to hammer this into your dense heads?" he asked us. "Badminton is a balancing act. You gotta have both strength and grace. You need to smash the shuttlecock with just the flick of your wrist. None of this tennis swing, use-your-whole-arm nonsense. And to create the gentle tap of a drop shot, you use the force of your entire body to lunge across the court. Then you halt your momentum right before impact and make the hit. You think your all-star is good, but I've seen him driving around in his fancy Mustang." For a second, we thought he would call us out for getting rides from Justin, for buying into his richness.

"He's a spoiled dipshit," Superking Son continued. "His dad walks around like his fancy pharmacy degree makes him better than the rest of us. And his mom doesn't shop here, you know. She thinks the store is beneath her. His parents are always bragging about how smart he is and how hard he studies and how he's gonna go to a real university. You should hear the way his parents talk about him at my mom's parties, like he's slaving away reading SAT books. Badminton takes work—real work. You gotta practice until your wrist feels like it's on fire. When I was your age, I used to curl every item my dad made me stock on these shelves. Ten reps each, using only my wrist, curling boxes of those fucking chips you're eating."

We had no response to Superking Son, partly because of his crazed logic, but mostly because we didn't agree with him. It was real work to do well in school. And weren't we supposed to want what Justin's family had? Weren't we supposed to go to college and become pharmacists? Wasn't that what our parents worked for? But we couldn't think of how to express this, how to reason against someone who carried so much emotional baggage we almost wanted to tip him for his labor.

"Shit." Superking Son dropped his face into his palms. "Badminton was the only thing that made me happy. What a fucking joke." He swung his arms in exasperation and knocked over a stack of dishes. "This place is so fucked."

We looked around the store—at the meat counter lined with blood and guts, at the sacks of rice piled to the ceiling, at the oily Khmer donuts Cha Quai Factory Son supplied, the ones that tasted so good it was hard not to eat yourself sick. All of a sudden, the building looked paler, sparser, empty, like the walls had caught the flu. Were the fluorescent lights dying above us and messing with our vision? Had we simply never looked at the store from this last aisle? We asked Superking Son why he didn't take a break from coaching, just for a couple of weeks. We urged him to focus on the store, assured him that we could run practices on our own in the meantime. We had Justin to watch over our drills and give us pointers. Something about the store seemed off, and we needed him to fix it.

"I can't stay here all day. There's no reason for me to anymore." We watched Superking Son slowly rise to his feet. He prepared himself to face whatever had driven him to this aisle in the first place. "This store disgusts me," he said, mostly to himself. "It always has." He brushed his shirt off, like he saw what disgusted him crawling over his torso, like the store's literal essence had laid claim to his body.

IT WAS QUIET the next few days. Superking Son canceled a week of practices, told us to stay at home and rest. Something strange was happening at the store, and no one, not even our gossipy Mings and Mas, knew what it was—why Superking Son closed the store randomly in the middle of the day, why he failed to appear at Kevin's second cousin's engagement party. Justin, too, was a mystery. He walked the halls in silence, calculating his next move against Superking Son. At lunch he talked our ears off about how canceling practice was an affront to his manhood.

The afternoon practice resumed, Justin bought us bean-and-cheese burritos from the gas station and splurged on a forty-four-ounce mango Slurpee we passed around. He didn't mention Superking Son once the entire day. Something seemed off, but we weren't about to turn down free food. We hadn't received a break since Kyle's oldest half-sister's other half-brother was promoted to assistant store manager at the nice Walmart and every Cambo in the hood got the hookup with a 10 percent discount.

Stretching and warm-up went as smoothly as ever, in the sense that Superking Son was typically late and not present. Justin offered to lead us through some drills. We were hesitant at first. "It'll be chill," he said, too eager in his expressions and voice to sell us on the "chill" factor. "What's the worst that could happen?"

Of course, shit went down when Superking Son walked in, looked up from his text messages, and found himself amid a shuttlecock tornado before getting whacked in the head with a racket by a freshman.

"What the fucking shit is going on here?" he yelled, after grabbing the freshman's racket and throwing it to the ground. In response, Justin began laughing—either hysterically or fake hysterically. His body hunched over, his arms wrapped across his stomach, it seemed like he wanted to piss off Superking Son. Superking Son pointed at him. "You wanna start something, don't ya? You're just trying to get me riled up."

"As a matter of fact, I am." Everyone turned to look at Justin. He walked through the crowd of players up to Superking Son, stepping on fallen birdies on the way. "I challenge you to a match."

Ken gasped for air, but that was probably his developing smoker's lung.

"Oh yeah?" Superking Son said, imparting to his words as much condescension as possible.

"Yes, and if I win, you have to make me rank one." Justin's posture was completely upright to emphasize his height over Superking Son.

"What's gonna happen when you lose?" Superking Son asked.

"Then I'll quit. As simple as that. You won't have to deal with me undermining your whole I'm-the-coach-and-I-demand-respect routine."

"That's boring," Superking Son said. "You're not offering any real stakes."

"Fine, if I lose, I'll not only stay at my ranking, but I'll also serve as designated birdie collector for every single practice and meet." Our ears pricked up at this proposal—cleaning up the mess of white feathering nubs was easily the worst thing about playing badminton.

"Deal." Superking Son grabbed a racket out of Kyle's hands.

We crowded around the centermost court, the only spot in the gym well lit by the crappy ceiling lights. Superking Son offered Justin the first shot, saying, "Show me what you got," as he handed over the birdie—and when Justin served, Superking Son charged. He smashed the birdie so hard it ricocheted off the ground and whacked Ken in the face, leaving a red welt. *Damn*s and *Ooooohhhhh*s came from the crowd as Ken yelled, "My face! My fucking face!"

For thirty minutes, Superking Son and Justin became dance partners. Their moves fed off each other with the intensity of two Mas shit-talking their grandchildren. Superking Son lobbed, Justin drove the birdie back. Justin lunged forward for a drop shot, Superking Son sprang forward in anticipation. Superking Son jumped for a smash, Justin crouched to retrieve it. Neither gained more than a two-point lead. Both were so effortless in their playing, so in tune with their own and each other's bodies they seemed half asleep, steered by some master puppeteer.

The most beautiful badminton unfolded before our eyes. Birdies flew impossibly close to the net. Feet glided across the court, bouncing, lunging, leaping. Racket strings trembled. We exclaimed at every point and every unthinkable shot. We rooted until their sheer athleticism became routine, until all the incredible smashes averaged out into the same shot. Our voices fatigued and our eyes stopped caring.

The second half of the match turned downright boring. Instead of paying attention, some of us opened our textbooks and studied. Ken lay down on the bleachers with an ice pack on his swollen face. Others busted out a deck of cards and started a round of big two. (If anything, the big two game became more riveting. Kyle squandered his ace of hearts, lost ten bucks, and completely upended his weekend plans—the bet required the loser to drive the other players' Mas to the temple, the one in the boonies next to the bad Walmart.) Superking Son and Justin were too good. They predicted each other too well. There was no drama, no tension or grit, no underdog who could bounce back and surprise us. And when Superking Son scored that final, winning shot, no one really gave a shit. Even Justin seemed apathetic.

But Superking Son gave tons of shits. He pranced around his side of the court, ran victory laps, and stomped his feet so hard we're pretty sure our half-deaf, half-dead, he-should-retire-but-tenure-is-cushy English teacher (it's no wonder kids barely make it to community college) heard him from across campus. He yelled, "Fuck yes!" over and over, like winning this badminton match against a high schooler was better than all the sex he'd ever had (which was probably true). He shifted into older-Cambo taunt mode, donning the same antagonism our moms did when we try to buy shoes not on sale, our dads when we prioritize our homework over the family business, our Mas and Gongs when they hear our shameful Khmer accents, and our older siblings when we complain about responsibilities they previously shouldered, about enduring what could never match what had already happened to everyone we know.

"Who else wants a piece of this shit!" Superking Son yelled, beating his chest with his racket-free hand. He traversed half the gym to direct his taunts not only at Justin but at every guy in the room. "None of you have what it takes. None!" He seemed blinded with misguided passion, the bulging veins in his fat neck pumping blood straight to his eyeballs. "Get out of my fucking face!" We felt spit fly from his slobbering mouth and into our faces.

Our memories go out around the time Superking Son began challenging us to matches, even the poor freshmen on the exhibition team, pointing with his racket at kid after kid and repeating, "Come on! Show me what you got!" like a robot stuck in an infinite loop. The next thing we remember is this: the shock of watching Superking Son's ego spurt all over the gym began to fade. Our bodies settled into pity. We looked at our coach, an overgrown son fed up with his place and his inheritance, perpetually made irritated and disgusted and paranoid by his own being, and we looked at each other. Right there in the gym, Superking Son screaming in our faces, we made the collective decision, silently, almost telepathically, that one, Superking

Son was an asshole—a tragic one, but still an asshole; two, we had too many assholes in our shitty lives; and three, we didn't have enough asswipes to deal.

LOOK, WHAT CAN WE SAY? We were busy. We had our own lives full of responsibilities and expectations we were always on the verge of failing. Sure, there were signs, tons of them. It's not like Superking Grocery Store was packed with customers. There were no lines of people throwing cash into the registers. Superking Son wasn't driving around a new Porsche. He wasn't decked out in Rolex watches and Ralph Lauren polos.

First our Mas started complaining about the lack of fresh vegetables, about papayas as old as their concentration-camp-surviving hands decaying on the shelves of the produce section. Then shadowy Cambos started rolling into the store, not to shop for rotting papayas, that's for sure. They rushed to the backroom, sometimes with loads of packages, sometimes in the middle of the afternoon, sometimes at closing, never to be seen leaving the premises. After a while, Superking Son stopped letting us into the backroom. That giant bulky guy, the ex-army Cambo who took Kevin's sister to the prom, guarded the door. Superking Son barely trekked back there himself, not even to play solitaire on his ancient HP computer.

We'd seen it happen to Cambo businesses before. We'd seen it when Angkor Noodles Lady hired a new cook who made soggy-ass noodles. (The old cook pulled a classic drunk dad move—he went on a bender for a week. When they finally found him, he was passed out at a roulette table in Reno and had gambled away his kids' college fund.) Angkor Noodles Lady borrowed more and more money from the higher-up Cambos. Each month she promised to pay them back with full interest once business picked up. Business never picked up (the new noodles were gross), and the restaurant floated on Cambo community money until Angkor Noodles Lady ditched town. She ended up nursing a boxed-wine addiction from her niece's guest room in Bakersfield until she died of liver failure.

Now Superking Son isn't dead, don't worry. We see him out all the time, usually at the good pho place, usually with Cha Quai Factory Son, who has been ranting about the same far-fetched business plan for years. (It involves mass-producing in neon party colors those weird suction cups that make Cambo moms look like they're getting abused to people with white savior complexes.) When the store closed and Superking Son couldn't even offer the higher-up Cambos his back storeroom to use as their headquarters, Superking Son's mom saved his skin by selling her house and paying back his debts.

We don't know how Superking Son makes a living anymore, but sometimes, if you're lucky, Superking Son will appear at an open gym. He'll play a match or two, give some pointers on form. His lunges and smashes will strike you as impressive for someone his age, someone who probably has knee and wrist pain. Halfway through the session, he'll leave the player queue and sit on the bleachers. He'll watch a crew of younger Cambos play the game that, according to him, was the only thing that made him worthwhile as a person. When open gym is over, you'll drive home, and if you're taking Pershing Avenue to Manchester Street, you'll pass what remains of Superking Grocery Store. And even though the building has been empty for years, gathering dust and gang signs like flies to a pile of bloody meat, even though the community has moved on to bigger and better things, like college degrees and Costco bulk food, you'll swear, on the graves of all those murdered Cambos, on every cupping bruise your mom self-inflicts to rid her body of trauma, we promise you'll swear that the lingering smell of raw fish never left the air. Trust us.

2018

MISSING TIME

ARI M. BROSTOFF

S. WAS THE ONE WHO USUALLY WROTE OUR FANFIC. IT'S ALL THERE in my files, packed into the box my mom sends me from the Valley when I decide to write about the show. It tends to be in screenplay form and leans toward the carnivalesque. It's 1970s night at the Haunted Mansion and we are all together: Mulder and Scully, me and S.; their nemesis the Cigarette Smoking Man, a deep-state puppeteer responsible for countless acts of terror, and our nemesis Ms. Simonds, an English teacher at Gaspar de Portola Middle School whose crimes I cannot recall. Exene Cervenka of the legendary LA punk band X makes a cameo appearance. After a few tequila-and-opiums, our gang throws open the gold-plated doors at a members-only club hidden in Disneyland's New Orleans Square and discovers we've passed through a portal to the Life Café, where everyone hangs out in *RENT*. We order soy dogs and sing.

My stuff sounds stilted and self-conscious by comparison. My one real contribution to the genre was a naive first attempt, a fanfic that could not yet speak its name, which appears as a notebook entry from the beginning of seventh grade.

9/22/97
Dear B.,

God, we have a lot of catching up to do. Well, first of all, between now and maybe a month ago or so, I became an obsessive *X-Files* fan. Call it hanging out with S. too much, but it is seriously the best show ever made. I even have a completely screwed up, totally bogus theory about it. This is it:

The X-Files is not a Fox 11 TV show as commonly thought by a vast majority of sane people in the world. It is instead written and produced by the secret government. Now, Marissa, you may ask, what the hell are you talking about? Well, according to my theory, this Secret Government began around the time of World War II. What they intended was to gradually build suspicion about their existence until people began rebelling. Then they could declare the rebels, who would be the majority of the American people, a threat to society, and have them vaporized. (Am I starting to sound just a wee bit like a militia member here?) Unfortunately for them, the cold war and McCarthyist policies and stuff started. So people got their attention off the Secret Government, and vented their anger at the Russians instead. OK, skip to the '80s. The cold war is almost over, and the SG (you figure it out) guys are thinking, OK, now we can get down to business. So they create fictitious people like George Bush and Bill Clinton to lure the people into a false sense of security. But all the while, they're dropping hints to get people neurotic. So there should be a surge of UFO sightings soon (which, of course, are just planted by the SG) and that's how The X-Files started!!!!! Don't you just love my logic?!?

Anyway. I started the coolest club. It's called the Messed Up People Club.

Things continue in this vein.

Sixth grade had not gone well. Around the beginning of the school year, I had become an ardent communist. I knew about communism from musicals and Jewish historical fiction and the night of the big earthquake when I was 8, when everyone left their houses at four in the morning to loop past the palms on March Avenue in silent procession because the location of safety had moved outside. A few months later, a big tacky house that appeared to have only cracked in a few places went on sale nearby, in the foothills at the far edge of the Valley, and we moved in. My mom spoke glowingly of our proximity to nature. Rabbits ate the lawn, and sometimes coyotes ate the rabbits. My parents hired a gardener to replace the grass with Astroturf. It was the mid-1990s, but like a lot of people, we lived outside historical time.

As for the ardency, who can say? Like everything I started wanting in the months before my first period, the desire for communism seemed both endogenous and alien, secret and self-evident. To me it seemed to explain a lot of things, but I tried to keep quiet about it because it was, as we said at the time, very random. I found a Marxist reader in the den among my father's college books; it was too hard for me, but I buried it like a fetish under my bed. It had always been my custom to hide the media that could hurt me, like novels with bees or Nazis, around the house. The philosopher Ernst Bloch distinguished between two currents of Marxism, one warm and one cold. The cold current—"the detective glance at history"—was about where capitalism came from, how it worked, and ways it could be overthrown, and about all this I knew very little. My current was the warm one, all strikes and hammers and bread and roses, a child's communism. Sometimes, if I started having too much fun being with other people, I laughed so hard I peed in my pants, and a warm current froze into a cold one down my legs.

People think that only adults felt groggy and homesick after the end of history, but children were sad, too. In the Valley, you could dress up as any decade. Kids were covered in meaning. Or, I thought we were. Obviously I was bullied. Every day after school I sat at my desk drawing automated rows of smiling girls and tried to divine who would eat whom, just from looking. My only friends, B. and the other fuzzy glowworms who lived in my stomach, formed a council to address the crisis but schismed. At the end of the school year, I addressed them sternly in my notebook.

6/5/97
A Letter to B.:

I am writing this because I don't think you should be a communist
any more. In that Marxist book or whatever it is that Daddy has it
says that the main idea in communism is to abolish private property.
Well, obviously, that has to do with economics and all that. I think
when we grow up we should focus on something less extreme and
something that will actually be paid attention to by regular people.
Here's a list of practical causes and stuff that I can protest/advocate
at some point in time:

> Fur
> Abortion
> Gun control
> Death penalty
> Drugs (but not heavy ones)
> Assisted suicide

love,
> marissa

The following entry, from August, concerns a birthday party to
which I was not invited. By September there was S., and *The X-Files*.

SOMETHING HAD HAPPENED, and we could not remember what it
was. In *Missing Time*, a 1981 best seller that helped establish the
conventions of the alien abduction memoir, ufologist Budd Hopkins explained that evidence of an extraterrestrial visitation often
took the form of precisely this sort of mysterious gap in experience.
Abduction was a way of describing rupture in its purest form, a
literal wrinkle in time. I could relate: it wasn't like I had a better

excuse for being such an old-fashioned girl. But I was not alone. In the 1990s, anyone could be abducted, though the aliens seemed to have a thing for white girls, and a way of making men feel like white girls even though they weren't. Weird syndromes coagulated everywhere. The deeper in the suburbs they appeared, the more mysterious they seemed, like signs from another world. A postwar infrastructure of office buildings and tract homes designed to cordon off the white middle class from the contagious city turned out to be built from noxious materials that made people sick. Asbestos, formaldehyde, and 4-phenylcyclohexene, or "new carpet smell," dewed up in moldy corners beneath the level of perception. Veterans returning from Iraq reported a rash of problems—memory loss, respiratory trouble—that they attributed to chemical exposure. When no physical marker could be found for Gulf War syndrome, mass psychogenic illness, a new term for hysteria, was extended for the first time to men.

The X-Files was born into this biosphere in 1993 on Fox, an upstart network trying to figure out how to undercut its more established rivals with niche programming like The Simpsons (1989 to present) and the Fox News Channel (1996 to the end of the world). A seriously ambitious program, The X-Files "made TV cinematic," as the critic Theresa Geller put it in a recent monograph, inspiring waves of cerebral genre programming and launching the careers of showrunners like Vince Gilligan (Breaking Bad) and Frank Spotnitz (The Man in the High Castle). But the show was also a quasi-respectable cousin of Jerry Springer at a time when reality, too, was remaking TV. In this sense the series wasn't science fictional at all, but took place in a world just like our own, where women being poisoned by their microwaves floated around with Lyndon LaRouche supporters and AIDS denialists and 12-year-old ex-communists in dubious pursuit of a history of the present. There they were, serially archived on a single flashing screen, from the Loch Ness monster and the chupacabra to the JFK assassination and the defamation of Anita Hill. In the last years of the 20th century, this solar system of conspiratorial thinking was where the postmodern condition lived its best life. You could find yourself in cozy exile there, social theorists said, if you'd tried too hard to picture technoscientific global capitalism and your brain broke. I'd barely begun to try, and mine already had.

On *The X-Files*, the United States government was a shell company for extraterrestrial interests in our GDP of biopolitical slop: neurons and wombs, oil fields and cornfields, radio towers and internet cables, Nazis and bees. The cold war wasn't really over, but it had also never really begun, the whole thing having been, as Thomas Pynchon put it in *Gravity's Rainbow* twenty years earlier, a front for the war of multinational technology cartels against everyone else. Now, in the Nineties, world-historical conflict farted in its fresh grave as hoax and scandal filled the deregulated airwaves. Cable news proved such a deadly carrier of "subliminal messages" that in one episode, people in a DC suburb watch TV pundits weigh in on Bosnia and are hypnotized into homicidal rage against their loved ones. In other words, paranormal activity caused by US–alien collusion manifested on a day-to-day basis as unaccountable violent symptoms bugging out the collective sensorium. In the parlance of the show, this sort of thing was an X-file, a local mystery with national implications that the federal government didn't *want* to solve. Such cases fell to an odd couple of FBI agents: Fox Mulder (doofy, irreproachable David Duchovny), a believer bent on avenging a government cover-up of his sister's abduction, and Dana Scully (acute, deadpan Gillian Anderson), a medically trained skeptic assigned to spy on him. Mulder and Scully spend the series investigating strange phenomena, from a 120-year-old serial killer who hibernates between meals of human liver to an American luxury liner perpetually invaded by Germans because it's always 1939 in the Bermuda Triangle, on behalf of a regime that wants to snort their brains. *The X-Files* may not have been the best postmodern novel ever written, but it was, despite stiff competition, perhaps the longest.

The show ran until a few months after September 11, 2001. It spawned two forgettable feature films and started up again as a series in 2016 in a painful nostalgia exercise; this spring, it was ostensibly laid to rest for good. *The X-Files*'s creator, Chris Carter—a SoCal boy who spent thirteen years at *Surfing Magazine* before he started the show—shot episodes like small movies where the sublime architecture of conspiracy in the post-Watergate thriller entered the orbit of Lynchian Americana: *All the President's Men Meet the Log Lady*. Some episodes layered one aesthetic atop the other: in countless scenes, girls in white nightgowns run barefoot through the woods illuminated by the glare of spacecraft or SWAT teams. Others seemed located halfway in between, in endless gray suburbs where Washington and Main Street alike flicker in between commercials on a half-watched screen before a working mom is gobbled up by a swarm of irradiated cockroaches. Either way, everything looks like Vancouver, where the show was shot through its fifth season, creating the uncanny impression that, in the Nineties, the entire country was a Northwestern logging town haunted by industry. The show's devotees created an online subculture largely populated by female X-philes, who debated the relationship between its conspiracy-driven "mythology" arc and its less sweeping but often more satisfying "Monster of the Week" one-offs, as well as the persistent question of whether Mulder and Scully should bang. ("Shippers" said yes, "no-romos" said it would ruin the show.) At a time when being obsessed with stuff on the internet was still the province of freaks and geeks, the show's producers winked back, turning losers into collaborators.

Teetering between police procedural and science fiction, *The X-Files*, Geller notes, forgoes the positivistic comforts of a regular forensic drama, in which truth can be discovered and justice served in the space of a single episode. The show's collision of genres, she writes, conscripts Mulder and Scully into the role of social detective—Fredric Jameson's term for a sleuth, sometimes a policeman or a journalist, but sometimes a Jane Q. Public or even a whole community—who, motivated by forces beyond the need to file a report, approaches "society as a whole" as "the mystery to be solved." As such, our heroes stumble through each X-file in a state of epistemological crisis. Halfway through the pilot episode, driving one stormy night down a back road in an Oregon town zapped with extraterrestrial enterprise, the agents are enveloped by a halo of light, and their car goes dead. When the light subsides, Mulder checks his watch and squeals that nine minutes have vanished into thin air. "Time can't just disappear!" Scully, panicked for the first time, stammers through the rain at her giddy partner. "It's a universal invariant!" Mulder, riveted beyond gloating, pants back, "Not in this zip code."

By granting impressive measures of scientific reasoning to one and gestalt interpretation to the other, the show gives its leads a basic measure of dramatic and intellectual equality. Neither agent is Sherlock to the other's Watson, and each contends with the harassment that befalls women who do autopsies and men who read tea leaves. Both are smart, stubborn, lonely, and brave. At the same time, a persistent sleight of hand gives *ontological* priority to Mulder: it's his world we're visiting, and in the final instance, his research methods tend to be the ones that work. (Not coincidentally, Anderson is a serious, thoughtful actress who would go on to play Lily Bart and Nora Helmer. Duchovny, at his best, just kind of *is* Fox Mulder. Had he not dropped out of Yale to play gender-bending roles in *Twin Peaks* and porny indie films, he might have finished his dissertation on Pynchon and his peers, "Magic and Technology in Contemporary Fiction and Poetry.")

To be Scully—or, in a more archetypal sense, to be "a Scully"—is to insist on the laws of physics even as the aliens stretch you out on board their ship. It's to begin a sentence, as she does in "Die Hand Die Verletzt" (The One Where Devil Worshippers Run the School Board), "I mean, there's nothing odd about—" only to be cut off by toads falling from the sky. It's to climb the rungs of an institution that seeks to push you off the ladder, to stoically salute your authoritarian father's coffin, to relax by studying the DSM-IV on a Friday night over a glass of wine, and still to somehow find yourself among mutants, the odd girl in a different boys' club than the one you'd intended to join. Like her predecessor Clarice Starling, Jodie Foster's dogged young criminologist in *The Silence of the Lambs*, Scully dares to look into the hearts of the coldest killers, and they alone dare to look back.

To be a Mulder, on the other hand, means your ears buzz with white noise but your sacred duty is to keep it Real. Because you're obsessed with getting outside, you take a job way on the inside, put on the gray suit you were born in, and work both for and against the (Cigarette Smoking) Man, who considers vaping you every eighth episode but then just maims you again like a favorite broken toy. Your basement office under the panopticon is so close to where the maps are made, it's off the map. You're a polonium-tipped dart's throw from knowledge but so far from power that they don't even bother harassing you half the time. So you curl up in the belly of your own surveillance, eat sunflower seeds out of the bag, and jerk off at your desk beneath your iconic poster of a grainy UFO with its block-lettered caption, I WANT TO BELIEVE. "It's interesting," a shape-shifting rapist tells him in an episode called "Small Potatoes" (The One Where Mulder Gets Impersonated by a Man with a Tail). "I was born a loser. But you're one by choice." To be a Mulder is to be a kind of idiot, and to be right. In many episodes, he crumples to the ground as though literally stricken by the force of terrible knowledge. I did that too, I bragged to my journal. And I liked to watch.

IN OUR BOOK, even in the late section titled "The Great List of Differences," S. and I never quite come out and say that she is a Scully and I a Mulder. This might appear in retrospect like a correction for the show's own bias, a critique of how contemporary metaphysics still estranges science from magic after all these years, or a mature recognition that Mulder and Scully aren't *real*. In fact, I think S. was happy to acknowledge her own allegiance to the latter, while I was too uneasy to admit to such a fundamental split.

I had known S. since the second grade. We liked each other because we were both serious, but for the same reason didn't play together much. Once I borrowed an armload of her books, then forgot about them for so long that we had outgrown them by the time I brought them back. In middle school we became part of the same carpool, and at the start of seventh grade she became what, had we been paranormal investigators, I would have called my partner. It was 1997. Earlier that year, the thirty-eight remaining members of Heaven's Gate, a UFO cult that started in the '70s, washed down phenobarbital with vodka for the same reason everyone did what we did in those days: the millennium was coming.

My mom, a special-ed teacher, diagnosed me with autism spectrum disorders only when I was getting on her nerves, which in those days I usually was. S. presented her with a complicated case. At school, most kids on the spectrum had trouble getting along, or only hung out with each other. S. gravitated in their direction, but she was as cool as an algorithm, or a brand, and could sense the same quality in the objects around us as disinterestedly as a nurse checking for fever. Later, when there were more of us, we spent years trying to account for her unaccountability, as though she had joined us from another planet. In retrospect, though, she was simply from a feminist cyberpunk future that never quite happened. She was a tiny child, pale with freckles and acne, who wore a spiked dog collar and soft bright T-shirts from babyhood and who seemed to have more processing power available to her than anyone anyone had ever met. She learned programming languages and, like the girls who took Korean lessons after school, turned her handwriting into a font. At one point she tried to make pocket protectors happen and almost succeeded; if we'd had more internet in those days, she might have. She was mean to boys and they fell in love with her; if we'd had more internet in those days, she might have become one herself. When she wrote about middle school as an adult, her alter ego was a secret robot.

To her great frustration, S. had to share a small room with her sister, but in my mind her house was, if not a portal to the Life Café, at least a peephole. Through it could be glimpsed a full-spectrum pastiche of cultural politics: her aunts and uncles on one side included Marxist art historians and a regional leader of the Objectivist society; on the other, a Sonic Youth producer with a bathtub full of records. It was her father, who drank wine and watched baseball and read John Barth, who informed me one day in our carpool, "Work is hell." S. and I silently agreed that I would come as close as possible to taking on her tastes, habits, and Myers-Briggs classification (INTP: the Logician) and use the results to establish our superiority to the normies around us. Throughout my files from this time, our belief in the typological power of codes we had made up ourselves appears with a conspiracist's selective rigor. ("I've finally figured out why my mom and I don't get along," I wrote. "She's an ESFP!") In the notebooks I manically maintained in the fall of seventh grade, I claimed that we had become so close, we seemed to be merging into one.

I kept, for those months, not one but two journals. In my regular journal, I fantasized about making a suicide pact with a boy in a Pearl Jam shirt, and global annihilation as an antidote to slow violence. I copied S. I complained about my mom, who compared me during one fight, I reported indignantly, to another young woman lacking in "fundamental values": Squeaky Fromme, the Manson girl who'd plotted murder from Spahn Ranch just a few miles up the canyon from our house. In my *X-Files* journal, which opens with an apology for "my ever-insistent urges to write even *more* rambling pages" about the show, I traced David Duchovny's face out of *Us Weekly*, hit critical walls (what was the proper level of detail to include in an episode recap for which I was the only reader?), and tried to suck a political education out of my television.

HISTORY, WE WERE TOLD in the 1990s, was something that happened to other people. The recent past was littered with code-named police actions that, rendered pointless by the evaporation of the cold war, no longer even had the dignity of the unmentionable. Conservatives kept building monuments to the death of communism that no one wanted to visit. Liberals wanted to forget the whole messy business and gave themselves endless Oscars for movies about World War II. Only fools with sheaves of xeroxed newsletters thought they were smart enough to construct a narrative out of a deafening drone. The more distant past, upon inspection, turned out to be much the same, leading some to suspect that history had never happened at all. There were, however, exceptions to the rule: events taken to be unique in their world-shattering horror, and exceptional people who had come near them and gotten away no longer quite themselves. We, too, could be exceptional: if we were good and listened hard, history could become something that happened, though only by proxy, to us. Every year on the Day of Remembrance, survivors came to Hebrew school and asked us to feel on our skin the licks of the Shoah's eternal flame and to guard with our lives its redemption in the birth of a handsome nation. In history class in regular school, we learned nothing at all. And yet the past kept ghosting through like reruns.

Reruns were the form in which I watched the show, already five seasons in and beginning its long decline by the time I got on board. Seeing its baffling conspiracy arc unfold out of order saved me the hassle of getting fully invested in a plot that often made no sense. True to its times, *The X-Files* lacked a show bible, the reference guide typically used to maintain consistency over the course of a series. Yet even at its most labyrinthine the program imparted the crucial thesis that cataclysmic violence was not merely the stuff of historical memory, but an ongoing process of natural history still ravaging lands and bodies zoned for continuous extraction. "Something just clicked about the whole Holocaust," I wrote, shaken, after watching season two's searing "Anasazi" trilogy (The Ones Where Mulder Gets Decolonized), in which we learn that the Kissinger-era State Department collaborated with ex-Nazi scientists on the production of human-alien hybrids, using tribal populations as test subjects.

When Mulder finds evidence, the government destroys the tape, but Navajo code talkers have already memorized its contents. The Final Solution, the episodes suggested, emerged not from the depths of an unfathomable hell but had a *logic* that preceded the camps and survived their dismantling; maybe it was even right at home in the United States. Here, if memory stood a chance at enduring through the body, it was lodged in throats intubated by colonial force.

Did I get all that, or did it go over my head entirely? Was it even there to begin with? *The X-Files*, a show whose social detectives are at the end of the day still cops, occupied a cunningly ambiguous slot in the ideological lineup of its equivocating era: symptomology without diagnosis, conspiracy without collectivity, paranoia for its own sake, a bossa nova accelerationism for a rainy evening with an eclectic drug collection and nowhere to go all night. Critics spanning the political spectrum loved it, especially those concentrated at its weirdo ends like S.'s aunts and uncles. The appeal to academics on the left of a series about intrepid hauntologists trapped in an institutional maze run by evil overlords perhaps goes without saying. The show was like Duchovny: if it hadn't landed on Fox, it would have just taught cultural studies. Many of its most poignant, sophisticated episodes are seminars on the power, and the limits, of Mulder's methods for patiently sifting through piles of cultural detritus on the lookout for connections between dubious Monsters of the Week and tortuous conspiracy arcs. On the dust jacket of her excellent cultural history of ufology, *Aliens in America: Conspiracy Cultures from Outerspace to Cyberspace*, the Marxist political theorist Jodi Dean broke the fourth wall of scholarly detachment entirely, posing in front of an I WANT TO BELIEVE poster and appearing to suppress a giggle. But the libertarian right boasted hardcore fans as well, and for similar reasons. The show represented resistance to neoliberal governmentality in the form of clandestine cells: hacker collectives, militias, cults practicing archaic magics bright and dark. In doing so, it seemed to beckon its own cult following, wrote the libertarian scholar Paul Cantor, who has devoted hundreds of admiring pages to

The X-Files, "as if the program were trying to replicate in its audience what it shows in the world at large."

For me, too, *The X-Files* held out the promise of subculture, the meaning of style. I studied Mulder's methods—suspend disbelief when doing fieldwork, wink at your interview subjects—and tried to make them my own. But because I was 12 and had never heard of anything, the show functioned even more literally as a dictionary of esoteric knowledge from which America could be inferred. The secrets made me giddy and desperate, like hearing an incredible bit of gossip over a wiretap. S. and I got on the phone every Sunday night after the show ended and talked for hours.

Fandom was a way of organizing knowledge and desire, a kind of epidemiology. You learned from the cluster of objects that drew near you what kind of person you were. The internet was like that, too: it sorted. S. loved it there and from it brought back news of our cult. From her I learned of the epic online battles between shippers and no-romos, and S. and I took up the cause of the latter with the passion of hardheaded agents who thought romance was for little girls. Around the beginning of seventh grade, men from the phone company had come to my house, too, and installed our own beeping, flashing modem. My journal makes no mention of the internet's installation, but by the end of the year, it's there in every entry, a thrilling, ugly hassle. I went through the motions of fury with my parents for limiting my access to its catacombs, but even S. knew I basically agreed with them: I wanted it to leave us, and hoped it still might.

Sometimes, through the entropy of perversion, curiosity, a hunch, I found myself in bad company. "I finally managed to subscribe to the INTJ page, and they're all Ayn Rand freaks!" I griped to my journal. "'Mercy is a trait that only an F can possess'!" And yet my diary itself, in the moments it draws most clearly from my *X-Files* notebook, sounds unnervingly like the adolescent fascism of 4chan. There is a short story about the Pentagon "vaporizing" rebels in Montana, a state my mother often used to illustrate the point that even in the Nineties, a Jew could not go everywhere. There is a poem called "Awaken" in which the speaker steps into reality, "where bureaucrats are not cheerful pink bunnies / And dreamers do not rule the world." It wasn't that I'd switched sides in my private political pantomime, where communists and fascists were still at war. If anything, I probably rested too easy in the assumption that I never could. It was simply that my enemies, who filled the web with paeans to the intellectual superiority of white men who liked to code, had the advantage of actually existing. I dabbled in their language because, as far as I knew, I did not.

On New Year's Day, I described a fight with my parents in which I lost access to language and became "a dead circuit." Chunks of the recent past had gone missing, and the cloud of absence threatened the borders of the present. The visitors had landed, Jodi Dean wrote that year: the internet was changing people; it had gotten into our blood, scrambling codes. Just as Budd Hopkins, the ufologist, had promised, we were no longer the watchers but the ones being watched. I still have information sickness. I don't know what it's really called.

On January 2, though, I had better news. I took out what amounted to full-page ads in both my regular and *X-Files* journals, indicating in giant purple letters that something had changed in my house, something that meant I would now be able to watch the show every night:

WE
GOT
FX!!!

And then, for months, I barely wrote at all.

WHEN MY JOURNAL picks up again around the start of eighth grade, a new kid has emerged, kind of hyper, in the midst of a determined cultural discovery process. I loved Sylvia Plath and the Violent Femmes and "anarchists" and my JNCOs. My mapping had become more focused; there were fewer global conspiracies and more genealogies of punk. An *X-Files* soundtrack had introduced me to Nick Cave, and a Nick Cave CD had a cover of "All Tomorrow's Parties," and "All Tomorrow's Parties" led me down the stairs to the Velvet Underground. At some point in the process I no longer needed the show: I could read lots of things now. It was 1998. In Calabasas, where the rich girls from Hebrew school lived behind locked gates, a new outdoor mall was built in the shape of a fake Umbrian plaza. They called it the Commons.

BY THE TIME S. AND I graduated from middle school, we had built a world together. *M. and S.'s Book*, made one long weekend after graduation in the summer of 1999, catalogued that world before it was destroyed, as we knew it would be, by our departure for different high schools: a math-and-science magnet for her, a humanities one for me. Like an eponymous first album, it did not have another name. Its cover is adorned with cutouts and stickers—a Lisa Frank palm tree, Beck, the Ayatollah Khomeini, a potato. Its handwritten pages are filled with song lyrics and comics and fanfic and assessments of our friends and endless inventories of our universe.

> Things We Want (in S.'s writing), No. 41: No tongue so I can sound like the Sex Pistols (M. thought of this first).

> Stuff That Scares Us (S. again), No. 31: Obsessive fans-turned-assassins. Where the hell is your brain, I'm talking to you, Mark David Chapman.

> Things That Depress Me (my writing), No. 14: How Columbine made all these shitty laws happen and now you can't wear trench coats and stuff.

> ____ No. 15: How my dad fucked my computer and I can't get in.

> ____ No. 16: How communism didn't work.

We wanted to distribute our book widely, but my mom read it, noted that it was, among other things, a burn book—"Oh, and her choreography sucks," S. wrote of one friend—and forbade this, instead driving us to Staples to print the only two copies in existence. "It's just me and S. again," I wrote in my journal at the end of that summer, "and god we had the most depressing conversation tonight. About how we're so worried about *everything*: high school, college, life. How this era totally sucks and even our parents admit they had it easy, but at the same time we are so lame cuz all our music is old and we act like it came out yesterday. We are obsessed with old dead people. Everyone is fuckin dead or they own stores in places like Silver Lake." On bad days, I admitted, "I completely lose myself in time."

MULDER AND SCULLY'S partnership could not survive the turn of the millennium and neither could mine and S.'s. In the show's final seasons, the agents finally seem to be sleeping together, ruining an important source of dramatic tension exactly as we knew it would. Both leads had pulled back from the series and were partially replaced by generic opposite-gendered investigators. George W. Bush was elected, the twin towers fell, and the national appetite for conspiratorial fantasy was sated, for a while, by the nightly news.

By that time I had stopped watching. S. stuck with the original series until the end; I quit when the going got tough. She wanted to remain an extraordinary child and I was trying to become a more ordinary miserable teenager. Neither of us could keep up with the other, and we suffered and quarreled. For S., computing offered safe passage to wonder; the beauty of form was on the inside. I remained locked out; computers break when I come near. At Armenian church camp one summer, she welcomed Jesus into her heart and kept him there for a few years, and I discovered my own bewilderment in the face of belief. She was celibate; I just couldn't get laid. We both loved other girls but not quite, we decided, each other. Later, she would study engineering, and I would study its critiques. Later still, she would move to the Pacific Northwest, build brains for a big company, and fill a mansion with marvelous toys and then children to play with them. I moved across the country to my city, where I wander around staring uncomprehendingly at objects and waiting for them to stare back. I still have my I WANT TO BELIEVE poster over my desk. It was the first thing I ever bought online.

What is easier to see with greater distance is that the epistemological tension that had held the show together—the coy flirtation between magic and science—had been consummated, just like the relationship between Mulder and Scully or between conspiratorial fantasy and political reality. We had been literalized into a strange new lifeworld entirely saturated by computer technology. *The X-Files* filled its characters with alien-manufactured microchips, but it never really caught up to a world with smartphones. Detective work on *The X-Files* had happened under the cover of darkness, the agents' flashlights casting single beams across a blackened screen. But by the turn of the millennium, the night was fading. In Russia, a space company made plans to dot the sky with satellites that would reflect sunshine back to earth at all hours, creating "daylight all night long." The satellites never launched, but it didn't matter. The new order of things had eliminated shadows, and with them, an entire methodology for seeing in the dark.

The *X-Files* reboot first aired in the early months of 2016, when the air was humid with denial. Fittingly, the real problem is the lighting. Anderson has a self-help book out; Duchovny, back from rehab for sex addiction, wrote a novel in which farm animals representing Israel and Palestine make friends, and has a Twitter account for his dog. In the new episodes, they uncannily seemed to be playing themselves—her with sharpened cheekbones, him with an open top button on a crisp white shirt—like they'd just come from brunch in Santa Monica. But an influx of daylight created a problem for the series on another level, too. In "My Struggle" and its sequels (The Ones That Felt Longer Than a Knausgaard Novel), the show's updated myth arc revolves around our protagonists' attempt to deal with a strange new bedfellow, a popular right-wing conspiracy peddler on the model of Alex Jones, who is both clearly odious and possibly onto something. For all the original program's storied self-reflexivity, the new show could not figure out how to live up to its twist, both jaw-dropping and enragingly inevitable, on the old one: *Fox Mulder Meets Fox News.* The call is coming, all too obviously, from inside the house.

The reboot rebooted again in early 2018, its problems further magnified by everything we've learned in the past two years. Season eleven, does, however, include one all-time great episode, "The Lost Art of Forehead Sweat" (The One Where an Alien Does a Trump Monologue), a bittersweet film essay on the impossibility of *The X-Files* in a "postconspiracy" age when power refuses to go through the motions of concealing its most brutal machinations. In one montage that spans the Reagan through Obama years, a nebbishy paper pusher evolves from a bored postal clerk to a napping Securities and Exchange Commission operative to a CIA agent casually waterboarding a bound man to a drone operator accidentally bombing a far-off wedding, all from the comfort of the same cubicle. At the episode's end, Mulder and Scully meet a bedazzled extraterrestrial ambassador who has arrived in a flying saucer to inform them that the aliens' study of Earth is complete; the intergalactic confederation no longer wants anything to do with us. "We are building a wall," he intones cordially but firmly. As a parting gesture, he gives Mulder a trim, leather-bound book called *All the Answers,* "in case you have any questions remaining."

"It's OK, Mulder," Scully reassures her stunned partner when the spaceship has whizzed off. "There will always be more X-files." "No! It's not true!" Mulder howls, hurling the book and crumpling to the ground.

The *New York Times* recently reported that the Pentagon has spent millions of dollars on UFO research in the past decade. Weird objects are appearing in the sky again, or maybe they're just Teslas. It's all been met with a collective shrug.

As usual, Mulder was right.

IN THE MONTHS BEFORE the election, I lost my method, too. I was trying to write my own dissertation about magic and technology in contemporary literature, and left my city to be alone with my devices. Keeping myself safe from stories and refusing to stumble on mysteries, my information sickness spread until I could not know things at all. A dead circuit. Instead of a map, Trump's giant face.

That November, the earth opened and we fell through the cracks, picking up speed. It wasn't one big hole but endless small ones, like gas coming up through the tundra, or like our house in the Valley with its network of hidden fissures that opened up one day twenty years after the earthquake. Broken clocks floated by. They were melted but no longer missing. I am a communist again, like lots of kids. As I write this, children across the country are marching out of their schools together because the location of safety has moved outside. The rich are planning missions to the stars.

The world felt strange in the late 20th century when politics congealed into fandom, like being haunted by ghosts. Now that fandom on the right has melted back into politics, it feels psychotic, like being stalked by monsters or chased by cartoon frogs. When we get accustomed to the political unconscious becoming conscious, the imperceptible perceptible, we say we are woke; the Nazis say red-pilled. It is uncanny to remember a time when we spoke only through the things we liked and wore, like looking back at cultists who think they have outgrown the swaddling of history, but in fact simply will not speak the names of their devils and gods. When alt-right thinkers complain about a specter they call postmodernism, I wonder if they miss it.

It's hard to say whether the new show we are living in is a sequel to the old one, or just its reboot. We were in the park at night, a different friend and I, a different time. I'd tangled myself in a swing and was spinning round and round when he told me about Roko's basilisk. The basilisk, born on an internet chat forum for the philosophical wing of the new tide of fascism, is a super-powerful artificial intelligence from the future. He wants you, earthling, to work toward his establishment as a supreme being ruling a neofeudal order. He will not bug you if you do not know his name, but once you do, you're in or you're out, and if you're out he will fuck you up, even if he has to rebuild your consciousness out of machine dust in order to do it. The basilisk is a folktale of our time. In him, we meet the ultimate conspirator in the shape of a chintzy Monster of the Week. Like a bit of malware in your head, he insists his story be passed on.

"Let him come," I said to my friend. "If we refuse to speak of him, we give him the power of our childhood phantasms. The enemy has revealed himself. Now we can fight."

"You are a white girl in the park on acid," he said. "On the border, they are building camps."

I put my foot out sharply and stopped spinning. One looks at one's friends and neighbors and wonders who will turn. One turns to oneself.

I do not know if we can organize from a place this disorganized. But I want to believe.

2018

ON LIKING WOMEN

ANDREA LONG CHU

ONCE A WEEK, FOR A SINGLE SEMESTER OF HIGH SCHOOL, I WOULD be dismissed early from class to board the athletics bus with fifteen teenage girls in sleek cap-sleeved volleyball jerseys and short shorts. I was the only boy.

Occasionally a girl who still needed to change would excuse herself behind a row of seats to slip out of her school uniform into the team's dark-blue colors. For more minor wardrobe adjustments, I was simply asked to close my eyes. In theory, all sights were trained on the game ahead where I, as official scorekeeper, would push numbers around a byzantine spreadsheet while the girls leapt, dug, and dove with raw, adolescent power. But whatever discipline had instilled itself before a match would dissolve in its aftermath, often following a pit stop for greasy highway-exit food, as the girls relaxed into an innocent dishabille: untucked jerseys, tight undershirts, the strap of a sports bra. They talked, with the candor of postgame exhaustion, of boys, sex, and other vices; of good taste and bad blood and small, sharp desires. I sat, and I listened, and I waited, patiently, for that wayward electric pulse that passes unplanned from one bare upper arm to another on an otherwise unremarkable Tuesday evening, the away-game bus cruising back over the border between one red state and another.

The truth is, I have never been able to differentiate liking women from wanting to be like them. For years, the former desire held the latter in its mouth, like a capsule too dangerous to swallow. When I trawl the seafloor of my childhood for sunken tokens of things to come, these bus rides are about the gayest thing I can find. They probably weren't even all that gay. It is common, after all, for high school athletes to try to squash the inherent homoeroticism of same-sex sport under the heavy cleat of denial. But I'm too desperate to salvage a single genuine lesbian memory from the wreckage of the scared, straight boy whose life I will never not have lived to be choosy. The only other memory with a shot at that title is my pubescent infatuation with my best friend, a moody, low-voiced, Hot Topic–shopping girl who, it dawned on me only many years later, was doing her best impression of Shane from *The L Word*. One day she told me she had a secret to tell me after school; I spent the whole day queasy with hope that a declaration of her affections was forthcoming. Later, over the phone, after a pause big enough to drown in, she told me she was gay. "I thought you might say that," I replied, weeping inside. A decade later, after long having fallen out of touch, I texted her. "A week ago, I figured out that I am trans," I wrote. "You came out to me all those years ago. Just returning the favor."

This was months before I began teaching my first undergraduate recitation, where for the second time in my life—but the first time as a woman—I read Valerie Solanas's *SCUM Manifesto*. The *SCUM Manifesto* is a deliciously vicious feminist screed calling for the revolutionary overthrow of all men; Solanas self-published it in 1967, one year before she shot Andy Warhol on the sixth floor of the Decker Building in New York City. I wondered how my students would feel about it. In the bathroom before class, as I fixed my lipstick and fiddled with my hair, I was approached by a thoughtful, earnest young woman who sat directly to my right during class. "I loved the Solanas reading," she told me breathlessly. "I didn't know that was a thing you could study." I cocked my head, confused. "You didn't know what was a thing you could study?" "Feminism!" she said, beaming. In class, I would glance over at this student's notes, only to discover that she had filled the page with the word *SCUM*, written over and over with the baroque tenderness usually reserved for the name of a crush.

I, too, had become infatuated with feminism in college. I, too, had felt the thrill of its clandestine discovery. I had caught a shy glimpse of her across a dim, crowded dormitory room vibrating with electronic music and unclear intentions: a low-key, confident girl, slightly aloof, with a gravity all neighboring bodies obeyed. Feminism was too cool, too effortlessly hip, to be interested in a person like me, whom social anxiety had prevented from speaking over the telephone until well into high school. Besides, I heard she only dated women. I limited myself, therefore, to acts of distant admiration. I left critical comments on the student newspaper's latest exposé of this or that frat party. I took a women's studies course that had only one other man in it. I read desperately, from Shulamith Firestone to Jezebel, and I wrote: bizarre, profane plays about rape culture, one where the archangel Gabriel had a monologue so vile it would have burned David Mamet's tongue clean off; and ugly, strange poetry featuring something I was calling the Beautiful Hermaphrodite Proletariat. Feminism was all I wanted to think about, talk about. When I visited home, my mother and my sister, plainly irritated, informed me that I did not know what it was like to be a woman. But a crush was a crush, if anything buttressed by the conviction that feminism, like any of the girls I had ever liked, was too good for me.

It was in my junior year of college that I first read the *SCUM Manifesto*, crossing over the East River in a lonely subway car. It exhilarated me: the grandeur, the brutal polemics, the raw, succulent style of the whole thing. Solanas was *cool*. Rereading *SCUM*, I realized this was no accident. The manifesto begins like this:

> Life in this society being, at best, an utter bore and no aspect of society being at all relevant to women, there remains to civic-minded, responsible, thrill-seeking females only to overthrow

the government, eliminate the money system, institute complete
automation and destroy the male sex.

What's striking here is not Solanas's revolutionary extremism per
se, but the flippancy with which she justifies it. Life under male
supremacy isn't oppressive, exploitative, or unjust: it's just fucking
boring. For Solanas, an aspiring playwright, politics begins with an
aesthetic judgment. This is because male and female are essentially
styles for her, rival aesthetic schools distinguishable by their respec-
tive adjectival palettes. Men are timid, guilty, dependent, mindless,
passive, animalistic, insecure, cowardly, envious, vain, frivolous,
and weak. Women are strong, dynamic, decisive, assertive, cerebral,
independent, self-confident, nasty, violent, selfish, freewheeling,
thrill-seeking, and arrogant. Above all, women are cool and groovy.

Yet as I read back through the manifesto in preparation for class,
I was surprised to be reminded that, for all her storied manhating,
Solanas is surprisingly accommodating in her pursuit of male extinction. For one thing, the groovy, freewheeling females of Solanas's
revolutionary infantry SCUM (which at one point stood for "Society
for Cutting Up Men," though this phrase appears nowhere within
the manifesto) will spare any man who opts to join its Men's Auxil-
iary, where he will declare himself "a turd, a lowly abject turd." For
another, what few men remain after the revolution will be generously
permitted to wither away on drugs or in drag, grazing in pastures or
hooked into twenty-four-hour feeds allowing them to vicariously live
the high-octane lives of females in action. And then there's this:

> If men were wise, they would seek to become really female, would
> do intensive biological research that would lead to men, by means of
> operations on the brain and nervous system, being able to be trans-
> formed in psyche, as well as body, into women.

This line took my breath away. This was a vision of transsexuality as
separatism, an image of how male-to-female gender transition might

express not just disidentification with maleness but disaffiliation with men. Here, transition, like revolution, was recast in aesthetic terms, as if transsexual women decided to transition, not to "confirm" some kind of innate gender identity, but because being a man is stupid and boring.

I OVERREAD, PERHAPS. In 2013, an event in San Francisco intended as a tribute to Solanas on the twenty-fifth anniversary of her death was canceled after bitter conflict broke out on its Facebook page over what some considered Solanas's transphobia. One trans woman described having been harassed in queer spaces by radical feminists who referenced Solanas almost as often as they did Janice Raymond, whose 1979 book *The Transsexual Empire: The Making of the She-Male* is a classic of anti-trans feminism. Others went on the offensive. Mira Bellwether, creator of *Fucking Trans Women*, the punk-rock zine that taught the world to muff, wrote a lengthy blog post explaining her misgivings about the event, characterizing the *SCUM Manifesto* as "potentially the worst and most vitriolic example of lesbian-feminist hate speech" in history. She goes on to charge Solanas with biological essentialism of the first degree, citing the latter's apparent appeal to genetic science: "The male is a biological accident: the Y (male) gene is an incomplete X (female) gene, that is, it has an incomplete set of chromosomes. In other words, the male is an incomplete female, a walking abortion, aborted at the gene stage." For Bellwether, this is unequivocal proof that everything *SCUM* says about men, it also says about trans women.

Yet these are odd accusations. To call Solanas a "lesbian feminist" is to imply, erroneously, that she was associated with lesbian groups like New York City's Lavender Menace, which briefly hijacked the Second Congress to Unite Women in 1970 to protest homophobia in the women's movement and distribute their classic pamphlet "The Woman-Identified Woman." But Solanas was neither a political lesbian nor a lesbian politico. She was by all accounts a loner and a misfit, a struggling writer and sex worker who sometimes identified as gay but always looked out for number one. The dedication to her riotous 1965 play *Up Your Ass* reads, "I dedicate this play to ME, a continuous source of strength and guidance, and without whose unflinching loyalty, devotion, and faith this play would never have been written." (It was this play, whose full title is *Up Your Ass, or From the Cradle to the Boat, or The Big Suck, or Up from the Slime*, that Solanas tried first to sweet-talk, then to strong-arm, Andy Warhol into producing.)

As for the matter of genetics, I suppose I ought to be offended to have my Y chromosomes' good name raked through the mud. Frankly, though, I have a hard time getting it up for a possession I consider about as valuable as a $15 gift card to Blockbuster. The truth is, if it's hard for contemporary readers to tell men and trans women apart in Solanas's analysis, it is not because she thinks all trans women are men; if anything, it's because she thinks all men are closeted trans women. When Solanas hisses that maleness is a "deficiency disease," I am reminded of those trans women who diagnose themselves, only half-jokingly, with testosterone poisoning. When she snarls that men are "biological accidents," all I hear is the eminently sensible claim that every man is *literally* a woman trapped in the wrong body. This is what the *SCUM Manifesto* calls pussy envy, from which all men suffer, though few dare to admit it aside from "faggots" and "drag queens" whom Solanas counts among the least miserable of the lot. Hence the sentiment Solanas expresses through Miss Collins, one of two quick-witted queens who grace the filthy pages of *Up Your Ass*:

> MISS COLLINS: Shall I tell you a secret? I despise men. Oh, why do I have to be one of them? (*Brightening.*) Do you know what I'd like more than anything in the world to be? A Lesbian. Then I could be the cake and eat it too.

Bellwether might object that I am, again, being too generous. But generosity is the only spirit in which a text as hot to the touch as the *SCUM Manifesto* could have ever been received. This is after all a pamphlet advocating mass murder, and what's worse, property damage. It's not as if those who expressed their disappointment over the tribute's cancellation did so in blanket approval of Solanas's long-term plans for total human extinction (women included) or her attempted murder of a man who painted soup cans. As Breanne Fahs recounts in her recent biography of Solanas, the shooting was the straw that broke the back of the camel known as the National Organization for Women (NOW), which despite its infancy—it was founded in 1966, only two years earlier—had already suffered fractures over abortion and lesbianism. As the radical feminists Ti-Grace Atkinson and Florynce Kennedy visited Solanas in prison, the latter agreeing to represent Valerie pro bono, then president Betty Friedan scrambled to distance NOW from what she viewed as a problem that most certainly had a name, demanding in a telegram that Kennedy "DESIST IMMEDIATELY FROM LINKING NOW IN ANY WAY WITH VALERIE SOLANAS." Within the year, both Kennedy and Atkinson had left the organization, each going on to found their own, ostensibly more radical groups: the Feminist Party and the October 17th Movement, respectively. Likewise, after the Solanas tribute was canceled in 2013, folks hoping to hash out the Facebook fracas in person held a splinter event called "We Who Have Complicated Feelings About Valerie Solanas."

This is simply to note that disagreement over Solanas's legacy is an old feminist standard, the artifact of a broader intellectual habit that critiques like Bellwether's lean on. This is the thing we call feminist historiography, with all its waves and groups and fabled conferences. Any good feminist bears stitched into the burning bra she calls her heart that tapestry of qualifiers we use to tell one another stories about ourselves and our history: radical, liberal, neoliberal, socialist, Marxist, separatist, cultural, corporate, lesbian, queer, trans, eco, intersectional, anti-porn, anti-work, pro-sex, first-, second-, third-, sometimes fourth-wave. These stories have perhaps less to do with What Really Happened than they do with what Fredric Jameson once called "the 'emotion' of great historiographic form"—that is, the satisfaction of synthesizing the messy empirical data of the past into an elegant historical arc in which everything that happened could not have happened otherwise.

To say, then, that these stories are rarely if ever "true" is not merely to repeat the axiom that taxonomy is taxidermy, though it cannot be denied that the objects of intellectual inquiry are forever escaping, like B-movie zombies, from the vaults of their interment. It is also to say that all cultural things, *SCUM Manifesto* included, are answering machines for history's messages at best only secondarily. They are rather, first and foremost, occasions for people to feel something: to adjust the pitch of a desire or up a fantasy's thread count, to make overtures to a new way to feel or renew their vows with an old one. We read things, watch things, from political history to pop culture, as feminists and as people, because we want to belong to a community or public, or because we are stressed out at work, or because we are looking for a friend or a lover, or perhaps because we are struggling to figure out how to feel political in an age and culture defined by a general shipwrecking of the beautiful old stories of history.

So when Bellwether condemns the *SCUM Manifesto* as "the pinnacle of misguided and hateful 2nd wave feminism and lesbian-feminism," this condemnation is a vehicle for a kind of political disappointment that feminists are fond of cultivating with respect to preceding generations of feminists. In this version of the story, feminism excluded trans women in the past, is learning to include trans women now, and will center trans women in the future. This story's plausibility is no doubt due to a dicey bit of revisionism implied by the moniker *trans-exclusionary radical feminist*, often shortened to TERF. Like most kinds of feminist, TERFs are not a party or a unified front. Their beliefs, while varied, mostly boil down to a rejection of the idea that transgender women are, in fact, women. They also don't much like the name TERF, which they take to be a slur—a grievance that would be beneath contempt if it weren't also true, in the sense that all bywords for bigots are intended to be defamatory. The actual problem with an epithet like TERF is its historiographic sleight of hand: namely, the erroneous implication that all TERFs are hold-outs who missed the third wave, old-school radical feminists who never learned any better. This permits their being read as a kind of living anachronism through which the past can be discerned, much as European anthropologists imagined so-called primitive societies to be an earlier stage of civilizational development caught in amber.

In fact, we would do better to talk about TERFs in the context of the internet, where a rebel alliance of bloggers like Feminist Current's Meghan Murphy and GenderTrender's Linda Shanko spend their days shooting dinky clickbait at the transsexual empire's thermal exhaust ports. The true battles rage on Tumblr, in the form of comments, memes, and doxing; it is possible, for instance, to find Tumblrs entirely devoted to cataloging *other* Tumblr users who are known "gender critical feminists," as they like to refer to themselves. But this conflict has as much to do with the ins and outs of social media—especially Tumblr, Twitter, and Reddit—as it does with any great ideological conflict. When a subculture espouses extremist politics, especially online, it is tempting but often incorrect to take those politics for that subculture's beating heart. It's worth considering whether TERFs, like certain strains of the alt-right, might be defined less by their political ideology (however noxious) and more by a complex, frankly fascinating relationship to trolling, on which it will be for future anthropologists, having solved the problem of digital ethnography, to elaborate.

OF COURSE, FEMINIST TRANSPHOBIA is no more an exclusively digital phenomenon than white nationalism. There were second-wave feminists who sincerely feared and hated trans women. Some of them are even famous, like the Australian feminist Germaine Greer, author of the 1974 best seller *The Female Eunuch*. Few TERFs curl their lips with Greer's panache. This is how she described an encounter with a fan, in the *Independent* magazine in 1989:

> On the day that *The Female Eunuch* was issued in America, a person in flapping draperies rushed up to me and grabbed my hand. "Thank you," it breathed hoarsely, "Thank you so much for all you've done for us girls!" I smirked and nodded and stepped backward, trying to extricate my hand from the enormous, knuckly, hairy, be-ringed paw that clutched it. The face staring into mine was thickly coated with pancake make-up through which the stubble was already burgeoning, in futile competition with a Dynel wig of immense luxuriance and two pairs of false eyelashes. Against the bony ribs that could be counted through its flimsy scarf dress swung a polished steel women's liberation emblem. I should have said, "You're a man. *The Female Eunuch* has done less than nothing for you. Piss off."

Little analysis is needed to show that disgust like Greer's belongs to the same traffic in woman-hating she and her fellow TERFs supposedly abhor. Let us pause instead to appreciate how rarely one finds transmisogyny, whose preferred medium is the spittle of strangers, enjoying the cushy stylistic privileges of middlebrow literary form. It's like watching Julia Child cook a baby.

Then again, Greer has long imagined herself as feminism's id, periodically digging herself out of the earth to rub her wings together and molt on network television. In 2015, she made waves when she criticized as "misogynist" *Glamour* magazine's decision to give their Woman of the Year award to Caitlyn Jenner, then fresh off her *Vanity Fair* photo shoot. In response to the backlash, Greer released this gem of a statement: "Just because you lop off your dick and then wear a dress doesn't make you a fucking woman. I've asked my doctor to give me long ears and liver spots and I'm going to wear a brown coat but that won't turn me into a fucking cocker spaniel." More surprising is when a second-wave icon like Atkinson, onetime defender of Solanas, trots out TERF talking points at a Boston University conference in 2014: "There is a conflict around gender. That is, feminists are trying to get rid of gender. And transgendered [*sic*] reinforce gender." That Atkinson's remarks arrived at a conference whose theme was "Women's Liberation in the Late 1960s and Early 1970s" only encourages wholesale dismissals of the second wave as the Dark Ages of feminist history.

Yet consider the infamous West Coast Lesbian Conference of 1973. The first night of the conference, the transsexual folk singer Beth Elliott's scheduled performance was interrupted by protesters who tried to kick her off the stage. The following day, the radical feminist Robin Morgan, editor of the widely influential 1970 anthology *Sisterhood Is Powerful*, delivered a hastily rewritten keynote in which she unloaded on Elliott, calling her "an opportunist, an infiltrator, and a destroyer—with the mentality of a rapist." Morgan's remarks were soon printed in the short-lived underground newspaper *Lesbian Tide*, where they could enjoy a wider audience:

> I will not call a male "she"; thirty-two years of suffering in this androcentric society, and of surviving, have earned me the title "woman"; one walk down the street by a male transvestite, five minutes of his being hassled (which he may enjoy), and then he dares, he dares to think he understands our pain? No, in our mothers' names and in our own, we must not call him sister. We know what's at work when whites wear blackface; the same thing is at work when men wear drag.

This is where reports of the conference usually end, often with a kind of practiced sobriety about How Bad Shit Was. Yet as the historian Finn Enke argues in an excellent article forthcoming in *Transgender Studies Quarterly*, many accounts leave out the fact that the San Francisco chapter of the national lesbian organization Daughters of Bilitis had welcomed a 19-year-old Beth Elliott in 1971 after her parents rejected her, that Elliott had been elected chapter vice president that same year, that she had been embraced by the Orange County Dyke Patrol at the Gay Women's Conference in Los Angeles, and that she had been *a member of the organizing committee* for the very conference where her presence was disputed by a vocal minority of attendees. As for the vitriolic keynote, Enke suggests that Morgan's attacks on Elliott were born of the former's insecurity over being invited to speak at a conference for lesbians despite her being shacked up with a man, whose effeminacy she often tried, unsuccessfully, to parlay into a basis for her own radical credentials.

This is to say two things. First, the radical feminism of the Sixties and Seventies was as mixed a bag as any political movement, from Occupy to the Bernie Sanders campaign. Second, at least in this case, feminist transphobia was not so much an expression of anti-trans animus as it was an indirect, even peripheral repercussion of a much larger crisis in the women's liberation movement over how people should go about feeling political. In expanding the scope of feminist critique to the terrain of everyday life—a move which produced a characteristically muscular brand of theory that rivaled any Marxist's notes on capitalism—the second wave had inadvertently painted itself into a corner. If, as radical feminist theories claimed, patriarchy had infested not just legal, cultural, and economic spheres but the psychic lives of *women themselves*, then feminist revolution could only be achieved by combing constantly through the fibrils of one's consciousness for every last trace of male supremacy—a kind of political nitpicking, as it were. And nowhere was this more urgent, or more difficult, than the bedroom. Fighting tirelessly for the notion that sex was fair game for political critique, radical feminists were now faced with the prospect of putting their mouths where their money had been. Hence Atkinson's famous slogan: "Feminism is the theory, lesbianism is the practice." This was the political climate in which *both* Elliott and Morgan, as a transsexual woman and a suspected heterosexual woman, respectively, could find their statuses as legitimate subjects of feminist politics threatened by the incipient enshrining, among some radical feminists, of something called lesbianism as the preferred aesthetic form for mediating between individual subjects and the history they were supposed to be making—call these the personal and the political.

So while radical feminism as a whole saw its fair share of trans-loving lesbians and trans-hating heterosexuals alike, there *is* a historical line to be traced from political lesbianism, as a specific, by no means dominant tendency *within* radical feminism, to the contemporary phenomenon we've taken to calling trans-exclusionary radical feminism. Take Sheila Jeffreys, an English lesbian feminist recently retired from a professorship at the University of Melbourne in Australia. In her salad days, Jeffreys was a member of the Leeds Revolutionary Feminist Group, remembered for its fiery conference paper "Political Lesbianism: The Case Against Heterosexuality," published in 1979. The paper defined a political lesbian as "a woman-identified woman who does not fuck men" but stopped short of mandating homosexual sex. The paper also shared the *SCUM Manifesto*'s dead-serious sense of humor: "Being a heterosexual feminist is like being in the resistance in Nazi-occupied Europe where in the daytime you blow up a bridge, in the evening you rush to repair it." These days, Jeffreys has made a business of abominating trans women, earning herself top billing on the TERF speaking circuit. Like many TERFs, she believes that trans women's cheap imitations of femininity (as she imagines them) reproduce the same harmful stereotypes through which women are subordinated in the first place. "Transgenderism on the part of men," Jeffreys writes in her 2014 book *Gender Hurts*, "can be seen as a ruthless appropriation of women's experience and existence." She is also fond of citing sexological literature that classifies transgenderism as a paraphilia. It is a favorite claim among TERFs like Jeffreys that transgender women are gropey interlopers, sick voyeurs conspiring to infiltrate women-only spaces and conduct the greatest panty raid in military history.

I happily consent to this description. Had I ever been so fortunate as to attend the legendarily clothing-optional Michigan Womyn's Music Festival before its demise at the hands of trans activists in 2015, you can bet your Birkenstocks it wouldn't have been for the music. Indeed, at least among lesbians, trans-exclusionary radical feminism might best be understood as gay panic, girl-on-girl edition. The point here is not that all TERFs are secretly attracted to trans women—though so delicious an irony undoubtedly happens more often than anyone would like to admit—but rather that trans-exclusionary feminism has inherited political lesbianism's dread of desire's ungovernability. The traditional subject of gay panic, be he a US senator or just a member of the House, is a subject menaced by his own politically compromising desires: to preserve himself, he projects these desires onto another, whom he may now legislate or gay-bash out of existence. The political lesbian, too, is a subject stuck between the rock of politics and desire's hard place. As Jeffreys put it in 2015, speaking to the Lesbian History Group in London, political lesbianism was intended as a solution to the all-too-real cognitive dissonance produced by heterosexual feminism: "Why go to all these meetings where you're creating all this wonderful theory and politics, and then you go home to, in my case, Dave, and you're sitting there, you know, in front of the telly, and thinking, 'It's *weird*. This feels *weird*.'" But true separatism doesn't stop at leaving your husband. It proceeds, with paranoid rigor, to purge the apartments of the mind of anything remotely connected to patriarchy. Desire is no exception. Political lesbianism is founded on the belief that even desire becomes pliable at high enough temperatures. For Jeffreys and her comrades, lesbianism was not an innate identity, but an act of political will. This was a world in which biology was not destiny, a world where being a lesbian was about what got you woke, not wet.

Only heterosexuality might not have been doing it for Dave, either. It seems never to have occurred to Jeffreys that some of us "transgenders," as she likes to call us, might opt to transition precisely in order to escape from the penitentiary she takes heterosexuality to be. It is a supreme irony of feminist history that there is no woman more woman-identified than a gay trans girl like me, and that Beth Elliott and her sisters were the OG political lesbians: women who had walked away from both the men in their lives and the men whose lives they'd been living. We are separatists from our own bodies. We are militants of so fine a caliber that we regularly take steps to poison the world's supply of male biology. To TERFs like Jeffreys, we say merely that imitation is the highest form of flattery. But let's keep things in perspective. Because of Jeffreys, a few women in the Seventies got haircuts. Because of us, there are literally *fewer men on the planet.* Valerie, at least, would be proud. The Society for Cutting Up Men is a rather fabulous name for a transsexual book club.

BUT NOW I REALLY AM overreading. That trans lesbians should be pedestaled as some kind of feminist vanguard is a notion as untenable as it is attractive. In defending it, I would be neglecting what I take to be the true lesson of political lesbianism as a failed project: that nothing good comes of forcing desire to conform to political principle. You could sooner give a cat a bath. This does not mean that politics has no part to play in desire. Solidarity, for instance, can be terribly arousing—this was no doubt one of the best things the consciousness-raising groups of the Seventies had going for them. But you can't get aroused *as an act of* solidarity, the way you might stuff envelopes or march in the streets with your sisters-in-arms. Desire is, by nature, childlike and chary of government. The day we begin to qualify it by the righteousness of its political content is the day we begin to prescribe some desires and prohibit others. That way lies moralism only. Just try to imagine life as a feminist anemone, the tendrils of your desire withdrawing in an instant from patriarchy's every touch. There would be nothing to watch on TV.

It must be underscored how unpopular it is on the left today to countenance the notion that transition expresses not the truth of an identity but the force of a desire. This would require understanding transness as a matter not of who one *is,* but of what one *wants.* The primary function of gender identity as a political concept—and, increasingly, a legal one—is to bracket, if not to totally deny, the role of desire in the thing we call gender. Historically, this results from a wish among transgender advocates to quell fears that trans people, and trans women in particular, go through transition in order to *get stuff:* money, sex, legal privileges, little girls in public restrooms. As the political theorist Paisley Currah observes in his forthcoming book, the state has been far more willing to recognize sex reclassification when the reclassified individuals don't get anything out of it. In 2002, the Kansas Supreme Court voided the marriage of a transsexual woman and her then-deceased cisgender husband, whose $2.5 million estate she was poised to inherit, on the grounds that their union was invalid under Kansas's prohibition on same-sex marriage. The sex on the woman's Wisconsin birth certificate, which she had successfully changed from M to F years earlier, now proved worthless when she tried to cash it in.

Now I'm not saying I think that this woman transitioned to get rich quick. What I am saying is, *So what if she had?* I doubt that any of us transition simply because we want to "be" women, in some abstract, academic way. I certainly didn't. I transitioned for gossip and compliments, lipstick and mascara, for crying at the movies, for being someone's girlfriend, for letting her pay the check or carry my bags, for the benevolent chauvinism of bank tellers and cable guys, for the telephonic intimacy of long-distance female friendship, for fixing my makeup in the bathroom flanked like Christ by a sinner on each side, for sex toys, for feeling hot, for getting hit on by butches, for that secret knowledge of which dykes to watch out for, for Daisy Dukes, bikini tops, and all the dresses, and, my god, *for the breasts.* But now you begin to see the problem with desire: we rarely want the things we should. Any TERF will tell you that most of these items are just the traditional trappings of patriarchal femininity. She won't be wrong, either. Let's be clear: TERFs are gender abolitionists, even if that abolitionism is a shell corporation for garden-variety moral disgust. When it comes to the question of feminist revolution, TERFs leave trans girls like me in the dust, primping. In this respect, someone like Ti-Grace Atkinson, a self-described radical feminist committed to the revolutionary dismantling of gender as a system of oppression, is not the dinosaur; I, who get my eyebrows threaded every two weeks, am.

Perhaps my consciousness needs raising. I muster a shrug. When the airline loses your luggage, you are not making a principled political statement about the tyranny of private property; you just want your goddamn luggage back. This is most painfully evident in the case of bottom surgery, which continues to baffle a clique of queer theorists who, on the strength and happenstance of a shared prefix, have been all too ready to take transgender people as mascots for their politics of transgression. These days, the belief that getting a vagina will make you into a real woman is retrograde in the extreme. Many good feminists still only manage to understand bottom surgery by qualifying it as a personal aesthetic choice: *If that's what makes you feel more comfortable in your body, that's great.* This is as wrongheaded as it is condescending. To be sure, gender confirmation surgeries are aesthetic practices, continuous with rather than distinct from the so-called cosmetic surgeries. (No one goes into the operating room asking for an ugly cooch.) So it's not that these aren't aesthetic decisions; it's that they're not *personal.* That's the basic paradox of aesthetic judgments: they are, simultaneously, subjective and universal. Transsexual women don't want bottom surgery because their personal opinion is that a vagina would look or feel better than a penis. Transsexual women want bottom surgery because *most women have vaginas.* Call that transphobic if you like—that's not going to keep me from Chili's-Awesome-Blossoming my dick.

I am being tendentious, dear reader, because I am trying to tell you something that few of us dare to talk about, especially in public, especially when we are trying to feel political: not the fact, boringly obvious to those of us living it, that many trans women wish they were cis women, but the darker, more difficult fact that many trans women *wish they were women, period.* This is most emphatically not something trans women are supposed to want. The grammar of contemporary trans activism does not brook the subjunctive. Trans women *are* women, we are chided with silky condescension, as if we have all confused ourselves with Chimamanda Ngozi Adichie, as if we were all simply trapped in the wrong politics, as if the cure for dysphoria were wokeness. How can you want to be something you already are? Desire implies deficiency; want implies want. To admit that what makes women like me transsexual is not identity but desire is to admit just how much of transition takes place in the waiting rooms of wanting things, to admit that your breasts may never come in, your voice may never pass, your parents may never call back.

Call this the romance of disappointment. You want something. You have found an object that will give you what you want. This object is a person, or a politics, or an art form, or a blouse that fits. You attach yourself to this object, follow it around, carry it with you, watch it on TV. One day, you tell yourself, it will give you what you want. Then, one day, it doesn't. Now it dawns on you that your object will probably never give you what you want. But this is not what's disappointing, not really. What's disappointing is what happens next: nothing. You keep your object. You continue to follow it around, stash it in a drawer, water it, tweet at it. It still doesn't give you what you want—but you knew that. You have had another realization: not getting what you want has very little to do with wanting it. Knowing better usually doesn't make it better. You don't want something because wanting it will lead to getting it. You want it because you want it. This is the zero-order disappointment that structures all desire and makes it possible. After all, if you could only want things you were guaranteed to get, you would never be able to want anything at all.

This is not to garner pity for sad trannies like me. We have enough roses by our beds. It is rather to say, minimally, that trans women want things too. The deposits of our desire run as deep and fine as any. The richness of our want is staggering. Perhaps this is why coming out can feel like crushing, why a first dress can feel like a first kiss, why dysphoria can feel like heartbreak. The other name for disappointment, after all, is love.

2018

AN ACCOUNT OF MY HUT

CHRISTINA NICHOL

IN 2017, THE WEATHER IN CALIFORNIA WAS THE HOTTEST IN HIS-
tory. It was hotter than in 2016, which was also the hottest in history.
The vineyard owners spoke nervously of how difficult it was to find
people willing to pick grapes in this heat. The apple trees dropped
all their apples. Over the summer the smoke from hundreds of wild-
fires burning throughout the state gave me a chronic cough, which
turned into walking pneumonia. People began to talk about how
illnesses are getting weirder these days. I decided to attend a climate
change action meeting I had seen announced in the local newspaper.

It was an experimental prototype course founded on the ideas in
George Marshall's book *Don't Even Think About It: Why Our Brains
Are Wired to Ignore Climate Change*. After spending fifteen years
studying climate change–denying microcultures, Marshall concluded
that facts don't change people's minds; only stories do. We're so motivated by wanting to belong that we'd rather risk the dangers of climate
change than the more immediate symbolic death of estrangement
from our peers. In order to address climate change in our communities, Marshall suggests, we must appeal to the same desires that
religion does: for belonging, consolation, and redemption.

For this reason, the purpose of the group—or "fellowship," as
the organizers called it—was to borrow the most effective tools of

religion to create a community of people who would work together when it was time to implement policy change, or even take to the streets. Their aim was to galvanize 3.5 percent of the local population—the number social scientists estimate is the tipping point for effecting social change.

You had to apply to the prototype course, so after the informational meeting I wrote the organizers the following email, thinking there'd be a lot of competition:

> I attended your Information Session last night at the Sonoma County Land Trust. I marked the sheet stating that I would like to take the course you are offering but I just want to reiterate how much. I grew up with a dad who would regale us with climate change statistics over the dinner table. If my brother said he was going to a Giants game, my dad would say that he better enjoy it now because there weren't going to be any Giants games in the future. Hanging on the wall was a color-coded map he created of what property values would be worth when ocean levels rose in the Bay Area. He terrorized all my friends by describing how the atmosphere would start to smell like rotten eggs as soon as the oceans warmed and started pluming carbon. In effect, I assumed that by 2020, life on Earth wouldn't exist anymore. I teach environmental studies and am looking for ways that I can bring hope to my students but also help motivate them (as well as myself). I found your session to be inspiring, especially in its emphasis on fellowship and taking concrete action, and I felt a newfound joy that I hadn't felt in a while. I feel ready to take on the commitment that this course asks for.

THE ORGANIZERS TRIED many methods for cultivating a feeling of fellowship. They'd start the session by banging a gong, or by reciting a poem by William Stafford or the former mayor. They encouraged us to discuss our vulnerabilities. But the most effective method was to scare the crap out of us with mini-lectures about the realities of climate change, which bonded us in common terror.

We were presented, at the beginning, with a self-proclaimed "humorless, brain-numbing deep dive into climate science." They told us it wasn't supposed to happen this quickly. Climate scientists had predicted that by 2017 we would be at 380 parts per million (ppm) of carbon dioxide in the atmosphere, but we were already past 410 ppm.

The man who presented this information was, like my father, a local architect. Scrunching up his face he said, "I don't want to depress you, but I want to tell it to you straight." He told us that when he designs a house he has to deal with very strict building codes, which are intended to prevent worst-case scenarios. By contrast, the Paris Agreement—whose purpose is to limit the temperature increase over the second half of the century to 1.5 to 2 degrees Celsius above preindustrial levels—doesn't address worst-case scenarios. "Would you put a loved one on an airplane if the airplane had a 50 percent chance of making it across the Atlantic?" he asked.

The most effective glue for bonding, our organizers said, was collaboration: we needed a goal we could all work toward. Our goal was to phase out the internal combustion engine in California by 2030. They gave us questionnaires so we could spend the next week testing the public's receptivity to this idea. Here are some of the responses we got:

What happens if the power goes out?

Where do the cars on the road go? Do we get a free car? What happens to the oil companies? Would you be punished for having a gas car?

Do I have to get rid of my brand-new car? How did we get into this mess? What can we do to ensure our children can understand so they know what is going on by the time they get through high school?

Why not just get everyone to stop eating meat instead? Agriculture creates as many greenhouse gases as automobiles. Haven't you seen *Cowspiracy*?

There are so many other issues. Why electric cars? We need to change our habits!

Our schools should feature human relationships and our relationship to the Earth. The 4 Rs: Reading, 'Riting, Rithmetic, Relationships.

Could I go to Nevada to buy a car?

Isn't solar production toxic?

What will I do with my beloved van that carries all my stuff day after day?

Would there be violent, emotional reactions to such a "radical" move? How do we deal with that reaction?

I like it. Get there!

Proud of you, Bill, for being involved. It's inspiring.

I'm not driving an electric car! I'm allergic to electricity and SMART meter rays!

2030 may be too late to avoid some of the most catastrophic climate & social issues.

We have such a gas + car culture. Why do we let high schoolers drive to school? We need to change the consciousness. Only HS kids who work should have a car.

I asked my friend who works as a photographer for the Red Cross for her take on the electric-car issue. She said it was a good idea and invited me to help her install smoke alarms on houseboats in Sausalito.

"You should come," she said. "Get to know the houseboat community."

It's true that I was looking for community. I'd recently sent my friend an email about Russian House #1, a restaurant on the Sonoma coast where all the waiters have PhDs and the owners post a daily philosophical question diners are encouraged to discuss with one another. But I was also looking for a house to live in. I started wondering if a houseboat could be the solution to my housing dilemma.

I scanned Craigslist and called my boyfriend, Bongjun.

"Guess what? There's a way to live in the South Bay without paying a million dollars!" I said. "It's possible to live there for only a hundred thousand dollars. But actually, I researched it and it's not possible."

"What is it?" he asked.

"A houseboat. Three bedrooms for a hundred thousand."

"I saw a houseboat on Zillow last week," he said. "It was the kind of boat you discover the New World in. In the picture, the seller was hanging off the mast in a Renaissance costume."

"But these ones are actual houses. You get to know your neighbors."

"I don't want to live in a boat. I'd rather live in a bus."

"But you're always talking about how you love water, how you need to live near a river. We could go out in a kayak at night. Row to a restaurant."

"I don't like soggy socks."

"The water doesn't come *into* the boat."

"But I would have soggy socks in my subconscious."

Anyway, it didn't matter. It turned out that residents of Docktown, the houseboat community in Redwood City, were being evicted. All the houseboats without school-age children were required to vacate by February. That's why they were so cheap. But now I was back to negotiating with another person about a place to live in the midst of a housing crisis. "Maybe we could buy the houseboat and put it on some land," I said. "Then we'll be all set for when the oceans rise."

In California, the only people who own houses are people who bought them in the 1970s, work for tech companies, or were on the receiving end of a miracle. In Oakland, the blocks of homeless tarp housing continue to expand. In the grocery store you overhear people talking about the housing crisis. "It's called BYOH," the bagger says to the checker. "We buy a piece of land together and you Bring Your Own House."

In his book, George Marshall writes that people like to point to the Chinese pictogram *wēijī*, claiming that the character for "crisis" (*wēi*) is always paired with the character for "opportunity" (*jī*). But it turns out that *jī* doesn't actually mean "opportunity" at all. It means "a moment," "an airplane," and, sometimes, "organic chemistry." I started to wonder if there is a Chinese character that links "trying to solve climate change" with "trying to solve California's housing crisis."

THE DAY TRUMP WAS ELECTED, the first thing my mom said was, "Is today the day we can start smoking marijuana?" One of the consequences of California's legalization of marijuana is that industrial agriculture is appropriating the weed business. There are a number of reasonably cheap former pot farms for sale in the Santa Cruz Mountains.

Bongjun went to look at one to see if it was an appropriate place to build a sustainable community. Part of the road had been washed away by last winter's flood, so he had to park at the bottom of the hill. "We'd have to get four-wheel drive to get up there," he said. "You would really like the house, though. It has a grow room."

"But I'm not interested in growing marijuana."

"Oh, is *that* what *grow room* means?" he said. "I thought it was a place where Californians go to meditate, and, you know, *grow*."

I ONCE READ A STORY called "An Account of My Hut," by Kamo no Chōmei, a 12th-century Japanese hermit. Chōmei describes how after witnessing a fire, an earthquake, and a typhoon in Kyoto, he leaves society and goes to live in a hut.

Seven hundred years later, Basil Bunting, the Northumberland poet, wrote his own rendition of Chōmei's story:

> Oh! There's nothing to complain about.
> Buddha says: 'None of the world is good.'
> I am fond of my hut . . .

But even if I wanted to renounce the world, I wouldn't be able to afford a hut in California.

A FEW MONTHS AGO, Bongjun and I found a house in Oakland. The real estate agent said we were competing against twenty-eight other bids. She suggested that we write a love letter to accompany our offer.

"A *love* letter?" my former roommate from Florida said over the phone. "And everyone makes fun of people from *Florida*? They're all, 'That guy put his head in an alligator's mouth because he smelled licorice in there, but actually the licorice was on his face!' But that's nothing compared to having to write a love letter to a house!"

"Well, it's to the owner of the house," I told him. "I have to write something like, 'I will only use biodegradable detergents. I will only plant native plants in the garden. I will keep the bird feeder well stocked . . .'"

"Those people need to cut the cord," he said. "It's a *house* for god's sake."

We made an offer well over the asking price and tossed in our love letter, but got outbid by somebody who offered $400,000 over the asking price.

Another day we found a former sheet-metal factory that we thought we could turn into a community performance space. It didn't have a sewage system, and it's possible that the previous owner had died from the black mold that encroached on all the surfaces. The factory needed a new roof, and if it burned down it couldn't be rebuilt because it was constructed in the 1940s, before the road got wider. We still got outbid by $150,000.

MY FRIEND FROM the Red Cross called to invite me to a pop-up house concert in Oakland called Songs of Resilience, a musical journey of sound healing, but I didn't feel like going. "Is it in a *community* house?" I asked. "Those people are going to look at me with that condescending look of pity that means they think I haven't set my willful intentions, that I haven't made that list of everything I want. But I made the list. It's just not working out."

"One of the problems is that Bongjun doesn't like to drive on curvy roads," I told my friend. "But the only cheap land available is at the end of a curvy road. There was one affordable place off Highway 17. It was more like an outhouse. The real estate agent was like, 'Oh, that one? Well, it's hard to make the turnoff. I might miss the turnoff.' Instead, he drove us to a house way above what we could pay."

"It sounds like you're not enjoying this process," my Red Cross friend said. "Looking for a house together should be a journey of joy."

For a moment I believed her and felt a slow sinking feeling. Then I remembered that she's always insisting that I need to be more open-minded about the tech world, because Silicon Valley offers many opportunities for storytellers.

"Like what?" I asked once.

"Like Fitbit. You track the Fitbit family users. After they exercise, some guys go to the sports bar; their girlfriends go to the frozen yogurt shop. Which user consumes more calories?"

"That's a story?"

BONGJUN AND I found a piece of land on top of a mountain, but it didn't have a single tree. "Why do you need a tree?" Bongjun asked. "There are plenty of neighbors' trees to look at." When I thought about it more, I realized that it wasn't really the top of a mountain so much as the side of a cliff. Maybe we could have put a yurt there.

The next time I talked to my friend from Florida I asked whether he thought I was doing something wrong because I wasn't on a journey of joy.

"Journey of joy? Ah hahahaha!"

I told him about the treeless mountaintop and the yurt. When he asked what a yurt was, I texted him a picture of the Lotus Belle yurt I'd found online.

"In California the only option is to live in a *smurf* house?" he asked. "A helicopter is going to be flying overhead and the pilot will look down and see this little puffball on the side of the cliff. 'What's that?' the pilot's gonna say. 'A giant Q-tip? No! It's a Journey of Joy!'"

ON OUR NEXT JOURNEY of joy, Bongjun and I visited a piece of land that turned out to be the receptacle for all the neighborhood runoff water. Black plastic pipes crisscrossed the marsh. Bring Your Own Boat. Here's where we could put the houseboat.

MEANWHILE, OUR CLIMATE change group provided a metastudy about the 97 percent scientific consensus on climate change. Because scientists never say that something is 100 percent true, and because scientists, by nature, are often poor at communicating on an emotional level and tend to resist alarmist scenarios, the climate-change deniers have been able to point to that 1 to 3 percent of doubt. (Ninety-seven percent is also the proportion of scientists who support the theory of plate tectonics.)

We also learned that 61 percent of Americans say climate change is important to them, but they rarely or never discuss it with people they know. Our homework was to become climate-change evangelists for a month. To prepare, we discussed how to raise the topic with a stranger. "Sure is hot these days," or "How often do *you* take the train? Trying to save on fossil fuels?" or "Do you *ever* remember it being ninety-seven degrees in October?"

I decided, as an experiment in humiliation, to discuss climate change everywhere I went. The following are methods I do not recommend.

1. Bumping into someone's shopping cart at Safeway. "Oh, sorry, I was just so distracted thinking about climate change." (Note to self: Try using the phrase "climate disruption," rather than "climate change." Or better yet, "global greenhouse gas chamber," the expression that Wallace Smith Broecker, the man who coined the term "global warming," wished he had come up with earlier.)

2. After complaining to my boss about the measly salary I make as an adjunct professor: "I apologize for expressing myself in such a heated manner about how impossible it is to live on this salary. I was just really distressed thinking about climate disruption."

3. During Hurricane Harvey, I was having dinner with my neighbor, whose car has bumper stickers like MY OTHER CAR IS A BROOM and NEVER FEAR, THE GODDESS IS HERE! So it was unsurprising to hear her say, "This hurricane is Earth Mama expressing her anger at the patriarchy!"

"Actually," I said, "I'm not sure if the hurricane has anything to do with the Earth getting angry. It might have more to do with greenhouse gases. I'm not saying that climate change is *causing* the hurricane. It acts more like a hormone, or an adverb, an intensification of the qualities already present. I'm afraid things are only going to get worse." She looked upset. "Wait, what's the matter?" I asked.

"You're triggering my PTSD!"

4. I went to my friend's *Blade Runner* party, which was filled with fortysomething guys who kept reciting all the lines and knew all the trivia answers. During the pee break, one guy started talking about how we'd all be wearing Google Glass in ten years. "If the Earth doesn't burn up," I added.

"Right!" someone interjected. I thought we might be on our way to a useful discussion.

"This party just turned into a real downer," someone else said, so we went back to the movie.

Oh, no, I thought. I'm turning into my dad. He often told stories about how the heartbeat of the ocean might stop, which would affect the wind and freeze parts of the Midwest and Europe. For this reason I think of discussing climate change as a relaxing family activity. My father's second wife, on the other hand, got so tired of hearing about global warming that she considered getting a STOP GLOBAL DOOMING bumper sticker for her car. When my brother announced that his wife was pregnant, my dad told him he wouldn't need a college fund since there wouldn't be any college in the future. My brother, who was tenderly grilling ribs, threw down his barbecue fork and said, "For once I want to talk about life, and not always be focused on the end!" After that, climate change became a forbidden topic on holidays. Now I was redis-covering what I'd understood as a kid: people don't respond well to threats, to cajoling, to end-of-the-world scenarios, to dystopian futures, to hopelessness.

But as I watched the news about Hurricane Harvey, I was aston-ished that not a single anchor mentioned climate change. Instead they blamed the flooding on Houston's pavement. According to George Marshall, those who don't believe in climate change are *less* likely to believe in it *after* a climate disaster. Every single member of our group was confounded by this. "That makes no sense!" we said to one another.

If a person believes that weather fluctuates regardless of car-bon dioxide in the atmosphere, or that catastrophes represent some kind of punishment from God, confirmation bias will lead him to view the latest climate disaster as proof. And after a climate disaster, people feel a heightened sense of community; they don't want to get into a politicized discussion with the neighbor who just saved their dog. Furthermore, Marshall writes, climate disasters operate accord-ing to the same psychological logic as lightning strikes. People who have been struck by lightning tend to believe they are statistically immune to it happening again, even as the actual odds remain the same. And if your house floods due to a changing climate, it is *more*

likely it will flood again. If your house burns down, it is *more* likely
it will burn again.

I WAS ALREADY MENTALLY and emotionally enfeebled from watching so much hurricane disaster news, but I still couldn't stop
watching the hypnotic swirl of Irma. The way the news was reporting it, I thought for sure that *this* hurricane was going to be the end
of America. I called up my friend in Florida. "I'm worried about you
and that hurricane," I told him.

"Oh, really? I haven't been watching the news." A few hours later
he texted, "Oh, shit!"

Later we exchanged emails. "Did I mention we are binge-watch-
ing our way through this hurricane with *Dexter*?" he wrote. "We
didn't stock up on food so we are eating scrambled eggs and chicken
potpies. But do you know what? I honestly *get* those guys who are
shooting into the hurricane. I swear to god. It's not about shooting
the hurricane. It's about blowing off steam. . . . I'd go outside and
fire off a gun if I had one. . . . It's not my go-to move, but there is
something about blowing a big ol' hole in something from a distance.
I used to be a pretty good target shooter. OMG. A new food update
from my fam. With a side of no concern for safety."

THE NIGHT THE FIRES STARTED in Northern California, Bongjun and
I had an argument. Afterward, he took out the garbage. "Come here,"
he said when he opened the door. "Check out how hot it is outside."
A little while later, the wind started to sound like airplane engines.

The following morning, my mom and my aunt both told me
that they'd thought we were being attacked by North Korea.

THIS IS HOW Kamo no Chōmei describes the fire that broke out
in Kyoto:

It was, I believe, the twenty-eighth day of the fourth month of 1177,
on a night when the wind blew fiercely without a moment of calm,

that a fire broke out toward nine o'clock in the southeast of the capital and spread northwest. It finally reached the gates and buildings of the palace, and within the space of a single night all was reduced to ashes. The fire originated in a little hut where a sick man lodged.

The fire fanned out as the shifting wind spread it, first in one direction and then another. Houses far away from the conflagration were enveloped in the smoke, while the area nearby was a sea of flames. The ashes were blown up into the sky, which turned into a sheet of crimson from the reflected glare of the fire, and the flames, relentlessly whipped by the wind, seemed to fly over two or three streets at a time. Those who were caught in the midst could not believe it was actually happening: some collapsed, suffocated by the smoke, others surrounded by flames died on the spot. Still others barely managed to escape with their lives, but could not rescue any of their property: all their treasures turned into ashes. How much had been wasted on them!

Sixteen mansions belonging to the nobility were burnt, not to speak of innumerable other houses. In all, about a third of the capital was destroyed. Several thousand men and women lost their lives, as well as countless horses and oxen. Of all the follies of human endeavor, none is more pointless than expending treasures and spirit to build houses in so dangerous a place as the capital.

And this is Basil Bunting's rendition:

On the twentyseventh May eleven hundred
and seventyseven, eight p.m., fire broke out
at the corner of Tomi and Higuchi streets.
In a night
palace, ministries, university, parliament
were destroyed. As the wind veered
flames spread out in the shape of an open fan.
Tongues torn by gusts stretched and leapt.
In the sky clouds of cinders lit red with the blaze.

Some choked, some burned, some barely escaped.
Sixteen great officials lost houses and
very many poor. A third of the city burned;
several thousands died; and of beasts,
limitless numbers.
Men are fools to invest in real estate.

Neither writer mentions the paper that falls from the sky.

ON THE EVENING of the eighth of October, in the seventeenth year of this century, severe gusts of dry winds blew across desiccated grasses and diseased trees caused by years of excessive heat and drought. A great flood that year had fattened grasses into combustible fuel. The wind knocked down power lines that lit the trees on fire. The firestorm destroyed a thousand homes in a single neighborhood. Neighbors pounded on neighbors' doors, honking horns, trying to rescue one another. It took hours to leave town. Most people reported that drivers were calm, though a few resorted to the sidewalk, the median, and the opposite side of the road. One woman managed to stuff her pony in the back seat of her Honda Accord. Another woman had to choose between saving her car or her horse. She jumped on her horse in her pajamas and rode away from the flames. The fires burned for over a week, killed forty-four people, and destroyed more than ten thousand structures and 380 square miles of land. It was the most destructive fire in US history to date.

DURING THE FIRES I took walks, and I tried to read the paper falling from the sky. I wanted to collect the scattered notes, but they disintegrated when I picked them up, leaving the smell of poison on the tips of my fingers. The paper pieces lay curled like chocolate shavings. They were all the size of my palm. I was looking for stories, but I could only find information. Bible pages (sections from Genesis); cell phone bills; pieces of romance novels (so many of those); perfectly preserved letters so meticulously burned around the edges they looked the way letters do when you burn them in fourth grade to make them look romantic; gold-embossed stationery with someone's name written over and over in tiny letters at forty-five-degree angles; musical scores; Swedish vacation package-tour brochures; pieces of phone books (people still have phone books); a kid's homework (he did poorly); journal pages (so many pages of people talking to themselves); as well as tar paper and bits of insulation burned thin as paper. I walked and walked and tried not to breathe. Why was the sky directly above me blue, while everywhere else it was gunmetal gray flickering with particulate matter? Everyone spoke of particulate matter. In the hardware store all you needed to say was "Where are they?" and they'd point you to the pile of N95 masks. Someone passed me on the trail. I imagined he was judging me for not wearing a mask, but I couldn't read his expression because he was wearing one. I looked at the dun, shoulder-high grass; that explosive fuel, the color of pale grasshoppers, was all that stood between an out-of-control fire and me. The news never reported where the active fire was. We only knew that it was completely uncontained and that all effort was focused on rescuing people, evacuating the hospital, getting elderly people out of their homes. All we could do was hope the winds wouldn't change. I walked into the grasses to get away, to get away from the panic on people's faces.

There was no digesting this fire. There was no beginning, middle, end. I couldn't stop thinking about Sugarloaf Ridge State Park, which was now decimated. I hadn't walked on Sugarloaf Ridge in years, but whenever I used the words *poison oak*, or *gallop*, or *fog* my mind flashed femtosecond images of the park. Now it was ash. My old high school had burned down, as well as everything along the roads to get there.

BEFORE THE FIRES I'd been teaching a class on ecology. We were learning about systems theory and the interdependency of ecosystems, how trees communicate and send messages and medicines to other parts of the forest, how trees draw up water to share with other plants. We watched the Stevie Wonder video about his journey to the secret life of plants. We read a book about how to enter the imaginations of plants. We read stories of how bees know the location of every flower in a sixty-mile vicinity. We learned how butterflies make tinctures of nectar-soaked pollen grains and how elephants concoct forest booze and get drunk. We learned how a chimpanzee will fold a leaf like an accordion and swallow it so that it scrapes away the worms in his digestive tract.

We learned how insects can digest the compounds in eucalyptus and create poop that inhibits the growth of encroaching plants, like mustard. This is probably one reason why the eucalyptus has been so successful as an invasive species here. But why, in the 1850s, when the government planted eucalyptus throughout California at maniacal speed because its fast-growing wood was essential for railroad ties and fence posts, did these trees, unlike the old-growth groves in Australia, twist when they dried and become so hard they were no longer suitable for building? And now the volatile oils in their leaves turned out to be extremely combustible. In seasonably dry climates, native oaks are fire resistant, but with the introduction of eucalyptus we introduced an extreme fire hazard. I stared at the eucalyptus twisting in the heat.

THE WEEKEND BEFORE the fires I attended a grief workshop sponsored by the climate change group. They told us grief processed on one's own turns to despair, but grief processed communally becomes medicine. Now that we knew the reality of climate change, we would grieve the Earth. That way grief wouldn't hold us back when it was time to mobilize. To prepare us, they drew two circles on the board. YOUR COMFORT ZONE was written inside one circle. In the second circle, some distance from the first, they wrote, WHERE THE MAGIC HAPPENS.

The day before the workshop I had gone to the ocean to prepare but realized I wasn't yet ready to grieve the Earth. When I looked at the sea and the tangled seaweed on top, all I could think of was the word *holdfast*, the name for the dangly part of seaweed that clings to rock. Our climate group had read a poem about holdfast, and we had been encouraged to use it to steady ourselves when things got rough. Instead of reciting poems about the sea and cliffs and black rock as I used to while walking this beach, I now thought about how the oceans have been absorbing more than half of the CO_2 in the atmosphere, along with 90 percent of the excess heat. I thought of pH balances and dying plankton, and of how the last time the oceans were this acidic, 96 percent of ocean life went extinct.

At the grief workshop we drummed and journaled. The facilitator said that because we are continuously bombarded by bad news, we live in a state of chronic secondary trauma. It starts as soon as we are born with our cave-child DNA, expecting to see forty pairs of eyes looking toward us, asking us what we dreamed that night, if we want to help collect firewood, if we'll be at the ceremony tonight with the elders. Our psyches were never prepared to deal with the isolation of American culture, nor the sadness of the tragedies we see every day, nor the reality of our dying ecosystems. For hundreds of thousands of years grief rituals recalibrated the fields of trauma. These days there is no communal cup of sorrow; there is only psychotherapy, which colludes with the privatization of property, the privatization of consciousness, and the privatization of grief—with "own your sorrow." These days, the great fear we have about grief is that we have to face it alone. And so people avoid it and it settles like sediment over our psyches. There is personal grief, but since we are all connected, there is also the sorrow we feel for the world right now. And that cannot be processed alone. We cannot think our way through this mess. Nor can we moralize our way through it. Our workshop leader suggested that the thing that will save us may be our own broken hearts, for true action can only come through these deeper feelings.

THE NIGHT AFTER the workshop, I got into an argument with Bongjun. I was sitting on the floor because all the other flat surfaces were covered by lab equipment and mechanical parts. There were boxes of electronics, wires, sensors, laser parts, and, in the kitchen, an old dentist's light he'd accidentally bought on eBay. On shelves were laser-diode-current supplies, an oscilloscope probe, a function generator, a piezoelectric transducer driver, a microscope, boxes of lab snacks (just the boxes, not the snacks), a laser temperature controller, and, his favorite item, Marvin, the perpetually depressed robot from *The Hitchhiker's Guide to the Galaxy*.

"What is this?" I asked, pushing aside some sort of mechanical part.

"It's a transmission gear piece. They were getting rid of it at my work."

"You should get out of the Silicon Valley rat race and dedicate yourself to transitioning to a green economy," I heard myself saying. "You're a scientist. You can help develop technologies. This article says we have to treat climate change like we are fighting World War II. For example, we have to start movements where everyone paints their roofs white to try to dissipate the heat before it reaches a 2 degree Celsius rise. We have to cut carbon emissions now," I said. "Here's an article about what we can do to stay below a 2 degree rise. There are solutions. If you were to really *internalize* that we are the first generation to see the effects of climate change and the last generation to be able to do anything about it, would you change your life?" Even while I spoke I could hear myself sounding like a maniac. I kept reminding myself that people don't respond well to threats, to cajoling, to end-of-the-world scenarios. But I couldn't help it. I was in a bad mood because it was so hot outside.

Many years ago I lived in Korea. During the summers it would get so hot by eight in the morning that I'd have to stop at 7-Eleven on my way to the subway to buy honeydew-melon popsicles, or cold cans of pine-bud sodas, the drink invented by Korea's forest service. On the radio station inside the 7-Eleven, the announcers would warn everyone to be careful and avoid arguments in their work environments because the "uncomfort" index was high. Studies have shown that people's tempers flare in high heat.

"Yes, it's the right thing to do," Bongjun finally said calmly, in response to my grief workshop–induced rage. "But if it were really that bad, as bad as you say, don't you think Google would be doing something about it?"

ON THE FOURTH NIGHT of the fires, the humidity plummeted again, and anxiety peaked. A dry wind was expected to blow almost as strongly as on the night the fires started.

I packed a suitcase full of clothes and looked around my room. Should I pack the vase I bought in Turkey? How about the old Soviet tourist books about Tbilisi? How was it possible to choose between items of sentimental value? Better to leave it all.

"At least we have the public pool across the street," my mom said. We'd heard about the couple who took refuge in their neighbor's pool while their own house burned. They stayed in the water for six hours, covering their faces with wet shirts whenever they had to come up to breathe. "How long does it take for a house to burn?" the woman had wondered underwater.

My sister-in-law called and said, "Remember how when your brother and I first got married and your dad was always talking about global warming? Turns out he was *right*!" My dad called: "I've been needing Ambien to sleep. I'll forgo that tonight."

THE NEXT DAY, having survived the night and craving fresh air, I drove to the ocean. I was searching for clean air, but smoke covered the soot-colored sea all the way to the horizon. I could have felt guilty for driving a car with an internal combustion engine, but guilt goes on hold during fires. I sped on my way home, because the rule of law no longer applies during fires. This is the wildness that descends. This is the triggered reptilian brain. During the fires we craved sugar and fat and ordered take-out pizza and didn't mention that we usually never order pizza. During the fires my neighbor, the goddess, forgot she was gluten intolerant. During the fires all I could think of was the word *holdfast*.

WE MADE A PLAN. It seemed perfectly reasonable at the time. If the wind blew the fire this way we'd get in our cars and head to the ocean. If the fire kept following us, we would drive *into* the ocean.

MY FRIEND WHO HOSTED the *Blade Runner* party texted me: "I bought a fog maker for my upcoming Halloween party. But now with all the smoke outside I don't need it anymore."

A STUDENT OF MINE complained that he still had to work at the bank during the fires, since his branch was the only one open in the region. In one day customers deposited $600,000 in cash—a record—which they must have been keeping under their mattresses. My student said that all day his nerves were on edge because people kept walking into the bank wearing N95 masks. The firemen told us that the masks don't actually help much.

A FRIEND WHO WAS evacuated said he grabbed his two dogs and two banjos and hustled into his car. Driving away he realized he had forgotten to pack any clothes. During fires you hear, over and over, "I lost everything, but at least I have my life." A couple of people, after losing everything, knocked on the door of a man whose house was for sale. They said, "We've lost everything. Can we buy your house and everything in it?" He left everything he owned to them, including his toaster and bath towels.

MY FRIEND FROM the Red Cross described the evacuation center in Napa where she worked. There was face painting, acupuncture, aromatherapy, medicinal teas, massages, a whole Sikh temple feeding five hundred people with blessed food. "And Dreamers," she said, crying over the phone. "You know the Dreamers? Red Cross doesn't take donations, but there were so many donations we didn't know what to do with them. And then this woman, this random woman off the street, came in and said she would organize it all. She took it all out to the racquetball courts, arranged care packages of shoes—different sizes—and food, put it in backpacks. And for three days cars would pull in, ten at a time, and these Dreamers, behind the scenes, afraid for their lives, distributed all these packages."

THE SONGS ON THE LOCAL radio stations were especially upbeat during the fires. They interspersed Tom Petty's "I Won't Back Down" with quotes from locals who had lost their houses. "Fires are burning in eight California counties," the news announcer said with the Tom Petty beat in the background. A woman's voice: "I came out to get my dog and looked down the ridge and saw a glow and I looked at the wind and I told my parents that they might want to pack up something just in case, and my mom said that the fire was already at the bottom of the hill . . . *No I won't back down, no I won't back down. You can stand me up at the gates of hell but I won't back down . . .*" Another woman: "I just want to thank all of you first responders. I love you all from the bottom of my heart. I thank you all for being there. For being away from your families, to help everyone else out there . . . *Hey baby, there ain't no easy way out. Hey . . .* we are Sonoma County strong . . ."

I cried when the song came on, though I'd already heard it five times. I cried while driving, and when I saw the banners on every highway overpass: THANKS, FIRST RESPONDERS. THANK YOU, FIREFIGHTERS. Or the signs in front of the cafés: FIREFIGHTERS EAT FOR FREE. Even as the fire raged on.

ALL THE MEXICAN RESTAURANTS were closed except one. I went in to get a burrito and found it full of evacuees. "Sure is busy here," people kept saying. One man said to the cashier, "It'll have to be bulldozed. Totally demolished. How was yours?"

"We're OK."

MY FAMILY DECIDED to go for a picnic. When we called the Point Reyes ranger station to check the weather and the recording said

"Smoke," we stayed home instead. But still had a picnic. Outside. In the smoke.

Over the beet salad, I brought up the need to join together to find climate change solutions to a young relative who works in tech. He said, "Evolutionary theory says that diverse species never collaborate. People only want to take care of their families."

"But humans have never encountered the reality of climate change," I said. "Maybe this will rearrange our biology."

He shrugged. "Why worry? Technology will take care of everything. If the Earth goes, we'll just live in spaceships. We'll have 3D printers to print our food. We'll be eating lab meat. One cow will feed us all. We'll just rearrange atoms to create water or oxygen. Elon Musk."

"But I don't *want* to live in a spaceship."

He looked genuinely surprised. In his line of work, he'd never met anyone who didn't want to live in a spaceship.

WHEN I TOLD MY AUNT that in my class we were trying to read the minds of plants, she said, "Can you teach me how to read the mind of a plant?"

"I haven't really figured it out yet, but according to the book, you first have to *believe* that you can do it."

Bongjun said, "The only way you'll be able to read the mind of a plant is if you slow your metabolism *way* down. Humans can't slow their metabolisms to the rhythm of a plant. Plant thoughts are too slow for humans to understand."

But I'd been practicing the long, slow view. Nature's metabolism works much more sluggishly than ours; the cumulative effects of CO_2 are slow but steady, like a tortoise, or a bionic woman in slow motion. I tried to listen. I took a rock and used it as a clock. I started thinking in geologic time. Started thinking one thousand years into the future, *after* the great extinction. Started thinking about the time after the age of heat and darkness when that other version of humanity would need solar and wind technology.

IN 2004, MICHAEL CRICHTON, the author of *Jurassic Park*, wrote *State of Fear*, one of the few novels about climate change. Crichton's book is about a group of "eco-terrorists" from the Environmental Liberation Front who set out to trigger natural disasters in order to foment mass panic about climate change and install a "green" dictatorship. It includes a dense technical appendix to "prove" climate change is a myth. George W. Bush spent an hour with Crichton in the Oval Office and then presented the novel as "scientific" evidence to the US Senate that climate change was a hoax.

In his book *The Great Derangement*, the novelist Amitav Ghosh writes that not too long ago, everyone who lived in the Sundarbans, the dense jungle along the Bay of Bengal, had a family member who had been killed by a tiger. Those who escaped would describe the weird, uncanny look of mutual recognition when they met the tiger's gaze: an expression of preternatural wildness and intimate communication with the nonhuman. Ghosh says that now, in the age of anthropogenic climate change, we will confront that wildness again, this time in the eye of the hurricane, the tongue of a flame. Stories will become more alien, less human, more strange. The stranger the stories, the more we will recognize them and be recognized in them. They will speak, in his words, of the "interconnectedness of the transformations that are now under way."

AFTER THE FIRES we watched Josh Fox's documentary *How to Let Go of the World and Love All the Things Climate Can't Change*. We realized that Indigenous movements are the most active in facing climate change. And every one of them knows how to dance. We realized that if we want to save the planet, we have to learn how to dance.

Bongjun finally read the peer-reviewed articles by climate scientists. He spent a long time studying the graphs, in the same way he once studied the medley of eight prescription medicines his mother had accidentally mixed together, and finally announced about the square-shaped ones, "Actually, these are chewing gum."

"It's scary," he said, pointing at the West Coast on the map. "The West Coast will burn up. Korea, and the rest of Asia, will go through a famine. The only problem with solar is storage capacity. I could try to get a job in a national lab experimenting with hydrogen fusion. But I don't know if they've made much progress on that since I was in the seventh grade."

It was still hot: ninety-five degrees in late October. We wondered if winter would ever come again. You can't get into a pumpkin-carving mood when it's so hot. On Halloween a few kids came looking for candy, but it seemed like everyone else went to the movies. The parking lot at the theater was full.

I had a dream that I had to evacuate, and the only thing I grabbed was the leftover bag of Halloween candy. I handed out Kit Kats to people as we ran from the fire.

After the fires people posted the most random item they grabbed when they evacuated.

daughter's piggy bank with $2.35 in coins in it
Grandmother's Christmas cactus
a wetsuit
an avocado
the cat-scratcher tree
a Hermione wand
the cookie cutters
tarot cards
all the beer
kids' pinewood derby trophies
the sewing machine
dog's ashes
the spice rack
Norton Anthology
son's Darth Vader alarm clock
husband's Hawaiian shirt collection
jury duty notice for the next day

the cat-litter box and all the cat litter
combat-ready lightsabers
a toothbrush (even though the man who grabbed this one was
    evacuating to a dentist's office)
a jar of Miracle Whip (because they were evacuating to a mayo-
    heavy household)

BONGJUN AND I finally found a hut in the Santa Cruz Mountains. It was part of a co-op with twenty other little houses. Maybe this was it! Maybe this was our sustainable community. The day we were set to drive down there, the whole region caught on fire. It burned for a while. "I can't take much more of this," I thought.

THE FIRES DIDN'T DISCRIMINATE between the houses of the rich and the poor. Everyone's pearls melted, no matter how large. Nor did they discriminate between the houses of the "realists" and the "idealists." After the fires, the realists wanted to rebuild as fast as possible with the same footprint. The original developers of Santa Rosa's Coffey Park, which was destroyed by the fires, offered to use updated versions of their old floor plans in rebuilding efforts. Homeowners were upset to learn that they were now required to rebuild in adherence with the 2016 California Green Building Standards Code. They argued that they shouldn't have to.

Before the fires, the builders who showed up to city council meetings were the same people every time—they all seemed to be on a first-name basis. But after the fires, something changed. People began presenting ideas to install rain-catchment and gray-water systems, community gardens, and bike paths. They wanted to revamp the land-use laws, change the zoning for tiny houses, use fire-resistant straw-bale construction and concrete and foam. The city council was inundated with people wanting to rebuild with green roofs and walls, to rebuild in a way that would promote bees and carbon-capturing methods, even permaculture methods and composting plants. City officials looked a little frightened as they listened to a large group of people talk about a town in Kansas that rebuilt with renewable energy after getting hit by a tornado. More than seven hundred people showed up for a breakfast sponsored by Daily Acts, an organization that builds community by working with neighborhoods to turn lawns into drought-tolerant gardens. A farmer who had lost his farm and all of his bees spoke at the podium: "Why can't Sonoma County *always* be able to feed its poor?" My neighbors started talking about "agrihoods," a new trend in which affluent, slow-foodie millennials move to neighborhoods surrounding a farm, instead of to the golf-course communities of their parents' generation. My dad even wrote an op-ed about it.

AFTER THE FIRES, I started reading a book by Alejandro Jodorowsky, the Chilean French filmmaker/poet/therapist who maintains an unusual psychotherapy practice. If someone feels poor in spirit, or even in material wealth, he'll prescribe that they glue coins to the bottoms of their shoes so that they feel like they are always walking on money. He describes how Chile, being "a poetic country," graciously accepted his poetic acts. He and a friend once decided to walk in a straight line across the city, disregarding any obstacles they encountered. Sometimes this would mean having to walk through people's houses. This is how he describes it:

> Having rung the bell of a house and having explained to the lady of the house that we were poets in action and that our mission required us to cross her house in a straight line—she understood perfectly and had us leave through the back door. For us, this crossing of the city in a straight line was a grand experience, the way we managed to avoid all the obstacles. Little by little, we went about inventing more extreme acts. . . . Another day, we put a large quantity of coins in a bag full of holes and traveled to the center of the city. . . .
>
> Also, we dedicated ourselves to very innocent acts that were no less powerful, like putting a beautiful shell in the hand of the conductor

when he came to take our bus tickets. The man stood there stupefied for a long time without saying anything.

He goes on to say,

> Life is like that, you understand? Totally unpredictable. You think things will happen this way or that way and, in reality, while standing on the corner talking to a friend, you can be run over by a truck; you can run into an old lover and go to a hotel to make love; or the roof can fall on your head while you work. The telephone can ring to announce the best or the worst of news. Our acts as young poets were performed to prove this, to swim against my parents' rigid world. . . .
>
> My father practiced Psychomagic without knowing it: He was convinced that the more merchandise he had, the more he would sell. He had to give shoppers the image of superabundance. . . .
>
> What is generally called "reality" is just a part, an aspect of a much greater order.

2018

WHEN A PERSON GOES MISSING

DAWN LUNDY MARTIN

WHEN MY BROTHER WAS A TEENAGER AND I WAS IN GRADE SCHOOL, he let some bullying kids from his high school persuade him to skip the day and invite them over to our house. He asked them to leave, but the boys refused. So my brother grabbed our father's shotgun and corralled them into the bathroom, the barrel pointed in their direction. The bathroom door now locked from the inside, my brother held the gun, luckily, up toward the ceiling, so that when his finger slipped and the mechanism went off, the shot with its massive force went through the second-floor ceiling, the attic, and then out the roof of the house into the sky. How the rest of the family received the details of the incident, I can't recall. But to travel home now is to walk beneath the hole in the ceiling stuffed with newspaper from 1978. To return is also to encounter the past lurking behind me, contorting its face so I can really feel it—its truncated force, whispering a ghost voice into my ear.

If I believed in omens, I'd say the shotgun incident was the worst of omens, literary in its foreshadowing. We can smell a hint of devastation, can't we, a scent we can't quite recognize on first whiff but turn our noses away from knowingly. Where will our characters end up? Our armed protagonist? The girl who tells the story? When I began writing this essay I wanted it to be about fate—how two black kids raised by the same working-class parents could have radically different life outcomes because, as fate would have it, divergent occurrences compel divergent paths. Bruce never went back to the high school with the bullying boys. He dropped out. It's around this time that my parents got a call in the middle of the night that Bruce was in custody at the local precinct for being caught in a stolen car. It was the 1970s and no charges were pressed, boys being boys. That night, my father beat my brother mercilessly with a washing machine hose in the dank basement of our house. The chaos of a violence like that is astonishing. The cacophonous screaming. The inability of anyone to stop it. The cold pallor that hangs in the air afterward. A chasm emerged between us—me, floating off like some wandering balloon; my brother tethered tightly to a familiar story of trouble and poverty, like most of the kids in our neighborhood.

But the question of fate is a fake question. It's a refusal to see how the good daughter is a part of the problem. As a kid, I was the exception, the one who would "make it out of the ghetto," the one bused out of town for school. I liked being the exception. I loved the ways people's eyes would glimmer when I told them any little thing about my life, or when I simply said anything aloud. "So well spoken," the middle-class blacks would say. I basked, annoyingly, in their glow. I didn't mind either when my brother failed, because his failure meant my light shone even brighter.

When Bruce is 17, already dropped out of high school, and I am 11, I'm allowed to go on ski vacations with the white families whose children I go to school with. I can't ski, but they are patient. I don't notice that I'm the only black face on the Vermont slopes. On the first trip, I've brought with me my beloved copy of Thoreau's *Walden; or, Life in the Woods*, not that I could understand much of it. I loved it anyway for its mysteriousness, and for how its *I* stands so solidly in the wilderness.

Public opinion is a weak tyrant compared with our own private opinion. What a man thinks of himself, that it is which determines, or
rather indicates, his fate.

When I return home, I look up each word that confuses in the hard-
cover *Webster's Dictionary*. I discover whole worlds of rebelliousness
in Thoreau's words, fascinated by the prospect of being "born in the
open pasture and suckled by a wolf."

I was drawn to orphan stories of all sorts, especially ones about
wolves raising children. To stoke that fantasy, I also read the novel
Julie of the Wolves, about an orphan Inuit girl, several times. After
being sexually assaulted by Daniel, whom she stupidly marries even
though he clearly has some kind of severe mental disability, Julie
runs off to live in the Alaskan tundra with a wolf pack. I had some
idea from *Walden* and *Julie of the Wolves* of a totalizing and enduring
freedom of the wild—one that can only be obtained outside human
society, particularly human family structures. By middle school, I
already had this idea of myself as a person akin to Thoreau's first
person, who would thrive by dropping out of the known social world.

Though literature is thick with this kind of adventure of the
individual, the protagonists of these narratives are rarely, if ever,
black. Toni Morrison's Baby Suggs makes the point: "Not a house in
the country ain't packed to its rafters with some dead Negro's grief."
In literature, being black is mostly about containment, or about the
body as an obstacle to the wild freedom of roaming adventure. But
it's a tricky containment because the black body is contained in
"blackness," and that blackness enables further containments. The
containment of the body in its skin is the means by which we, as
black people, are identifiable. This ability for us to be ID'd also facili-
tates our disappearance in plain sight. To disappear is opposite to the
self-discovery made possible by encountering, with any measure of
purity, a vast nature, no matter how badly we want it.

THE NIGHT OF BRUCE'S washing-machine-hose beating, the images would not leave me, and have not left me still. I sat with him upstairs in his room watching his body swell up into big, bulbous bruises. He had not fought back. Instead, he hunkered and cried like a small boy, when in fact he was nudging up on manhood. This reduction was one result of his training by our tyrannical father. It was a private opinion made manifest in Bruce's body, a transference of thought into matter, a tyranny all supreme. Before this night, my brother was swallowed already—a person trapped within a person. He had ambitions that were entirely unrealistic: architect, golf-course designer, business owner. He had begun to accumulate masses of random objects until his bedroom was so cluttered with things collected from yard sales and traded from friends that he was forced to sleep on a twin mattress on the floor. Though there were others less severe, this beating in particular seemed to cement him inside a very small world he'd likely never leave. One would think that the smaller your world, the safer you are.

What happens when a person goes missing?

My brother goes missing for almost two days in February 2017.

I find out on the Megabus en route from Pittsburgh, where I teach, to New York state, where I mostly live. It's a regular Megabus night, the cab darkened and quiet and most of us staring into the glow of our phones or watching something on our larger screens. I don't want to talk too loudly, so my voice is low, but since my mother is going deaf it's difficult for her to hear me. Mostly, I listen.

My mother tells me the story of him being gone all night and her worrying. She says she thought maybe his car broke down on the side of the highway and since he can't afford a cell phone he couldn't call. She also speculates that my brother's sudden disappearance is in some way connected to his owing past-due child support from a time when he was not working. There was a hearing, but where? She does not know. He could be dead by some sleight of hand, aggression, or accident. He could be in the hospital. Last year he became disoriented and dizzy at the wheel of his car, his hand tingling, which I revealed to him was likely a ministroke. My mother does not call the police. What would the police do? And anyway, as most black people understand, it is our work to stay clear of the police, as far from their notice as possible. My mother calls *me*. Absorbed by my busyness I didn't, as is my habit, bother to answer or check my messages. I didn't answer until the next day, when the calls became more frequent, blowing up my phone.

To account for my brother's missingness is to put ideas together that in our United States don't ordinarily belong together. If we follow conventional knowledge, we follow a path that suggests that the *missing* black body is its very condition: the overt presence of the black body is an imposition. Any indication of "difference," particularly that which marks the black body as black, is an offense punishable by a range of containments, from regulation and imprisonment to death and genocide. The racist alt-right writer Colin Liddell put it very plainly when he wrote, "We should be asking questions like 'Does human civilization actually need the Black race?' 'Is Black genocide right?' and, if it is, 'What would be the best and easiest way to dispose of them?'" He wants to make a connection between genocide and order, the subtext being: allowing these niggers to exist causes chaos. Look how they run around stealing, selling drugs, and raping, and killing. To "dispose" of something is to arrange it, to put it in place, to regulate it by containing it. Death, of course, is the ultimate containment; other, less final containments are conversely strategies toward genocide. Perfect chiasmus. Liddell's words are not simply rhetorical bluster. He wants to place the ideas in the room, uncloaked for the white readers who are looking for some language on which to hang their hatred.

When we were kids, our parents would drive from Connecticut down south to Florida once a year for a vacation to see our extended family. Our mother spent the entire day before travel cooking and preparing what seems to me now an extravagant cooler of potato salad, fried chicken, ham-and-cheese sandwiches, homemade pies, and grape and orange sodas. Our parents shared driving responsibilities, cursing at each other under their breath, while my brother and I lay in the way-back of the station wagon, sometimes with our feet dangling out the giant rear window. The middle bench seat between Bruce and me and the driving section gave us a feeling of being in our own world. We played games dividing up the junkyards filled with smashed cars, so that the first of us to spy a yard filled with metal junk could claim it was theirs. Bruce's and my aspirations of owning the virtually worthless filled our heads as we slept sweaty dreams in Carolina parking lots pretending not to exist in case the cops or the Klan came tapping on the window. We were lucky. No one ever came tapping.

"Where is he exactly?" I ask, but at 84 years old my mother can't fathom a way of finding out. I spend over an hour frantically searching Google for information using my phone. Eventually, after searching the Connecticut Department of Correction Inmate Information database, I find Bruce's inmate name, number, and "Controlling Offense: purge civil commitment." His ex-wife confirms with my mother that my brother was arrested at the courthouse for some reason related to the unpaid child support.

How can he be put in jail for owing child support, I wonder, when he's been unemployed and unable to find a job? How can he look for a job to pay the child support he owes if he's in jail? What are the chances of getting a job to pay child support if you've been incarcerated? These are the times, says the President, when work for what we used to call blue-collar workers has been replaced by automation and the shipping away of jobs overseas—to Mexico and China. So where is the compassion for the American worker who, for a year, has no income? When Bruce was working, almost all of his paycheck went toward child support. His take-home pay was less than $100 a week. But this last point is not the point at all.

According to the Separated Parenting Access & Resource Center, once the court has determined that there is a valid support order (a valid claim that child support is owed), it's up to you to prove that you can't pay the amount owed and that you have no access to the money. If you fail to prove this, or if the judge believes you do have the money but don't want to cough it up, he or she can decide to slap you with criminal contempt and throw you in jail. On the other hand, "if the court agrees that your conduct is not willful and you don't have the ability to pay you won't be found in contempt." That's the way it's supposed to work, anyway. A "purge" is the amount the court orders you to pay to "purge" you of contempt. In my brother's case, my mother had given him $10 for parking that morning. The judge finds my brother in contempt when he asks Bruce if he has any money. Bruce says no, thinking that the judge meant any amount of measure against the $13,000 he owes his ex-wife. The judge asks what Bruce used to pay for parking this morning and if he has any change in his pocket. He has six dollars' change. "Then you have money, don't you?" the judge says. Bond is set at $1,500 and off he goes in handcuffs, easy as pie.

In the movies and once upon a time, the newly incarcerated were granted a single phone call. This call would be used to reach a loved one or a lawyer, presumably a person who needed to know about the jailing or could help. But I'm here to tell you there is no right to a single phone call, just as there is no black man hiding in the bushes in your front yard. When the phone rings, my mother tells me, a computer voice says that Bruce is trying to reach her from jail, but that in order for her to receive that call, she is required to add money to a prepaid account using her credit card. Something about the recorded voice signals "scam" to me, too, so I do a quick search to make sure the company is legit.

The "inmate phone service" they use at the Hartford Correctional Center, which, incidentally, has the same abbreviation as Hartford Community College, is called Securus—pronounced "secure us"—Technologies. It's like two cruel jokes at once. To load an account for my mother, I first must listen to a long, complicated recording detailing a rate system that befuddles me. Finally, I proceed through the steps and add $25 thinking that should be enough for a single quick phone call from my brother to my mother, so that he knows that she knows what's happened. That's the bone of it. Bruce became missing because, though there is an online record of where he is, for a while he is unreachable. He has no means to contact anyone to alert them to his whereabouts. My mother, whom the current technological moment has left in some other age, hasn't the ability to locate my brother beyond imagining him inside this vague concept, "jail." For her, it's like he's fallen inside a deep hole in the earth. As she likes to point out, if I had been out of the country, as I sometimes am, or hadn't just been paid from writing gigs, he might still be inside that hole.

Miss, the verb, has several definitions. To fail to hit, reach, or contact. To pass by without touching. To be too late to catch. To fail to attend, participate in, or watch as one is expected to or habitually does. To fail to see. To be unable to experience. To omit. When the word emerged in the late 12th century its association was with regret, occasioned by loss or absence. But the adjectival version of *miss*, as in *missing*, was not recorded in English until the 16th century, and by 1845 became a way to describe military personnel not known to be present after battle. Whether missing soldiers were killed or captured is inaccessible data. In some parts of the world, we have transformed this state of indeterminacy into *disappeared*. Let me use this modified part of speech in an American sentence: "If recent trends continue, one in three black men in the United States will be disappeared into jail or prison in his lifetime." It strikes me that to miss or be missing, in my brother's case, requires a part-of-speech modification, too—one that could perhaps help me, at least, understand his particular condition, meaning the Condition of Bruce as it intersects with the subjugated identities we know are related, race and gender. To be *missing*, as a noun, would be the designation itself, like *a black*, the racial category without the noun *person*. A failed sight. A passed by without touching. A failed inclusion. An unattended. A missing.

Thoreau argues that the "mass of men lead lives of quiet desperation." It's an easy case to make when you can count on the centrality of your own unquestioned *I*. My brother, who is now 55, in jail for the first time, is not singular in his missingness. Many of my first cousins have been incarcerated at some point in their lives, some serving long sentences for drug-related charges, others for more serious crimes. I, myself, once went missing for 24 hours—years ago, returning from the Washington DC party for my first book, swept up by the airport police for having (I didn't know) the tiniest bit of marijuana in my carry-on bag. My girlfriend at the time awaited me at Bradley airport, but of course I never emerged from the gate. One cousin, Dwayne, died of a heart attack after having chest pains for several days. He didn't have health insurance and was leery of going to the emergency room and racking up a bunch of unpayable bills, as he had once before. He might be called *an untouched*. In 2014, the Black and Missing Foundation reported that 64,000 black girls and women were missing in the United States. Passed by without noticing.

MY BROTHER AND I grew up in Hartford, Connecticut, a small poor and working-class city in one of the richest states in the country. The racial segregation, after my parents purchased their house in what was then a neighborhood equal parts black and white, began to anchor itself, thereby dividing us from all the thems. The Puerto Ricans in one neighborhood; the US-born black folks in another; the recent West Indian immigrants gaining a foothold around Albany Avenue, the artery connecting Hartford to the small, wealthy corner bordering West Hartford, where the white families from another time resided in their multiroom mansions with circular driveways. The whole of Hartford for me, though, was always a place I was set on leaving. By middle school I was desperate to roam, and by high school I was sneaking off to Manhattan, two and a half hours away, in order to experience what I understood as "the world." It occurs to me now that I don't think my brother has ever been to New York City. He has been locked in place while I have been profoundly out of place. Places uncomfortable and foreign felt more like appropriate contexts than the place where I was raised.

And here is the hard truth of the matter. If I am missing in any sense, it is a missingness I created for myself in order to be free, to reach toward Thoreau's solid *I*, roaming the world in wild adventure. I removed myself from the messy missingness that engulfs my own family—my brother, of course; my heart-attack-dead cousin; my 10-year-old niece already tracked by police whom her school principal sent to her house in search of a stolen cell phone. Whenever I return home, I do so in a casual manner, just passing quickly through, so that I might avoid any contagion that might corrupt my good life. I am a welcomed ghost, but a ghost nonetheless, one called to a place forever fraught, the wallpapered walls peeling, the basement damp with wet clothes. It makes me feel bad to drive through the city where I lived for eighteen years. I get a sinking feeling. I often forget that the woman suing my brother for child support now is his second wife. I missed his marriage to his first wife entirely while I was living in the Bay Area after college. When I said before that the trick of the system is that it relies on the black exception, the thing is that I play right into it. I want to be your exception because that means that I get to escape, at least in part. I can be your shining example, and if I am, you can ignore the mass incarcerations, other disappearances, murders in plain internet view, what have you.

Via telephone I reach the officer on duty, who confirms, finally, that my brother is at the Hartford Correctional Center. While we're here, I'll pause and note the benign associations of the word *correction*, as if this place of punishment were a positive adjustment where humans are brought for the setting right of something previously misaligned. The logic is that the criminal element will be contained, rehabilitated, and released anew into society after the sentence is served. Jail, though, is mostly a holding tank for people too poor to post bail while they await their trial or hearing. Sixty-three percent of people in jail have not been convicted of any crime; they have been arrested and are trying to post bail. Under the law, they are presumed innocent. Bail, when it comes to minor crimes and civil infringements, is basically the freedom tax on the poor for being poor. The word *correction* is simply one of the many mindfucks of the way things work. If your jail has a population of 73 percent pre-trial, in this case men, then why do you call it a correctional center, when there is nothing clearly determined that needs to be corrected?

All I have to do to get my brother "corrected" is to bring $1,500 cash the next day for his release pending a new hearing in a month. My mother's voice sounds small and tired when she hears the news. "Did you talk to him? Is he OK?"

I think of a photo of Bruce I found recently when scrounging through my mother's old photo albums. He is about 20 years old and standing in the driveway of my parents' house wearing a crisp white T-shirt, jeans, and a silver watch. His face is soft, thoughtful. He does not appear to know his picture is being taken. He seems, in the photo, relatively "free." Not lost. I guess sometimes you can't tell. I am writing this story because it is impossible for me not to write it. It's my story too. And I keep trying to pull myself authentically into it. The photo albums themselves tell a story of an intense desire to capture our lives, the lives of my mother and her four sisters, my grandparents, my father, my brother, me. A record of existence like everyone's, but also a kind of testimony to black life, even and especially when we become uniquely aware of the multiple means by which black life is confined, made irrelevant, and eradicated.

What happens when a black person goes missing? I know that *I* am not missing in the same sense as my brother, but I also know that I am not entirely free. When I lived in Western Massachusetts in graduate school, I was pulled over by police regularly. One night after a late-night fight with my then girlfriend, I went for a drive, and was pulled over by police who asked me simply, "What are you doing out at this hour?" What should we say in these moments of encounter? I am human. I breathe and eat and shit. I have ambitions. It is as ordinary and extraordinary as the first words of any 19th-century slave narrative: "I was born." I contribute something to society. I am not a vagrant. I sweat and ache and love and mourn. There will be many who will mourn for me if I die.

The literal opposite of *missing* would probably be *present*, but in my mind it's *free*, the radical opportunity to be present. This brings me back to *Walden*, which honestly, I despise now, for its naive arguments about what is necessary for life. Thoreau never asks a basic question: What is a livable life? What does a human need to enact one's not-lostness, one's freedom? Though Bruce was incarcerated for only two days, it was for a civil offense, not a criminal one. What's recognized in the moment of random, unexpected jailing is the fragility of one's freedom.

THE NIGHT BEFORE I found out about Bruce's being in jail, I hosted the writer Maggie Nelson in one of the university's big reading series. As it turned out, she read from a work in progress on freedom. Freedom, she asks: What is it?

I, too, have been attempting to think through the possibility that freedom—real freedom—might not be possible within society. We hardly even know ourselves in our ongoing encounter with the other, producing on the one hand what Du Bois calls double-consciousness, and on the other, for black people in 2017, a radically distorted version of black selfhood. What else is possible given the prolific, penetrating, and ongoing looking at oneself through the eyes of an other?

To answer the question "What is freedom?" Nelson turns to lots of thinkers, including Hannah Arendt. Arendt notes a difference between political freedom and "inner freedom," the "inward space into which men [sic] may escape from external coercion and *feel* free." In my own work I have referred to this idea as a "freedom feeling," a sensation of freedom even when actual freedom might not exist. What I love about Arendt's distinction is that, for her, in order to experience inner freedom you must first know outer, political freedom. We like to think about this inner, "nonpolitical" freedom, she basically says, but we wouldn't know anything about it had we "not first experienced a condition of being free as a worldly tangible reality."

Neither I nor my brother is free in the way that Arendt describes. As a teenager, I often sat in front of my bedroom mirror in an attempt to recognize myself. Many distortions from other people's perceptions needed to be smoothed out. Something about an attempt to see my face as it was without mediation became, I believe, important for my growing sense of self, and thereby a sense of my own power, real or imagined. Feeling free is a relationship to *being* as much as it is to movement, travel, a sense of one's own body in unfamiliar places. When Bruce moved away from home, he moved in with a woman he'd just married. After he and his wife divorced, he moved back into our mother's house, our father long dead, and settled sadly into his old bedroom—the most familiar, perhaps, of places.

THE NEXT NIGHT, instead of heading to East Hampton for a weekend away from the university, I end up staying the night in Brooklyn and waking up at 5 AM to catch a 7 AM Amtrak train to Hartford. My mother and I do some maneuvering around the ATM withdrawal limits and pull together $1,500 in 20s and 50s, which I stuff into a zippered compartment of my computer bag. In the waiting room at the jail, the windows one approaches to talk to an officer on duty are blackened so that you cannot see whom you are talking to. Through a muted talk hole, the cop tells me that it's going to take two to three hours to process my brother's release and that once I start the paperwork I cannot leave the premises. There's no vending machine, so I run across the street and grab fries at Burger King, then put my elderly mother in an Uber home. I have magazines and set up my iPad connection via my personal hot spot. At one point, I go into the bathroom and guzzle the Patrón nip I have in my pocket. Time passes quickly. The gate opens dramatically when anyone leaves or enters the door where I believe the release will occur. People, women only, actually, come to visit relatives. The guard comes out. The women go through the metal detector. The gate closes. I feel a tickle on my neck and realize that the rosary beads I bought in Mexico even though I have no religion have snapped, and the Jesus has fallen down into my bra.

After only an hour and a half, the officer on duty takes my cash and gives me a receipt. He instructs me to drive around the building and wait on the side of the road for Bruce to exit. I wait at Gate 5. You'd think there would be an official pickup area, but it's just a dead-end street, nondescript save the random fact that my father and I would often pass by that jail before the street was blocked. We'd drive over the railroad tracks on our way back from the bowling alley where we went on the off Sundays I wasn't forced by my mother to attend church, noticing but not really noticing the stone building with the barbed-wire fencing. Whenever I thought about who might be locked inside I imagined rapists and murderers, or psychopaths like Charles Manson after I'd snuck and read my mother's copy of *Helter Skelter*.

Bruce comes out carrying a small, transparent plastic bag and a calendar. He hugs me long and hard. I can feel his body shaking as he towers over me and says, "Thank you, thank you, thank you." He tells me that his cell contained more than thirty men, all in similar situations to his, unable to pay bail. "Did you talk to each other?" I ask. "Not really," he says; "mostly we just slept. There were no windows or clock so you never knew what time it was." The stench of bodies was overwhelming, he tells me, very stuffy, the air stale and hot, the smell of shit and piss from the open toilets. We drive down streets familiar and drenched in the memory of the life I lived before I left home. On Tower Avenue, the long street that leads to my mother's house, we pass Mrs. Alberta's old house, a friend of my mother's so frightening to me as a child that I never addressed her in any way. She'd whack her children right in front of us, demanding their respect and discipline. The house looks so much smaller than it did when we were children. We pass a once-grand house on a hill, boarded up now, that belonged to a preacher and his typing-teacher wife. He was scandalized after being caught stealing money from his own church. When we finally pull into my mother's driveway, I'm staring at the shabby decay of her house, the three shutters that remain demanding paint. My brother says, "Seriously. I don't know what I would have done."

The bail system for nonviolent, misdemeanor offenses is currently under intense scrutiny in this country. More and more media outlets are reporting on jurisdictions that have increased their jailed population exponentially over the past two decades by locking up people who can't afford to post bail. Some, like Kalief Browder and Sandra Bland, suffer the direst consequences. At the less fatal end of the spectrum, pretrial detention keeps the poor poor. They get a choice: We'll release you if you plead guilty. It's a systematic and some say *illegal* practice that keeps commercial bail bond corporations making profit off poor people and coercing guilty pleas from those who may or may not have done the crime. As it happens, during day two of my brother's jailing, he received a voice message on our mother's landline for a job interview that day. It was a good job, paying well over the $10 minimum wage he'd been making at his last position. During his eventual quick Securus phone call with my mother, she alerted him to this fact. He thought about that, he said, from his stuffed jail cell—the missed opportunity.

AT MY MOTHER'S HOUSE, things are surreally normal. She's propped up on the couch watching Martha Stewart on TV. "She's making something with 'ramps,'" my mother says. "What's a ramp?" I tell her it's a wild leek, like a kind of onion. Suddenly we're all in a discussion about Martha Stewart's recipes and her friendship with Snoop Dogg. "Are you spending the night?" she asks. "No," I say, "I have to get on the road in an hour or so, need to catch the last ferry. Deadlines tomorrow. Need to work." I am, in fact, desperate to disappear. But I need my brother's help in order to do so. I don't have my car, and my mother can no longer drive the hour and a half to New London and back.

To reach the freedom feeling, I must first reach the dock in New London where the ferry departs to travel across the Long Island Sound to Orient Point. But in order to do that I need to ask Bruce to come with us so that he can drive the car back home. I ask this of the very recently incarcerated brother whose wallet and other personal effects are still in custody at the Hartford Correctional Center. To retrieve these objects he must return to the jail during an appointed time window on a weekday, and since he was released on a weekend, he is not in possession of his driver's license. My mother and brother and I reason it out, ignoring certain facts. We say, "Well, he *does* have a license and he's accompanied by two people with licenses. That should be enough." We say, "What are the odds that he's pulled over?" The risk we all take together is great. It's a risk I facilitate to some degree, unwilling as I am to stay one night in Hartford. I drive the fifty minutes to New London in my mother's aging Dodge Neon with a rebuilt engine so loud we can barely hear each other speak.

Above the engine's grumbling roar, I lecture my family on the school-to-prison pipeline and the systematic, institutional effort to disappear as many black people as possible. As the volume of my voice increases to drown out any protestations by my mother, who's always been more a bootstrap-theory gal, despite the evidence supplied by Exhibit A, Bruce, I feel an old impulse taking over: the impulse to dominate the situation, to control it. It's all swirling out of control so I do what I do best, which is to try to analyze things to death. I gain my footing at the expense of my mother, who still has optimism for some long-annihilated black American future, and my brother, who is nodding heartily at everything I say. Repression occurs on the infinitesimal level. It becomes so much a part of you that you hardly feel it. Your heart rate increases when you see the police drive by, but you feel relief the second the car turns the corner. You've been spared, however temporarily, and that gives you peace.

2018

NOTES ON TRAP

JESSE MCCARTHY

They are the music of an unhappy people, of the children of disappointment; they tell of death and suffering and unvoiced longing toward a
truer world, of misty wanderings and hidden ways.

  —W. E. B. Du Bois, *The Souls of Black Folk*

  Sometimes I really can't believe this shit happened
  Who woulda thought I'd make it rappin'?
  I almost lost my life when I was trappin'

  Numb the pain with the money, numb the pain with the money
  Numb the pain with the money, numb the pain with the

  —21 Savage, "Numb"

*For Lil Snupe (1995–2013), L'A Capone (1996–2013), Chinx (1983–2015), Bankroll
Fresh (1987– 2016), Lor Scoota (1993–2016), Da Real Gee Money (1995–2017), the
many thousands gone.*

1.

THE BEAT, WHEN IT DROPS, is thunder, and causes the steel rods in whatever you're riding to groan, plastics to shudder, the ass of the seat to vibrate right up into your gut. The hi-hat, pitched like an igniter, sparks. Snare rolls crescendo in waves that overmaster like a system of finely linked chains snatched up into whips, cracking and snapping across the hull of a dark hold.

2.

It is only in his music, which Americans are able to admire because a protective sentimentality limits their understanding of it, that the Negro in America has been able to tell his story.

—James Baldwin, "Many Thousands Gone"

3.

Rubber band man, like a one-man band
Treat these niggas like the Apollo, and I'm the sandman

—T.I., "Rubber Band Man"

HOWARD "SANDMAN" SIMS had a standing gig at the Apollo for decades as a tap performer who would "sweep" failing acts off the stage. It's stuff like this that makes up what Henry Louis Gates Jr. calls "motivated signifying," the inside joke that's on you before you know it, the razor wit—always the weapon of the underdog. The pleasures of dialect, hotly pursued by the holders of capital, the clout chasers of Madison Avenue, enclose a self-referential universe, a house of belonging in sound and word. A statehouse of language for a stateless people. Trap is an extension, a ramification of that vocabulary of radicalized homelessness: people creating a living out of a few grains of sand, hustling, sweeping anything that can't compete out of the way.

4.

TRAP, SOME DEFINITIONS from the *Oxford English Dictionary*:

> A contrivance set for catching game or noxious animals; a gin, snare, pitfall: cf. MANTRAP, MOUSETRAP, RAT TRAP.

> *transf.* and *fig.*, and in figurative expressions. Often applied to anything by which a person is unsuspectingly caught, stopped, or caused to fall; also to anything which attracts by its apparent easiness and proves to be difficult, anything deceptive.

> A concealed compartment; *spec.* (*Criminals'*), any hiding-place for stolen or illegal goods, etc.; a 'stash.' *U.S. slang.*

5.

> I just wanna get that money
> I just wanna get that money—flip that money
> I just wanna stack them hundreds,
> I just wanna spaz out—cash out

> —Kodak Black, "Spaz Out"

Q. What is the subject of trap?

A. Money, a.k.a. skrilla, paper, green, gwop, currency, stacks, bands, bundles, racks, currency, fetty (confetti), ends, dead presidents, bankrolls, $100,000 in just two days, fuck-you money, fuck up some commas, money long, run up a check, fuck up a check; a master signifier in falling bills, floating, liquid, pouring down on bitches in the proverbial rain, exploding like cold fireworks, screen-printed or projected onto surfaces human and otherwise, occasionally burned, often tossed into the impoverished streets left behind, kids trailing the whip their arms outstretched, often bricked up in bundles held in a grip, or cradled to the ear like, say, a call from the highest authority in the land, or fanned out in a masking screen, or caressed, the cold frisson of Franklin morbidly displacing the erotic potential of sexual attraction.

6.

AN ATTITUDE TOWARD LUXURY. Brands of old-world "foreign" opulence sound better in the escaped slave's mouth. The "Go-yard" bag, the "Phi-lippe" watch, "the Lambo" supercar pronounced like a Creole dish, every accoutrement of inaccessible lavishness smashed into pinball frenzy, a world where everything is always dripping, VVS diamonds are always dancing, every swatch of color given the player's ball touch, the planet WorldStarHipHop, a black satellite circling around a diamond white sun where the Protestant work ethic is always being converted into its rhythmic opposite, "You get the bag and fumble it / I get the bag and flip it and tumble it" (Gucci Mane feat. Migos, "I Get the Bag"). From the SoundCloud backpacker to the superstar trapper, the ideal of a supremely luxurious attitude toward luxury. "I'm spittin' fire like an arson / Hop out the Lam and don't park it" (Migos, "Forest Whitaker").

7.

NIGGA: AS RHYTHM, A TROCHEE (from the Greek for *running*, at root a runaway) coursing through the verse marking soundings, like a heartbeat; the nasal occlusive a vocal withholding, a negative that releases into a velar plosive, a voiced relief; as person, a real one; as word, a neologism indigenous to the American crucible, the umbilical cord of blackness: raw, intimate, original, word as bond.

8.

TRAP IS THE ONLY MUSIC that sounds like what living in contemporary America feels like. It is the soundtrack of the dissocialized subject that neoliberalism made. It is the funeral music that the Reagan revolution deserves.

9.

THE MUSICAL SIGNATURE embedded in trap is that of the marching band. The foundation can be thought of, in fact, as the digital capture and looping of the percussive patterns of the drum line. The hi-hats in double or triple time are distinctly martial, they snap you to attention, locking in a rigid background grid to be filled in with the dominant usually iterated instrumental, sometimes a synth chord, or a flute, a tone parallel that floats over the field. In this it forms a continuum with the deepest roots of black music in America, going back to the colonial era and the Revolutionary War, when black men, typically prohibited from bearing arms, were brought into military ranks as trumpet, fife, and drum players. In the aftermath of the War of 1812, all-black brass bands spread rapidly, especially in cities with large free black populations like New Orleans, Philadelphia, and New

York. During the Civil War, marching bands would aid in the recruit-
ment of blacks to the Union. At Port Royal in the Sea Islands, during
the Union Army occupation, newly freed slaves immediately took to
"drilling" together in the evenings in public squares, men, women, and
children mimicking martial exercises while combining them with
song and dance—getting *in formation*. The popularity of marching
and drilling was incorporated into black funerary practice, nowhere
more impressively than in New Orleans, where figures like Buddy
Bolden, Louis Armstrong, and Sidney Bechet would first encounter
the sounds of rhythm and trumpet, joy and sorrow going by in the
streets of Storyville. This special relationship, including its sub rosa
relation to military organization, persists in the enthusiasm of black
marching bands, especially in the South, where they are a sonic backdrop of enormous proximate importance to the producers of trap, and
to its geographic capital, Atlanta.

10.

> But closer to home, Traplanta is saddled with too much of the same
> racial baggage and class exclusion that criminalizes the music in the
> eyes and ears of many in power. The same pols who disgrace their
> districts by failing to advocate for economic equity find themselves
> more offended by crass lyrical content than the crass conditions
> that inspire it. Meanwhile, systemic ills continue to fester at will. It's
> enough to make you wonder who the real trappers are in this town.

> —Rodney Carmichael, "Culture Wars"

11.

TRAP'S RELATION TO HIP-HOP retains the construction of a song
around bars and hooks, but the old-school chime and rhyme, the

bounce and jazziness of Nineties production, is gone. Instead, empty corners space out patterns that oscillate between compression and distension. The drum machine popularized by the (black and gay) "jacking" sound of Eighties Chicago and Detroit is put to use in a way that is less mechanical than its forebear, more syncopated, wavy, elastic. But it retains the overall flatness of effect, the orientation toward the (strip) club, a music to obliterate self-consciousness and the boundaries of the self. Bass is the place and when the 808 drops, or one should say detonates (an effect imitated in the proliferation of amateur dance videos by a jagged shake of the camera), the signature is quickly established and the pattern rolls over. Songs don't develop or progress. Sometimes, as in an iconic track like Future's "Stick Talk" or "Wicked," the song appears to materialize and dematerialize out of a vacuum. A squealing siren pops out of the ether. His roving, overdubbed voice rides slightly off or apart from the pattern playing off a few variations. The track begins, then ends, like weather.

12.

HOW WILL CULTURAL HISTORY come to grips with the fact that the era of the first black presidency is also the era of trap—a metaphor for a suckering, illusory promise one falls for, only to realize things are worse than ever before?

13.

I'm 'bout to fuck this cash up on a new toy
'Bout to fuck this cash up on a new toy
You can't understand us cause you're too soft
Taliban bands, run 'em straight through the machinery

—Future, "Stick Talk"

TRAP INDEXES THE FEVER DREAMS of a declining imperial power. It irrupts within a wounded unconscious, seeking scapegoats, boasting, lashing out, categorically refusing any sense of responsibility for its actions. The frustrations and failures of military adventurism on the frontiers and borderlands are internalized; they find sites for expression in the fractured, neglected wastelands at the periphery of the power capital, in the ghetto, the hood, the slums, the bricks, the barrio, the mud, the bando, the trap house. The metaphors of imperial fantasy, of limitless power and wealth—and its nightmare, endless, and pointless wars without issue—cross-pollinate and mutate. In rap of the Nineties, the memory of Vietnam still resonated; Capone-N-Noreaga (C-N-N) gave us *The War Report* of the Persian Gulf War years. By the mid-'00s the war abroad and the war at home would fuse into the hard edges of a bloody portmanteau: Chiraq. The pressure of the proliferation of high-powered weapons, the militarization of everyday life, an obvious and pervasive subtext in trap, is also one of the most obvious transformations of American life at the close of the American century: the death of civilian space.

14.

> That music, which Miles Davis calls "social music," to which
> Adorno and Fanon gave only severe and partial hearing, is of
> interdicted black social life operating on frequencies that are
> disavowed—though they are also amplified—in the interplay of
> sociopathological and phenomenological description. How can
> we fathom a social life that tends toward death, that enacts a kind
> of being-toward-death, and which, because of such tendency and
> enactment, maintains a terribly beautiful vitality?
>
> —Fred Moten, "The Case of Blackness"

Trap is social music.

15.

CONSIDER THE VOICE OF Meek Mill. The inscription of dreams and nightmares in the grain. Its breathlessness, always on the verge of shrill hoarseness, gasping for air, as if the torrent of words can't come fast enough—as if there might not be enough time to say the things that need to be said. Every syllable eked out through grit, the cold facts of North Philly firing through a monochromatic hollow, like a crack in a bell.

16.

TRAP VIDEOS FOR OBVIOUS reasons continue an extended vamp on the visual grammar developed in the rap videos of the Nineties, a grammar that the whole world has learned to read, or misread, producing a strange Esperanto of gesture and cadence intended to signify the position of blackness. In the "lifestyle" videos, the tropes are familiar, establishing shots captured in drone POV: the pool party, the hotel suite, the club, the glistening surfaces of dream cars, the harem women blazoned, jump cuts set to tight-focus Steadicam, the ubiquitous use of slow motion to render banal actions (pouring a drink, entering a room) allegorical, talismanic, the gothic surrealism of instant gratification. In the harder, street-oriented version, luxuries are replaced by what one has, which is only one another: gang signs interlock, boys on the verge of manhood huddle and show they have one another's back. Women occasionally appear in an accessorizing role, but more often are simply absent. In the video for L'A Capone's track "Round Here," the indication is blunt: "Whole block got cane / But stay in your lane / Cause niggas getting changed." Like David Walker's graphic pointers in his *Appeal*, one of the key punctuation marks of this gestural grammar is the trigger finger, pointing into the camera—through the fourth wall—into the consuming eye.

The very motion of the arm and finger are perversely inviting and ejecting. You are put on notice, they say. You can get touched.

17.

TRAP IS THE SOUND TRACK to America in the years of the "opioid crisis." The drug crisis initially thought to be merely a breach in the hull of the underclass confined to the black ghetto spilled out into white rural America with meth and prescription painkillers, segueing to black tar heroin as the pill mills (but not Big Pharma) finally came under legal scrutiny. It now exceeds, as all great social disasters do, the class boundary. The hyped-up drug war of the 1990s and early '00s began to morph under the tenure of the great campaigner of hope into a normalized social fabric, a generalized landscape of dope. For the middle and upper-middle classes, Molly became a favorite, whether consumed casually at unabashedly corporate festivals or in warehouses not yet colonized for gentrification at the edge of town. An antidepressant, it could be said to provide the softer psychiatric analogue to the morphine class of painkillers that relieve the body or allow relief to occur passively with limited consent (its popularity being closely associated with the allure of sexual willingness).

For the ambitious children of the bourgeoisie, high achievers raised on Adderall, Xanax, and a raft of discreet legal narcotics, drugs are the norm just to get to sleep, to deal with anxiety, to avoid crushing bouts of abjection and the relentless pressures to exceed and excel. In the hood, promethazine, the syrup of Houston, became the fashionable coping agent for those living in the free-fire zones of America, where turf wars regulated with cheap handguns cut down lives in a vicious spiral. From so many points of view, then, one looks out into the Trump era with a prevailing numbness, nihilism, cruelty, ambient anxiety, disarticulation seeping in from all sides.

The music records all this. It sounds like this. Future's lyrics are mocked for their lack of sophistication, but the veritable pharmacopeia in his verses is not dishonest or inarticulate about an affect that is pervasive, or its origins: "Percocet keep 'em motivated / Good drank keep a nigga motivated / Lortabs on my conversation / Talk a lot of bands then we conversatin' / I was on my way to Rice Street in the paddy wagon and it had me numb / The pain from the slum had me numb" ("56 Nights"). A preoccupation with depression, mental health, a confused and terrible desire for dissociation: this is a fundamental sensibility shared by a generation.

18.

JUST PAST THE SLIDING DOORS in a Rite Aid in Manhattan about 2 AM, Mike WiLL Made-It's producer tag and the familiar melancholy two-tone of Rae Sremmurd's "No Type" announces that soon Swae Lee's Floydian vamp on the trap sound will remind you of what you don't need to hear: "I ain't living right." The bored cashier there to assist you with self-checkout murmurs the chorus lightly tapping at her side as she assists you: "I make my own money, so I spend it how I like." Among other things, it's clear there has never been a music this well suited for the rich and bored. This being a great democracy, everyone gets to pretend they, too, are rich and bored when they're not working, and even sometimes, discreetly, when they are.

19.

IMAGINE A PEOPLE ENTHRALLED, gleefully internalizing the world of pure capital flow, of infinite negative freedom (continuously replenished through frictionless browsing), thrilled at the possibilities (in fact necessity) of self-commodification, the value in the network of one's body, the harvesting of others. Imagine communities saturated in the vocabulary of cynical postrevolutionary blaxploitation, corporate bourgeois triumphalism, and also the devastation of crack, a schizophrenic cultural script in which black success was projected as the corporate mogul status achieved by Oprah or Jay-Z even as an angst-ridden black middle class propped up on predatory credit loans, gutted by the whims of financial speculation and lack of labor protections, slipped backward into the abyss of the prison archipelago where the majority poor remained. Imagine, then, the colonization of space, time, and most importantly cultural capital by the socially mediated system of images called the internet. Imagine finally a vast supply of cheap guns flooding neighborhoods already struggling to stay alive. What would the music of such a convergence sound like?

20.

TRAP IS A FORM OF SOFT POWER that takes the resources of the black underclass (raw talent, charisma, endurance, persistence, improvisation, dexterity, adaptability, beauty) and uses them to change the attitudes, behaviors, and preferences of others, usually by making them admit they desire and admire those same things and will pay good money to share vicariously in even a collateral showering from below. This allows the trap artist to transition from an environment where raw hard power dominates and life is nasty, brutal, and short to the world of celebrity, the Valhalla of excess, lucre, influence, fame—the only transparently and sincerely valued site of belonging in our culture. It doesn't hurt, of course, that insofar as you're interested in having a good time, there's probably never been a sound so perfectly suited to having every kind of fun disallowed in conservative America.

21.

A SOCIAL LIFE STRICTLY organized around encounters facilitated by the transactional service economy is almost by definition emotionally vacant. Hence the outsize importance of the latest black music (trap) in selling everything: Sweetgreen salads prepped and chopp'd by the majority minority for minimum wage, real estate roll-outs, various leisure objects with energetic connotations, the tastefulness of certain social gatherings. In the city of the mobile user and their memes, signs, processed and recoded desires, the desperate energy and beauty produced by the attempt to escape the narcocarceral jaws of death becomes a necessary raw fuel, a lubricant for soothing, or rather perfecting, the point of sale.

22.

"MASK OFF": AN INAUGURAL processional for the Trump years. Some were inclined to point to Taylor Swift's "Look What You Made Me Do" as signaling the bad feeling, the irruption of a nasty, petty, and reactionary whiteness willing to bring everyone down, to debase everything, including oneself, in order to claim victory. But Metro Boomin heard something more. He went back to the Seventies, to Tommy Butler's "Prison Song," a soulful chant intended to accompany the marchers in Butler's 1976 civil rights musical, *Selma*. The counterpoint of Future's openly vacuous and nihilistic pursuit of power and the undercurrent of an unbroken spirit of black resilience, resistance, and hope—the old news meeting the news of today—creates an intoxicating, gothic aura, the sound of a nation not under a groove, but underwater, trying to hold onto the shores of light, but decidedly heading out into dangerous and uncharted depths. "Fuck it, mask off . . ."

The game of polite power politics is up. The veneer is gone. America will show its true colors; Amber Rose and Future will drive a Terminator-chrome Bentley through streets where "mere anarchy is loosed upon the world." It is the hour of radical disillusionment. As Walter says in Lorraine Hansberry's *A Raisin in the Sun*, "There ain't no causes—there ain't nothing but taking in this world, and he who takes most is smartest—and it don't make a damn bit of difference *how*." The grand years of the Obama masque, the glamour and pageantry of Ebony Camelot, is closed. *Les jeux sont faits*. The echo of black resistance ringing as a choral reminder to hold out is all that stands between a stunned population and raw power, unmasked, wielding its cold hand over all.

23.

RAINDROP. IF THE MARK of the poetic, of the living force of lyric in the world, is the ability to change the inflection and understanding of a single word, to instantly evoke and move speech into song, then what better example do we have than the poetics of Migos and their breakthrough album, *Culture*? "Like a wreath, *culture* is a word we place upon the brow of a victor," William H. Gass once wrote. As the title attests, Migos crowned themselves, like Napoleon. Their trap trips off the tongue, three steps to get it poppin', three more to get it started. Everything done in triplets. Quavo, Offset, Takeoff, their supergroup a triad. The message of the massive hit "Bad and Boujee" is simple and, thanks to its lullaby-rocking lilt, irresistible: the cosmopolitanism of the underclass is good enough for them. In this, everyone wins. The fetish of class and racial transgression is given a smooth membrane across which to exchange approving glances. Hence the appropriateness of Donald Glover's role in assisting the song to the top of the charts. No figure better represents the amphibious role of blackness slipping back and forth across lines of class, taste, and career.

The Migos lyric, with its love of onomatopoeia, annotating itself like comic speech bubbles, offers itself up as a kind of doubled, mirroring space for ludic play. The drug world of the streets is sublimated, neutralized as a background of merely referential content that has no bearing on the tenor of life that has been achieved. In the video for the single "T-Shirt," Migos are figured as "trappers"—the hunting and gathering kind—on a supermodel-clad Siberian steppe. It is the linguistic turn applied to the Atlanta music machine. Opening an entirely new horizon for expression. An attitude might be expressed with just a shift in emphasis, a teasing chiasmus: "Raindrop, drop top" ("Bad and Boujee"). The language of the corporate record label exec slashed with the syntax of the trapper blossoms into the office catchall phrase you never knew you needed but now can't stop murmuring under your breath: "Hold up, get right witcha (I'ma get right witcha)" ("Get Right Witcha"); "Bitches need to call casting" ("Call Casting"). The flavor of the South, the sauce, the endless capacity for flow, reimagines the bourgeois subject—even makes being one, under this conception, seem badass.

24.

I have always heard him deal with death.
I have always heard the shout, the volley.
I have closed my heart-ears late and early.
[. . .]
The red floor of my alley
is a special speech to me.

—Gwendolyn Brooks, "The Boy Died in My Alley"

25.

It's a lot of violence round here
So a lot of sirens round here
A lot of people dying round here
A lot of people crying round here

—L'A Capone, "Round Here"

THE CONNECTION BETWEEN martial drilling, funeral drilling, and recreational drilling finds a haunting but fitting contemporary expression in the so-called drill scene, a more aggressively bleak subgenre of trap that emanates from the post-Cabrini-Green teardown of the housing projects in Chicago. Drill trappers like Montana of 300 refer knowingly to the streets as "the slaughterhouse." They celebrate the same qualities that Sandburg did when he said, "I have seen the gunman kill and go free to kill again," and that he found the Windy City's inhabitants "proud to be alive and coarse and strong and cunning." Only they are not so optimistic or romantic about the implications of living in the maws of lawless, unregulated industrial capitalism. There is nothing uplifting about G Herbo's view of the season of violence, which is the only season his city knows. In "Red Snow," a strident song with thundering and throbbing orchestral groans, he denounces the staggering cost of violence in his hometown:

I know I rap a lot 'bout being dead or dead broke
But my city starving, it's the 'Go, that's just the way it go
They stealin', robbin', living heartless, never hit they target
The summers long and winters harsh cause we got red snow
Red snow, red snow
The summers long and winters harsh cause we got red snow

A track like "Everyday," by S.dot, is typical: simple and alluring, conflating fraternity and fratricide, a bass line boosted like a massive heartbeat ready to give skinny boys in jeans toting weapons the courage to keep going outside, to step off the relative safety of the porch, to numb oneself to fear, to ready oneself for the repetitive and cyclical encounter with fatality. The hook slams down the facts of life like dominoes connecting an inevitable pattern to a breaking point:

> Gangbangin', chain snatchin', card crackin'
> Closed caskets, trap houses, drug addicts
> Chiraq, everyday somethin' happen
> Bodies droppin', red tape, guns clappin'

The deep patterns of the funeral drill, the bellicose drill, the celebratory drill overlay each other like a sonic cage, a crackling sound like a long steel mesh ensnaring lives, very young lives, that cry out and insist on being heard, insist on telling their story, even as the way they tell it all but ensures the nation's continued neglect and fundamental contempt for their condition.

26.

TRAP IS INVESTED in a mode of dirty realism. It is likely the only literature that will capture the structure of feeling of the period in which it was produced, and it is certainly the only American literature of any kind that can truly claim to have a popular following across all races and classes. Points of reference are recyclable but relatable, titillating yet boring, trivial and très chic—much like cable television. Sports, movies, comedy, drugs, *Scarface*, reality TV, food, trash education, bad housing: the fusion core of endless momentum that radiates out from an efficient capitalist order distributing itself across a crumbling and degraded social fabric, all the while reproducing and even amplifying the underlying class, racial, and sexual tensions that are riven through it.

27.

Riding through the city, windows tinted, AC blast
I got bitches wanna fuck me, so so wrong, do me bad
I got cash in my pants, I got cash on her ass
AP dance, bitches glance, cause my diamonds look like glass

—Young Thug, "With Them"

When young black males labor in the plantation of misogyny and sexism to produce gangsta rap, white supremacist capitalist patriarchy approves the violence and materially rewards them. Far from being an expression of their "manhood," it is an expression of their own subjugation and humiliation by more powerful, less visible forces of patriarchal gangsterism. They give voice to the brutal, raw anger and rage against women that it is taboo for "civilized" adult men to speak.

—bell hooks, *Outlaw Culture*

THE EMO TRAP OF Lil Uzi Vert, his very name threading the needle between the cute, the odd, and the angry, might be thought, given his Green Day–punk styling and soft-suburban patina, to be less invested in the kind of misogynistic baiting so common to trap. But this is not the case. Like the unofficial color-line law that says the main video girl in any rap video must be of a lighter skin tone than the rapper she is fawning over, there is a perverse law by which the more one's identity is susceptible to accusations of "softness" (i.e., lack of street cred), the more one is inclined to compensate by deliberate hyperbolic assertions of one's dominance over the other sex. When Lil Uzi says of a woman who has given herself to him—

> Suckin' me up, give me brain now she dumb
> Tell her it's repercussions
> Play her just like a drum
> Make in a night what you make in a month
>
> ("Erase Your Social")

—the percussion lands on a cymbal crash aimed at a "you" that is really "us," the audience, who are invited to voyeuristically watch his performance (wordplay as foreplay), of which the unnamed woman is the desensitized object, but "we" are ultimately the target, the losers in the winner-take-all game of life, the suckers who work for a monthly paycheck who can't possibly compete with the value the market has bestowed on the speaker.

28.

THE QUIRKY PARTICLES coming out of the cultural supercollider of trap prove the unregulated freedom of that space: that in spite of its ferocious and often contradictory claims, nothing is settled about its direction or meaning. The hard-nosed but unabashedly queer presence of Young M.A; the celebratory alt-feminist crunk of Princess Nokia; the quirky punkish R&B inflection in DeJ Loaf; the Bronx bombshell of Cardi B: to say that they are just occupying the space formerly dominated by the boys doesn't quite cut it. They are completely changing the coordinates and creating models no one dared to foresee. The rise of the female trap star is no longer in question; an entire wave of talent is coming up fast and the skew that they will bring to the sexual and gender politics of popular culture will scramble and recode the norms of an earlier era in ways that could prove explosive in the context of increasingly desperate reactionary and progressive battles for hearts and minds.

The boys are not quite what they were before, either. Bobby Shmurda's path to "Hot Nigga," before landing him in prison, landed him on the charts in no small part because of his dance, his fearless self-embrace, and his self-love breaking out in full view of his entire crew. People sometimes forget that for the latter half of the Nineties and the early Aughts, dancing for a "real one" was a nonstarter. Now crews from every high school across the country compete to make viral videos of gorgeous dance routines to accompany the release of a new single. The old heads who grumble about "mumble rap" may not care for dancing, but the suppression of it as a marker of authentic masculinity was the worst thing about an otherwise great era for black music. Its restoration is one of the few universally positive values currently being regifted to the culture by trap.

29.

YOUNG THUG ENACTS a Charlie Parker theory of trap. Virtuosity, drugginess, genius, vulnerability, an impish childishness almost as a compensation for the overabundance of talent, the superfluidity of imagination. A Cocteau from East Atlanta, he teases the beat, skipping off it like a yo-yo, yodeling, crooning, blurting, squawking, purring, working his game on you, finessing, playing ad libs like Curtis Mayfield worked strings, or scatting and growling low like Louis Armstrong if he were sweating it out in a freestyle battle with James Brown, bouncing back and forth between personalities. His polymorphously perverse sexuality is so insistently graphic and deadpan that it has virtually zero erotic charge, au courant pimp talk channeled through a kind of private board game of his own imagination, a Candyland fantasia slimed in promethazine. By contrast, his persona oozes sex. In leather jackets, ultratight jeans and Janet Jackson piercing arrangements, he's a Mick Jagger–ish rake on the make who is also shy and easily wounded, suddenly open for a hug. A favorite and telling picture posted to Instagram account thuggerthugger1 (5.2 million followers) captures him with his arm around Sir Elton John, posing like a polite politician in photo-op mode (Obama-alt) next to Sir Elton, who is dressed in a gold-trim Adidas tracksuit and a black THUGGER cap.

If the outlandish persona were all there was to it, he might be written off as a variant to Weezy that went nowhere. But the music really does, somehow, sound like the future, like something that's never been tried before, a radical experiment. His concern for innovating, like his persistent concern for his kidney health, is a marker of identity, not just a lifestyle. The boundaries he pushes are only partly for our benefit; his chameleon love affair with the frisson of the louche, the lawless elasticity of language, and the plasticity of the self-fashioning body in motion is all of a piece. He insists on being the soloist and chorus all at once; his is an orchestral impulse, a surround sound lyricizing every inch of space on the track. Words aren't about what they mean, but, in the spirit of Baraka's "Black Dada Nihilismus," only how they sound. They are rhetorical and lyrical ammunition, raw material to freak like Jimi, not satisfied until the instrument wails, weirds out, trips over itself with a surplus that is no longer within respectable or even recognizable bounds—hence Thugger's fundamental *queerness* in the most capacious sense of that word. Free spirit from day one: "When I was 12, my feet were so small I wore my sisters' glitter shoes. My dad would whoop me: 'You're not going to school now, you'll embarrass us!' But I never gave a f— what people think." The music critic for the *Washington Post* writes that "if he lived inside a comic book, his speech balloons would be filled with Jackson Pollock splatters," which is halfway there (why not Basquiat?). Thugger is more exciting than Pollock, who never wore a garment described by *Billboard* as "geisha couture meets *Mortal Kombat*'s Raiden" that started a national conversation. Thugger's work is edgier, riskier, sans white box; if anything it is closer to Warhol in coloration, pop art without the pretension. It is loved, admired, hated, and feared by people who have never and may never set foot in a museum of "modern art."

30.

He . . . loved that he could look out of his window and see an open
horizon over the water, where the waves from the Gulf quietly
lapped the shore, where the oak trees in the median stood witness
over centuries to wars, to men enslaving one another, to hurri-
canes, to Joshua riding along the Coast, blasting some rap, heavy
bass, ignorant beats, lyrical poetry to the sky, to the antebellum
mansions our mother cleaned whose beauty we admired and hated.

—Jesmyn Ward, *Men We Reaped*

31.

THE OPPOSITION: TO SEEING the next man get ahead, the zero-sum
game, crabs in a bucket, colors, gang gang, the division of self against
other, the envy that breeds envy, Girard's triangle of mimetic desire,
the division of self against self. Everyone has the wants that they
want, and so everyone universally has opposition. Generic, unspecified in name, number, location, or time. A condition of belonging.
Opposites attack. Those who you don't fuck with. Who don't fuck
with you. The opposition. Opps.

I grew up in the projects which is one room
So I had to sleep on the floor in the front room
Me and my cousins on the block tryna thug
Nigga you a school boy, nigga we was sellin' drugs
I grew up in Jonesboro, it was straight wildin'
I hung out with the older cats, so it was straight violence
And the niggas I looked up to was hustlin' or robbin'
So I hopped up off the porch too and started gettin' it popping

—Lil Snupe, "Rap Battle"

Came up with jack shit up out that wishing well
Left with this black skin and a digital scale
I pray I be okay when I grow up a little bigger
If I don't, tell my babies daddy was a real nigga

—Chinx, "Die Young"

DJ SMALLZ EYES: Now, why is there always beef, especially amongst rappers—and this has been going on for years and years and years, from what I can see—it's always beef amongst rappers, and I've been to Baton Rouge before, it's a very small town—city—whatever you want to say, but it just seems always like a lot of animosity, a lot of hate between different artists—not all the artists hate each other, but there just always seems to be something in the air, right? Why is that?

DA REAL GEE MONEY: See, that goes exactly back to what I was saying, like—don't nobody want to see the next man ahead of him, so like . . . it really be hate for no reason. Like, if you just get to doing your thing, like if you just get to moving forward, it's going to be uninterested in beef coming from anywhere, because this man might be rapping and you then passed him up, so now he got all this kind of animosity built up . . . Just be real on something like that . . . 99 percent of the beef . . . don't have no real, real street meaning behind it. It be like, something, you know, something like that.

DJ SMALLZ EYES: So it's competitive?

DA REAL GEE MONEY: Basically, it's like, it's like basically competitive.

DJ SMALLZ EYES: Now, let me ask you this. Can this be stopped? Can this be fixed? Do you see this ever changing? Like, from what I've known of Baton Rouge, it's always seemed to be some sort of beef.

DA REAL GEE MONEY: Right. I always, I used to feel like, me person-ally, I always used to feel like maybe one day . . . they'll just stop and maybe we can all get money together, you know. But like, the way it's going? Like, the way it's been going for years? It looks like it ain't going to change, you know. I don't know. Me, I just stay in my own lane, though.

(Da Real Gee Money, YouTube interview with DJ Smallz Eyes, April 9, 2017)

RIP to Eddie B wish I could bring you back
Swear I smoke a thousand Black and Milds to bring you back
My nigga used to smoke them bitches like they cigarettes
My trap buddy every morning first ones on the trap
We used to fuss about who get to hit the first pack
Do any thing to bring ya nappy head ass back

—Lor Scoota, "Perks Callin Freestyle"

They killed my lil nigga Snupe
My lil nigga was the truth
And all he wanted was a coupe
All he wanted was a coupe

—Meek Mill, "Lil Nigga Snupe"

I love my niggas unconditionally
I just wish that they was present with me physically

—Mozzy, "I Love My Niggas"

32.

Black-boy blues articulated pitch-perfect
If nothing else your words make the whole world worth it

—Joshua Bennett, "16 Bars for Kendrick Lamar"

33.

What if this music, Future's *DS2*, the Drake/Future *What a Time to Be
Alive*, Vince Staples' *Summertime '06*, Kanye West's *Life of Pablo*, the
numerous individual points that are sounds and words that emerge
from laptops, artists who live within this surround, the formation
that is trap music. . . . Let's call it "possibility"—let's call it *now*,
cracked time of where we are and where we are going now. We
don't have the words for how broken. And yet we are warned.

—Simone White, *Dear Angel of Death*

THE PROBLEM OF THE overdetermination of blackness by way of
its representation in music—its tar baby–like way of standing in
for (and being asked to stand in for) any number of roles that seem
incongruous and disingenuous to impose upon it—is the central
concern of *Dear Angel of Death*, by the poet Simone White. Her target is the dominantly male tradition in black literary criticism and
its reliance on a mode of self-authorization that passes through a
cultivated insider's knowledge of "the Music," which is generically
meant to encompass all forms of black musical expression, but in
practice almost always refers to a canonical set of figures in jazz. It's
clear that she's right, also clear that it's a case of emperors with no

clothes. It may have been obvious, but no one had the courage to say so. Take these notes on trap, for example: they neatly confirm her thesis, and fare no better under her sharp dissection. Though she could easily not have, White makes her point in a spirit of care and generosity. "We must agree to think about the work we have asked the Music to do," she writes, "whether it is still able to do that work, and how that work might be done elsewhere."

What would that elsewhere be? I ask seriously, even as I agree with the urgency of alternatives. Could black intellectuals abandon wholesale our favored set of metaphors, drop our reflexive turns to improvisation, to discursive riffs meant to signify a kind of mimetic relationship to the sound? Could we begin our conversation over again, at a tabula rasa of black creative freedom, and, importantly, one that would avoid the circle jerk that Simone White correctly implies? Surely the answer is yes, especially in terms of who is talking to whom and about what. And yet part of me thinks the answer is also partly no—or at least not without what I would think is an irresponsible and even decadent relationship to the very cultural forces that have guided black thinking, feeling, and interest, much of it informally political to be sure, but a form of talking about all things, including formal politics nonetheless. Who, after all, should be in a place to characterize and define the daily grind of contemporary life under the post-Reagan US internet tech empire to which we have set the musical tone? Would we consign that sprawling undertaking to the ash heap, would we accept the view that the white bourgeoisie holds of it? That it is cheap, trashy music, useful for frat parties and little else, the usual jitterbugging of "the blacks" who can't help themselves, the great sly replacement of minstrelsy by an even better show, to which the only prohibition, and this not even necessarily followed, is that one mouth along all the lyrics except for *that one*—passed over in thrilling hum?

Let's be clear: White's larger point stands. Looking to trap music to prepare the groundwork for revolution or any emancipatory

project is delusional and, moreover, deaf. If we start from the premise that trap is *not* any of these things, is quite emphatically (*pace* J.
Cole) the final nail in the coffin of the whole project of "conscious"
rap, then the question becomes what is it for, what will it make possible. Not necessarily for good or ill, but in the sense of illumination:
What does it allow us to see, or to describe, that we haven't yet made
transparent to our own sense of the coming world? For whatever
the case may be, the future shape of mass culture will look and feel
more like trap than like anything else we can currently point to. In
this sense, White is showing us the way forward. By insisting that
we abandon any bullshit promise or pseudopolitics, the project of a
force that is seeping into the fabric of our mental and social lives will
become more precise, more potent as a sensibility for us to try and
communicate to ourselves and to others.

34.

TRAP IS WHAT GIORGIO AGAMBEN calls, in *The Use of Bodies*, "a form-
of-life." As it's lived, the form-of-life is first and foremost a psychology, a worldview (cf. Fanon) framed by the inscription of the body in
space. *Where you come from*. It never ceases to amaze how relentlessly black artists—completely unlike white artists, who never seem
to come from anywhere in their music—assert with extraordinary
specificity where they're from, where they rep, often down to city, zip
code, usually neighborhood, sometimes to the block. Boundedness
produces genealogy, the authority of a defined experience. But this
experience turns out to be ontology. All these blocks, all these hoods,
from Oakland to Brooklyn, from Compton to Broward County, are
effectively *the same*: they are the hood, the gutter, the mud, the trap,
the slaughterhouse, the underbucket. Trappers, like rappers before
them, give coordinates that tell you where they're coming from in
both senses. I'm from *this* hood, but all hoods are the hood, and so I
speak for *all*, I speak of ontology—a form-of-life.

The peculiar condition of being ceaselessly co-opted for another's profit could arguably point to an impasse, to despair. But here's the counter: the force of our vernacular culture formed under slavery is the connection born principally in music, but also in the Word, in all of its manifold uses, that *believes in its own power*. That self-authorizes and liberates from within. This excessive and exceptional relation is misunderstood, often intentionally. Black culture isn't "magic" because of some deistic proximity of black people to the universe. Slavers had their cargo dance on deck to keep them limber for the auction block. The magic was born out of *a unique historical and material experience* in world history, one that no other group of people underwent and survived for so long and in such intimate proximity to the main engines of modernity.

One result of this is that black Americans believe in the power of music, a music without and before instruments, let alone opera houses, music that lives in the kinship of voice with voice, the holler that will raise the dead, the power of the Word, in a way that many other people by and large no longer do—or only when it is confined to the strictly religious realm. Classical European music retained its greatness as long as it retained its connection to the sacred. Now that it's gone, all that's left is glassy prettiness; a Bach isn't possible.

Meanwhile, in the low life of blackness, there is a running fire that even in the midst of its co-optation exceeds the capacity of the system to soak it up. Mozzy is not a tragedian for the ages, but he is closer to the *spirit* of tragedy, as Sophocles understood it, than David Mamet.

The people who make music out of this form-of-life are the last ones in America to care for tragic art. Next to the black American underclass, the vast majority of contemporary art carries on as sentimental drivel, middlebrow fantasy television, investment baubles for plutocrats, a game of drones.

35.

Coda: What is the ultimate trap statement?

Gucci Mane: "I'm a trappa slash rappa but a full-time G."

2018

THE KEEPER

CHRISTINE SMALLWOOD

DOROTHY WAS TAKING A SHIT AT THE LIBRARY WHEN HER THERAPIST called and she let it go to voicemail. For three years running they had been meeting every Tuesday (save a New Year's holiday and the thirty-one days of August) in the stuffy fifteenth-floor studio on Central Park West, with its treetop view and standard-issue decor: African masks, Oriental rugs, Afghan throws, South American flutes. Dorothy was comforted by the therapist's warmth and womanliness, her aging but elastic skin, the way she clucked and wiped her hands like someone who had seen it all and intended to save you the trouble of seeing it for yourself. Still, more and more it worried Dorothy to have entrusted her mental health to one who made such little effort against the tide of cliché. It was one thing for problems—even solutions—to be unoriginal; another for presentation.

When the worrying got too intense, Dorothy had a choice of palliatives arrayed in pouncing distance of the saggy patient sofa: stress balls, beads, figurines for rubbing and handling, various-size pillows for pounding and embracing, and the eternal tissue box, draped in its hand-knitted elephant-gray cover. The box was always full. The therapist must be keeping watch on the box's levels. Dorothy respected her attention to detail. Fullness, plenitude, preparedness, a material well of empathy—excellent clinical values all. But where did the therapist hide the half-full boxes? Or did she cram new tissues into the same old box between sessions? How old was the box, and how old were the tissues at the deepest, most archaeological substratum, and what might happen if Dorothy had a particularly lachrymal session and made it all the way down to the bottom?

The therapist was calling because Dorothy, who at this moment was rereading the flyer for student health services taped to the wall above the receptacle for used feminine-hygiene products, had left a voicemail at eleven o'clock last night canceling today's session. It wasn't that the miscarriage was such a big deal or that she was broken up in grief about it; it was that she hadn't told the therapist she was pregnant, and didn't want to have a whole session about her tendency to withhold. In the asymmetrical warfare of therapy, secrets were a guerrilla tactic. Dorothy was not belligerent by nature. She almost certainly would have told the therapist everything, except a few weeks ago, when it was on her tongue to do so, the therapist had interrupted a story that she was telling about her boyfriend, Rog, to remark that Rog was "a keeper." Dorothy saw at once that after the language of "keeping" had been introduced into the room, it would be impossible to keep it from becoming attached to the pregnancy, to define the pregnancy in terms of a keeping or a not-keeping, when in fact Dorothy was not ready to talk about retention, even as a future decision toward which she was inevitably hurtling, and so she, driven into a cul-de-sac by a linguistic overdetermination that would have been rich material if she only could have borne it, said nothing.

FINALS GOT YOU STRESSED? the flyer quizzed. DON'T DESPAIR. TEXT TO TALK IT OUT. A sad stick figure in one corner, a smiling stick figure in the other. KILL YOURSELF, someone had written in green ink above the smiler. STOP THE HATE, someone else had written alongside. Then the hand in green ink had returned to draw a drooling penis with a thick beard and a natty top hat. Dorothy wondered if she had taught any of these students. It was possible.

There were other things that Dorothy had kept from the therapist, questions that lingered unasked, doubts she had failed to articulate.

She had never expressed her aversion to the decor, never raised the matter of the tissues. And why, Dorothy had often speculated, had she never once—never in three years running—seen another person in the therapist's waiting room? Did the therapist never run behind schedule? Was the next patient never early? Who were these masters of time? What had begun as Dorothy's private joke—that she was, in fact, the therapist's only patient, that the tissue box was refilled for her benefit alone—had blossomed into a suspicion that had evolved into a conviction that was reaching maturity as full-blown fact.

The therapist naturally went to great lengths to put up a front that Dorothy was one of many, an item in a series that had no beginning and no end. There were, first of all, the references to other patients. "Some of my other patients find it useful to . . ." "When you've been in this game a long time you learn . . ." That kind of thing. There was the overstuffed appointment book that the therapist consulted if Dorothy needed to move her session time. There was the gentle, patient smile the therapist issued whenever Dorothy complained of being in "crisis," a wordless sign intended to make plain that Dorothy was a model of normalcy compared with the mentally ravaged hordes that were beating down the therapist's door all the live-long week, except during the precise times that Dorothy was traversing the hallways, elevator, and lobby of the doorman building on Central Park West. The upshot of all this was that Dorothy was sure she was the therapist's only patient but had not yet determined why this was so. Was the therapist not good at her job? Was she lazy? Who paid the rent? Perhaps she was merely a hobbyist therapist, or—and this was a new theory, whose kinks Dorothy was still ironing out—perhaps she had retired just before Dorothy was referred to her, and for deep psychological reasons of her own had not been willing to admit that she was no longer taking new patients, and thus the farce had begun, and thus had spun, ever so slowly, out of control.

Not long ago Dorothy had started seeing a second therapist, on the side, in whom she confided her doubts about the first therapist, but this was only a temporary situation. Dorothy wasn't a millionaire.

MARTIN LUTHER THOUGHT UP the 95 Theses while on the toilet.

Dorothy couldn't remember where she had read that.

She wiped, examined her fingernails, wiped again. She wiped back to front. She knew this was incorrect, but she had been doing it her whole life, and there are habits that one gives up on breaking.

The second therapist had never called her. Dorothy didn't even have her number in her phone. Her office was downtown: abstract art, leather furniture. She dressed business casual and steered the conversation away from any topic that wasn't Dorothy's first therapist. These topics included:

1. Work: A 4–3 teaching load. A ticking tenure clock. Her first book was more difficult to complete than she had expected. What was supposed to be a simple clean-up job was turning into a total rewrite. Dorothy didn't understand why her first drafts were so often failures. She hated producing so much waste.

2. Family: Alternately suffocating and distant. Proportions difficult to establish, boundaries unevenly maintained. The fear of turning into one's mother. The guilt engendered by the fear. What was so bad about our mothers, that we should avoid their fates at all cost?

3. Money: There was not enough of it.

From time to time Dorothy raised one or all of these issues with the second therapist, who responded by pursing her lips and smiling gently, much like the first therapist did, which made Dorothy wonder where therapists learned to smile like that.

"That's not why you're here," she would say. "Why are you here?"

Yesterday, unusually, the second therapist had asked a direct question. She wanted to know what the first therapist—they never used her name; it was a professional courtesy—had said about Rog, why she had called him a "keeper."

The word sounded foreign in the second therapist's mouth. Dorothy thought of fish, which ones you take home for frying, which you throw back. She had never been fishing. She turned her head to look out the window, but there was no window in the second therapist's office. The shock of rediscovering this lack of window was comparable to turning over in the night and finding Rog's head replaced with a watermelon, which had happened once, in a dream. But Dorothy often had these little perceptual mix-ups in the second therapist's office. It was only to be expected, when having an affair.

"I like my meat very rare," Dorothy began. "I like it undercooked."

The second therapist nodded. Her hands were folded in her lap respectfully. She never wrote anything down while they talked.

Dorothy explained that Rog, without asking her, had purchased a sous vide machine. The way it worked was that it submerged cuts of meat, sealed in airtight plastic bags, into a water bath. It made the meat so tender that it could be cut with the dullest, oldest knife. The color was indescribable. The flesh turned to paste in the mouth. Before serving, you seared the outsides with a flame, as when making a crème brûlée.

"Sous vide machines are expensive," Dorothy said to the second therapist. "I was telling her how wonderful it felt to be given such an expensive gift. I love receiving gifts. I wish I could receive gifts every day. That's when she said that he was a keeper."

The second therapist nodded.

What Dorothy did not say to the second therapist, as she had not said to the first, was that she had learned, after thanking Rog for the lavish gift, that he had bought the cheapest sous vide machine on the market.

"Did you like eating the meat that the machine cooked?" the second therapist asked.

Dorothy said yes, but that was a lie to make herself appear grateful.

STILL ON THE TOILET. Still sitting, crossing legs, uncrossing them. The toilet didn't have an automatic flush, so Dorothy could sit for hours if she chose and never be sprayed with water.

She opened her phone and scrolled through her photos. There was one that she liked a great deal, of Rog playing with his brother's dog. Rog was at peace, and the dog's face was a rictus of joy. It was a few years old. Rog had long hair then. The dog in the photo was now dead.

The library toilet was very clean. Dorothy did not frequent the large women's room by the water fountain, with its row of six open-bottomed stalls under which could be passed fistfuls of paper or whatever else a person required. She used the single-occupancy bathroom by the critical-theory reading room. It had been designed for the handicapped, but Dorothy knew the able-bodied made use of it. Sometimes two undergraduates went in at once. She had seen it happen.

The handle of the bathroom door shuttled back and forth.

"I'm in here!" Dorothy called.

It was day six, and she was still bleeding. Not the unceasing hemorrhage of the first ten hours after the second Cytotec suppository had kicked in—now it was thick, curdled knots of string, gelatinous in substance. If she had opted for the in-office procedure, they would have vacuumed her clean. But she had wanted to bleed at home. It had seemed less official that way. She hadn't known how degrading the dribble would be. Dorothy was starting to fear it might never end; that until the last of her days, whenever she wiped, the tissue would come back bloody and brown.

She didn't have much experience with blood, abscesses, sores, things of that nature. She had never broken a bone or needed stitches. Once she saw a cyst explode. Her college roommate, Alyssa, had developed a soft lump on her elbow that over several weeks expanded like a balloon being pumped with water until one afternoon she bent her arms to put her hair in a pony and streams of white confetti burst out, decorating the books, pencils, et cetera on her desk, as well as her denimed lap, with foamy spray. Dorothy ran from the room in horror, but Alyssa, fascinated by the materials of the body, took photographs.

Alyssa had a "natural" approach to life. Dorothy had learned this early in their friendship, when during a wild party for "spring fling" they fell into an embrace. Dorothy would estimate the number of

CHRISTINE SMALLWOOD   259

rum-based drinks she enjoyed that evening at five. When she imagined having five drinks now she was aghast, but back then she was a
young person with a young person's liver and a young person's courage. She and Alyssa kissed and groped and were soon scouring the
building, whose name was Trotter, for a place to be alone, pursuing
like two moles the feeling of being shut in, unobservable, burrowed.
The classrooms were locked, but the spacious, single-occupant bathroom on the ground floor was open.

The floor was cold and blindingly white, like the lavatory's other
features: the walls, the sink, the toilet, the light, the grout that separated and conjoined the tiles. Alyssa jerked down her pants, exposing
a tangle of hair, and reached a hand inside. She pulled out a maroon
latex cup that came to a point like a nipple. It was called, Dorothy
remembered, a keeper. Hippies used them, vegans, people like that.
In her drunken enthusiasm Alyssa was clumsy and spilled the blood.
It left a trail like drizzled syrup on her blond leg, across the clean
tiled floor. Alyssa's reaction was merry. She tossed the cup into the
sink and wiped the blood away with toilet paper, leaving smudges
everywhere, and without pausing to apologize showed Dorothy how
to form her first two fingers into a rod and ram it back and forth in
the place where the keeper had been, and as Dorothy did this for
Alyssa she was overcome with a feeling of desolation and loneliness
and fatigue. Dorothy wasn't used to being so active, sexually speaking. She preferred lying down on something soft and warm like a bed
and letting someone else do the ramming.

The knocking at the door became importunate.

"I'm in here!" Dorothy called again.

When the footsteps receded down the hallway, she listened to
her voicemail. The first therapist had a pleasant speaking voice. She
enunciated clearly but without exaggeration. "I'm sorry that you're
not feeling well," she said. "Rest up and I'll see you next week." There
was no distrust in the voice. Before she could put her phone away,
Rog texted to ask how she was feeling. She wrote back, "Still bleeding." She flushed. She inspected her fingernails.

Thinking back on it now, Dorothy marveled at how clean the Trotter bathroom had been. Other than the spatter, which was not really so big—the keeper cup could only hold thirty milliliters, less than a shot of liquor—there was not a speck of dirt or grime anywhere on any part of the toilet. Not the lid or the lip or the rim or the trunk. The library toilet was similarly pristine. You could lie down with your face pressed up against the ceramic base and it would be incommodious but not repulsive. But Dorothy's toilet at home was always dirty, and covered in her own hair. Some days it seemed like Dorothy's hair was threaded with magnets and the toilet was burnished in stainless steel, the way they attracted each other. And how does she have any hair left at all, now that she thinks of it, considering how it clogs the drain and collects around the edges of the bath mat, how it fills the crooks of her fingers when she tugs on the ends in concentration, how so much of it has been falling out, day after day after day?

2018

NOT EVERY KID-BOND
MATURES

GABRIEL WINANT

Malcolm Harris. *Kids These Days: Human Capital and the Making of Millennials*. Little, Brown, 2017.

ON A RECENT VISIT TO MY PARENTS, MY MOTHER ASKED ME WHETHER I want to have kids. Being 30 and single, an uncle to a niece and a nephew through both my siblings, I've started to get questions from older generations about my plans to reproduce. This began later for me than it does for women and is a fraction as oppressive, but to be honest I'd thought male privilege would shield me from it entirely. When this defense failed, I forestalled a line of inquiry from my mother by talking about climate change. Even as I said it, I knew it was an already hackneyed form of stonewalling. You can defend any uncertainty these days by evoking melting ice sheets and disappearing permafrost.

But she'd never heard anyone take this tack before—at least not since her own generation's "population bomb" version of the same story. "That," my mom said slowly, "is so heavy." Over the course of the rest of my visit, she mentioned it to others my age for confirmation, to others her age in incredulity. "Gabe says nobody in his generation wants to have kids because of climate change. Did you know about this?"

How could the gap between us be so great? What seemed to me such a commonplace as to be evasive and impersonal appeared to my mother as a serious human quandary—which, in fact, it is. I'm more politically optimistic than my mother, yet I was taken aback to realize how much darker the future seems to me than to her. Then I remembered: she's a boomer, I'm a millennial, and this is the song of the season.

There hasn't been a generational divide this pronounced since the 1960s. The flare-ups that have occurred have been aftershocks of the 1960s—as in the 1992 confrontation between World War II veteran George H. W. Bush and draft dodger Bill Clinton with the wife who didn't want to bake cookies. Generational analysis rarely got beyond generic psychobabble: the "greatest generation" were stoic, laconic survivors, boomers the spoiled offspring of Dr. Spock, et cetera. The actual "life chances" of the generations were not meaningfully different, and politics did not line up with the generations. Clinton's best generational slice of the electorate in 1992 was the senior vote, but he performed pretty evenly overall, winning between 41 and 50 percent in every age category. Neither party enjoyed any significant preference from the young or the old in particular.

The contrast with today could hardly be starker. Republicans have consolidated the elder vote and Democrats enjoy the default support of the young, who largely don't vote anyway: as we know from the maps on our social-media feeds, Hillary Clinton would have won something like forty-five states if 18–25-year-olds had cast the only ballots. And she was the distant second choice of these so-called young millennials in the Democratic primaries, far behind the left-wing challenger. The reawakening global left of the past decade, of which Bernie Sanders was the American electoral incarnation, is, in terms of its age distribution, uniform: the Indignados and Podemos, Syriza (alas), the Arab Spring, Occupy, the Gezi Park protests, South Africa's Economic Freedom Fighters, Hong Kong's Umbrella Movement, the Kurdish revolution, Black Lives Matter, Nuit Debout and La France Insoumise, Momentum and Jeremy

Corbyn, the Democratic Socialists of America—all are or were movements of the young.

While striking, this massive political generation gap is a symptom of something deeper. Whatever it is, we register it in complaints about the supposedly "bad" work ethic of young employees or scolding about keeping good habits: our smartphone-induced fidgetiness; our infamous predilection for avocado toast over mortgages; the decline of Applebee's and Buffalo Wild Wings, laid low by millennial distaste. (Cf. the swelling genre of listicles about what consumer brands millennials are killing. Cf. also all the articles about millennials and their love of listicles.) You hear it in stories of adult children who move back in with their parents. It's in the 52 percent of teenagers who have told surveyors that they don't identify as straight, and the perplexing—if encouraging—news of resurgent youthful interest in public libraries. For good or ill, something has gone profoundly awry in the intergenerational transmission process.

Under ordinary circumstances, the institutions built by the old are repopulated by the young, who adjust them for new circumstances but leave them basically the same, in turn handing them over to the next generation. The possibility of successful passage through the institutions of society is what makes a person follow a normative rather than deviant life course: being a woman or a man roughly the way she or he is supposed to, partnering and reproducing in the socially standard fashion, trying to get ahead or at least get by according to prevailing ethics of education and work. In our society, this has meant (in ideal-typical middle-class terms) homeownership, an occasional vacation, sending your kids to college, and retirement. Historical continuity—the integrity of social institutions over time— works itself out on the individual level: people may feel they are making distinct, agonizing life choices, but for the most part they are living out those institutions predictably. An institution is, at the end of the day, just a pattern of social behavior repeated long enough. On the other hand, if the institutions aren't processing enough people into the proper form—if too many can't or won't do family, school, work, and sex approximately the way they've been done before—then large-scale historical continuity can't happen. The society can't look tomorrow like it does today.

WHILE IT FEELS as though we are heading toward some such break, there have not yet been many serious efforts to understand our national crisis in terms of generations. This is why Malcolm Harris's new book, *Kids These Days: Human Capital and the Making of Millennials,* is a landmark. Remarkably for an author of a trade book on such an on-trend topic, Harris makes a politically radical argument, undergirded by a coherent and powerful Marxist analysis. You can very well imagine buying this book in an airport, and because Harris is a compelling and funny writer, you'd get through it before you landed. But you might land a different person: the book is devastating. "American Millennials come from somewhere—we didn't emerge fully formed from the crack in an iPhone screen," Harris writes. In his view, we are, down to our innermost being, the children of neoliberalism. The habits so often mocked and belittled in the press are in fact adaptations to tightening repressive and exploitative pressures, the survival strategies of a demographic "born in captivity."

Capitalism's generation-long crisis, in Harris's diagnosis, has imposed enormous competitive pressure on the young to produce "human capital." This concept, a core one in neoliberal economic thought, is meant to quantify the bundle of economically valuable human qualities—education, skills, discipline—accumulated over the course of a life. It's in the book's subtitle because it's the key to Harris's argument. The hidden hand that shapes millennials, producing our seemingly various and even contradictory stereotyped attributes, is the intensifying imperative—both from the outside and also deeply internalized—to maximize our own potential economic value. "What we've seen over the past few decades is not quite a sinister sci-fi plot to shape a cohort of supereffective workers who are too competitive, isolated, and scared to organize for something better," writes Harris. "But it has turned out a lot like that." Capitalism is eating its young. It's only feeding us avocados to fatten us up first.

Harris works through this argument by following the millennial through the stages of life—as far as we've yet gotten. A remarkable feature of the book is how Harris is able to apply this single explanation to dozens of disparate if familiar symptoms. Again and again, he yanks the disguise from some behavior seeming to belong to a discrete field—parenting, education, pop culture, or the labor market—and finds that it was actually neoliberalism all along. Harris points out that, beginning in childhood, so-called helicopter parenting and the measurable decline of unstructured play are actually forms of risk management. Given how social inequality in the world at large has worsened competition to get ahead, "parents are told—and then communicate to their children—that their choices, actions, and accomplishments have lasting consequences, and the consequences grow by the year."

From the preoccupation with bullying to the design of playgrounds and the school policy of zero tolerance, Harris finds the world of childhood increasingly redefined by actuarial caution. Most of all, though, he finds it in the classroom. School is just a form of unwaged work, masked by the ideology of pedagogy. The surplus that kid-labor creates, rather than going to any immediately present boss, pools up in the students themselves, to be tapped by future bosses. When children do schoolwork, they labor on themselves. "By looking at children as investments, we can see where the product of children's labor is stored: in the machine-self, in their human capital." The steady increase in homework, the growing apparatus of testing and school accountability, and the pressure for longer school days and school years are just what you would expect once children have been turned into financial assets. Many of the observed social-psychological attributes of the young generation result from undergoing such processing into a human commodity form. Childhood is a "high-stakes merit-badge contest," teaching kids to be "servile, anxious, and afraid."

At the end of childhood, some millennials go to college to continue accumulating human capital. Harris is a peerless observer of the harrowing economic costs of "meritocracy," and his chapter on college abounds in withering aperçus. "College admissions offices are the rating agencies for kids," he writes. "And once the kid-bond is rated, it has four or so years until it's expected to produce a return." Because the pressure to accumulate human capital is so intense, students will bear enormous costs to do it. Far from the coddled children of stereotype, Harris points out, most college students are "regular people—mostly regular *workers*—who spend part of their work-time on their own human capital, like they've been told to." Exhaustion, overwork, and even food insecurity are common. Colleges themselves, meanwhile, reap obscene rewards from their gatekeeping position by offering a worse product for a higher price: hollowed-out pedagogy from exploited adjuncts and graduate students, masked with "shiny extras unrelated to the core educational mission." Aggrandizing administrations bloat on student debt, the key to the whole scheme. Student debt, Harris argues, is a blood-sucking Keynesian stimulus, turning the value of the future labor of young borrowers into the capital to build stadiums and luxury dorms today, jacking up tuition even higher and allowing another round of borrowing and building.

But not every kid-bond matures. Students who can't keep up are diagnosed, drugged, and punished. The extraordinary proliferation of mood and attention disorders among the young, and their development into a lucrative pharmaceutical market, is only the logical complement of the human-capital-accumulation regime of testing, supervising, and debt collecting. Depression, Harris notes, is up 1,000 percent over the past century, "with around half of that growth occurring since the late 1980s." While there's always a question about changing diagnoses with this sort of figure, Harris is convincing that there's more to this phenomenon than an artifact of measurement. So too the growing punitive apparatus waiting to catch kids who fail: "We can draw a straight line between the standardization of children in educational reform and the expulsion, arrest, and even murder of the kids who won't adapt." On this account, mass incarceration, too, is a generational phenomenon, and it makes its first appearances inside schools, which are now heavily policed zones, as are the public spaces in which working-class kids congregate. "Millennials are cagey and anxious, as befits the most policed modern generation," Harris writes. In this way, the book effectively argues that widely different experiences of neoliberalism—from the grasping student's anxiety for good grades to the young person of color dodging the cops—are nonetheless part of the same social process.

The immediate impulse driving human-capital accumulation is the need to compete in a labor market more unforgiving than anything in memory. This is one of the most familiar elements of the millennial critique of the world we've inherited, perhaps best embodied in the meme of "Old Economy Steven"—a yearbook image of a smug and blotchy young white man with an echt mid-'70s look: pageboy haircut, wide-lapeled shirt, some kind of necklace. "Why don't you call and ask if they're hiring?" says the supertext on one version; the subtext reads, "Hasn't been on a job hunt since 1982." "Pays into social security," offers another. The kicker: "Receives benefits." The story Harris tells here isn't new, but it lies at the core of millennial experience: "It's harder to compete for a good job, the bad jobs you can hope to fall back on are worse than they used to be, and both good and bad jobs are less secure. The intense anxiety that has overcome American childhood flows from a reasonable fear of un-, under-, and just plain lousy employment." The meme itself conveys something distinctively millennial: not just precarious employment but awareness of our own precariousness, which our elders refuse to accommodate or even acknowledge.

Though media stereotypes often portray millennials as brittle, wheedling, and demanding, for the most part young workers are docile enough to have bent themselves into whatever shape capital has required. Millennials aren't fragile—they're overstretched. This is the most human-capital-intensive generation in history, productive far beyond the wages it garners. "From our bathroom breaks to our sleep schedules to our emotional availability, millennials are growing up highly attuned to the needs of capital markets," Harris writes. "We are encouraged to strategize and scheme to find places, times, and roles where we can be effectively put to work. Efficiency is our existential purpose, and we are a generation of finely honed tools." Racing to stay ahead, young workers accept low wages, sweatshop working conditions, and insecure arrangements. They do not expect that their employment will grant access to the social benefits enjoyed by their parents and grandparents—written off by Harris as history's most entitled generations, anomalies not likely to occur again. Rather, the emblematic figure of the millennial workforce, the clearest expression of its tendencies, is the intern: the worker whose labor is disavowed entirely, made out to be for *her* benefit, like the labor of schoolchildren.

For Harris, even millennial forms of creativity and self-expression are captive to this logic. The young are transforming the entire culture, he argues, through the way that their human-capital-accumulation strategies are working themselves out in the culture industries. Pointing to professional and college athletes, musicians, tween entertainers, online pornographers, and YouTube stars, he repeats his point: depressed entertainment profits have produced an arms race, causing aspiring performers, actors, and writers to laboriously produce their own stardom rather than wait to be discovered. He tells the story of Chicago rapper Chief Keef, who released more than forty songs for free online and created his own label at age 16 without any corporate involvement: "By the time Interscope signed Keef, he was already a bona fide star, with the kind of brand they would have otherwise had to spend money developing."

While the restructuring of these industries allows for some Cinderella stories, its overall effect is to intensify exploitation, by others or by oneself. For Harris, this is both a way of interpreting mass culture today and a metonym for a classic millennial habit. "Older Americans like to complain about the way many young people obsessively track our own social media metrics, but it's a complaint that's totally detached from the behavior's historical, material causes," he writes. "Personal branding shifts work onto job-seekers."

On social media—the heart of the matter, naturally, for a book on millennials—personal branding becomes indistinguishable from social life in general. The destruction of childhood as we once knew it by parents, teachers, and police has driven kids into social media for their "flirting, fighting, and friending." Once online, these formerly free activities can be commodified, the living activities of childhood vacuumed up as data and monetized. Despite cyclical moral panics over new drugs or hookup culture, teens—busy engaging in their social lives online when they're not doing homework—actually use fewer recreational drugs, drink less, and have less sex than their equivalents in prior generations. It's risk aversion again, says Harris—fuel for Silicon Valley profits now and more disciplined workers later.

The summation *Kids These Days* gives us is harrowing: here is a generation hurrying to give in to the unremitting, unforgiving commodification of the self. Harris predicts a future of debt servitude, confinement for the "malfunctioning," worsening misogyny (though his gender analysis is less coherent than the rest of his argument), and total surveillance. Millennials, that is, are the first generation to live in the dystopia to come. Harris's politics are revolutionary, and he dismisses any lesser mode of collective response to the thoroughgoing crisis as—to use his simile—akin to playing with a toy. Ethical consumption, electoral politics, philanthropy and nonprofits, and social protest are all just switches and buttons, yielding fun noises and flashing lights but having no effect: "The series of historical disasters that I've outlined, the one that characterizes my generation, is a big knot. There's not a single thread we can pull to undo it, no one problem we can fix to make sure the next generation grows up happier and more secure." What you do with a knot that you can't untie is cut it.

HARRIS EMERGED AS a writer with anarchist politics over the past decade, particularly in the New York milieus of Occupy Wall Street and the *New Inquiry*, though one can find his writing in this magazine and early issues of *Jacobin* as well. The window of possibility, the feeling of historical openness, that was generated by the Occupy moment did not stay open. The halves of the anticapitalist left, embodied on the one hand by Harris's anarchism and on the other by the emergent democratic socialism of *Jacobin*, became incompatible—a rupture to which Harris's work feels like a partial response. You can actually watch this happen in real time in a video of a 2011 panel at Bluestockings bookstore on the Lower East Side. The same day that thousands had rallied to defend the occupation against a police raid, anarchists Harris and Natasha Lennard squared off against socialists Jodi Dean, Doug Henwood, and Chris Maisano in a contentious exchange off which one can read much of the substance of intra-left developments and conflicts of the past six years. Periodically, the camera pans around the packed bookstore, and a sharp eye can pick out a large number of prominent figures from New York's left-wing world of letters.

The whole thing quickly takes on a generational tone. "The sitdown strike was invented decades ago by unionists," says Maisano. "It wasn't a bunch of kids running around the University of California writing stuff on the wall." (Off to the left, Harris and Lennard roll their eyes and laugh.) The socialists propose workplace and student organization and campaigning for free higher education. Harris answers the socialists with a slogan from the 2009 University of California occupation: "A free university in a capitalist economy is like a reading room in a prison." Henwood—a man nearing 60—mimes masturbation in response to Harris, at the time 22 years old. One moment, though, stands out as particularly prescient. It's a question from an older man in the audience. This isn't going to last forever, he points out. "What happens when the occupation ends? What happens when the tumult and the shouting of the ecstatic moment dies? Who remains? Who maintains the continuity? Who draws the lesson? Who draws the lesson—what a question for a school abolitionist.

About a year later, Harris sniped at the Chicago Teachers Union during its 2012 strike against school closures, widely seen as a rare instance of heroism and victory on the left. He wrote on Twitter that teachers don't "like or care very much about the kids," comparing them to prison guards whose word we wouldn't accept about the best interests of prisoners. His line, that he supported the strike but opposed the school system itself, was hard for many comrades to swallow. Earlier the same year, he mounted a defense of his generational analysis, in which he mocked his critics, especially Henwood, for missing the point because they were 'old.' Henwood shot back that readers should check in with Harris in ten years, by which time he'll have transitioned from revolutionary anarchism to marketing.

In many ways, Henwood could scarcely have been more wrong about Harris. Five years later, the younger writer has published a book calling for youth revolution and recently seemed to risk his book contract by publicly rooting on Twitter for the death of the Republican congressman Steve Scalise. Harris doesn't seem to have mellowed. But there's something more interesting at stake in this debate than male-writer egos, old and young. In a less ad hominem register, Henwood might have raised a valid question: can the political impulses that Harris represents, the ones that come out of our generation's distinctive experience, mature into potent collectivity? Or are they individualist from the root, bound to decay into posture and then a racket—absent the guidance of more seasoned activists, or without connection to struggles more deeply historically or socially grounded?

While there are of course old and young anarchists and socialists alike, the political division that has reemerged over the past decade on the left still pivots on this question: What is the proper relationship to the past for those of us who want to make a new future?

The more traditional socialist left argues for continuity. We've been doing occupations since forever, Maisano said; let's rebuild social-democratic institutions like CUNY, Henwood said. Socialism may be embraced by the young now, but in this version it still looks and sounds like Bernie Sanders—still a project of recuperation as much as invention, resuming an effort interrupted by the neoliberal caesura. In some guises, such historical continuity is humbling and useful. In others, it's boomer narcissism run amok, reducing every left-wing proposition from a young person to an opportunity to force the past into the present. "Don't repeat my mistakes," cries the old socialist to the new one. The result can be formally radical but quite often conservative in affect and mood, dabbling soberly in the far-fetched notion that you can change the structure of society while everyone stays the same kind of people. This is one way of understanding why whiteness and masculinity continue to bedevil the socialist left, even in its committed antiracist and feminist quarters. A left that maintains a tether to a usable past is bound more tightly to the historical American nightmare. It can't rush toward utopia, because it's committed to engaging with people as they are and nudging them along.

The insurrectionary left, on the other hand, wants year zero. The power of the occupation, Lennard pointed out, is that when you step into it, you become someone else. The problem with becoming someone else, though, is that you're disinherited from your history, so you can't wield it effectively to understand the present or get ready for the future. It's life in a permanent now, a condition reflected in anarchism's traditional weakness when it comes to strategic calculation and engagement with state institutions—those durable, blunt objects. What was predictable about Occupy's destruction—in fact, what was predicted at Bluestockings that night—was for this reason hard to prepare for until it was already under way.

It is, in its way, a generational question. If you kill your parents, you won't hear their warnings, and then you'll eventually just become them without realizing it. If you listen to them, you'll become them on purpose. The question is how to become new and stay that way, how to be a stable point moving steadily from past into future without a neurotic relation to either—neither clinging nor leaping. This is the existential core of the strategic question on the left. It's a question about growing up.

HARRIS IS A LEAPER. There are no preparations to make, for him, no slow and steady work to chip away at power structures and create strategic opportunity. He imagines no source of transcendence in the millennial experience itself. If things break our way, it will be simply the intrusion of events. He anticipates some great departure, seemingly coming all of a sudden as Occupy did. In the book's rushed coda, Harris points vaguely to some approaching test of unknown shape for the millennial soul. "We don't know for sure when or where our crucial moments are coming, but we do know that they are." We will, he predicts enigmatically, become "fascists or revolutionaries, one or the other." What determines the timing of this reckoning or its outcome is unspecified, except that it would help if we can be "lucky and brave." This much I agree with.

Since the days of Occupy, Harris has gotten older, and like most of us as we've gotten older, he's hardened some. *Kids These Days* wants to be a political economy of millennials the way *Capital* wanted to be a political economy of the working class, a story of how structural processes produce abjection, then crisis, then transformation. But—like Marx, though not for the same reason—he doesn't quite close this circuit. Harris experienced defeat, and he can't help but telegraph the hopelessness it created. *Kids These Days* is the story of the objectification of millennials, not the subjectivity that they make from that objectification. At the end, we're still playthings of history, not its agents. Addressing the deunionization of the American workplace, he describes his cohort as "the perfect scabs." Of acquiescence to the internship, he writes, "Only a generation raised on a diet of gold stars could think that way." Millennials are captive to fantasies of upward mobility, a "fool's errand." We're "so well trained to excel and follow directions that many of us don't know how to separate our own interests from a boss's or a company's." We are, in his telling, incapable of trust, crippled by anxiety, unwilling to stand up for ourselves or one another, and sexually stunted: "Like Calvinists who thought the heaven-bound were preordained but unknown, everyone has to act as if they are saved, even though most are damned."

While the diagnosis is persuasive in its way, Harris seems unusually willing to set aside our generation's quite impressive record of resistance in the streets and at the ballot box. (On Twitter and in his published record he is visibly a regular, passionate observer of international social movements.) The catalog of movements of millennials, if not yet thick with victories, is nothing to sneeze at either. Moreover, it's clearly a work in progress. His own experience at Zuccotti, mine in the labor movement, and those of millions of our comrades around the world in social and political struggles of all kinds sit uneasily with the existential skepticism that the book avows.

The problem may be that Harris seems to see our generation as the whole of the question. He's right that one can see the crystallization of our world in what's happening to our generation. But this clarity is possible exactly because it's only a part of the picture. Without engaging with the larger social landscape, Harris can't get a view of what exactly might dislodge the current pattern. This, one supposes, is why such a sharp analysis concludes with a hand wave about future "crucial moments." Millennials are not alone, and we are not the only ones facing life changes of momentous social consequence. Generation is not actually just an identity. It's a relationship: no children without parents, no millennials without boomers. And all of us should have noticed by now that our parents are starting to get old. This will impose new obligations on us and open up new opportunities.

The aging of our parents' generation will produce a new peak in the country's age structure. When the boomers were young, less than 10 percent of the population was over 65. Today, we're around 15 percent, and we'll get to 20 percent as quick as 2030—then stay there for some time. Our society has never gone through anything like this before. It's likely to slow economic growth significantly all on its own—in addition to whatever other drags will be operating at that point. It certainly will put enormous pressure on social support and caregiving systems, likely beyond what they can sustain in anything like their current form. Harris writes that millennials have been written out of the social contract of midcentury American liberalism, whose crown jewels are Social Security and Medicare, social-insurance programs for the elderly. But the beneficiaries whose entitlements he resents, the boomers, may end up being written out, too.

The sharp pressure on elder-care and health-care systems engendered by the boomer demographic decline will be more than a statistical outlier. Health-care prices, already rising, will skyrocket as demand spikes. Medicare and Medicaid, if they're still intact in anything like their present form, will face attempts by the right to impose steep cuts. Nursing homes will become overcrowded, leading to the torture of old people—something that the Trump Administration recently moved to weaken elders' legal power to sue over, not coincidentally. (The old folks left behind in California and Texas and Florida nursing homes after recent disasters—lethally in the latter case—are a precursor of this coming nightmare.) The demand of older Americans on fixed incomes for affordable places to live will collide with housing markets that, if current conditions still obtain, will probably be even more out of control than now. What you should imagine is not debates in Congress over Medicare reimbursement policies, though these will happen. What you should imagine is homeless shelters packed with octogenarians.

Many of these processes are already under way. Today, health care accounts for nearly one-fifth of the economy and one-seventh of the labor market. It expanded right through the Great Recession. Home health aide is the fastest-growing job in the country. It's a 21st-century job—unregulated by labor law, afflicted with falling real wages, taking advantage of the heightened desperation for work of women, immigrants, and people of color. Usually it involves caring for Medicaid patients—in other words, people still shielded (if barely) by parsimonious 20th-century social protections.

The young and the old don't become who they are, and live the lives they live, independently of each other. In Harris's bad future, we're all the home health aide. But as the old grow in number, we'll have to make a choice. The right will probably attempt simultaneous attacks on programs for the old and on the working and living conditions of the young, arguing that screwing over the young (though they will call it increasing opportunity) is the only way to sustain the threadbare safety net for the old. Grandma can only have a decent twilight if her home health aide's wages get pushed down to $7 an hour. Further unraveling of the welfare state, falling wages, worsening inequality—this is the route to Harris's apocalypse. Maybe it ends well, but if the old are reducing the young to peonage and the young are abandoning or torturing the old in their nursing homes, it's a bit hard to imagine coming out the other side happy with who we are and what we've done.

The need to replace parents and care for the old always marks a watershed in the life course, but it isn't usually a mass event capable of rewriting the social contract. A crisis of such breadth and intensity as we are likely to face seems the only possibility for breaking the political deadlock currently pitting young against old. If there's a path to political resolution short of apocalypse, it runs through the young growing up and assuming the caretaking role, and compelling the old to accept care on our terms—and with it, our political hegemony. Either we rebuild democracy around care provision, as the political theorist Joan Tronto argues we must, or we lose it as Harris predicts.

This is not an idle fancy. One sees it nowhere more clearly than in British politics, upended by action from both ends of the age structure at once. On the left, the Labour Party was transformed by a movement of the young, a movement emerging from the 2010 student protests, which installed Jeremy Corbyn as the party's most left-wing leader in a century. Corbyn then escaped his universally predicted demise in the general election, holding the Conservatives to a hung parliament and setting himself up for victory down the road. By all accounts, the turning point in the campaign happened when the Tories unveiled their party manifesto, which included a proposal widely derided as a "dementia tax." This idea would have required long-term-care patients to forfeit all assets above £100,000, including their homes. (We do a version of this in the US to the Medicaid recipients who make up two-thirds of the population of our nursing homes.) The response was so withering that Prime Minister Theresa May stumbled to reverse herself almost immediately, but the damage was done. The "about-face awoke a largely dreary election campaign," as the *New York Times* put it.

In the end, the old still voted for May in huge numbers—69 percent of those over 70. It was the young, perhaps imagining the way that care burdens would be dumped onto them, who brought the socialist Corbyn within reach of power. The age structure of the vote was almost perfectly symmetrical: for every ten additional years of age, a voter was 9 percent likelier to support the Tories. The old will certainly never enact social transformation themselves. They are even likely to obstruct it. But it is nonetheless our relationships with them that may lead us to a sustainable program for its pursuit—a way to move forward in our lives and in history at once. If we see our millennial identity as a relationship to our elders, rather than an abject identity, then an avenue of transcendence short of apocalypse opens up: in this collective relationship, new solidarities may form, new varieties of care, love, and responsibility may take shape—and, from them, power. Millennials may yet figure out what we need to do politically from the labor we'll need to perform in our lives.

We have our examples in this country, too. In that famous picture from Charlottesville, we see a young black man—Corey Long is his name—shooting fire from a spray can at a wormy white fascist brandishing a Confederate flag like a club. So far, we're in Harris's world here—in fact, I believe I first learned the term *antifa* from his

Twitter page some years ago. But if you look at the photo, you see over Long's right shoulder a frail-looking older white man, whom Long, it emerges, stepped forward to defend against the physical menace facing them, including the actual discharge of a gun in their direction.

This is an image, then, not only of the escalating racial and ideological confrontation gripping the country but also of intergenerational solidarity and protectiveness. In this sense, it is quite far from the fantasy of antifascist defense as irresponsible youthful adventurism. The scene is made all the more tender by the fact that the 23-year-old Long is actually an elder-care worker. This, care for the old, is his job. He probably doesn't usually do it with fire, but it's good to know that's part of the skill set that this particular millennial has accumulated. One can be quite sure that his job is a shit job, but he appears committed to the principle, and in that, there's something more.

2018

SPADEWORK

ALYSSA BATTISTONI

IN 2007, WHEN I WAS 21 YEARS OLD, I WROTE AN INDIGNANT LETTER
to the *New York Times* in response to a column by Thomas Friedman. Friedman had called out my generation as a quiescent one: "too
quiet, too online, for its own good." "Our generation is lacking not
courage or will," I insisted, "but the training and experience to do the
hard work of organizing—whether online or in person—that will
lead to political power."

I myself had never really organized. I had recently interned
for a community-organizing nonprofit in Washington DC, a few
months before Barack Obama became the world's most famous
(former) community organizer, but what I learned was the language of organizing—how to write letters to the editor about its
necessity—not how to actually do it. I graduated from college, and
some months later, the global economy collapsed. I spent the next
years occasionally showing up to protests. I went to Zuccotti Park
and to an attempted general strike in Oakland; I participated in
demonstrations against rising student fees in London and against
police killings in New York. I wrote more exhortatory articles. But it
wasn't until I went to graduate school at Yale, where a campaign for
union recognition had been going on for nearly three decades, that I
learned to do the thing I'd by then been advocating for years.

By the time I started organizing so much that it felt like a full-time job, it was the spring of 2016, and I had plenty of company. Around the country there were high-profile efforts to organize magazines, fast-food places, and nursing homes. Erstwhile Occupiers became involved in the Bernie Sanders campaign and joined the exploding Democratic Socialists of America, whose members receive shabby business cards proclaiming them an "official socialist organizer." Today's organizers—not activists, thank you—make clear that they are not black bloc participants brawling with police or hippies plotting a love-in. They are inspired by a tradition of professional revolutionaries, by Lenin's exhortation that "unless the masses are organized, the proletariat is nothing. Organized—it is everything." Organizing, in other words, is unembarrassed about power. It recognizes that to wield it you need to persuade untold numbers of people to join a cause, and to begin organizing themselves. Organizing means being in it to win.

But *how* do you win? Historical materialism holds that crises of capitalism spark revolts, perhaps even revolutions, as witnessed in the eruption of Occupy and Black Lives Matter; uprisings in Spain, Greece, and Egypt; and the British student movement against tuition fees. But there's no guide for what happens in the long aftermath, as the left has often learned the hard way.

In previous moments of upheaval and promise the left has often turned to Antonio Gramsci, who sought to understand why working-class revolts in Europe following the Russian Revolution had led to fascism. Gramsci concluded that on some level people *consent* to subservience, even take it for granted, when the order in which they live comes to seem like common sense. Hegemony was subtler than outright coercion, more pervasive, permeating the tempos of daily life.

It was hegemony, Stuart Hall argued in 1983, that was key to understanding the disappointment of his own generation—why Thatcher and the new right had triumphed in remaking common sense after a decade of labor union revolt. Hegemony shaped how people acted when they weren't thinking about it, what they thought was right and wrong, what they imagined the good life to be. A hegemonic project had to "occupy each and every front" of life, "to insert itself into the pores of the practical consciousness of human beings." Thatcherism had understood this better than the left. It had "entered the struggle on every single front on which it calculated it could advance itself," put forth a "theory for every single arena of human life," from economics to language, morality to culture. The domains the left dismissed as bourgeois were simply the ones where the ruling class was winning. Yet creating hegemony was "difficult work," Hall reminded us. Never fully settled, "it always has to be won."

In other words, there is no economic deus ex machina that will bring the revolution. There are still people, in their stubborn, contradictory particularities, as they exist in concrete space and time. It is up to you to figure out how to act together, or not; how to find common ground, or not. Gramsci and Hall insist that you must look relentlessly at things and people as they are, face your prospects with brutal honesty, and act in ways that you think can have an effect. In these ways they are an organizer's theorists.

BUT IN FACT, one doesn't become an organizer by reading theory, or at least I didn't. I went to graduate school to study political theory, in hopes of figuring out what to do about the dilemmas that weighed on me. But it took something else to give that theory meaning in my own life. This was the experience of graduate school, which wasn't necessarily your typical workplace—so the Yale administration kept telling us.

I'd joined the union as a matter of course, stopping by the Graduate Employees and Students Organization (GESO) table at the extracurriculars fair before I'd gone to a single day of class. Politically, it seemed obvious: I supported unions in general, so why not join? Plus my college roommate had been at Yale and organizing for years already: I'd heard from him of struggles and triumphs, of how he'd knocked doors all summer to help a slate of union members and supporters take over city government the year prior. A few days after I signed my card, I went to a union pizza lunch in my department to welcome our new cohort—I was one of just three people who'd showed up, out of seventeen—and nodded along with the organizer's rap about why the union was good. I didn't need convincing.

Yet when another organizer asked me to join the union communications team a few weeks later, I burst into tears. I was already completely overwhelmed with hundreds of pages of reading I couldn't possibly hope to complete, response papers to write and presentations to give on said reading, obligatory departmental workshops and talks to attend. Doing one more thing seemed impossible. She talked me down from panic and I agreed to do something small—an interview with a union member for a newsletter we hoped to revive. I took on a series of other projects—more interviews, filming testimonials for a new website. At the end of our first year, my closest friend in my graduate cohort ran for a municipal office on the union slate, and I spent the summer knocking doors for his campaign. I met up with other organizers for "visits," where we walked around campus looking for members to sign whatever petition we were running at the time, and joined my department's organizing committee. I cried in many more meetings.

Graduate school, I came to realize, was not the place to go to learn about politics. I was bewildered by its rituals, which counterintuitively seemed structured around avoiding intellectual conversation in favor of gossip and shoptalk. At house parties and department receptions, we rarely talked about the things we'd read or thought about; instead we complained about how many papers we'd written that week, how many deadlines loomed for funding applications or summer programs, how little sleep we'd gotten. We tiptoed around more sensitive conversations: access to mental-health care, caring for children on a stipend, the cratering job market and growing pool of adjunct labor. I was desperate for those conversations, and organizing, I found, was the way to have them. Like a consciousness-raising group, organizing conversations allowed you to air grievances long suppressed in the name of politeness or professionalism, to create a space for politics where it wasn't supposed to be. The point was to locate the fundamental experience of powerlessness lurking beneath the generalized misery. Yet for all that we griped about how much we worked, in organizing conversations the question of whether we were really workers came up constantly.

Why was it so hard to see ourselves as people who might need a union? Gramsci had observed that any individual's personality was "strangely composite," made up of a mixture of beliefs, thoughts, and ideas gleaned from family history, cultural norms, and formal education, filtered through their own life experiences read through the prevailing ideology of the time. Hall had taken this up to argue that when the working class failed to espouse revolutionary thought, women to embrace feminism, or people of color to advocate anti-racism, it wasn't because they suffered from false consciousness. The idea that consciousness could be true or false simply made no sense: it was always, Hall stated, "complex, fragmentary, and contradictory." This was just as true for those on the left as for anyone else. "A tiny bit of all of us is also somewhere inside the Thatcherite project," Hall had warned in 1988. "Of course, we're all one hundred per cent committed. But every now and then—Saturday mornings, perhaps, just before the demonstration—we go to Sainsbury's and we're just a tiny bit of a Thatcherite subject."

The Thatcherite project was since then much advanced, and we had internalized its dictates. For our whole lives we had learned to do school very well; in graduate school we learned to exploit ourselves on weekends and vacations before putting ourselves "on the market." Many of us still believed in meritocracy, despite learning every day how it was failing us. The worse the conditions of academic life became, the harder everyone worked, and the harder it became to contest them. Plus, we were so lucky to be there—at Yale! Compared to so many grad students, we had it good, and surely jobs were waiting on the other side for us, if for anyone. Who were we to complain? Organizing a union of graduate students at Yale seemed to many like an act of unbearable privilege—a bunch of Ivy League self-styled radicals doing worker cosplay.

Then there was the prevailing ideology. Many people liked unions in the abstract, for other people, but had reservations about whether one made sense for us. We worked independently for the most part (getting paid to read!); we exercised control over our own work—or at least hoped to one day. Nearly all of us had grown up hearing about how bad teachers' unions were for our own precious educations. Few of us came from union families; almost no one had belonged to a union before, and those who had sometimes cited bad experiences. Even among those who were nominally sympathetic, "I think unions are good, but . . . " was a common refrain.

The really controversial thing, though, wasn't joining the union but organizing it. We asked people to help build the union, and to help lead it. We asked them to sign a card, then to ask a friend to sign one, too; to commit to meeting regularly with an organizer; to join the organizing committee and bring the people they knew to meetings and to rallies. We asked a lot—too much, some thought. Many people were happy to sign a membership card and a petition from time to time but didn't want to go to more meetings or talk to colleagues about the union: they were already busy, so busy. They supported the union, they said, but they wanted it to leave them alone.

This seemed like a distinctive challenge of organizing graduate students, who on the one hand were notoriously overworked and never really off the clock, and on the other were not quite immiserated, at least at Yale. (In fact, this was partly because the university had increased graduate stipends and benefits over the years in order to undercut the union; it was the price of success.) Yet I came to think it was part of the challenge of organizing more generally. Reading Charles Payne's *I've Got the Light of Freedom*, about civil rights organizing in the Jim Crow South, I was struck by the list compiled by Student Nonviolent Coordinating Committee (SNCC) canvassers of reasons black Mississippians gave for not wanting to register to vote in the early 1960s, which could by and large have been given by grad students: "Just not interested." "Don't have the time to discuss voting." "Feel the politicians are going to do whatever they want, regardless of votes cast." "Too busy, engaged in personal affairs." "Wants time to think it over." "Satisfied with things as they are."

We were not, of course, fighting Jim Crow. Yale was miserable and feudal in many respects, but we were there temporarily and by choice; many of us feared our advisers but did not fear for our lives. We might give the same excuses, but they didn't mean the same things. Still, certain dynamics of the two organizing campaigns were similar, despite the obvious differences. People often told you why they weren't going to do something, often with perfectly good reasons, and you tried to convince them that they should.

We *were* all too busy, but the too-busyness wasn't really about time, or at least not only. Being too busy meant people didn't see why the union was worth making time for. Your job as an organizer was to find out what it was that people wanted to be different in their lives, and then to persuade people that it mattered whether they decided to do something about it. This is not the same thing as persuading people that the thing itself matters: they usually know it does. The task is to persuade people that *they* matter: they know they usually don't.

"THE BEGINNER WHO has learned a new language always translates it back into his mother tongue," Marx observed in *The Eighteenth Brumaire of Louis Bonaparte*, "but he assimilates the spirit of the new language and expresses himself freely in it only when he moves in it without recalling the old and when he forgets his native tongue." Organizing requires you to learn the language of politics so well that it becomes your own. Like any other language, it takes a lot of practice, during which time you often feel awkward and unsure. For this stage there are exercises like "stake, take, do," which lays out a sequence of questions for you: What is at stake for you? What will it take to win? What will you do about it? You have to start with what matters to you and the person you're organizing before jumping into how hard it's going to be and why they should do it anyway. These exercises are useful, but they can be stiff and artificial, because you're not really speaking politics yet: you're still translating. It's why new organizers often sound slightly robotic, repeating something they've clearly learned from someone else. But eventually you learn to leave this scaffolding behind and speak as yourself.

Often, however, you have to learn to speak differently—to speak as a different version of yourself. This means discarding many of your most familiar habits. Like many women, for a while I managed to get by on likability; I was already good at a certain kind of emotional labor. But as the asks got bigger, I hit a wall: people might spend thirty seconds signing a petition they didn't think mattered much because they liked me, but they weren't going to piss off their boss just to stay in my good graces. So I had to learn something else. "An axiom of organizers," writes Jane McAlevey, "is that every good organizing conversation makes everyone at least a little uncomfortable." The most awkward part is what McAlevey calls "the long uncomfortable silence"—the moment when you make an ask and let someone think about their answer. For a long time my biggest weakness was my tendency to shy away from making sure people knew that winning the things they said they wanted was up to them. Too often I tried to gloss over the discomfort instead of letting it sit. It was a lot easier to talk about our brilliant plan or how much support we had from our allies than to insist with the people I was organizing that whether we won our own union or not depended on them. As a result, people saw me as the union person who would deliver information and lay out a plan and keep them posted; they did not see themselves as union people who were also responsible for helping to win the things they said they wanted. McAlevey would call this a shortcut; we called it protecting people from the organizing. To soften the ask seems compassionate, but like any other protective measure, it condescends, and like any other shortcut, it makes things harder in the long run.

Realizing that it was not enough for people to like me was revelatory. I had to learn to be more comfortable with antagonism and disagreement, with putting a choice in front of people and letting them make it instead of smiling away tension and doing the work myself. I had to expect more from other people. With other organizers, I role-played the conversations I feared most before having them; afterward, I replayed them over and over in my head. I struggled to be different: the version of myself I wanted to be, someone who could move people and bend at least some tiny corner of the universe.

It's not easy to be the site of a battle for hegemony. It's not a beatific Whitmanesque "I contain multitudes"; it's an often painful struggle among your competing selves for dominance. You have one body and twenty-four hours in a day. An organizer asks what you'll do with them, concretely, now. You may not like your own answer. Your inner Thatcherite will raise its voice. You can't kill it off entirely; you will almost certainly find that it's a bigger part of you than you thought. But organizing burrows into the pores of your practical consciousness and asks you to choose the part of yourself that wants something other than common sense. It's unsettling. It can be alienating. And yet I also often felt I was finally reconciling parts of myself I'd tried to keep separate—what I thought, what I said, what I did. To organize, and to be organized, you have to keep in mind Hall's lesson: there is no true or false consciousness, no true self that organizing discovers or undoes. You too, Hall reminds us, were made by this world you hope to change. The more distant the world you want to live in is from the world that exists, the more deeply you yourself will feel this disjuncture. "I'm not cut out for this," people often say when they struggle with organizing. No one is: one isn't born an organizer, but becomes one.

THE SOBER, UNSEXY CHARACTER of organizing is often reromanticized in paeans to the "real work." Organizing's defenders are the most likely to insist that it is boring. For a generation maligned as flighty and self-absorbed, the mundanity and dullness signify authenticity, like political normcore. Organizing signals heroic commitment rather than faddish dilettantism, a noble resolve to do something in real life rather than trade memes in Facebook groups or dunk on Twitter enemies. It's true that organizing is the day-to-day work of politics—what Ella Baker called "spadework," the hard labor that prepares the ground for dramatic action. But I've never understood the charge of mundanity. Canvassing on a slow day can be tedious, but no other part of organizing has ever felt dull to me. Quite the opposite: nothing has ever felt more thrilling or more wrenching. Nothing has ever been harder to do, or harder to stop thinking about.

In *The Romance of American Communism*, Vivian Gornick tells a story I think about often, about a young woman tasked with selling the Communist Party newsletter *The Daily Worker*. "My God! How I hated selling the *Worker*!" she recalls. "I used to stand in front of the neighborhood movie on a Saturday night with sickness and terror in my heart, thrusting the paper at people who'd turn away from me or push me or even spit in my face. I dreaded it. Every week of my life for years I dreaded Saturday night. . . . God, I felt annihilated. But I did it, I did it. I did it because if I didn't do it, I couldn't face my comrades the next day. And we all did it for the same reason: we were accountable to each other."

No one ever spat in my face, but the rest I recognize. Though I didn't always dread organizing, I often woke up with a pit in my stomach, thinking of the phone calls I'd have to make that day and the people I was supposed to catch in the hallway after class. If anything, it was worse: the people I was talking to weren't strangers on the street, but friends and colleagues. It hurt when they stopped picking up the phone or looked away in the halls. Why on earth did I keep doing it?

Why did anyone? Because of their political beliefs? Maybe at first—I didn't want to be an armchair revolutionary. But sheer ideological conviction is rarely a predictor of someone's organizing stamina. More importantly: because your father was in a union, or—more likely—your mother needed to be; because your friend needed child care or you needed a therapist. These things genuinely mattered. But at some point you took a leap into excess. Was I really organizing forty hours a week because I wanted dental? At the rate we were going, I was unlikely to see any of the benefits anyway.

If much of my daily struggle was against the experience of grad school itself, I had also been looking for something like the union for a long time. I had ended up at the community-organizing nonprofit all those years prior after a few months spent volunteering with an anarchist collective in the ruins of New Orleans after Katrina, frustrated with the limits of mutual aid in the face of total state breakdown, and had been grasping for some kind of political activity that was both transformative and pragmatic ever since. Organizing was all about that dialectic. The union connected our demands—which were real but not exactly world-historical—to the long history of labor struggles, contemporary efforts to rebuild worker power, visions of a radically different future that we could play a role in bringing about.

So we demanded bread and butter, but we were ultimately organizing for the future of academic life, which was visibly crumbling around us; or for the revival of the labor movement, which had mostly already crumbled; or because it was intolerable to live in a city as segregated as New Haven and not do something about it. That our union had been organizing for three decades was both motivating and burdensome. We knew the past triumphs and failures, attachments and wounds; we inherited hope and melancholy. In this, it was not unlike the broader left: so much history, so much struggle—sometimes too much. We knew we had tuition waivers and stipends and health care because of the union; still, the fact that no one yet had won the whole thing in the end could be sobering. Why would we be the ones to succeed where so many others had failed? But it was also comforting: as there was GESO before us, so there would be GESO after. The campaign to unionize US Steel had taken nearly fifty years; more recently, Smithfield Foods had taken twenty-four.

Sometimes I felt I was organizing for the future of the entire world, in a deductive train that went: capitalism was going to devastate the planet; to fight it we needed strong unions, which meant new organizing, particularly in low-carbon fields like teaching, which meant building the academic labor movement—which meant that I needed to unionize the Yale political science department. It was absurd. Could I have been more quixotic, more grandiose, more self-important? Our style of organizing was intense, often all-consuming, and I knew that, too. I didn't always like it. Often I longed for a nice life, an easy life, the life of the mind that academics were supposed to have. Couldn't I just go to demonstrations here and there on the weekends before stopping off for groceries, the way I had before?

But that hadn't worked. And the gap between the smallness of everything I could realistically do and the largeness of everything I wanted to happen was so immense. I was deeply pessimistic, intellectually. The time in which to transform the global economy in order to prevent untold death and destruction shrank daily, and the forces of reaction grew stronger just as fast. So I *wanted* to do something ambitious and hard: something commensurate with the monstrosity of the world, with the distance of utopia and the nearness of catastrophe. There was so much I wanted to change, so many people I wanted to move. In the daily struggle to build the union and beat the boss and the odds, I saw something I desperately wanted to learn.

THE RELATIONALITY of organizing is maybe the hardest thing to understand before you've done it. But it is the most important. This is not because people are governed by emotions instead of reason, though they sometimes are. It's because the entire problem of collective action is that it's rational to act collectively where it's not to act alone. And you build the collective piece by piece.

Organizing relationships can be utopian: at their best, they offer the feminist dream of intimacy outside of romance or family. In the union, I loved people I did not know very well. In meetings I was often overcome with awe and affection at the courage and wisdom of the people there with me. I came to count many of the people I organized with as my dearest friends. When I needed help, there were always people I could call, people who would always pick up the phone, people I could and did talk to about anything. These relationships often served as a source of care and support in a world with too little of those things. But they were not only friendships, and not only emotional ballast. The people I looked to for support would also push me when it was called for, as I would them; that, I knew, was the deal.

Our relationships forged the practical commitments to one another that held the union together. They made us accountable to each other. They were difficult and multifaceted, often frustrating, intensely vulnerable, and potentially transformative but no less prone than any other relationship to carelessness, hurt, and betrayal, and always a lot of work. We were constantly building them and testing their limits, pushing each other harder the closer we got. They had to bear a lot of weight. In more abject moments, I wondered whether they were anything more than instrumental. More often, though, I wondered what was so menacing about usefulness that it threatened to contaminate all else.

The word *comrade*, Jodi Dean argues, names a political relationship, not a personal one: you are someone's comrade not because you like them but because you are on the same side of a struggle. Comrades are not neighbors, citizens, or friends; nor are they any kind of family, though you might call them brother or sister. The comrade has no race, gender, or nation. (As one meme goes: "My favorite gender-neutral pronoun is comrade.") Comrades are not even unique individuals; they are "multiple, replaceable, fungible." You can be comrades with millions of people you have never met and never will. Your relationship is ultimately with the political project you have in common. To many noncommunists, Dean readily admits, this instrumentalism is "horrifying": a confirmation that communism means submitting to the Borg. But the sameness of the comrade is a kind of genuine equality.

Being an organizer is like being a comrade in some ways but different in others. The people you organize alongside may be comrades, but the people you are organizing often aren't; the point of organiz-ing, after all, is to reach beyond the people who are already on your side and win over as many others as you can. So you can't assume the people you organize share your values; in fact, you should usually assume they don't. This means that unlike comrades, organizers aren't interchangeable. It matters who you are. McAlevey's theory of the organic leader is that people have to be organized by people they know and trust, not by strangers who claim to have the right ideas. The SNCC looked for "strong people"—not necessarily tra-ditional leaders, but people who were respected and trusted among their peers, on the logic that people would only take risky political action alongside people they trusted. When organizers reflect the people they organize, they win: when women of color organize other women of color, a 2007 paper by Kate Bronfenbrenner and Dorian Warren shows, they win almost 90 percent of elections. This cuts both ways: when women and people of color led the organizing in my department, we often struggled to get white men to take us seriously.

Yet the comradely element of organizing can also open up space for building relationships with people beyond those boundaries. It's not that class and race and gender disappear, transcended by the cause—but the need to work together to achieve a shared end provides a baseline of commonality that makes it possible to relate across difference and essential to figure out how. That's why you meet people one-on-one and talk about what you both care about, why you open up to someone you only know as a colleague or share with a stranger things you hardly even discuss with your friends. It's why I cried about the humiliation of the grad-school pecking order with my organizer when I wouldn't admit to anyone else that I was struggling. One-on-ones are countercultural: the conversations you have in them challenge your default expectations of who you can relate to, force you outside of the demographic categories that organize most of your life and the scripts you've learned for inter-acting with people accordingly. You build trust with people you have no prior reason to trust not simply by affirming your commitment to the shared project, your devotion to the Borg, but by coming to understand what brought someone else to it.

IN AUGUST 2016, the National Labor Relations Board issued the decision the academic labor movement had been waiting on for nearly the entire Obama presidency, declaring graduate workers eligible for labor protections. Graduate students across the country had been saying we were workers all along, but now the government agreed, and cited our efforts as part of the reason why. Our union filed for elections in ten departments the next week. It had suddenly become very real to everyone.

The first meeting in my department after we filed went nearly two hours over schedule. Almost everyone in political science was a union member on paper, but not all of them were sure they would vote yes. How much would the dues be? What would we get in a contract? Would the union make us go on strike? Would the other Yale locals make us go on strike? Would the international union we were affiliated with make us go on strike? What decision rules would we operate by? What decision rules were we operating by now? Did we have bylaws? Would Yale retaliate? Why mess with something that was pretty good already? Who had appointed us organizers anyway? Many were suspicious of organizing itself: we said that grad students should be able to choose for themselves whether they wanted a union, but here we were trying to convince people that they did. It didn't seem very democratic. Why not just take a vote right away? We could even do it online—the software was pretty good these days.

I thought the union was intensely democratic—we were, after all, seeking some amount of self-rule in our workplace and asking more people to take part in it. But democracy was more than aggregating our individual preferences or adhering to procedures; it was more like the attempt to find the general will. We were declaring ourselves a people, and that meant coming to see ourselves as part of a collective, not just a sample of rational actors. We want nondomination, another political theorist in the department said; things are pretty good now, but we're vulnerable to arbitrary power. This went over surprisingly well with the empiricists. Finally—the academic discussion I'd been waiting for! In any case, it was true that I wanted to persuade people of my position. I thought the union was good, and important, and I wanted them to vote for it. But I didn't just want their votes; I wanted them to want the union. There was no union without them.

Through the fall I organized like my life depended on it. An inveterate night owl, I began getting up early to go to morning meetings. I'd wake to a cluster of messages about plans for the day—where things stood with a petition, who I needed to talk to about signing it, who I needed to talk to about talking to someone else, when updates on my progress were expected—and try to shake off my anxiety in the shower. I dreaded everything in the morning. But once I was out of the house, I often loved my days.

They were long and exhausting. It was astonishing how much work everything took, how many minor crises could erupt in the course of a day, how many long-planned events came down to arrangements made at the last minute. I met the people I organized; I met my organizer; I met groups of organizers—in my department, across the union, across the city. I was constantly on the phone. I scarfed down protein bars between meetings and greasy slices at the pizzeria that served as the unofficial union hangout. My last meetings ended around eight; I went to the gym afterward and ran on the treadmill while simultaneously texting updates, cursing at presidential debates on CNN and fuming at whoever had most recently ranted about politics on Facebook but not called me back. I shared my apartment with two other grad students and a rotating cast of friends who had left New Haven long ago but now were returning to organize, crashing at our house on an air mattress in what was essentially an oversized closet. When I got home late at night I ate eggs on toast, the only meal I could be bothered to make, and wrote emails—so many emails.

Often I was resentful: How had I let this happen to my life? I had started out asking a couple of people to sign the occasional petition and stepped up gradually to pitch in where needed, and had somehow ended up responsible for my whole department. I sometimes felt trapped: if I quit, which I often wanted to do, I'd let down my fellow organizers, my department, the whole union, members of the other unions at Yale, our allies in New Haven, the housekeepers in hotels across the country whose dues were paying for our campaign, every grad student who'd ever worked to organize the union for the past thirty years. In my angriest moments I blamed the people who had gotten me started organizing in the first place. They hadn't told me it'd end up like this, that organizing would take over my whole life. I understood why people were reluctant to start doing this themselves. I realized all too well how it could spiral. But I was often angry at them, too. How did anyone expect anything to happen? Who did they expect to do all the work?

It wasn't fair: in fact, many people were up for doing a lot of things. As the election loomed, our people came to rally after rally, talked through update after update. They sat through NLRB hearings, in which faculty said we contributed nothing to the university, and went together to administrators' offices to deliver petitions saying they wanted a union. They took their pictures for the union, wore union buttons in class and while teaching, filed grievances and wrote op-eds about the things they wanted in a union contract. They were honest about their misgivings but also about why they really did want to win.

On the night of the 2016 presidential election I stayed up very late. I woke up a few hours after Trump's victory speech to go to a union meeting, hungover and exhausted but grateful to have something to do. Our election, at least, was still to come, and I was more determined than ever to win it. I went to meetings every day for the next six months, usually more than one, and I was grateful for nearly all of them. Family and friends elsewhere described feeling despair, depression, fear. But I wasn't mourning—I was organizing! I rode a wave of righteous exhilaration. I was sure that if everyone in the country who thought as I did was doing what I was, things would be very different. We would show that the left could win despite Trump.

But if the wave of history was still cresting, it increasingly seemed more likely to crush us than carry us to victory. We had expected to vote at the end of 2016; we had also expected a Clinton presidency. Trump had pandered to workers, but labor still had a huge target on its back. We finally got our election order at the end of January, a few days after Trump's inauguration. We voted a few weeks later.

On the eve of the election, I realized I had never wanted anything so much in my life, and had never wanted so badly something over which I ultimately had so little control. I had organized all I could, but at the end of the day, people would make their own choices. It was a strange feeling, after a life spent chasing individual achievement, to want something that I could only have if other people wanted it too. And if on the one hand organizing was an exercise in learning that you could do so much more than you thought—that you could talk to people, find out they wanted the same things you did, and fight together—it was also a lesson in limits. You simply could not make someone do something they had decided not to do.

We won in my department, with exactly the number of yes votes we'd counted on. And we won in all but one of the other departments in which we'd filed, most in a blowout. That night, we sang "Solidarity Forever" while hugging one another in the university building where the election had been held and, later, walking down the street on the way to my house once the bar had closed, mumbling the verses but bellowing the chorus.

IT WASN'T THE END. We needed a contract, which meant we needed to make Yale negotiate with us, something they clearly had no intention of doing. Our best shot was to get the NLRB to certify our election result before Trump appointed a Republican majority: at that point, Yale would have no more legal recourse and would have to break the law to bust our union. But in the meantime, they could simply run out the clock through months of legal appeals. (We had all by now become experts on the dysfunctions of federal labor law.) We would have to force the administration's hand—but only a few weeks remained of the semester. The thirty-odd members of the union's cross-departmental decision-making body, nominally elected by our departments but realistically in our positions by virtue of our willingness to do an ungodly amount of organizing, decided to do what we could with the time we had: we would undertake a month of intensive action in order to shame Yale into backing down. At the center of the campaign would be a group of union members who would fast on a rotating but continuous basis. The fast was the really controversial thing, debated over two intense days of meetings; it was the thing that seemed to aggravate the tension between our relatively comfortable position and our commitment to full-blown combat with the administration. Weren't hunger strikes the tactic of prisoners and others operating from a position of weakness, with nothing left but their bodies to use? Wasn't this a step too far, even for us? I'd been skeptical at first; a fast didn't seem inappropriate so much as embarrassing, like something a small group of overeager undergrads would do. We were a well-organized union with hundreds of members coming fresh off an election victory; surely we could do better. But I couldn't imagine organizing a strike in a month. UNITE HERE had a history of using fasts as a tactic, following Cesar Chavez's fasts for the United Farm Workers. I came to think it was our best shot, and set about convincing other people.

Our union overnight became an insurrectionary outfit engaged in quasi-guerrilla warfare. Every day for a month we did everything we possibly could to disrupt the daily life of the university and make ourselves impossible for Yale to ignore. We staged feint actions to distract Yale's cops, built a massive structure in front of the president's office on Beinecke Plaza, and camped out around the clock to defend it, prepared to take arrest if it was dismantled. The first night, dozens of people—union members, faculty, students, friends, supporters—stayed at the structure all night, reading and talking and grading and playing games in some kind of prefiguration of academic utopia that I felt I would have done anything to preserve. Wisely, Yale let it be. Playing up Yale's union-busting, we dropped banners reading TRUMP UNIVERSITY in the business school library and got a faculty member to write about our hunger strike in the *New York Times*. We chanted outside the president's house, fresh off a $17 million renovation, and outside the Greenwich mansions of Yale Corporation board members on Sunday mornings while their neighbors literally rode by on horseback. I believed that we would win: my intellect and will were in perfect alignment. I didn't think twice before fasting for nine days. In many ways it was easier than organizing: all I had to do was not eat. In a manic email I wrote to a friend six days in, I called it "weirdly serene." My mother worried but also pitched in: she publicly confronted Gina Raimondo, a trustee of the Yale Corporation till then favored by my mother by virtue of being Rhode Island's first female governor, for failing to back the union while her daughter wasted away.

The university waited out the barrage of negative press and took down our structure after the semester had ended, when campus was quiet in the wee hours before alumni weekend. Later that summer, my organizers asked me to take a leave of absence from school and organize full-time for the continuation of the contract campaign in the fall. Any day now—any day now!—the NLRB would hand down our final certifications. We would be in a strong position to escalate again when school started up again in the fall.

I realized we had to escalate; I recognized that I could help. I just didn't want to do it. Once the euphoria of the month of action had subsided, I had crashed. I was exhausted. My will was flagging. I didn't want to spend my days calling people who were pissed off about all the drama of the fast and asking them to talk it through with me, to talk about how even though we hadn't won yet we still could, if they just did a few more things. I didn't want to spend every day in low-level combat, absorbing everyone else's bad feelings and trying to generate the energy to fight some more. There was always a next step; I was finally beginning to realize there always would be. I wanted to move to New York and finish my dissertation and take weekends off, or at least spend them working on my own projects like everyone else. I gave up my apartment in New Haven and started planning my move.

BUT I DIDN'T LEAVE. To some it looked like I had been brainwashed: I had insisted I absolutely wasn't coming back. And yet there I was. What had the union done to me?

No one was making me stay; no one really could. Other organizers could tell me why they thought I had to stay, but if I had really made up my mind to leave, I could live with that. I'd decided not to go on leave to organize once before. But this time I had agonized over the decision. The exhilaration of the spring had tilted wildly in the opposite direction. All I could see was fear and guilt in all directions. I was certain that I would regret either choice.

Why did I stay? Ultimately, for the same reason I had done everything else. I liked who I was when I put myself out there with other people again and again. I was braver and kinder, more generous and more confident. I wanted to live in a world where my voice mattered, where I could see the people around me as comrades instead of competitors. The union was imperfect in ways that I knew as well as anyone, but it was the closest I had come to that kind of world, and I simply could not convince myself that at that moment, for those few months, there was anything I could do that mattered more than trying to bring it into being.

We didn't win. All summer the NLRB was silent. In the fall, Trump's appointees were confirmed. Inside the union, things fell apart. We had been in what was supposedly the home stretch for months. We had asked a lot from people for a long time, pushed each other hard to hit our goals for rally turnouts and petition signatures. In the drive to force Yale to the table, our group of ultracommitted organizers had gotten out ahead of the rest of the membership and kept going; most of us had stretched our relationships in our departments as far as they would go, on the expectation that once we won, everyone else would come along. We had accepted these difficulties as the price of winning. But winning always seemed to be around just one more corner. Why would this time be any different? As our prospects faded, so did trust in the union leadership, which was predicated at least in part on the idea that we knew what we were doing. All the frustrations, criticisms, and resentments suppressed in the name of victory resurged: the union was undemocratic, delusional, instrumentalizing, manipulative. I struggled to hold things together through the worst few months of my life, and in the winter, I moved to New York, just a little behind schedule.

WHEN I STOPPED ORGANIZING, my life returned to normal—at least, to the normal of my life before grad school, where I read about politics and thought about politics and talked about politics and wrote about politics but did politics hardly at all. I read more, I slept more, I ate better. I watched more TV. My life was nicer in many ways. With Brecht, I would gladly be wise. But you don't get to choose your times. And in dark ones, I knew I was doing nothing that mattered.

I waited for someone to invite me to a meeting. No one did. Many days I talked to no one: it was astonishing how much time you could spend alone. I cried less; I laughed less. I worried about the job market and what people I didn't know would think of me. Was this anxious, self-absorbed person really a more authentic self than the one I'd tried to forge? I hoped not.

I still thought about organizing all the time. I read and read, trying to understand what had happened, what had gone wrong. I saw different situations, different organizing styles, different stakes, but the same conflicts, the same tensions, the same breakdowns. *The Romance of American Communism* ends on a note of tragedy: Gornick finally understands the heartbreak of the Communists among whom she grew up as she watches the feminist movement to which she belonged dissolve into acrimony. Their fate, she comes to think, revealed the "agony at the heart of radicalism," the "magnificent sorrow" of self-creation. But this isn't the part of the essay where I conclude that political life is tragically impossible. It's where I try to figure out how to get back to it.

The Labor Notes manual *Secrets of a Successful Organizer* ends with a secret for the unsuccessful one: "One hard reality about organizing: you're going to fail a lot. You'll lose more often than you win." If the secret to winning isn't really a secret—you just keep organizing and organizing and organizing so that along with all the losses and setbacks some victories start to pile up—then maybe the question of how to win is just a question of how to keep doing it, after you win and after you lose.

The union kept on. I worry I'll never do anything like it again, and I worry that I will.

2019

THE FEMINIST

TONY TULATHIMUTTE

IF YOU ASK HIM WHERE HE WENT TO HIGH SCHOOL, HE LIKES TO boast that, actually, he went to an all-girls school. That was sort of true—he was one of five males at a progressive private school that had gone co-ed just before he'd enrolled. People always reply: Ooh la la, lucky guy! You must've had your pick. Which irritates him, because it implied women would only date him if there were no other options, and because he hadn't dated anyone in high school. One classmate junior year had a crush on him, but he wasn't attracted to her curvaceous body type so felt justified in rejecting her, just as he'd been rejected many times himself.

Still, the school ingrained in him, if not feminist values per se, the *value* of feminist values. It had been cool, or at least normal, to identify as asexual. And though he didn't, he figured it was a better label than "virgin." His friends, mostly female, told him he was refreshingly attentive and trustworthy for a boy. Meanwhile he is grateful for the knowledge that *female* was best used as an adjective, that sexism harms men too (though not nearly to the extent that it harms women), and that certain men pretend to be feminists just to get laid. After he graduated he started to feel slightly sheepish about never having even kissed anyone. Everyone knows, though, that real dating starts in college, where nobody will be aware of his track record.

But in college, he encounters the alien system of codes and manners that govern flirting, conveyed in subtextual cues no more perceptible to him than ultraviolet radiation. Learning in high school about body positivity and gender norms and the cultural construction of beauty led him to believe that adults aren't obsessed with looks. This turns out to be untrue, even among his new female friends, who complain about how shallow men are. Now that he's self-conscious, he realizes he can't compete along conventional standards of height, weight, grip strength, whatever. How can he hope to attract anyone with his narrow shoulders?

The women he tries to date offer him friendship instead, so once again, most of his friends are women. This is fine: it's their prerogative, and anyway, lots of relationships begin platonically—especially for guys with narrow shoulders. But soon a pattern emerges. The first time, as he is leaving his friend's dorm room, he surprises himself by saying: Hey, this might be super random, and she can totally say no, but he's attracted to her, so did she want to go on a "date" date, sometime? In a casual and normal voice. And she says, "Oh," and filibusters—she had *no idea* he felt that way, and she doesn't want to risk spoiling the good thing they have by making it a *thing*, she just wants to stay . . . and he rushes to assure her that it's valid, no, totally valid, he knows friendship isn't a downgrade, sorry for being weird. Ugh!

Right? she replies, dating's so overrated and meaningless in college anyway, and she knows that *he* knows he'll find someone who deserves him, because he's great, really great, so thoughtful, *so* smart, not like these SAE sideways-hat-wearing dudebros, but of course he already knows that, and she really appreciates it. Then he thanks her for being honest, because it's proof their friendship is real, and don't worry about him, he gets it.

He does get it. It sort of kills him, but he knows his rejector was only trying to spare his feelings, since men often react badly to "hard rejection." So he validates her condolences and communicates them back until she's convinced he'll be fine. "Grrr, friend-zoned again!" he says, shaking his fists toward the ceiling, and they laugh together and hug and he walks back to his dorm just before sunrise.

He gets into bed and sighs. While he's confident he handled everything respectfully, the girl's praise only reminds him that none of his ostensibly good qualities are attractive enough to even warrant him a chance, which makes them seem worthless. He also suspects that her flattery was . . . exaggerated, and a bit . . . patronizing? If she didn't think friendship was a downgrade, she wouldn't have said she "*just* wanted to stay friends." By persuading him to reject himself, was she just offloading her guilt? He stews at the familiarity of the situation: once again, *he's* got to be the one who accepts, forgives, tolerates, pretends not to be wounded, pretends he has stopped hoping—all this sapping emotional labor not just to preserve his dignity and assuage her guilt, but also because he doesn't want to spoil his chances of dating her in the future, since it's her prerogative, after all, to change her mind.

Still, he respects her decision. He gets out of bed, feeling compelled to let her know where he stands, to check in, so he composes a long postmortem email, reconstructing everything that happened from the beginning, assuring her that he knew nobody was to blame for a lack of attraction, and that if it isn't clear, yes, he *is* interested in her, but he's not one of those fake-feminist guys who snubs any woman he can't fuck, so, sorry if this is com*plete*ly graceless and exhausting, by no means is he making his embarrassment her problem, he just wants to get everything out in the open. He hits send.

An hour later he sends a second email: Just out of curiosity, could she say a little about *why* she rejected him? It'd be really helpful for him. Is it because he's narrow-shouldered? Is that a deal breaker for her? Because he can't help that, as she knows. Or is it a specific thing he did or said, because if so, they could discuss that, clear up any miscommunications. Anyway, he'll be fine, hopes everything's cool—and if she ever changes her mind, he'll be around!

Considering his tremendous effort to be vulnerable, it seems unfair when a day passes with no reply. Fearing that he might not get one at all, he writes a third email clarifying that she's by no means obliged to reply, though if she wants to, he'd love hearing her thoughts. He is somewhat annoyed when she again doesn't reply, though he's glad to have given her that option. At least nothing's been left unsaid.

This exact scenario happens four or five more times. Later, when he relates these incidents, lightheartedly, to his other female friends, they assure him he's interesting, smart, thoughtful, good-looking (though they never say *hot*), that nothing's wrong with him. "It's so bizarre that you're single," they say, trying to mollify him with optimism, as if experience has made them objective. But they have no experience of having no experience. He figures that even bad relationships are better than none, since they prepare you for future relationships, and heartbreak is romantic and dignified, whereas rejection just makes you a loser. Short of outright abuse, the worst case is to be in his position.

Anyway, he doesn't want pity; he wants not to need it. He drops hints to his friends to set him up with their friends, but for some reason they never follow through.

Lacking other options, he decides there are other ways to stand out and be attractive. He cultivates academic achievement, surmising that income and status and intellect will enhance his appeal. And they do, but not for him: the same standards prevail in his field as everywhere else. The rich, beautiful, and broad-shouldered still get all the attention.

Then again, so do the terrible and ugly! His female friends keep dating men with cratered skin, awkward manners, poor hygiene; talentless schlubs identified by their hobbies and tastes; philandering worms; controlling, abusive dirtbags. Even his awkward gay college roommate had had a girlfriend in high school, before he'd come out. Maybe they all deserved love—but surely no more than him? At a house party, one friend talks about going home with a guy the night before who said he just wanted to sleep next to her, but around 1 AM she awoke to him grunting as he completed the process of jerking off on her leg. When she cussed him out, he claimed he was "overcome by raw animal passion" and "couldn't help it," and she still let him stay. "Whatever, we'll probably be married in three years," she says, rolling her eyes.

He's just about to insist she shouldn't devalue herself like that, that she's just been violated and maybe shouldn't be out tonight, should go home and practice self-care—and is astounded when everyone, including her, starts laughing. He joins in, figuring that this is all part of the cathartic process, even though it sounds to him like a clear case of SA. He'd asked her out once before; a literal *rapist* is more appealing than him? But he keeps silent as another female friend says, "Men are dogshit." And sure, fair, he understands they mean the patriarchy and not him specifically—but why'd she say that with him standing *right there*, unless he didn't count as a man? Not wanting to seem fragile or impugn their judgment or center the conversation on himself, he instead files this incident away in a thickening dossier of unfairness, privately reasoning that if they're going to keep dating assholes, what do they expect.

He gut-checks himself to make sure his concern for his trauma-tized friend is legitimate before texting her later: "Hey, I'm around if you need to talk about what happened. or even just watch trashy TV :) whenever wherever!"

She doesn't reply.

Dragging his virginity like a body bag into his midtwenties, he watches a certain amount of dom-oriented porn, probably due to internalized sexism, but he's read that porn is a safe, healthy venue to explore kink, that sexuality is neither a choice nor shameful, espe-cially if the studios follow good labor and aftercare practices. His female friends agree, though he does not mention that he seeks out actresses that look like them, which he deems acceptable as long as he consumes it critically, demarcating fantasy from reality.

He's more worried about *physical* desensitization: he doesn't use lubrication, because his roommates would overhear it. He comes to prefer the intensity of this "dry" method, but feels the friction is somehow eroding his psyche, and possibly dulling his penis nerves. He resolves to masturbate with a condom to wean himself. He wonders in what other ways touch, or the lack of it, has warped him. He's read about that study of baby monkeys who were denied soft physical contact and grew up disturbed and sickly. It's hard for him to believe chastity was ever associated with purity, when it feels like putrescence, his blood browning and saliva clouding with pus, each passing day rendering him more leprously foul to the senses. What about those venerable virgo intacta like Kant, Dickinson, Newton? Their virginity was a matter of will. They believed God loved them for it.

At lunch one day, two of his male coworkers offer unsolicited dating advice, relishing the chance to showboat their sexual proficiencies. He's too honest and available, not aggressive enough—friend-zone shit, they say unironically. Just don't be a fucking pussy is all! You gotta challenge them, be a puzzle for them to work out, that's just how girls' brains work, it's evolution. They offer grotesquely specific advice about eye contact and hair touching. Learn palmistry, they say, bitches love getting their palms read.

Then they ask him how he makes a move; he says he just asks. "Wait, you *ask* if you can kiss them? My man," one says, laughing and slapping his back, "you don't *ask*." With jagged touchiness, he calls them out, insisting that consent is nonnegotiable, that even if they're joking, it's textbook rape culture.

"Well, what makes you think you can speak for them," one says, smirking. "You're a guy too. Why do you know better than us what women prefer? Especially considering they're dating us."

He's *not* speaking for women, he says—unsure of how he'll answer, but certain he has something to say—he's . . . speaking *against* men who're speaking against women.

"Go ahead then," his coworker smirks, "ask your *female friends* what they think."

Bristling, he calls his QPOC agender friend from his college co-op, whom he's always gotten along well with, in part because he's never been attracted to them. He repeats what his coworkers said, using a "dumb guy" voice. His friend says, "Well, that's gross," and makes him swear never to become a mind-gamey asshole. They say that the friend zone is obviously a sexist canard that lets losers (like who, he wonders) blame their own unattractiveness on women. He agrees; then asks if it isn't true that some guys lack charisma or attractiveness, and are thus more prone to getting befriended? "Maybe," they say. He asks his friend if mind games work. "Sometimes," they say, "that's why it's so common. But it's not good." Never, he asks? "OK, yeah, shit's complicated. Some people are old-fashioned, or mistake abuse for affection. Doesn't mean we should *encourage* it." He asks if it's wrong to ask permission to kiss someone. "Depends more on how you ask." He asks if they personally would prefer it. "No, but I'm not all women. I'm not even *a* woman." He asks if they believe most women would prefer it. "Maybe, maybe not, but things are changing. Listen, I'm not sure what you're trying to get out of me here. Again: I'm *not* a woman." Of course he knows that, he replies, but it's important to him, especially as a privileged white man, to avoid placing the burden of educating him about women's experiences on a woman, which was why it's so great to have friends of other genders. His friend says, "Yeah, I guess." He thanks them for taking his call so late at night.

Despite the ambiguous advice, he decides that sheer experience and exposure will improve his odds. So he resorts to online dating, cropping out his narrow shoulders from his photos and carefully wording his bio:

> He / him. Unshakably serious about consent. Loves books, Thai cooking, a glass (or three) of Vinho Verde on my balcony, endless conversation . . . did I mention books? ;) Trans women are women (duh). All body types very welcome!

He suspects some of it risks sounding tryhard, but he prefers clarity over fake mystique, and why wouldn't women prefer a vocal ally?

He sends brief but thoughtful, grammatical messages, like a link to a *Psychology Today* article about limerence, followed by: "Fascinating topic. I'm a total sucker for the intersections of psychology and romance. Would love to talk it over at the venue of your choosing!" The few dates this brings only yield more rejection: three postpone indefinitely, then ghost; three more are no-shows. One leaves while he's in the bathroom.

Dating online, he realizes, one has to choose either fraudulence or honesty that can't compete with fraudulence. But then he thinks: Isn't the idea that women don't know what's best for them sexist, informed by his own petty resentment? Troubled by this paradox and unable to sleep, he texts his QPOC friend: Be honest: has he actually been a creep this whole time? Is that why he's been single for thirty years? His friend texts back, "okay but can you really count the first 16 years," then says that he *should* feel weird about his concerns, but that he hasn't done anything, and a creep probably wouldn't agonize so much over whether he was a creep, good night. He's still unnerved, but relieved that someone who was once female-identified has given him a pass.

He withdraws into work. Whereas before he only went out in hopes of meeting someone, now he stays in so he won't have to see the couples, the inaccessible women, the broad-shouldered men; even a passing whiff of plain aloe lotion on a woman's skin makes him feel structurally unsound and shivery through his linings.

At age 32, he has sex. One day on social media he catches a photo of the girl—the woman—he rejected in high school. She's cleaned up; her body type is no longer curvaceous, and he likes how she always wears a skirt and leggings, a thin dark cardigan over a blouse—a personal uniform suggesting fidelity to figured-out principles—but dislikes how her dyed red hair pinches off in a tiny bun that reminds him of the meaty tail-nubs on docked pit bulls, though that's fixable. They live in the same city. He messages her and suggests they meet.

She arrives at their date forty minutes late, which he tolerates, knowing that women's time is taxed by the pressures of female grooming. For about fifteen minutes their catch-up chat is small but promisingly pleasant. He insists on paying for drinks, joking that it's not chivalry, it's reparations for sexism. But he regrets it because, on her third whisky ginger (and his first), she starts rambling about a guy who dumped her years ago. Jokes about her eating disorder. Every few minutes her face scrunches like she's about to cry, then reverts weirdly to normal. Her blouse untucks, and when a guy playing pool nearby positions his cue close to her face, she slaps it to the floor.

Lonely as he is, does he deserve someone unstable? He'll have to reject her again, like in high school. What will he say? That he doesn't want to waste her time, that he thinks she's super great but isn't feeling a vibe . . . whatever he says, he wants to make her reaction feel valid.

But hours later he has not figured out a compassionate enough way to phrase it, and at this point, as they're leaving the bar, he decides he might as well kiss her good night for the sake of casual experience, and let her down over text message when he finds the right phrasing. So he asks if he can kiss her. She says, "Uhhhh, no." He asks why not. "What do you mean *why not*?" she says. "Because I don't *want* to. Who the fuck asks 'why not'? Fucking asshole."

He wonders if she is testing him. He asks if she is testing him. This time she gives him a two-armed shove, sending him to the ground, and instead of yelling, her mouth opens into a smile and she says, "Oh my god are you wearing *shoulder pads*?"

Getting up, he briefly considers shoving her back, which would only be fair. But she is doubled over and clutching her calves laughing, and then says, with unbelievable nonchalance, "OK, wait, I'm sorry dude, I didn't mean to push you that hard. Come on, is this happening or what?"

The sex disappoints; her moans and arches feel contrived, and something—maybe his dulled nerves—keeps deferring his orgasm; she gets impatient and pushes him away. He acquiesces, not having finished, his embarrassing frustration mitigated only by the unburdening of his virginity, and the prospect of telling everyone about it. To reassure her that his sexual awkwardness was not her fault, he tells her he thinks she's beautiful. She waits nearly ten seconds and replies, "Yeah, well, uh, you have a beautiful mind."

After this incident, he develops thoughts of self-harm, which are curbed by his awareness that rejection, loneliness, and sexual frustration are nothing compared with institutional and historical oppression. He knows sadness is a symptom of his entitlement.

Being a thirtysomething, he feels too young to give up and too old to adapt. His self-reliance has ossified into a lifestyle of craved, defended solitude. He can't imagine having to share a bed every night, not being able to read or stay in or leave parties when he wants. Solitude is fine, unwantedness is not. And as he's aged, has his intimacy with his female friends deepened? Did these friends, who always maintained that romantic love is overrated, provide an alternative to monogamous romance? No. They've all found partners and moved on to mature, cohabit, fuck, get married, spawn. Even if they're miserable, at least they're living real lives, with partners who prioritize them. Lately he sees them once a month tops, even though he's known them *far* longer than their partners. They've stopped inviting him to dinner parties because *It was a couples thing and you would've hated it*, which, while true, was still exclusionary, backed by the hegemonic, regressive institution of monogamy. He realizes that these female friends have, at last, completed their long-term rejections of him; that, without ever having had a girlfriend, his life is strewn with exes, friends without benefits. But he can't complain about his friends to his friends. His male friends would roast him, or pretend to sympathize but secretly think he's a pussy. His female friends might think he's passive-aggressively implicating them, and also think he's a pussy.

Since any rejection now paralyzes him with rage for weeks, he stops dating. He resents his married friends, his contently single friends, his unhappily single friends who nonetheless have casual sex, and his parents when they gently ask about his dating life. He also resents the grotesque fixations that have cropped up lately, like: If he's only ever used condoms and *the epidermis of his penis* has never contacted *the mucous membrane of a vagina*, if he's never *ejaculated into a birth canal*, does that technically make him a virgin? Was masturbation lowering his testosterone count, contributing to his narrow shoulders? And does that give women the impression that he has a small penis, which he objectively does *not*?

All he's doing is sharing some of these gripes at a picnic one afternoon when his QPOC agender friend asks him why he doesn't just call that girl from high school he went on that date with? He replies that just because he wants to be in a relationship doesn't mean he has to settle for a sociopath.

"See, you're moving the goal posts," his QPOC friend replies. "It's easy to feel sorry for yourself when you keep redefining rejection, because you won't let go of it. You refuse pity but crave it so much that you won't admit how strongly you invite it."

He says they're being facile, though he knows their point is rather nuanced and specific, he just hasn't considered it before, but he can't walk it back now.

"I'm *facile*?" his friend says. "Nah, I'm tired. That's what it is, I'm tired," they say from behind their sunglasses, waving their mimosa. "I know you identify as a reject, I know that's, like, your 'brand,' like it's some unprecedented form of suffering that gives you secret wisdom. All this nonstop high-frequency whining, that's what's *facile*."

He presses his lips shut while his brain feels like a swirling case of lottery balls, as his friend, pausing to hit a spliff, continues: "I mean, what the fuck do you want? Somehow you got a shit deal. Nobody knows why. Maybe it's like you never really grappled with this shit because you thought you were exempt. But you refuse to change and are *shocked* when nothing changes. It's not like you enjoy it, but you *do* enjoy pushing other people's faces in it, that's your main consolation. Weird how you're always right about rejection, since nobody's ever had it worse, nobody's as pure and as wronged as you. Yo everyone! Check out the Woman Respecter! Last principled man right here! And that's why you need it, because you get to convince yourself you're being rejected for your virtue, not cause you're a bummer. You've turned your loneliness into this, like, fetish necklace of martyrdom. And all of us," they gesture around to other picnickers, "have to sit here and rubber-stamp your feminism. If we don't indulge your wallowing, we're being callous and, like, complicit with some diabolical global conspiracy that's keeping you from getting laid. But if we do, then we're 'disingenuous' because none of us will fuck you ourselves. Right? Am I right, everyone? Hands up, who agrees?"

Three women's hands shoot up, followed more slowly by the rest.

His QPOC friend gestures at them like, *Behold.* "I just, like . . . I'nno what to say man, except, motherfucking cishets! I for one am bored of your scab collection. I'm sorry your dick is sad or whatever. Suck it up, you bitter little boy, and move on."

Oh, fantastic. That's fucking great. The clearest example yet of how even his friends dismiss him with straw-man arguments. Because he refuses easy consolation, they'd rather call him self-sabotaging, instead of thinking critically for *one second* about the bullshit social biases narrow-shouldered men suffer under, which originate in the same toxic masculinity they supposedly abhor. He doesn't have the luxury of having fun fresh relationship drama like theirs, so they got bored of him, even though listening to his problems is far easier than *living through* them.

Vitrified with outrage, he replies to his friend that they were minimizing his problems just because rejection wasn't on some Official Registry of Politicized Traumas. He can't address his feelings just because worse things happen? By that logic, he could say that their stupid anxieties about dating bi women aren't important because they're not being rounded up and pushed off rooftops like queer people in Syria. But *he* wouldn't say that to a QPOC friend! He would listen!

"Wo-ow-ow. You really don't want to press this," his friend warns, removing their sunglasses. "And BTdubs, I'm not your 'QPOC friend.'"

Are you fucking kidding me, he shouts, unsure if his exasperation is mock or real, you took it there, *you* made it about identity, all
I'm doing is reflecting *literally the same exact* sentiment as you, so
don't evade the point, and don't get the idea that framing it as a call-
out puts you in the right! And *I* brought those mimosas, by the way!

He grabs at his friend's drink. Everyone scrambles. His QPOC
friend's friend, a much larger man, gets up and tells him, "OK, my
guy, time to move along." It defies all reason that he's getting ejected
from a picnic just for airing opinions in good faith, by this swollen
alpha dickhead flaunting his gallantry. This was the male ally they
preferred: not the intellectual who challenged them as equals in an
open dialogue, but this muscle-confused fucking silverback *gorilla*.
They're all happy to hide behind patriarchy when it suits them. He
snatches up his READ MORE WOMEN tote bag and leaves.

On his way home, with jittering fingers, he gets on his phone to
block his drunk QPOC friend on social media and sees they've posted:
"smh @ 'woke' men who squawk abt their feminism but rly hang out
with women bc of the gendered power advantage foooooooooh."

One of the women who was at the picnic replied "omg dead-
assssss," which got thirty-six likes. The thought of thirty-six people
reading this petty, unsubstantiated accusation, siding with the
QPOC, and spreading gossip leads him to mass-block everyone who
did nothing to help him at the picnic.

He counterposts, "smh @ performative 'woke' 'queer' ppl who
pretend to care abt equality but rly just get off on humiliating strong
male allies who are trying to help and consequently punishing and
alienating them for fervently upholding the basic tenets of contemporary feminism foooooooooh," but deletes it because he can't figure
out how to make it sound good, which is unfair, because the point
is valid.

It would be pathetic now to keep seeing those friends. Maintaining friendships costs his female and agender friends nothing, but
it costs him a daily toll of endless triggering, which they've never
once acknowledged. They liked having him around to benefit from

his insight and generosity, but the moment he had genuine feelings for them as equals, it's like his attraction was some morsel of filth he'd tried to trick them into swallowing. Yet, free-falling into his late thirties, it's harder to make new friends. Whenever he stays in, he feels anxious about not meeting new people, but whenever he goes out, he spends the whole night scanning some depressing bar or art space for potential mates, then goes home alone, weary and dark-minded, to face the sight of his empty bed, which is even emptier after he gets in it, lying awake with pangs of loneliness that feel like getting stabbed through a very soft pillow. He lost his virginity so long ago it's grown back.

On one of these long nights, an ugly curtain lifts in his head: he's old enough to know that relationships don't guarantee happiness, that the source of his pain is an illusion agonizingly elaborated over decades. His mental habits are so ingrained that even if he got a girlfriend, he'd still feel rejected. Around this time he starts to feel breathless, a constant compression garment around his lungs. His stomach is tense and swollen as a basketball, he urinates frequently, his heart skitters and rushes, he has trouble swallowing. He can seldom achieve full erection even while masturbating: he's finally managed to sexually bore even himself. One day at work, while he's waiting for the microwave to finish heating up a cheese-and-mushroom tartlet, a quantity of urine dribbles out unbidden.

His PCP refers him to a blood lab and a urologist, who conducts an ultrasound and diagnoses him with a levator spasm, probably stress related. In his own online research, he reads that loneliness can indeed manifest psychosomatically, and even shorten your life span. He also reads that children bear trace amounts of the DNA of all their mother's sex partners in their own DNA—so it was true, confirming suspicions he didn't even know he had, that sex partners matter *biologically*; they leave a mark.

The findings send him into action. He takes zinc sulfate, lysine, and arginine to increase seminal volume, horny goat weed and pumpkin-seed extract for libido. The goal is to get his ejaculate to "arc" again. When after three months he sees no enhancements except for a longer post-JO cleanup, he begins using a penis pump, no matter the vascular damage. If it's going to be numb and useless it may as well be big.

He knows he is sick and must find relief. He wants so badly to believe that his life isn't broken and can still bring satisfaction. He eats healthy, exercises, takes improv classes, and consolidates his reputation at work, though he'd long since lost his relish for it when he realized it didn't magically improve his dating odds. None of it does.

At work, when he isn't thinking *This is all I'm good for*, he thinks *I should kill myself.* But he imagines his female ex-friends hearing of his death and not caring, or even laughing; it wouldn't be tragic. This maddening thought keeps him dismally alive. In each second is the slow fizz of cell death, telomeres shedding their base pairs two by two like an ignited fuse.

He tries paying for sex, hoping more experience will give him confidence, and while he is strongly pro–sex workers' rights, he still resents having to pay for something that someone, somewhere, ought to offer enthusiastically. Even while having sex, it comes freighted with so many expectations, such intense anticipation of disappointment, that he doesn't enjoy it much. To finish he silently imagines the woman is pregnant and that his more potent semen is killing off the other man's embryo and displacing it with his own. He tips well.

Sometime after turning 35, he makes a rare excursion from his apartment to visit his old favorite tapas restaurant in a hip neighborhood he lived in a decade ago. The foyer is crammed and it's a forty-minute wait. This place never used to be crowded, it had been a quiet place to read without feeling lonely; now it is massed with couples and their offspring colonizing yet another space, basking in the triumphalism of love, instead of confronting the real ugliness of their prejudice and superiority and, yes, the *privilege* that they profit from.

He waits out on the muggy sidewalk until his name is called, and at the entrance, a fleet of strollers exits the restaurant through the narrow vestibule. He flattens against the plastic wall to let three, four strollers pass, then tries to enter the restaurant when a fifth woman approaches, pushing an enormous three-wheeler with BMX tires and a crusty-eyed baby scrunched inside it. He expects her to let him through, but instead she pushes the vestibule door open and he feels and hears a crack, looks down at his leather sandals and sees his big toenail folded up at an astonishing angle, says, Ow ow ow. Instead of apologizing, she trades an eyeroll with her husband, who says, "Buddy, she can't get *through* if you don't *move back.*"

Your convenience doesn't outweigh mine, he asserts to the father; instead of replying, the father pushes him by the shoulder out onto the sidewalk, violating his bodily autonomy.

Being civil and slow to anger, he says nothing, even as fury chain-reacts down through his chest. The pack of parents recedes down the block, spanning the sidewalk's whole width, and now, first limping then sprinting, he catches up to them and (carelessly, with his injured foot) delivers a solid righteous side-stomp to the stroller's chassis, which the mother catches just before it tips over, and he gives another wild kick before he shoots off through traffic across the street. Their shouts degrade into noise as he rounds the corner at a hobbled gallop, and he makes sure they hear him laughing.

At home, legs trembling full of acid, grimacing, he peels off the bloody broken half toenail and dabs the wound with alcohol, and the pain pierces an opening inside him through which more tearful laughter escapes. Naturally he feels somewhat guilty about what he did, yet he will not deny that it felt good to ruin the evenings of the tyrannical assholes who loved dehumanizing innocent single men. Just a quick startle, no harm done. *He* was the one hurting. The only thing that bothers him is that he knows no one would condone what he did.

Years pass, all alike. Something goes wrong in the bathroom: it was not a levator spasm after all. His doctor repeatedly assures him it is not a death sentence but will require significant immediate changes to his lifestyle. The diagnosis clears his head like a window continuously opening. Finally it's happened: they've killed him. He might as well be dead already. It is now certain he'll never get the one thing he's ever wanted. All because he internalized and accepted his unwantedness, languished too long in mealymouthed consolations, let himself be deceived into pitying those who would never pity him. Nothing can be done.

He's never wanted to admit it, but with his hard-won lived experience and the stark authority of his disprivilege, he can declare that women in aggregate are just—wrong. That either they have failed feminism, or feminism has failed them. Yes, it's complicated, and no, no woman in particular is to blame, but it's irrefutable that in general, a *preponderance* of women harbor the very double standards feminism sought to eliminate and a narcissistic victim complex by which they tolerate and even solicit aggro misogyny in romantic partners, while relying on men of conscience to handle the emotional scut work. In his newfound online communities of narrow-shouldered men he finds life stories that align near unanimously with his, in the comments of blogs like The Empirical Agnate and Seneca's Revenge, on message boards like Rationally Rude and NSOM (Narrow Shoulders / Open Minds), and while he disagrees with them about many things, they confirm that it isn't just him: the problem is systemic.

Now that he is mostly confined to his bed, in one late-night tour of the NSOM forums, which he now moderates, he notices one thread attracting dozens of replies. Some outsider has discovered NSOM and has been admonishing the entire community. This has happened before, but never at such length:

coldshoulder02
Unregistered User
Location: BC
Age: 23
Posts: 1
Rep Power: 0

just found this board and I'm fucking obsessed yall. not even just by the misogyny, or the term-paper talk yall use to hide it. no, what's mesmerizing is, no lie, I'm *one of you*. I'm 23 and a virgin, never had a gf or even a date, mostly just solo queue League and work at Staples. I stumbled across this place because I have real narrow shoulders, hell I'm built like a closed umbrella, and I've always wondered if other guys feel insecure about it too. I work out sometimes but I'm not crazy fit or anything and wish I were bigger. I think racist/sexist jokes are funny but I feel bad about it. so, probably like you.

then I come here and WOW. what happened, boys? I can't lie that it isn't nice to find other NS guys, but this place is like staring into a fucked up cursed mirror where the longer you stare at it the uglier you get, but it's so fascinating you keep staring. go head and call me white knight / betafag / lib or whatever weak shit you got called in gym class in sixth grade. I'd rather die a sane virgin than fall for this mess.

maybe it's more about what happened to me. maybe it's bc I'm talking to a therapist and figured out some meds that work for me, or bc I have female friends (grew up with four sisters) or haven't had my brain bleached by the internet as much. I'm not saying I'm better than any of yall, if I did I'd be the same as yall. so women either reject you or they don't act 100% the way you want them to (the term for that is "slavery"). bottom line is nobody's hurting or stealing anything from you. yall just hitched your psychosexual angst to your self-worth and it's women's fault somehow. however unfair you think it all is, you're MAKING IT WORSE. hope yall logoff and find peace.

He scrolls down through the ensuing dogpile, watches seehawk1488 post memes of skinny guys labeled "OP" lifting two-pound weights, reads michaelJ_fux's post "obvious radfem psy op piss off." By the end of the thread, sweat is crawling through his hair. He feels that same flushed, hangdog supervisibility, that cleansing shame he would feel when being scolded by his QPOC friend or reading feminist literature that diagnosed his privileges and corrected his gaffes. He used to think, If a stranger can so accurately describe what I've thought without even knowing me, they must be right, and I should listen to them. Now he wants to do likewise for this online stranger, whose familiar and bracing conviction, uncompromised by experience, floods him with nostalgia. It's painful seeing this poor chump misled, as he himself was, like a running dog about to hit the end of its leash. He feels a responsibility to awaken him to reality even if it's too late for himself. Words appear as if pushed onto the screen from his eyes.

You may think you get me, he posts, but I've been you far longer than you have. I want to tell you about the reality of having lived four decades of silent virtuous pain and never asking to have your humanity and desirability recognized, he posts. It's not that I haven't done the intellectual labor to empathize with a broad spectrum of female perspectives, I've read Sanger and Friedan and MacKinnon and Dworkin and Firestone and Faludi and Winterson and Butler and Solanas and Schulman and hooks and Greer. I understand them, and they understand the viewpoint of the patriarchy—but what have they read to understand *us*? My entire life I've been nothing but useful to everyone else, especially women, so selfless that my entire self will evaporate without residue, with no one left to know what I've had to endure absolutely by myself. Think of all the times you've been ill, with no one to bring you soup. Those nights you wake up with no one to talk to. Every unshared apartment. Every expired condom. The couples laughing together and going home and fucking in every conceivable position: it will never be you. *It will never be you.* This is why you are wrong that they haven't stolen from us: they've stolen our lives. Our future and the people in it. You will never have a woman, and you will never have a son. Women's fucked-up preferences may have been ingrained there by the patriarchy, but women, as moral agents fully equal to men, are no less accountable for them. Me, I've done more than my part: I've combated misogyny both in the world and within myself, donated monthly to Planned Parenthood, marched and canvassed and forwarded emails for women's rights, am commitment friendly, wealthy and successful, not ugly, in fact a solid eight from the neck up and nipples down, six-inch penis from base of shaft, high seminal motility, veritably a straight flush of stable-pair-bonding qualities, AND I have never ONCE cat-called, gaslit, interrupted, microaggressed, or mansplained, taking every single rejection in stride without any of the social support, shared costs, mutual care, inside jokes, pet names, intimate confes-sions, indeed any fond romantic memories whatsoever, none of the bliss of puppy love unspoiled by bitterness, nor the naive love that knows no betrayal, the trusting companionship that weathers hate and temptation, nobody waking up nestled in your elbow, no one to try new restaurants or take selfies or travel with, to say nothing of the conveniences, stability, or tax breaks enjoyed by the conjugal, on top of enduring the taboo stigma of bachelorhood; I've never com-plained, objected, or harassed anyone all these years no matter how cruel or senseless the rejection, if anything I *enabled* their rejections, and even kept a sense of humor about it, he posts. What's worse is they want to pretend it's not happening, or doesn't matter, that's right, *they're gaslighting YOU*, just to absolve themselves of guilt, at the cost of our lives. By now my bachelorhood, and yours, cannot be ascribed to circumstance or indifference—only injustice. We can't accept it anymore. Like my many female friends always used to say, nothing's wrong with me, I've only asked for the same modest redamancy that everyone else, including chauvinists, liars, abusers, rapists, and low-IQ men, enjoy everywhere. I'd be the last to demand any special treatment for my still impeccable feminism, and to be sure, no specific woman is *required* to be attracted to us . . . but the fact that not *one* has been, out of *billions*, is proof of a categori-cal failure, a *mass abrogation of the social contract* by the legions of treacherous, evasive, giggling yeastbuckets, he posts. I have always, always been there for women; when have they ever been there for us? How, after decades of relentless refusal, can they ever recompense this silent androcide, the calamity of our suffocation?

He receives no reply. The stranger probably didn't read his post. Examining what he'd written, scouring it with an unsparing eye toward logic and tone, he finds no error. He closes his laptop, surveys his dimmed room: humidifier, prescription bottles, weights he can no longer lift, bedside wastebasket full of phlegm-wadded tissues. It can't happen again—all this nothing. The nothing that was made of words, the reading and discussing and journaling and posting he's defined himself by, just wasted effort composing a wasted life. Words were only ever meant to underscore acts; they have no substance. Being correct is its own reward and no reward at all. He must commit himself to action, pull out the serrated knife that's been in his chest for decades. Before he dies he must stop nothing from happening.

Weeks later, after some false starts, he is standing in the vestibule of his former favorite restaurant when a woman enters behind him, a short young twentysomething in a yellow smock with little pin-tucked ruffles, her collarbones lightly pied by sunburn. He stands aside to hold the door for her, and she thanks him. In spite of his resolution he smiles back and nods courteously at this small final vindication, before pulling on his mask, shrugging the backpack from his narrow shoulders, and following her in.

2019

WE USED TO RUN THIS COUNTRY

RICHARD BECK

LEARN FROM HISTORY, THEY SAID. SEVENTEEN YEARS AFTER THE decision to invade Iraq did more harm to America's global interests than any other since the Vietnam War, a similar confrontation with Iran remains one of the Republican Party's most cherished hopes. It is a desire often expressed in strange ways or at odd moments. In the weeks after September 11, Iran signaled its support for the American military campaign in Afghanistan, and the US secretary of state Colin Powell shook hands with Iranian foreign minister Kamal Kharazi at the UN—engagement between the two countries had not happened on such a high level for more than two decades. Two months later, George W. Bush declared Iran part of the "axis of evil." In 2007, an audience member at one of John McCain's campaign stops asked the Arizona senator when America was going to stop tolerating Iranian support for Shia extremist groups in the Middle East. McCain responded by repurposing a Beach Boys song: "Bomb bomb bomb, bomb bomb Iran." In 2015, as the Obama Administration negotiated its nuclear deal with Iran, Republican House speaker John Boehner invited Israeli prime minister Benjamin Netanyahu to address Congress. America's legislators showered the foreign head of state with twenty-six standing ovations as he accused their President of all but handing nuclear weapons to the Iranian government, whose members he characterized as the functional equivalents of Nazis.

After withdrawing the United States from the nuclear deal in 2018, Donald Trump spent two years alternately threatening Iran's final destruction and attempting to convince President Hassan Rouhani of his deal-making prowess, with his national security adviser John Bolton piping up to amplify any threats and grumbling ominously in response to any gestures of conciliation. Trump reportedly had Bolton removed in September 2019 because of serious disagreements on foreign policy—Bolton seems to have been a bit too principled about his rabid militarism for Trump's liking—but in the first week of 2020, the President made Bolton very happy by ordering the assassination of Qasem Soleimani, the commander of Iran's elite Quds Force and one of the country's three most powerful people. This brought the US and Iran closer to war than at any point in the past forty years. At a private fundraiser with campaign donors in January, Trump said he had approved the drone strike because Soleimani was "saying bad things about our country." This didn't sit well with Trump. "How much of this shit do we have to listen to?" he said to the crowd at Mar-a-Lago. "How much are we going to listen to?"

The unruliness of the Republican desire for this particular war—the theatricality of its expression, the obsessiveness with which it's pursued, and the willingness to do and say the ridiculous in pursuit of it—suggests some degree of awareness that war with Iran would be insane. When Republicans talk about cutting corporate taxes, they talk like people making a policy proposal. When they talk about war with Iran, they sound like people daring themselves to ride a barrel over the falls. The invasion of Iraq is the best model for what a war with Iran would look like, and that was a disaster for everyone other than oil company executives and, ironically, the Iranian government. There is every reason to believe that a full-scale military confrontation with Iran would be worse. Iran today has a stronger military, economy, and political system than Iraq did in 2003. Its armed forces are among the most formidable in the Middle East, and they have been built and trained specifically to wage a defensive war that would be as costly as possible for any invader. Iran has the second-largest oil reserves in the region (behind Saudi Arabia), and whereas American economic sanctions had totally cut off pre-invasion Iraq from the world economy, similar sanctions levied against Iran have not yet had the same crippling effect. (They have, however, both pushed the country's economy into a still-deepening recession and seriously hampered its efforts to deal with the coronavirus pandemic.) Public political life in Iraq had atrophied to nothing under the dictatorial rule of Saddam Hussein; the same cannot be said of Iran's political system, no matter how many times Lindsey Graham tries to say it. Iran's government is insufficiently responsive to democratic input, and it often suppresses dissident political activity with deadly violence. It is clear that these two facts make many Iranians furious, but there is no evidence that most Iranians want their government overthrown, least of all by the United States. Something on the order of a million people took to the streets of Tehran for Soleimani's funeral procession the week after his killing. This extraordinary demonstration of national solidarity should not be any kind of surprise. Plenty of Americans feel similarly excluded from the institutions responsible for their own governance, and you can ask those who protested in Ferguson, Missouri, or who found themselves "disappeared" to a black site run by Chicago police, about their own encounters with deadly violence. For all that, there is little clamor in the US for a foreign invasion.

It is not just that a military confrontation with Iran would be more difficult and more costly than its 2003 predecessor. Leaving aside, if only briefly, the moral outrage of the death and destruction that any war with Iran would entail, at the moment there is no plausible case to be made that such a war would serve even the most Manichean conception of American interests. The argument for war with Iraq was fatally flawed and based on lies, but it had a coherent internal logic. Saddam Hussein's government lacked both regional and internal popular support, which meant it could be brought down without too much opposition. Once Saddam was overthrown, America could install and oversee a democratic government, and foreign investment would ensure the privatization of Iraq's economy and its integration into the world market. Joining Saudi Arabia and Israel, a prosperous, US-allied Iraq would allow America to stabilize politics in the Middle East and then manage the region for decades.

None of that happened. Reality utterly discredited the idea that the US could simply ship secular, democratic government and liberal market economics to the Middle East and then assemble them like so much Ikea flat-pack furniture. Yet America's neoconservatives, loitering furtively around the Senate Committee on Foreign Relations or the Fox News studios in the hope that Donald Trump will catch one of their appearances, have not even bothered trying to explain how Iran would be different. The likeliest outcome of war with Iran is a hellish regional power vacuum, one that countries like Russia and China would be better positioned to exploit than the United States. The drumbeat goes on anyway: the insistence that Iran cannot be "tolerated," that the solution to its malign influence must be military, that "the mullahs" must pay. The persistence of this fantasy reveals something irrational in the practice of American foreign policy, some impulse that asserts itself independent of the usual questions of proportionality and geopolitical strategy. If a war with Iran is to be avoided—and it *must* be avoided—it is that impulse that has to be understood.

AMERICA'S CURRENT HOSTILITY toward Iran stems in part from a simple and acute feeling of betrayal. For the first three decades of the postwar period, Iran was America's most reliable and valued ally in the Persian Gulf. The US inaugurated this special relationship in 1953 by working with the British to overthrow Iran's democratically elected government. That government's leader, Mohammad Mossadegh, had nationalized the country's oil industry, a situation Western oil companies naturally found unacceptable. In Mossadegh's place, the coup's organizers settled on Mohammad Reza Pahlavi. He had become shah of Iran in 1941, but until the coup his political power was subordinate to that of the prime minister and the Majlis, the country's legislative body. The shah was chosen to replace Mossadegh not because of any particular charisma or leadership ability, but because none of the four Iranian military generals who would officially lead the coup had the necessary standing and prestige.

Henry Kissinger wrote in the first of his three memoirs (on page 1,261) that the shah "was for us that rarest of leaders, an unconditional ally." He readily agreed to Western demands for fifty-fifty profit sharing in Iranian oil operations and cracked down hard on internal opposition, arresting more than three thousand members of the communist Tudeh Party in the year or so following the coup and imprisoning a handful of officials for decades (he also granted American military advisers immunity from Iranian law). The shah worked with the CIA to set up a secret police force, SAVAK, that carried out the day-to-day work of political repression. He also became an avid purchaser, even a connoisseur, of American arms. By 1977, 35 percent of Iran's annual budget was going to the military; a joke circulated among arms dealers that the shah read defense equipment manuals the way other men read *Playboy*. He placed orders for F-16 fighter jets, naval destroyers, nuclear-powered submarines, and more than a thousand tanks. The US even agreed to throw in nuclear reactors, with the shah reassuring American officials that he had no interest in pursuing nuclear weapons. Congress appreciatively estimated that Iran's arms purchases from the US were "the largest in the world."

The shah's military buildup went hand in hand with a series of initiatives that he called the White Revolution, a project of rapid state expansion, land reform, and industrialization that began in 1963. Results were mixed. The industrialization had to be financed by oil, making Iran increasingly dependent on the success or failure of a single export, and the land reform created an underclass of more than a million sharecroppers who did not own enough land to survive, while failing to materially improve Iran's agricultural capabilities. Iran's economic growth during the 1960s was impressive, but most Iranians never saw its benefits, and the shah had no talent for managing the social fissures that opened up as a result. By the 1970s, migrating unemployed workers had tripled the population of Tehran, most of Iran's food came from outside its borders, and wealth was more unequally distributed than in almost any other country in the world.

With not much to show in the way of domestic achievements that benefited his people, the shah doubled down on monarchy, styling himself as a descendant of the ancient rulers of the Persian Empire. In a global period of nationalism, republicanism, and communism, this was a quixotic project. In 1971, he spent at least $100 million celebrating twenty-five hundred years of monarchy in Iran, feting important heads of state and other foreigners in enormous air-conditioned tents at the historic sites of Persepolis and Pasargadae, with catering by Maxim's of Paris, twenty-five thousand bottles of imported wine, and the premiere of an electro-acoustic composition by the avant-garde composer Iannis Xenakis. This spectacular orgy didn't make much of a positive impression on Iranians, who identified more with Shia Islam than with ancient Persia, but Westerners came away impressed. In 1974, a US task force evaluated relations with Iran and concluded the following:

> Iran is the most powerful, politically most stable, and economically most developed state on the Persian Gulf. It shares with us an interest in promoting moderate elements in the area and in limiting the influence of the Soviet Union and radical forces. Prospects are good for Iran's long-term stability and a continuation of its present international orientation, even if its present leadership leaves the scene.

President Jimmy Carter came to Tehran for a state dinner on New Year's Eve, 1977. "Iran, because of the great leadership of the shah, is an island of stability in one of the more troubled areas of the world," he said. "This is a great tribute to you, your majesty, and to your leadership and to the respect and admiration and love which your people give to you."

His majesty would flee Iran just over a year later. During the 1970s, as the shah lurched from one initiative to the next in a doomed effort to alleviate Iran's social tensions and stabilize its deteriorating political system, the sociologist Ali Shariati and a cleric named Ruhollah Khomeini were articulating a new kind of populist, nationalist, religious radicalism that eventually culminated in the world's first Islamic revolution. Shariati's writings, addressed to the students and intelligentsia who had always counted among the shah's fiercest opponents, advanced a vision of Shia Islam as a revolutionary force opposing all forms of oppression, especially capitalism and imperialism, with the goal of bringing a classless society into being. To Shariati, the Iranian clergy were apologists for capitalism who, in the words of historian Ervand Abrahamian, "[diluted] Islam's radicalism into watered-down paternalism." Khomeini had been exiled in 1964 because of his opposition to the shah's White Revolution and pro-Western policies, but as a member of the clergy, he wasn't going to sign on to Shariati's specific denunciations. Still, both men saw Islam as the only force in Iranian society capable of forcing out monarchism and the West's decades-long grip on the country. The shah was attempting to suppress politics as such in Iran. In Islam, Iranians found an avenue by which politics could breathe once again.

In early 1978, a government newspaper published an editorial denouncing Khomeini. Iranian students in the city of Qom flooded into the streets in response. Some of them were killed by police, and what followed was a cycle of protest and mourning, every forty days, that swept across the country. The shah did what he could to crack down, but it was too late: his regime, and monarchy as a system of government, were finished. The revolution was a period of violence and uncertainty. Rallies, strikes, marches, and clashes with police steadily ground down what remained of the shah's ability to govern. But it was not a revolution like Russia's in 1917, in which the government was ultimately overthrown only because of the tactical ingenuity of a small cadre. The shah had ignored the needs of the majority of Iranians for so long, and alienated so many sectors of Iranian society, that his downfall was inevitable. When Khomeini returned from exile in February 1979, some three million people were on the streets to greet him.

In the space of little more than a year, the foundation of American influence in the Middle East had crumbled to nothing, and America had not seen it coming. "We used to run this country," one US diplomat told a *New York Times* reporter on his way out of Iran. "Now we don't even run our own embassy." That was in February 1979—the diplomat didn't know how right he was about to be. For most of that year, American policymakers stewed in their bewilderment over what had happened, while the Iranian Revolution's victors hashed out a new constitution. The result was a hybrid system of government, tilted steeply if not quite decisively in favor of the religious radicals. It was a full-fledged theocracy alongside robust elements of representative democracy, a mostly authoritarian system that was unusual in carving out space for serious debate and the operations of various political interest groups. As supreme leader and imam of the Muslim ummah, Khomeini could declare war and peace, "determine the interests of Islam," and appoint half of the members of the Guardian Council, itself endowed with the power to veto bills passed by the legislature if it judged them to violate either the constitution or Islamic law. As a counterbalance, all Iranians were given the power to elect the president, members of the legislature, regional and local councils, and so on. The president, limited to two terms over eight years in office, was granted the authority to appoint cabinet members, ambassadors, and the head of the national bank, among other offices. The legislature could debate any issue it wanted, call a referendum to change the constitution, and appoint the other half of the Guardian Council.

Tensions between the near infallibility of religious rule and popular demands for democracy had been present throughout the revolution, and the drafting of the constitution brought them to a high pitch. Sticking with the insensitivity to Iranian domestic politics that had characterized America's relationship to the country in the years leading up to the revolution, President Carter picked this fraught moment to allow the shah to enter the US for cancer treatment, thanks in part to an intense lobbying campaign organized by executives at Chase Manhattan Bank, of which the shah was a highly valued client. (Not satisfied with securing his entry, the Chase team, led by bank chairman David Rockefeller, also acquired visas for the shah's associates and found a mansion for him to live in.) American officials justified the decision on humanitarian grounds, but they treat cancer in other countries, too. Politically, it was idiotic, providing a boost to the militant wing of the Iranian government at a moment when the shape that government would take was still unclear. Hard-liners seized on the gesture as evidence of a plot: America was biding its time and preparing to reinstall the shah, with the CIA running operations out of the American embassy in Tehran. On November 4, 1979, some four hundred university students overran the embassy and took the Americans hostage.

The crisis would last for 444 days, and if the revolution had caught US officials by surprise, this was something worse. It was an abject humiliation, an indictment of both the State Department's alleged expertise and the capabilities of America's security forces that crystallized, in especially mediagenic fashion, the damage the revolution had done to America's strategic interests in the Middle East. Leading up to the revolution, the American embassy in Tehran had a staff of almost a thousand people, and some forty thousand US civilians prowled the streets of the capital on behalf of American defense contractors. Now there were just fifty-two Americans left, held against their will and unable to do anything about it. A BBC documentary about the crisis, made decades later, features interviews with a number of the hostages, and even with all those years behind them, they still vibrate with confusion and anger. "To actually come onto the grounds, take the embassy hostage, and take the diplomats hostage—I mean, this was the worst part of all," says

Charles Jones, who was there working as a communications officer. "It was like being raped."

The hostage crisis was a boon to Iran's religious radicals. Khomeini hadn't organized the taking of the embassy or even been aware of the plan beforehand, but on November 5 he announced his support for the students; Iran's moderate prime minister, Mehdi Bazargan, resigned the next day. Purges followed, as documents found at the embassy revealed that this or that moderate Iranian political official had met with a representative of the US government. In early 1980, negotiations to secure the hostages' release progressed to the point that Vice President Walter Mondale felt able to discuss them with journalists, but then Khomeini delivered a radio address praising the students and demanding the return of the shah to Iran so that he could face justice. That hadn't been part of the deal, and negotiations fell apart. In April, President Carter approved Operation Eagle Claw, a special-forces raid on the compound that would kill or subdue the students and free the hostages. The helicopters never even made it to Tehran—three broke down in the desert, and one crashed after the mission had been aborted, killing all its occupants. The operation's only achievement inside Iran was to provide Khomeini with further evidence of America's disdain for negotiations and determination to impose its will by force.

Inside the US, the crisis was experienced as a collective trauma, the intensity of which can be difficult to understand in retrospect. People started tying yellow ribbons around trees—a ritual practice that has persisted through the Gulf and Iraq Wars—and the ABC news program *Nightline* was cooked up specifically to provide updates on the crisis. *Nightline*'s original title was *The Iran Crisis—America Held Hostage: Day X*. An on-screen counter made sure viewers never forgot how many days it had been since the crisis began. "The State Department is doing what it can," Ted Koppel said in his first televised report on the crisis, "but for the moment at least, that doesn't appear to be much." These reports were saturated with what have become stock elements of American news coverage of Islamic extremism: shots of chanting crowds and references to fanatics and madness. Each new day on the counter was a blow to the US and to President Carter, and Iran knew it. Carter's administration did eventually succeed in negotiating for the hostages' release in January 1981, after he lost reelection to Ronald Reagan. (The shah, who died in Egypt in July 1980, was by then a moot point.) Iran didn't announce the release of the hostages until January 20, the day of Reagan's swearing in. By refusing to release the hostages while Carter still held the White House, Iran drove the point home: not only had the revolutionary government successfully defied its longtime nemesis by deposing Iran's autocratic ruler, it had ended the political career of a US President.

The end of the crisis was followed by a frantic effort to recast trauma as a redeeming triumph. "America was looking for a reason to be proud, or a reason to be American again," one of the hostages told an interviewer years later. "We had lost it." Another hostage said that the American people had used the end of the crisis "to release itself of this burden of Vietnam." It had been less than a decade since the last American civilian and military personnel had been evacuated from Saigon via helicopter—undoing, or at least papering over, this string of retreats would in some ways constitute the whole project of Reagan's presidency. Ten days after the inauguration, hundreds of thousands turned out for a ticker-tape parade in New York, with yellow ribbons and American flags waving in the air as twenty-one of the former hostages cruised down Broadway, waving back.

BRUCE LAINGEN, the chargé d'affaires for the Tehran embassy, said of the crisis that "the American people as a whole . . . were all hostage to that drama." What were they hostage to, exactly? For all the election-cycle rhetoric about how domestic issues are the only ones Americans care about, foreign affairs have determined much of America's self-image over the past century, with greater or lesser degrees of mythologizing lacquered onto the story as circumstances demand. Broadly speaking, many Americans believe that their country is both perfectly dominant and perfectly benevolent. This self-image originated in World War II, when America sought to justify its new and very real position of global preeminence—and especially economic preeminence—with the myth that it alone had "saved the world from fascism." The story went through many permutations: the anticommunism of the '50s and '60s, which pitted freedom against soulless repression; the Carter Doctrine, which militarized America's relationship to the Middle East so as to prevent the Soviet Union from cutting off the capitalist world's oil supplies; the Balkans and the notion of humanitarian intervention, which recast America's pursuit of its own interests as a fight for all of humanity; the war on terror. Each of these has been underpinned, both emotionally and in concrete political terms, by Americans' twinned beliefs in their country's supremacy and goodness.

Iran successfully undermined both. America had spent decades pointing at Iran's growth rates and congratulating itself on supporting the Middle East's exemplary modernizer, but when the revolution came, it was a genuine popular revolt, and its overriding message was that America had to get out. How could America be benevolent if a mass mobilization said otherwise? On its own, this challenge was serious but probably manageable; many countries have cast doubt on the nobility of America's international intentions since World War II without being able to do much about it. But now here was an entirely new form of government that could back up its anti-American rhetoric with resistance, physically imprisoning dozens of representatives of the world's most powerful country. The US was helpless. American diplomats failed to achieve the sought-for breakthroughs, the military literally crashed and burned, and the revolutionary government refused to budge in the face of an embargo on Iranian oil. In her memoir, First Lady Rosalynn Carter recalled helplessly pleading with her husband: "Do something! Do something!" Not just Carter but the office of the presidency itself seemed to be diminished.

The end of the Carter era is understood to be the nadir of 20th-century American self-confidence. The recession that began in

1973 ended the country's post–World War II expansion—and in a particularly painful way, with high unemployment and high inflation battering economic growth from both sides. The trauma of Vietnam also loomed over everything; like Iran, the North Vietnamese Army had successfully undermined both of America's cherished myths about itself. Under the surface, however, things were not quite as dire as they seemed, and in some ways the prospects for American global dominance were actually improving. Nixon's triumphant 1972 visit to China inaugurated a process that would culminate in the reestablishment of full diplomatic relations in 1979, gradually depriving the Soviet Union of the support of its most important cold-war ally. The Nasserite dream of secular Pan-Arabism had begun its long retreat in 1967, when the Six-Day War established Israel as a pro-American military power in the Middle East. And though Marxist heads of state sporadically popped up to trouble the picture, as Salvador Allende did with his 1970 election as president of Chile, a little economic warfare and covert CIA support for a coup could usually take care of things. Even the failure of the Vietnam War didn't lead to what its most fervent proponents feared: communism wasn't going to conquer the world just because it had conquered Saigon. By no means was the US successful across the board in the 1970s, but being the preeminent global power doesn't mean you don't have any problems—it just means that you can handle them.

Iran was different. An international revolutionary movement based not on nationalism or Marxism but religion, Khomeini's pan-Islamism is the major political innovation of the last half century. It exploded many categories of "modern" political thought, including both the liberal democratic ideal of secular government and the Marxist characterization of religion as the opiate of the masses. Foucault was in Iran before the shah's overthrow to report on the spreading protests for an Italian newspaper, and in his view, Islam was providing the revolutionaries not with a set of rules but with a means of political organization: "a way of being together, a way of speaking and listening, a means of understanding each other and sharing each other's desires." That view was excessively rosy—with theocracy in place, Islam in Iran would very much turn toward providing people with a set of rules. But Foucault's point about Islam as a conduit for politics, in a country where other conduits to politics had been systematically repressed by the shah, remains.

Khomeini's political aspirations were not limited to Iran. He wanted Islam to foment revolution throughout the Middle East, so that Muslim-majority countries might be able to step outside of the cold-war system structured by the two great external powers and inhabit a geopolitical space of their own. The Soviet Union never came to grips with political Islam over the course of its final ten years of existence, and the US hasn't done much better in the three decades since. But Khomeini's project to unite the world's Muslims hit a snag almost immediately, when Saddam Hussein invaded Iran in September 1980. Saddam had come to power as Iraq's president the year before as a secular nationalist leader ruling over a country with a Shia-majority population. Worried that the Iranian Revolution would inspire Iraqi Shias to overthrow his government (and also interested in annexing Iran's oil-rich Khuzestan province), Saddam attacked quickly in the hope of capitalizing on the chaos of Iran's immediate postrevolutionary period. That worked for a little while.

By the middle of 1982, Iran had retaken all of the territory lost to the initial invasion, and what followed were six more years of ugly fighting as Khomeini tried to overthrow Saddam: trench warfare, bayonet attacks, chemical weapons. Iran resorted to full mobilization in the style of World War I, and the conflict allowed the state to both expand and consolidate its power in ways that may have otherwise been impossible. Militias were transformed into the now notorious Revolutionary Guard, a force that numbered some one hundred and twenty thousand by the war's end. Public support for the government surged, price controls and ration cards were introduced so that the poor did not go hungry, and the industries ministry nationalized dozens of factories that had been abandoned by their wealthy owners in the run-up to the revolution. The war decisively swept away the world of the shah, and an intense Islamicization of Iranian society followed, with the censorship of all media, the enforcement of an Islamic dress code, and the removal of women from the judiciary. Political purges brought about the deaths of hundreds of dissidents and former government officials in the first years of the revolution, and then again just after the end of the war, in 1988, on an awful scale. Khomeini organized the execution of twenty-eight hundred prisoners, many of them leftists. "We are not liberals like Allende," a prominent figure of the revolution named Ali Khamenei had warned in 1979, "whom the CIA can snuff out."

The US adopted an official position of neutrality at the war's outset but soon pivoted to supporting Iraq. Donald Rumsfeld traveled there to shake Saddam's hand in 1983, and full diplomatic relations between the two countries were restored the next year. Coming out of the war with Iran's national borders unchanged, Khomeini could now claim to have repelled the world's superpower yet again, and this time on an enormous scale. But if the 1980s allowed Iran's revolutionary government to consolidate power, it also required the country to scale back its international ambitions. Iran's economy was in terrible shape after eight years of continuous war, with insufficient foreign currency reserves and declining oil revenues, on which Iran was financially dependent. Khomeini's dream of a pan-Islamic revolutionary movement was also dead: a conflict pitting the Middle East's most powerful Shia government against its most powerful Sunni government had deepened the region's sectarian divide.

Having lost confidence in its ability to manage the situation through proxy governments, the United States had begun the process of militarizing its relationship to the Middle East. Billions of dollars poured into Afghanistan to help the mujahideen fight the Soviets, who had invaded in 1979. CENTCOM, or United States Central Command, was founded in 1983 to manage America's military commitments across the region. The US sought and received access to ports and airfields in North and East Africa, and kept military equipment stored on cargo ships in the Indian Ocean, ready to deploy if needed. Diplomacy still played a role, of course, but the Iranian Revolution had scrambled the region's dynamics to an extent that made it difficult for the US to get a handle on things, as was highlighted by the "Iran" component of the Iran-Contra affair. In its final shape, the Reagan Administration's scheme involved selling arms to Israel, which in turn sold those arms to the Iranian government, with the US funneling some of the proceeds to the Contras, right-wing rebel forces fighting the leftist government of Nicaragua. This was so Reagan could get around an explicit congressional prohibition on materially aiding the Contras in any way.

But the Contra issue had nothing to do with why the US decided to facilitate the sale of arms to Iran in the first place, which was also prohibited under America's own embargo on Iranian arms sales. The US was originally approached about selling arms to Iran by an Israeli diplomat and an Iranian intermediary. Israel wanted to sell arms to Iran because it was interested in keeping the Iran-Iraq war at a stalemate for as long as possible. The Iranian intermediary, Manucher Ghorbanifar, was a freelance arms dealer and former agent with the shah's secret police. And despite being such a notorious liar that the CIA itself issued a "burn notice" against him in 1984, he was able to get the Reagan Administration's attention by claiming access to a "moderate" faction, led by one of Khomeini's advisers, Hassan Karoubi, that hoped to slowly reorient Iran toward open markets and the West. Using arms sales to inaugurate a working relationship with this faction was tantalizing, but Ghorbanifar's unreliability made for a very unstable foundation on which to justify covert and illegal arms sales, as Reagan would discover when Iran-Contra became public in late 1986. When it came to Middle East diplomacy in the 1980s, the US was in over its head, and so it was America's military footprint in the region that continued to expand. The original justification was the need to counter a broader Soviet invasion that never actually materialized, but once Iraq invaded Kuwait and the Soviet threat disappeared for good in 1991, the pretext changed. Now Saddam was the great regional bogeyman against whom Saudi Arabia's oilfields had to be protected.

Iran's leaders understood that a direct confrontation with this American show of force was hopeless. Instead they turned to regional proxy groups, a strategy on which Iran has relied ever since. The Iranian government founded Hezbollah in the early 1980s to fight the Israeli occupation of Lebanon, where Yasser Arafat's Palestinian Liberation Organization was based. A kind of umbrella organization for Shia militant groups, Hezbollah became one of Iran's primary means of projecting its regional influence, engaging in guerrilla warfare against Israel—which Khomeini had termed the "Little Satan" for its support of the shah, treatment of the Palestinians, and dependence on the US—and carrying out, or working closely with affiliated groups that carried out, terror attacks against Israeli and American forces. The most spectacular of these killed 241 American military personnel in Beirut in 1983. This support for proxy groups allowed Iran to oppose America's growing military presence in the Middle East without having to risk an unwinnable conventional war. And if Hezbollah and other militant groups like Hamas and the Islamic Jihad Movement in Palestine weren't capable of forcing the United States out of the region, that was fine. As the 20th century neared its end, it increasingly seemed that you didn't actually have to defeat the United States to disrupt the smooth functioning of its foreign policy machine—all you had to do was throw a few wrenches into the gears. It was as though American power got more brittle even as it grew.

Khomeini died in 1989. Ali Khamenei, the mullah who had warned that "we are not liberals like Allende," became Iran's second supreme leader, and Akbar Hashemi Rafsanjani became its fourth president. Following the end of the war the pair embarked on a program of economic liberalization that was in tune with the neoliberal policies that were sweeping across the globe: shrinking the government here and there, opening a handful of free-trade zones, printing less money, and lowering business taxes. Wealth inequality increased, and in the mid-'90s a steep drop in oil prices triggered a recession. What emerged out of this economic crisis was a reform movement led by Mohammad Khatami, who won a presidential election in 1997 on promises to cultivate civil society, fix the economy, and replace a "clash of civilizations" with a "dialogue of civilizations." The cultural transformation that unfolded over the next several years was remarkable. The share of university graduates who were women topped 60 percent, a new generation of intellectuals began to favorably cite Western philosophers, and religion more or less stopped policing the daily lives of most Iranians. By 2000, the *Economist* was reporting that according to Iran's own clergy, fewer than 2 percent of Iranians attended mosque on Fridays. On the economic side, the neoliberalization of Iran intensified; small-scale factories were exempted from labor laws, and state-owned industries were privatized (loosening the state's grip on the economy was thought to be the best way of decreasing state interference in Iranians' private lives). Iran's relationships with foreign nations, even the US, also improved considerably. President Clinton eased up on the economic sanctions that Reagan had put in place in 1987, and Khatami appeared on CNN to talk about his admiration for the American nation and people. Al Qaeda's attack on the United States on September 11, 2001, was met with a massive outpouring of sympathy for America in Tehran, with enormous crowds holding candlelit vigils and some sixty thousand people observing a moment of silence at a soccer match on September 13.

It continues to strain belief that it was *this* version of Iran, an Iran going out of its way to endear itself to the US and other developed world nations, that George W. Bush described as part of the axis of evil in January 2002. Bush's decisions to invade Iraq and Afghanistan were obviously the most consequential of his presidency, but the decision to include Iran in the axis of evil may be his dumbest. Nothing more clearly illustrates the Republican Party's irrational bloodlust with respect to Iran than this move, which alienated a committed enemy of both Saddam Hussein and Sunni extremist groups at a time when the US was simultaneously preparing for war against Saddam Hussein and Sunni extremist groups. Bush's speech surprised the Iranian government. It surprised America's allies. It even surprised people at the State Department, who for good reason are accustomed to getting a heads-up about this sort of thing. Overnight, Iran went from a state working assiduously to improve relations with Western powers to, in the Bush Administration's words, a "totalitarian" nightmare whose citizens were held hostage by "unelected leaders." The speech demoralized Iran's reform movement, which soon split over disputes about how to respond to Bush's provocation, and it provided an enormous boost to the country's hard-liners, who were once again able to make the case that you couldn't ever trust the Great Satan.

The invasion of Iraq only accelerated the rightward shift that began after Bush's speech. Conservatives in Iran campaigned on national security concerns—with the US military wreaking havoc just next door, who wouldn't be worried about where they might invade next?—and won elections for municipal councils in 2003 and for the Majlis in 2004, with turnout plummeting in urban areas and among women and students. The shift culminated in 2005 when a populist son of a blacksmith named Mahmoud Ahmadinejad won the presidency. Censorship increased, important government positions went to members of the Revolutionary Guard, and Iran's foreign policy entered the realm of the grotesque, with Ahmadinejad stating that Israel should be wiped off the map and that the Holocaust was a myth. The fifteen-year-long standoff between Iran and the Western powers over its nuclear program dates from Ahmadinejad's election. It can be tempting to view this outcome as ironic—Bush gave a speech denouncing the Iranian government as autocratic, which only pushed that government further toward autocracy! But this temptation should be resisted, because it is founded on the myth that all of America's political parties value representative democracy as such, a myth President Bush may even have tricked himself into believing. The Republican Party works tirelessly to suppress democratic influence on the political process, through gerrymandering, the closure of polling stations, cynical hand-wringing over the nonexistent issue of "voter fraud," and efforts to dismantle laws that protect voting rights. It clings to the Senate filibuster to ensure that not even majorities in Congress are sufficient to pass legislation. George W. Bush himself was made President not, in the end, because of a vote, but because five unelected judges decided he was President. The success or failure of representative democracy in the Middle East is of little interest to America's political system as a whole and of no interest whatsoever to the Republican Party. What mattered to the Bush Administration was that the oil keep flowing and the geopolitics of the Middle East remain unchanged, except for the transformation of Iraq into an ally. Just as autocratic regimes like that of Saudi Arabia have been America's most valued allies in the Middle East, so have autocratic governments been the preferred enemies. Questions of political morality had no bearing on why the Republican Party launched the war on terror, and with Ahmadinejad in power, Bush had an ideal enemy. The differences between the two regimes are less striking than their similarities: Abrahamic religious extremists whose political fortunes were founded and dependent on fossil capital (Bush Jr., of course, got his start as an oilman in Texas). What remained was a conflict waged on the Republican Party's preferred terms—a naked contest for economic and military power, tipped steeply in favor of the US.

THE IRAQ WAR and the larger war on terror constituted a major setback for Iran's relationships with the Western powers, but America's destructive crusade also opened up all kinds of opportunities for Iran to expand and solidify its position in the Middle East. The most significant of these appeared in Iraq itself, where Bush Jr.'s troops deposed the Sunni leader of a Shia-majority country without any viable plan for the political aftermath. In the words of the political scientist Amin Saikal, the invasion transformed Iraq "from a strong dictatorial state with suppressed societies to a weak state with strong but rival societies." In the years since, Iran has devoted enormous resources to Shia Iraqis, investing in everything from infrastructure to tourism to the renovation of holy sites. When US troops left Iraq in 2011, the country was led by a mostly Shia, pro-Iranian government. Iraq and Iran have signed more than a hundred cooperation agreements since the invasion, and Iran is now Iraq's largest trading partner. The two countries' regional alignment, after decades of violent hostility, is among the most consequential outcomes of the US invasion.

Looking to put the brakes on Iran's growing influence, the US escalated its sanctions program and then added a mix of targeted military operations, warmongering, and hysteria over Iran's nuclear program, none of which has done much to encourage a productive working relationship between Iran and the US. Over the past fifteen years, there has been only one period of relative realism with respect to Iran: Obama's nuclear deal. The US didn't get everything it wanted in the deal, and neither did Iran. That's OK—it's what usually happens at the end of a negotiation conducted in good faith.

Republicans ostensibly opposed the nuclear agreement on the grounds that it was a "bad deal." But their idea of a good deal was a total and unconditional capitulation on the part of Iran. The fact that it was a negotiation may be precisely why Republicans found the nuclear deal unacceptable. After all, can you really call yourself the world's superpower if you have to *negotiate* with people? This posture is arrogant, to be sure, but arrogance alone can't explain it. The great historian Ellen Meiksins Wood has described America's odd investment in what she calls "surplus" imperialism, the belief among America's foreign policy establishment that it is not enough for America to be the most powerful country in the world—it must be the most powerful country by such a disproportionate margin that the very idea of anyone else overtaking it is unthinkable. In the words of Colin Powell in 1992, the US needs to be powerful enough "to deter any challenger from *ever dreaming of challenging us* on the world stage" (emphasis added). Or, in the words of George W.

Bush's 2002 National Security Strategy, "strong enough to dissuade *potential* adversaries from pursuing a military buildup *in hopes* of surpassing, or equaling, the power of the United States" (again, emphasis added).

This may sound like the mindset of a comic-book villain, but America's investment in surplus imperialism has a concrete, material basis. Since the end of World War II, the United States has been not only the world's most powerful capitalist nation but the global custodian of capitalism itself. (That task had previously fallen to the system of European colonialism, which at its height occupied some 80 percent of the world.) In exchange for the privilege of enjoying the highest rates of consumption on earth, the United States also invests more than any other country in the direction, supervision, and maintenance of global capital flows. These investments take many forms, including the spearheading of free-trade agreements, the establishment of financial institutions like the World Bank and the International Monetary Fund (IMF), support for governments that adhere to the capitalist consensus and the undermining of those that don't, and the use of military force to pry open markets in cases where diplomacy and economic pressure aren't enough. The "surplus" aspect of America's imperialism is crucial, because capitalism requires stability and predictability *through time* in order to function smoothly. Investments need months, years, or decades to produce their returns, and people are only willing to invest their capital if they feel confident that the future is going to unfold in the way they expect. You don't start producing almonds until you're confident that almond milk isn't just a passing fad, and you don't move one of your factories to a new country if there's a chance a leftist government will come to power and expropriate the factory. Financial markets move every day in response to changes in these ephemeral moods, and the financial press has names for them: uncertainty, consumer confidence, business expectations.

Surplus imperialism is an effort to keep uncertainty to a minimum. It's good to be strong enough to defeat a country that attempts a military land grab against one of its neighbors (as with Saddam Hussein and Kuwait in the Persian Gulf War). But from the perspective of capital markets, it's much better for the US to be so strong that nobody even thinks about attempting the land grab in the first place. And in a sense, the surplus imperialist mindset isn't only or even primarily aimed at America's enemies. Countries like Venezuela and North Korea are already perfectly aware that they have no hope of equaling American power. Rather, the psychological force of surplus imperialism is aimed squarely at America's friends—countries on the make, like Turkey, India, and Brazil, which are discouraged from getting any big ideas about creative new alliances even as the brute facts of America's declining power unfold in full view, year after year—and frenemies like Russia and China, regional powers with whom a full-scale military confrontation remains unimaginable, but only so long as Vladimir Putin and Xi Jinping agree there's no upside to imagining it.

American imperialism is not a recent development, and neither are American military interventions in pursuit of imperialist goals. But the kind of surplus imperialism to which the US is now committed, accounting for nearly 40 percent of global military spending on its own, is new. It dates roughly from the end of the cold war, and it has produced a doctrine under which the US can take military action anywhere in the world whenever it wants, with no explanation required. The tradition of "just war," which previously dominated political rhetoric about military action, was flexible to the point of near incoherence, but at the very least it demanded that war be declared with a specific goal in mind, that it be declared by an appropriate authority, and that the destruction inflicted be proportionate to the aims one hoped to achieve. All of that went out the door with George W. Bush and the global war on terror. The country's new rationale for military action became a part of American law when Congress passed the Authorization for Use of Military Force in September 2001. As Wood puts it, "military action now requires no specific aim at all."

It may be, however, that the goals of American war-making haven't disappeared so much as they have been generalized to such an extent that they are now hard to make out at all. The end of the cold war also produced Francis Fukuyama's *The End of History and the Last Man*, in which the political theorist argued that the spread of liberal market democracies and the collapse of the Soviet Union signaled "the end of history as such: that is, the end point of mankind's ideological evolution and the universalization of Western liberal democracy as the final form of human government." This is probably the most controversial claim made by a political theorist over the past thirty years, and Fukuyama himself has since amended it with so many qualifications and caveats that he may as well have repudiated it entirely. But imagine the "end of history" thesis not so much as a description of the world but as a goal of US foreign policy—something to be achieved, preferably through the movements of global capital, but also by force wherever necessary. As the region on which the capitalist world most depends for its oil supplies, the Middle East can do more to disrupt the smooth functioning of America's global dominance than anywhere else on the planet—it is the place where history most threatens to break out. And so the United States has gone there, again and again, to stop history in its tracks, to demonstrate, in the paraphrased words of Mark Fisher, that there is no alternative.

The United States has been trying to keep Iran frozen in place for almost seventy-five years, whether by helping to depose Mossadegh, subsidizing the shah even as he lost any semblance of domestic political support, prolonging the Iran-Iraq War by playing each side off the other, or foreclosing real opportunities for diplomatic engagement with the axis of evil speech and the militarization of the Middle East in general. Over the past two decades, the US has worked diligently to maintain its stranglehold on Iranian politics and society, and not just in material terms. American politicians and media personalities have effectively banned any discussion of Iran that tries to move beyond the war on terror binary. To hear Americans tell it,

Iranians either support freedom on American terms or favor the tyranny of an Islamic dictatorship. They want nuclear weapons because their leaders want to blow up American cities and wipe Israel off the face of the earth. (*If* they want nuclear weapons and not just nuclear power, which remains a matter of debate, it is certainly not to embark on a suicidal global offensive.) Homegrown civil rights protests, like the Green movement that convulsed Iran after the disputed results of Ahmadinejad's reelection in 2009, are described as attempts to overthrow the regime. But the Green movement was nothing of the kind. It was a nonviolent *reform* project seeking the expansion of Iranian civil rights. Its leaders no more wanted the revolutionary government abolished than Martin Luther King Jr. wanted to abolish Congress and the presidency.

After a decade of boiling tensions between the two countries and military adventurism on both sides throughout the region, Obama decided that the best path was a deal that would at least make a disastrous war with the largest country in the Middle East less likely. Obama made the safe bet that easing up on the international panic around Iran's nuclear program and reintegrating the country into the world economy could mitigate the Iranian government's sense of its nuclear program as a key locus of nationalistic pride. The deal was another chance for the United States to allow politics and history to unfreeze in Iran, a chance to give Iran the security and breathing room it needs to address some of its long-simmering political problems. One of Iran's increasingly urgent problems is the outsize influence of the Revolutionary Guard, the branch of the military specifically focused on protecting Iran's political system. It is composed of the country's most dedicated hard-liners, and over the years it has acquired a level of power over Iranian society, including its economy, that may eventually threaten the very political system it was founded to defend. The political sociologist Hazem Kandil has warned that further extension of the guard's influence "could override all other regime institutions and transform Iran from a popular theocracy to a military dictatorship, or worse, a police state." By providing a clear path for Iran to politically and culturally reintegrate with the rest of the world, the nuclear deal would have eroded the guard's influence and boosted the reformist wing of Iran's government.

Obama even saw the nuclear deal as a means of unfreezing politics in a wider, regional context. Talking about Saudi Arabia and America's other Sunni Arab allies with the *New York Times*, Obama said, "I think the biggest threats that they face may not be coming from Iran invading. It's going to be from dissatisfaction inside their own countries. . . . That's a tough conversation to have, but it's one that we have to have." It is entirely Obama's fault that he didn't do more to help that process along, and that he actually did a lot to hinder it, increasing drone strikes instead of ending them, sending troops to Afghanistan instead of bringing them all home, and doing so little to meaningfully address Israel's destructive role in regional politics. But the larger point stands—the nuclear deal would have helped. It would not have ended America's military adventurism at a stroke, but it was a step in that direction and would have set the US on a path to engaging with the region as something other than a violent empire spouting transparently disingenuous rhetoric about self-determination. That outcome is now impossible. Inside Iran, an opportunity for political liberalization has been gutted, and a sharp turn to the right is certain to follow. In pulling the US out of the deal, Trump joined the long tradition of helping out the Iranian right wing by demonstrating once again that only a dupe would put their faith in the goodwill of the United States. His decision was exactly what Republicans wanted, and now that Trump has managed to assassinate Qasem Soleimani, they are salivating for war.

For the Republicans, rejecting the nuclear deal and advocating for war is the correct political decision. Caught off guard by the Tea Party movement in 2009 and lacking even a cursory interest in addressing the wealth inequality that has generated so much fury since the financial crisis, the party is weak. It clings to power thanks to voter suppression, gerrymandering, and, in Donald Trump, a real-life version of a bit player in a sub-Scorsese Mob movie. Domestically, its constituencies are held together by a shared commitment to patriarchy, racism, and the freedom of capitalists to make as much money as they can while treating workers and the environment however they want. But foreign policy platforms have constituencies as well, and a bedrock commitment to imperialist violence as America's primary means of interacting with the Middle East is also crucial to the Republicans' political fortunes.

This constituency has several elements. There are the capitalists, people with an ownership stake in the economy who are looking nervously over their shoulders at a decade of anemic growth and declining rates of profit (our most recent economic expansion, now brought to an end by a global pandemic, was the longest on record but also the slowest). This group will not tolerate any reluctance whatsoever on Republicans' part to use military force to pry open new markets. Republicans know that capitalist support is provisional—Democrats are committed capitalists, too, and much of Wall Street was happy to throw its support behind Hillary Clinton's free-market militarism. And so the only way for Republicans to keep the ownership class in their corner is to make sure that Republican militarism remains the gold standard.

There are also the nationalists who provide the party with much of its energy on the ground, the Steve Bannons and Stephen Millers and other adjacent figures who happily assert that America isn't merely the greatest country on earth, but that all the other countries are, in the words of their hero, shitholes. There isn't much risk of this group swinging over to the Democrats, but mobilizing them requires that their energy be kept at a fever pitch, a task for which war is useful. Losing the popular vote by three million in 2016 was bad, but it would have been much worse had the Republican Party been run by a group of respectable and well-spoken Mitt Romneys or Jeb Bushes, droning on about values and hard work and the importance of family.

Finally, there are the evangelicals. Abortion may be the main reason they turn out so reliably for Republicans each election cycle, but Christian Zionism, according to which the founding of the state of Israel is a biblically prophesied precursor to the Second Coming of Christ and the Rapture, also plays a role. Secretary of State Pompeo and Vice President Pence are both strong supporters of the Christian Zionist group Christians United for Israel, whose leader claims to have helped in persuading the Trump Administration to move the American embassy in Israel from Tel Aviv to Jerusalem. In an interview with a Christian television network given while he was visiting Jerusalem, Pompeo agreed that Trump could be a modern-day Queen Esther, sent to save the Israelis from what the interviewer called the "Iranian menace." These evangelicals refuse to see America's Middle East crusade end with a whimper.

Losing the support of any of these groups would be catastrophic for Republicans. Like patriarchy and racism, imperialism is nonnegotiable. It will be at the foundation of the Republican Party's project for as long as the Republican Party is a national political force.

And what about the Democrats? There is a lot to say about them, but also, there isn't. Their objections to Republican foreign policy amount to pleas for "smarter," "more strategic," "more thoughtful" imperialism. The only thing these pleas signify at the level of the party as a whole is that while Democrats may have begun to perceive the question facing American foreign policy, they have taken no meaningful steps toward answering it. To their credit, they did not join the Republicans in active warmongering after Soleimani's killing, even after Iran responded by carrying out missile strikes on American bases in Iraq, proportional attacks that injured but did not kill American troops. However, Democrats have raised no meaningful objections to the part of Trump's Iran policy that most increases the likelihood of war: the economic sanctions. If left in place indefinitely, these sanctions will destroy the Iranian economy, just as similar sanctions did to Iraq in the 1990s.

Under the current sanctions regime, all Iranian assets based in the US have been frozen, and almost all forms of trade between the US and Iran have been banned, including trade in oil, on which the

Iranian economy is dependent. The US also has ways to discourage other countries from economic engagement with Iran. After Trump pulled the US out of the nuclear deal, the European Commission encouraged the EU's main investment bank to invest in Iran as a way to provide the country with some relief. The bank refused, on the grounds that a third of its funds have to be raised on US capital markets, meaning that investing in Iran would expose the bank to crippling sanctions itself. What this means for Iran is that its economy shrank by almost 10 percent in 2019, according to the IMF. To make matters worse, Iran is currently in the midst of a severe coronavirus outbreak, with more than eight thousand dead and some 160 thousand infected. The sanctions program, along with American threats to penalize companies found in violation of it, have hampered the Iranian government's efforts to increase its stock of crucial medical supplies.

Protests have occurred as a result; in November 2019, Iranians took to the streets to object to an increase in the price of subsidized gasoline, which the government implemented because it is now desperate to raise revenue wherever it can. Mike Pompeo pointed to the protests as evidence that Iranians en masse are finally getting fed up with their own government, but Iranians aren't idiots. They know who is to blame for their economic problems. Trump's "maximum pressure" campaign is an exact repeat of Bill Clinton's sanctions against Iraq. If left in place, its only effects will be to make life harder for the people of Iran. Frustration will continue to break out in public, and when it does, the government will continue to send in police to clear the streets and jail protesters. Those protesting will feel their government only wants them to keep quiet in the face of an economy that is increasingly in crisis. The government will feel that their old enemy, the cause of this crisis, has left them with no real choices outside of repression. This will poison the relationship between the two countries to an extent that will make negotiations impossible. If Democrats are sincere in their desire to avoid war with Iran, they will have to work to dismantle America's sanctions program before it is too late.

OUTSIDE THE US, the consensus is clear: international polls consistently show that America is viewed as the world's most serious
threat to peace. Inside the US, the myth of America's benevolence
continues to hold sway, especially among those in government, with
ritual expressions of wounded outrage in response to any suggestion
that America's intentions could be anything less than pure. Since the
Iranian Revolution, a particularly favored ritual of this type has been
the furor over the phrase "Death to America," which Americans
associate as closely with Iran as they associate "life, liberty, and the
pursuit of happiness" with themselves. "Death to America" was first
popularized by Khomeini, and it has since become a staple of Iranian
protests and marches. Americans take it literally, seeing it as a call
for the destruction of their country, the killing of soldiers based in
the Middle East, and attacks against civilians like those carried out
on September 11. As the Obama Administration worked to convince
Congress to ratify the nuclear deal, Democratic and Republican representatives alike threw the phrase in his face.

In US politics, the persistence of "Death to America" symbol-
izes all that is supposed to make negotiation with the Iranian regime
hopeless: the bloodlust of the Iranian government, the unwillingness
of Iranians to see reason, Muslim "fanaticism." But as with much of
American political rhetoric about the Middle East, this reading is
willful ignorance at best. The fervor backing the slogan has been
wildly overstated. "Saying 'Death to America!' has been a permanent
fixture of the revolution that we don't listen to anymore," a deputy oil
minister with the Iranian government said recently. "It comes out as
a matter of routine." A political scientist at the University of Tehran
estimated that only a fifth of Iranians bother to chant the phrase
at all, and that "only a teeny percent" of that fifth actually believe
in it. And in any case, Iranian officials have long insisted that the
target of the chant is American policy, not Americans themselves.
"These slogans," President Khatami said in a 1998 interview with
Christiane Amanpour, "symbolize a desire to terminate a mode of
relations which existed between Iran and the United States." This

understanding is shared by the current Iranian president's chief of staff: "It's not the people of America, per se. . . . It's not a nation. It's a system of behavior."

Most Iranians have little or no direct experience with America or the people who live there, and little or no reason to wish them harm. But they do have decades of direct experience with American foreign policy. There can hardly be an Iranian on earth whose life has not been shaped by it in some way. Of course the slogan is incendiary: it came to prominence as Iran ousted a dictator who had the full and explicit backing of the US government, and it has persisted over forty years during which America has been consistent in its view that Iran's effort at self-determination should be ground into dust. The slogan is outrageous because the American actions that brought it into being have been more outrageous. Also, it's a *slogan*, a catchy way to sum up and condense feelings of frustration and anger that are widespread because they are based in experiences that all Iranians have shared. What are they supposed to chant? "We take issue with core aspects of American foreign policy"?

The American government's refusal or inability to understand what "Death to America" means is symptomatic of a foreign policy that must blind itself to the anger it arouses around the world in order to function. If the US can do the bare minimum of beginning to recognize that anger as reasonable, a different foreign policy is possible. If it can't, then the US will be just as bewildered by what's to come as it was when Iranian students stormed the embassy forty years ago.

2020

ROME CORONAVIRUS DISPATCHES

FRANCESCO PACIFICO

Stop Making Points
March 12, 2020

Listen to me. The problem is your imagination. Stop using dystopia as your compass. Stop using metaphors. You have to live through this. We've been inside the house, inside the quarantine, for five days, and it is totally unreal even for people used to lying in bed writing. This is a proper quarantine, a real one, not just a brief dimming of everyday life. The newspapers are posting pictures of the empty Spanish Steps on their websites. They shouldn't enjoy this too much, that messes up your defenses. You need them. I know this because I am endocrinologically impaired, and I know you have to stoke your immune system all the time to stay healthy. I left a WhatsApp chat of fellow writers and intellectuals the other day because they were posting and scrolling through photos of the apocalypse like children. I couldn't stand it. No takes. No points. Stop making points.

Go back to Tolstoy, forget the dystopias you got secondhand from crappy TV, say your prayers, buy a block of pink salt shaped like a bar of soap and cleanse your energy with it. It burns. Buy limes and lemons and learn the proportions for sours: three quarters of an ounce of lemon juice, the same amount of simple syrup or any sweet

357

liquor, two ounces of spirit. The margarita is a sour. The vodka sour is a sour. Alcohol keeps your family happy, and the citrus keeps the virus away. (This last bit is unconfirmed, but I love it.)

Let me go back to Tolstoyan basics and tell you about my father's hip replacement operation. My father decided to do the dramatic, momentous thing of retiring in the summer he turned 70. That was last summer. This after forty years of life as an IT entrepreneur, as the man who sat quietly at dinner with his arms crossed, eating while his two children were kept from talking by his wife's electric eyes. All work and no play with the kids, for decades. We were obviously scared that retiring from the only thing he'd done consistently throughout his life—and doing it at this fateful moment—would be too much. Too much drama.

If I remember correctly, the messed-up hip all goes back to when he screwed up his knee a decade ago. It was the trickle-up effect: the jumbled knee put pressure on the hip. I may be mythmaking here, but I think the trouble began at my sister's wedding reception at his house in the country. The catering people got their car stuck in mud, and though he'd been an unathletic guy his whole life, he decided he had to help out and push the car. He fell, of course, and when he accompanied my sister to the altar he had a leg-brace over the left leg of his suit. At the time I decided this was a symptom of his overly conflicted feelings about my sister getting married. A shaman I know thinks my sister was my father's slave in another life.

Ten years later, he's retired and has been hobbling, or maybe even crippled, going on two years now. He is a resourceful man, especially in times of distress, or maybe only in times of distress, when he suddenly conjures a jovial attitude he otherwise never displays. It's mystical, almost hippyish, impossible to square with his day-to-day sternness. He's ready for the surgery: he wants to use the hip replacement as the fresh start his retired life hasn't provided. Though of course he'd say that it's a compelling life even under the constraints. He lives next door to his three quirky and handsome grandchildren—my sister's children. He is a poet at heart. He can make the most of a stroll.

When the outbreak happens, three weeks ago, our society's reckoning comes in spurts. In very slow spurts. I remember feeling panic on a train from Paris to Milan to Rome, and I remember the panic receding, but after that it hasn't ever been so linear, going up and down on a whim. Now that we're stuck at home it's flattened out—yesterday, March 11, was my most serene day. The analogies aren't right, but none of them could be. What we have in our minds are the soundtracks to Christopher fucking Nolan movies, a thousand action movie trailers blurring into a single mass, the GIF of goddamn Peggy's reaction shot from *The Handmaid's Tale* on loop forever. We think everything is ramping up, but it's not ramping up. Writing the narrative of this thing feels like each of us is writing a novel. It's not a linear process. But I can remember thinking: alright, my father is not canceling his operation, he's not afraid of the prospect of the epidemic escalating like it has in Lombardy, or he must feel that if he doesn't do it now he'll have to wait for six months, because the hospitals will have become off-limit war zones in the meantime and his plan to be a healthy, retired senior citizen will be delayed. He must have thought—we'll never talk about this—that six more months as a crippled man in pain would do him in.

THREE DAYS BEFORE my father's due to be admitted to the hospital, Rome gets its first cases. The day before his admission they find a coronavirus case in his hospital. My sister and I don't budge. My father and my mother—a very anxious person, tall and devilish and candid and childish and tricky to be around when you're weak—decide to go.

I've been telling people my age that we have to let my parents' generation go. I say that since these people never relinquished their power, we feel like their tragedy is our tragedy. We're not an independent generation, I declare emphatically. My pep talk resonates well with my receptive and lonely audience of me and me alone. My anguish lifts. I think to myself that these people—these parents—are even cool. They've decided that they're willing to risk being killed in order to avoid being lame. I don't know if that pun works, but I'm asking you to be generous during this difficult time.

So they go. On the day of the surgery my mother's anxiety is world-historical. The day begins at 6:30 AM and drags on forever, though it's a comfort—sort of—that the delays are due to the surgery prep and not the virus. My parents say that everything in that fantastic, state-of-the-art hospital is safe. And you want to believe them, because their life is a fantasy. Their generation's life is our porn, so I believe them. I'm praying and letting go at the same time. In the meantime, you have to understand that my wife, a hypochondriac, is dealing with the situation by crying for everyone's safety. We get drunk at home on martinis and tiki cocktails that we have for lunch and dinner and after dinner. I have nine different rums on my shelf, and I'm experimenting with a recipe book from Smuggler's Cove, the San Francisco tiki bar.

The surgery goes well, and my mother is less antsy. My father's nagging pain has ceased and he is very happy.

The first night is fine. We're on a family WhatsApp chat and are kept updated. My father's IV drip is making him happy. Jokes and memes are exchanged. The doctors, we're informed, are switching to a blander painkiller. It's a Catholic hospital, so I assume they're against recreational anesthesia. He has very low blood pressure.

OK, so the next day is a Saturday, and my wife and I are driving to the country with friends to breathe some good air. That night the government will decree its full-China response to the situation, and of course that's all we'll talk about. Even before that, my wife is miserable. We're all scared. We have arguments, we drink, we have acid reflux. But that morning, before the worst goes down, my mother does this thing that is so her. "Some pics of the grandkids to cheer up a heavy day. *Please*," she writes. No context and no additional information. My mother's style. My sister posts a pic of her son recklessly launching himself from the fence around the park.

I talk to my mother that afternoon. My father was in too much pain from the blander painkiller. Hence the demand for grandkid content. I know it could have been worse—and she does, too—but I assume him screaming all night must have been a serious scene.

The next day my mother writes: "There was a moment of panic when a security person stopped me to tell me they were shutting down our sector, and I had to go home. I'm staying, though, because us family members are helping out the nurses with a lot of minor things. But we are stuck in our room. I was able to sneak into mass. The hospital is a desert."

Hours later: "This soap opera of them trying to kick me out is still going on. We're waiting to see if I can stay until tomorrow, or if a guard is going to escort me out right now. Dad told them that if they kick me out, he's going, too. The nurses are helpless."

Twenty minutes later. "The head nurse has agreed that I'm staying but they'll have to bury me alive." Buried alive, like the architects of pyramids trapped forever inside the walls. "They'll decide on Dad's dismissal tomorrow."

As it turns out, even in the midst of dystopia you can still want to kill your mother, like in a comedy. I've been spending my days making cocktails for my wife. We wrote to the cleaning lady and the yoga teacher and told them we'd keep paying despite the shutdown. It's a strange time when you want to give people money.

On Monday I get a call from my father, who's much friendlier on the phone than my mother. He asks if I can pick up the walker he's renting from this pharmacy ten kilometers away from my place, because he's coming home. (Home is eight kilometers away.) The thing is, Monday is the first day of real awareness in Rome. My wife is bleak when I tell her I have to go do this. I feel heroic and skinny, if that makes sense. I feel like a sexy 20-year-old hero. I put on a tracksuit, sneakers, sunglasses and a fleece collar on my mouth and nose. I'm ahead of the curve of on the panic, but I think people will understand. I drive down the on-ramp to the eastern freeway and put on some Joyce Carol Oates online classes I've downloaded onto my tablet. She's soothing as hell, and her commitment to explaining Virginia Woolf's diary is making me cry.

I get off the freeway and end up on a tame little road in a very residential part of town. This must be the neighborhood's main street.
A lot of double-parked cars, not many people around. I get cash at
an ATM and enjoy the experience of giving five times what I usually
give to a young African man standing on the corner and an old Eastern European guy sitting on the curb. I'm a young, skinny cowboy
doing apocalyptic errands for my father. There are three people in
line outside the store where they're waiting for me and my 100 euros
and my ID. Everyone is keeping their distance, but I'm the only one
there not looking for face masks. When it's my turn I ask the store
owner about availability and turn to inform the people behind me.
I'm never about being good, and this heroic day of errands is making
me want to be good. I take the green walker to my car. I buy a Danish
at a bar. I wait thirty minutes before eating it, hoping that the virus
it's obviously infected with will die out in that time.

I have a new book out, and I'm proud of it. It's an essay about
how *Mrs. Dalloway* can offer men today a new kind of sentimental
education, how she can free us from our bad habits. I have a book out
but I don't care.

I drive to my parents' house, where I wait for them to arrive in
a black car. When they get there, I argue with my mother as I help
my father slowly get acquainted with the walker. He moves slowly,
but he's not in pain. People on the street say hi and are clearly puz-
zled by this new development—so now the virus is also crippling
people? In the deserted street his slow, assisted walk can't help but
look ominous.

I bicker with my mother about whether my father should start
using the walker immediately, or stick to his crutches for this short
walk to the elevator.

"Stop bitching," she says. "I'm the boss."

"Fair enough," I say. "And then when it's June, we'll shake hands,
and I'm never going to see you again."

We go upstairs and briefly check on my father. He's so relieved, I
can tell. I start saying that I'm afraid my wife could fall apart, she's so

scared. Her father has been hanging out with his best friend, whose daughter works in Milan and just came back to their hometown, which is near Rome.

"What can we do to help?" my mother asks.

"Nothing," I say. "I just needed to vent my fears, or I'll develop something psychosomatic, please just listen."

Marriage Story
March 18, 2020

The woman living with me was my wife until two weeks ago. We got married for different reasons: she wanted a big party, and I wanted to secure what was still, at that point, an alliance built on strengthening our positions. I'm a political science major and a novelist. I believe in shapes, forms, and tendencies—not in values. She studied theater and cinema, she's a feminist. When we started living together she had a job that was making her miserable, but she wouldn't quit: she had always made a point of never leaving a job without first securing the next one. As a result she'd never had the chance to regroup or retool.

Our Catholic heritage compels us Italians to believe that between marriage and divorce lies an interesting gap of time called the "separation." During the state of separation you are still married, but some of the effects are suspended. (The coincidence between this and our current predicament is unintentional, but I'm acknowledging it anyway.) I told her that if we got married either of us could take time off work, and we'd still be safe, and if we broke up during a work hiatus, whoever was employed at the time would have to keep buying the other person food. "And clothes, too?" "Oh, for sure!" I said to her, with what I recognize now as tone-deafness, that according to my understanding being a feminist shouldn't feel like punishment, or self-punishment. It shouldn't force someone to remain in an abusive workplace. If we get married and you're out of work, I said, I have to pay for both of us until we're divorced. And since you'd have to cosign the divorce papers, you can remain in a state of separation until you find a job you actually like.

We got married, and I myself have taken advantage of this deal. I took our first year of marriage off to write a novel; she—and a very meager amount of magazine work—fed me throughout that time.

She was my wife until two weeks ago. That's how I started this story, because what I want to stress is that marriage is a social thing. Even if you're a fan of vows and complicated weekends in the country full of rituals and pageantry, marriage isn't set up to compose the entirety of your life within society: it acquires its value from context. Now there is no context, especially not for two hypochondriacs who have been piling up garbage in the yard because they're afraid of making the very short walk to the neighborhood dumpsters and have seen one friend and no relatives in the past ten days. She is not my wife, and I am not her husband. In the wedding vows there is always an allusion to bad times, but I'm not sure that includes total separa- tion from the society that gives the social contract its meaning.

Who are we when we're alone? I have time to study her. She's sad half the time, scared most of the time. She is capable of experiencing her fears all at once, in a bundle, like an all-access subscription ser- vice to her nightmares, whereas I can only concentrate on one fear at a time. So I put all my energy into, say, avoiding social contact, or checking my bank account for signs that anyone in publishing who owes me money has actually gotten around to paying me what they owe me before early April, when I have to pay my credit card bill. I never think about what editors and translators and podcasters and writers will be paid after the pandemic, while she has a lush, six-screen setup in her mind where she monitors every contingency all the time: she'll lose her job; she'll lose her parents; she'll lose me; she'll die; and then the economy will collapse.

The neurotic comedy of married life has a completely differ- ent feel these days. The jokes feel like they're written by SUNN O))), who've slowed the dialogue down and buried it in reverb and echoes. I'm writing about the pandemic in a language that is not my own because I don't want to deploy my usual tools. I don't want to repeat things I learned and said at a different time. If the government ordered us to use a different language to express ourselves during the pandemic, it wouldn't even be that strange. Being stuck is a different language, too.

The above digression is my homage to the woman I live with and her fears. Her fears are so real and so present. I no longer tease her for lumping them all together. I watch her curl up on the couch and weep and I thank God for my stilted childhood and android-like reactions. (My response to the pandemic feels like a malfunction: my faint but ever-present tinnitus has become a monumental drone, low and jagged. When I try to go to sleep it's just me and my disintegration loop. I looked up tinnitus online, and apparently it has some psychosomatic wrinkles I wasn't aware of.) But when she hears that one of her close friends has been laid off, she doesn't encrypt and disperse the revelation via drones and tinnitus. She keeps it in front of her, all day long. When a friend tells her that everyone who works for her company will be subject to the *cassa integrazione*, the temporary lay-off scheme, and that she's still not sure if they'll survive, and who knows whether the government's stimulus package will be successful, anyway, the woman who lives in my house, the woman lying on my couch, keeps the information front and center and places it onto the pile, just on top of the previous piece of news. And when another friend tells her that her mother has to keep going to the hospital for chemotherapy and that her sister is a nurse, she projects this new information onto a new screen next to the other information that occupies the other screens.

When the writing really slows down for me, like it has this morning (the birds are chirping, it's sunny), there is no distraction or temptation to open Twitter or Facebook. At moments like this I can use writing the way I did when my family wouldn't let me do anything that wasn't related to the church, when I developed the hermit skills that are serving me so well these days.

I want to tell a story from last weekend, but it requires so much context. The main thing you need to know is that the woman who lives with me hasn't been working, because she is in the event industry. This alone would be enough to provoke constant nightmares, but there's more things, and it's not related to the virus. Her new job, which she started shortly before all this started, is her dream job. This self-actualization provoked a lot of inner turmoil over the past few months, because no one who grows up and realizes their desires is ever really happy, especially not us Catholics. On top of this were two new realities that would inevitably shatter the reality of the married life we'd known. She would have to spend some of her time in Turin, commuting back and forth and threatening her Roman routine and her Roman community in the process (and I would have to go with her, because I'm a wimp, and I miss her all the time). And even worse, when in Rome, for the first time in her life she would be working from home.

This was our major problem around the time she was last my wife, two or three weeks ago. We were worried about both of us working from home, and she was afraid that she would go crazy without an office to go to every day. A few days before all this started, she told me that I was allowed to spend my days in spandex only until I submitted the Hanya Yanagihara novel I was translating. After that I was going to have to start dressing like a normal person again.

On Saturday morning, the power went off and our alarm started blaring. She later told me, after we'd made up, that I freaked out as soon as the noise began. I didn't notice my reaction, but I know I felt guilty because I was the one who hadn't chased down the electrician weeks ago, when she'd implored me to. Without a fresh battery, the alarm was bound to erupt with the most violent noise because the living beast that it is thinks that every time the power goes out it's because there are thieves around, scheming and breaking and entering. A few weeks ago, someone in the neighborhood called the power company people, and they had to disconnect the power on our block a few dozen times. On that occasion, our alarm went off every single time, until 4 AM. We ended up driving around in the middle of the night, mortified. There were people walking down the next street over from us, trying to figure out where the noise was coming from. Nobody had ever told us that you have to change that battery every two years. It had died five years ago.

So when the alarm went off again, in a neighborhood now frozen by quarantine, I must have freaked out because I hate to bother the neighbors, it's something my mother etched into my brain. I got out of the house and stared at the alarm high up on the outside wall, its orange light blinking frantically. The woman I live with saw that I was freaking out and started screaming "You're no good! It's your fault!" So I felt the urge to go out, for the first time since Monday, and check the electrical box on the block to see if I could make it stop from over there.

There were two men drilling into the pavement in the narrow alley where the electrical box is located. I asked them if the power outage had anything to do with them. They said no. "My wife is about to kill me," I said. I apologized for pulling my hoodie all the way up, to cover my nose and mouth. "She's a hypochondriac," I said. "No, of course," they responded, "our wives are like that, too."

I was at a safe distance from the men, staring helplessly at a box I couldn't remember if I even had the key to. Right at that moment, the woman who'd been my wife appeared and started shouting from a safe distance, about ten meters: "I can't believe it!" she yelled. "What are you doing over there with them? We've spent a whole week alone to make sure we're healthy, and now we have to start from scratch!"

Her voice was a canyon full of caves where horses had gone to die. It was so scary. When I was growing up I had a kind of falsely symbiotic relationship with my mother. Everything she said became a truth I had to accept, but which I remained wary of. That happens with partners, too. I went back inside thinking that she was right, that death had entered our house.

I told her that it was going to be fine, that I had taken all the necessary precautions. My voice was feeble and unpersuasive. She was miserable, she was crying. (The alarm had shut off at some point.)

I called the power company but was interrupted mid-conversation by my neighbor, who grew up here. It was his house the men with the drills were working on. He told me through the window that we were probably using too many appliances, because after all we weren't used to spending all our time at home. The man on the phone told me that the power company had recently started to limit usage at peak times. I can't be more specific about any of this now because I was in a state and don't remember.

The idea of a power outage is scary at a moment like this. The woman who had been my wife got on the phone and found a different electrician who brought a new battery the following day and solved the problem. He and I stayed three to four meters apart the whole time he was here and were happy to have the chance to chat. He told me he'd been able to buy the battery at a wholesale place that was still open because it wasn't a neighborhood store and so was exempt from the restrictions. If the sale and distribution of things like batteries had been interrupted, too, we would have ended up in a much darker place, watching as everything we needed eventually stopped working. We left him an envelope with cash in various denominations on the table in the yard. He helped himself to it and left.

But something else happened before that, on Sunday night. You have to know that Sunday was our day of peak sadness. The weekend felt so lonely, and also the numbers were climbing. Most people don't read what the scientists say and only participate in the commentary. There isn't enough herd immunity to bullshit, and I feel like I'm the only one who swears by the graph that says that things have been invisibly changing for the better from the minute we went on lockdown. But the thing is, the official numbers change slowly, it's inevitable, and you have to have hope. And hope is what some people started to have yesterday, on Monday, when, for the second time in a row, public announcements went with what the scientists had been writing—the numbers were showing promise.

What happened on Sunday night is a small thing that doesn't have to do with the virus, and that's why I'm focusing on it. My parents are at home, and a man from a clinic comes to see my father every day to help him with physical therapy after his hip replacement surgery. Then my parents watch the rosary and the mass on TV. I cannot focus on this—on the fact that this man leaves the clinic and comes to my parents' house and puts his hands on my father. I might be an orphan in two weeks. I can't be like the woman who lives with me and keep this thing in front of me all day. I can still love her, maybe I love her more than I did before all this, but for the first time I feel that we're on different dimensions. I don't want to be that human. I'm using this foreign language to allow myself to briefly feel things and consider things, and I can't wait for this piece of writing to be over so I can go take a shower and be my old self, in Italian, clunky and silly in the face of adversity.

Sunday night my baby, my fantastic life partner, was getting ready for bed. She sleeps with a heated pad you have to plug into an outlet. She had told me days earlier that the pad was taking forever to charge. On Sunday night, she plugged it in, and I saw the light in the living room dim. We checked everything: the wall sconces were OK, but the lamps you plug directly to the wall had gone dark. I looked at the electric panel; the switch for outlets was in the off position. I tried to flip the switch back to On, and there was a spark somewhere inside the wall.

This time around, I asked my love not to freak out, and I smiled in a way that conveyed natural, hopeful goodwill. The risk of fucking up the power in our hermitage made us experience deep, strong emotions. We both had low battery on our phones, but we discovered that the sockets in our kitchen worked—they were grouped on a different switch on the panel. We plugged our phones, then dumped the heating pad in a corner after carefully pulling it from the socket it had short-circuited.

My beloved housemate and I looked each other in the eyes and realized that our collective not-freaking out was an important moment in our woozy journey. I told her I was sure the spark wasn't dangerous, but we shouldn't risk setting off the alarm in the dark. The next morning, though, we'd flip the general switch off, then flip the outlets switch on, then flip general on again.

On Monday, the news finally arrived. The mid-May event my wife had been so happily working on, her perfect assignment, has been postponed. Monday was a sad day. The next day, yesterday, the office in Turin called her up for an online meeting. She was so happy at that meeting. It was a joy to watch her sitting at the table waving hi to everyone on her camera. Before we went to sleep, she casually dropped the news that her team had decided that she was going to take on part of their social media work soon. She felt so happy saying that, and now I'm marveling at my unearned ability to concentrate intensely on only one thing. Last night, it was her smile. This morning, it's a foreign language that takes me on a two-hour stroll in the garden of my feelings.

The Toothache
April 10, 2020

At the end of my second week of isolation my teeth started to ache and I was plunged into my body, where I spent the next two weeks in a state of blissful retreat from my conscience.

My body took over at the end of a long speech I was giving to some of my students, whom my colleague and I had gathered on Zoom. The speech was about how crucial it is to identify the thin line that separates one's work hustle from the examined life. You are more than intellectual capital, I told them. You don't have to be invested. I logged off when the pain snatched me from my mind and threw me back inside my body, a body that hadn't had sex or gone for a run in some time. I wrote to my dentist and asked her for advice. It had been years since we'd spoken. On my last visit, which involved a cavity, she had asked me to come back a couple months later because she wanted to monitor a situation involving a couple of molars that were rubbing each other. I hadn't.

During the call I mentioned my collection of essential oils. She told me that her go-to disinfectant is tea tree oil. I could, she said, dilute it in water and use it as mouthwash. But the question of the pain remained before us: was it a cavity, or just gingivitis? The tea tree oil wouldn't cut it. I bought mouthwash, floss, and interdental brushes and spent the weekend trying to fine-tune my mouth's pH level. My mind was haunted by my wife's response to the situation: a surge of panic. If it was a cavity, I'd have to go to the dentist's office, where I'd catch the virus and die, and then she would die, too. By this point I was already mostly my body, but there was enough mind present for me to feel like I was being pulled down, down into that dark place of hers.

The very first thing I tried was a few drops of the tea tree oil in a glass of lukewarm water. I was barely into the first sip when my knees buckled under a chromelike pain that coated my teeth and penetrated them all at once. I knelt down in front of the bathtub, the glass still in hand. I wanted to be able to spit out into the tub and avoid crushing my head on the floor in case I passed out. The spike of pain that hit just then, on the floor, felt like somebody was holding a big blueprint of my teeth in front of my face. My teeth were finely detailed renderings of buildings, a starchitect's dream project in a faraway place.

During those first three days I had to pop a bunch of Okis, a brand of ketoprofen. Ketoprofen is an NSAID, a nonsteroidal kind of painkiller. According to the WhatsApp groups I'm in, if you catch the virus, NSAIDs can make things worse, but during our phone calls my dentist didn't try and talk me out of it. We kept in touch all weekend long as she examined me based on the words I said to her. Finally, on Monday morning, she came to the conclusion that it was a cavity and she had to treat it.

As soon as she made up her mind she delivered a speech she must have given to other clients in my situation:

> I'm only seeing people who are in desperate need for my help. We don't have anyone in the waiting room. We only schedule one appointment at a time, and there's time to completely sanitize the office between patients. My hygienists, who take the bus to work, aren't coming in right now. Only my daughter is, and she lives around here. We've got all the right equipment: the fabric, the masks, the glasses. There's no risk. The risk is on the street. I am tending to my very old mother, who is ill. She has a bad leg I'm trying to help with, so I see her every night. I myself cannot afford to catch the virus.

When my wife found out I was going she started crying. She didn't stop for two hours. That was one of the last moments I spent not fully inside my body. I am the sort of symbiotic being who has to buy into his partner's tragic vision, whatever it might be, but this time I felt very confident that I was not going to catch the virus in the dentist's office, and I said that to her. She's never been the type of person who is defiant in the face of trouble—to her, every form of resistance is an act of hubris.

I left her crying in the house and got into the car. The afternoon was cold and sunny. No jacket, just a wool sweater, fleece gloves, sunglasses, and a makeshift mask made of parchment paper tucked inside my scarf. The drive only took fifteen minutes, but it felt endless: the roads were terrifying and unfamiliar. My breathing was mechanical and fogged up my lenses. I turned into a quiet street near the train station and found the office. The door was open for me. My dentist was covered from head to toe in sage green. We said hi to each other and both laughed dryly.

The dentist and her daughter examined my cavity, cleaned it, and inserted a filling. They assessed the gingivitis. She said I also seemed to have sinusitis, and trigeminal nerve inflammation, and I was grinding my teeth in my sleep, and my jawbone was tense. But at least she had been able to take care of the cavity. An ominous ping of pain made my teeth hyperreal again as I was rinsing my mouth at the end of the appointment. The dentist gave me a worried look. I was at the door and itching to leave as she insisted that she had to see me again in a few months, when everything was back to normal. But at least the cavity was cured.

On the way back the roads were a little busier. It was 5 PM, the ghost of rush hour. I undressed in the yard and dumped my clothes right there. I entered the house naked except for the sunglasses and presented myself to my wife like a proud toddler who had just learned how to take care of himself. But she was on Zoom for work and didn't smile back. Work was probably going to stop for a while, and the fears associated with that imminent reality had distracted her from the fact that death had returned from the dentist's office and had just entered the house.

All this washed faintly against my mind, because there was no longer a mind left. I was only a naked body who longed for the shower, and that's where I went. I washed away the fear from the streets, and the cold sun, and the pallid fluorescent vibe of the dentist's office, and the assortment of mouthwashes I had tried, and the quiet haste of the procedure.

THE PAIN DIDN'T STOP, as my dentist's face had suggested at the end of my visit. In my effort to avoid making a big deal out of it, to normalize it, I commented on it aloud, constantly. "Oh, see? Now the pain is doing this." "Huh, now it's doing that." I was inside my mouth, all of me, all the time. I could barely sense how my wife was reacting. I knew she was mad: "You never heal," she said. "Every time you have a problem, it goes on and on and never ends. Do the doctors not know what they're doing, ever? Are you just nuts?"

By then I was somewhere in the remote region of my back molars, but in a moment of clarity I realized that there'd been a misunderstanding. "You know I have mental issues," I said. "I always have strong psychosomatic reactions to everything. My family never wanted me to emote, so I developed weird, nagging, physical issues. You shouldn't make too much of this, you know the process. The trigeminal nerve is triggered by stress. The sinusitis has to do with allergies. It's a perfect storm."

She brought up our trip to Iceland last year, which I spent so stressed out that my head started buzzing and then kept buzzing for two weeks straight. I had to drive our rental Jeep for hours every day through the stoned gray cloud between my eyes. The only thing that made it go away, briefly, was when I would stop the car and break down crying. During the long trip we'd taken a year before Iceland, she'd been in mourning for a relative, and this had wreaked havoc on her body. The trip had been ridden with IBS and panic attacks, and more than one hospital visit. On one particularly scary afternoon in a Los Angeles hospital, the doctors had suspected a blood clot. They got it wrong, but had tested her with appropriate urgency. The Iceland trip had unearthed a sorrow I had kept quiet in California. Now my wife was saying that my prolonged toothache during the lockdown reminded her of the psychosomatic buzz that had needlessly worried her on the Iceland trip. She was right, I told her, but this was who I was and she should simply stop paying attention. "In that case," she said, "you must stop informing me of every variation in your pain."

My body perceived the sophisticated reasoning she had concealed behind what only seemed like harshness, and so I started to pretend I wasn't in pain. I asked to be excused from all meals, because I knew I wouldn't be able to eat at a normal pace, and that would upset her.

Two days after the trip to the dentist's office, while juggling paracetamol; a lesser drug; and the occasional dangerous, happy, trippy Oki, I remembered that the acupuncturist I'd been visiting for the past two years was also a doctor and that she could help me with the toothache, the trigeminal nerve, and the sinusitis. (I realize now, as I write this, that I met her when my wife was trying to cure the physical breakdown brought on by the mourning I mentioned.

The doctor had solved her kidney issues and her colon issues in a single sitting. My wife stopped seeing her after that because the visits reminded her of death, but I had become a regular, monthly client. I didn't go for specific reasons—I just liked the tweaking. Acupuncture can give you a high that will arouse you and make you write a chapter of your novel in your mind and make you feel love for humanity and energize your liver all in the span of a brief nap. All it takes are those weightless needles in the ankles and face.)

I wanted to call her because the Oki and the paracetamol were worrying me, and especially the amount of time I'd been taking them. Oki is dangerous for the heart and paracetamol bogs down your liver. My liver was already bogged down thanks to an intense cocktail-mixing regimen during the first two weeks of quarantine. Paracetamol gives you a tiny, gentle buzz but doesn't last, and Oki feels like dancing while lying down, like a robot geisha at your bedside.

One night I wake up at 2 AM, pop an Oki, and spend time reading about painkillers. According to the site I'm looking at, paracetamol is the least dangerous of the bunch, which says a lot about the heaviness of the entire painkiller genre. The rest of the list is made up of the most dangerous stuff. There's fentanyl and that whole family. I've been practicing yoga and qigong since I turned 40 and have found out that any pain that comes from inflammation—lower back pain, for instance—can be healed either with slow continuous exercise that helps you find new dimensions in what your body can experience, or with the most dangerous drugs. Those are the two teams, the two opponents. On one hand, the most boring practices—but also the most rewarding; on the other, drugs that kill you with pleasure.

My acupuncturist hears my story and gives me some natural drugs that will cure the inflammation of the trigeminal nerve. There's a boswellia-based thing that tastes harsh and wizardlike. It functions as a painkiller, but a bland one. All these drugs play the long game, and the pain is such that I still wake up at night and take paracetamol.

When I pop an Oki it feels like cheating on your girlfriend when you're young—a sudden urge that cancels everything else.

The doctor knows my liver, though, and writes to me that the maximum amount of paracetamol I can afford to take is two grams a day, a bit lower than what the box says, three grams.

She invites me to a free video qigong session with the other clients. The physical work is very light, aimed only at stirring the energy inside you and boosting your immune system by stimulating some pressure points in your arms and shoulders that can jump-start your lungs and intestines.

The next night I wake up in pain and start pressing on my jaw, warming it and numbing it, and I manage to fall back asleep. That happens three times, on and off until 10 AM. I wake up smiling.

This pain I'm writing about, it's time to put it into words. It's a ghost. Sometimes it's in the lower molars. When it's there, it starts when I unwittingly clench my jaw and one of the lower molars touches the upper molar just above it, the one that had the cavity. It's deep, it feels like dirty gold. Then the pain moves to the jaw. That must be the trigeminal nerve. It arrives at the juncture of skull and jaw, at which point it seems to take the shape of a halo: I feel it reaching all the way out to the temple. From time to time it retreats and moves toward the front teeth. At other times, the pain limits itself to the sinusitis, concentrated on my right cheekbone, in particular.

I am confined to my house for the duration of the quarantine, and I now have a deeper understanding of the different vibes every room offers. I can tell how the light of one specific day's sun will affect the spirit of each room. But also, I am not really allowed to be in the house anymore, because I spend all my time forced to explore the brutalist villa that has been expanding rapidly: a wing in my cheekbone, a wing near my ear, and a basement in my mouth.

THE STORY NOW GETS TO its happy ending, and to redemption. Thursday, March 26, is the seventh day since the pain started; the trip to the dentist's took place on Monday. In the meantime, Italy's

Covid numbers have started to improve, and Rome's case growth is no longer exponential. We might soon emerge from the first stage of this new life, at which point we'll have to figure out where to go next. Inserting this Covid recap into my narrative feels so abstract. I have detached myself from my mind, which was the last thing in me that had been connected to society, through my friends' and relatives' preoccupations.

From the moment I put an end to the neurotic shtick of describing my pain and began keeping this journey to myself, my life entered a different stage. It feels as if life has become mine again, after decades. This place at the intersection of the jaw, the sinuses, and the molars, this tense place where paracetamol can come and comfort you the way masturbation can on a depressed day, this place where the vapors of fumigation—boiling water in a pot, baking soda, eucalyptus oil—can create a miniature spa under the towel that I hold over my head, this place has created something that is mine. It is mine like writing was mine when I had two friends in the whole world and I didn't like the life my parents forced me to live, when writing became a place where I could stop being inside society, that false friend who was calling me over and always leaves me unhappy and hollow. This place, my jaw and my cheek, this model house is my new safe space, generous and loving and rich with possibilities.

On Friday afternoon, I realize I haven't taken paracetamol since 9 AM and I'm managing. Around 5, the pain comes back, so I write to the acupuncturist and say: maybe there are some pressure points you can teach me that will ease the pain? Otherwise I will have to take more painkillers than you want me to.

Five minutes later we're on Zoom and she's pointing at her face. There's one pressure point where my jaw seems to form an angle. A half-inch above it, there's a ligament thing, and when I touch it it makes me feel like my face is a roast chicken. It's turgid and it gives me an entirely different idea of what a face really is. I keep pressing onto it with my index finger, mimicking her. There's this other "secret" point, she says, this off-the-grid pressure point that will help, too. It's right under this sort of small rock that you have at the far-thest end of your cheekbone, near your ear. A small jutting rock, like a cliff. Press a finger in the hollow right under that cliff.

I should also touch the base of the nostrils. And I can look for that hollow place right under the center of each cheekbone.

I'm only ever imitating what she's doing. I'm touching my face with intention, going through these new yet familiar motions. It occurs to me that if we had all been taught to touch ourselves in order to get more diverse, assorted kinds of satisfaction and well-being, then stroking your genitals would be a simple part of a bigger regimen focused on how to love yourself.

Twenty-odd minutes into this Zoom session, I have one of the strangest realizations ever. I was completely absorbed by imitation, I wasn't even thinking of succeeding in what I was doing, and suddenly I find myself telling the doctor, "Oh . . . the pain is gone."

A whole week has passed since that supremely emotional moment. I have started doing qigong every other day, and I have kept touching my face anytime I've needed to, and I can now predict the result. It's not a prayer, I'm not keeping track of when I do it, but I am still well aware that there's a pain in front of me that has come in with the tides, and I have let it drown me. So even now that it's not coming, it's there.

I live on this imaginary beach that has a sea of pain in front of it. The tide has come and gone, and now I'm lying here watching the sea, its salt still on my lips. A week of pain was followed by a week of touching-induced pleasure, and it has left me on that beach, away from the quarantine, in a buzz of my own, occasionally distracted by work calls, but for the rest just here, in the body, alone with the writing.

2020

MAGIC ACTIONS

TOBI HASLETT

LEST WE FORGET. THE FEAR, THE WEEKS OF WAITING, THE VIVID force of the eyewitness testimony; the replaying of grisly footage and then the shock of the conviction: the whole drama of the Derek Chauvin trial—its obscenity and thin catharsis—would not have *taken place at all* were it not for last year's riots. Police trials are rare. So is national uprising. Looting, acts of vandalism, and the nightly carnival of torched police cars are what vaulted George Floyd's death from single cruelty to American crisis, as the fires of Minneapolis swept through every major city. It feels both near and far now.

It's been a year: long enough for the events to be flattened and foreshortened; long enough for the authorities to paint their account over the true one. The statements by Nancy Pelosi et al. after the trial exposed the hope that a guilty verdict for Chauvin will be enough to end this episode, sating the popular fury and killing the memory of the rebellion. We shall see. Even now, an official narrative has yet to emerge from the chaos of last spring. But it was stunning to watch the corporate media try to summon one and fail, confounded by the images they flashed in the public's face. At the DNC last fall we saw how the uprising may be remembered: a sunny, noble blur of soaring rhetoric and "peaceful" crowds—a fabulous alternative to the rawness on the ground.

But certain facts remain; some things can't be wished away. Too much was born and broken amid the smoke and screams. The least we can do is remember—to try, after the riots, after the speeches, after the backlash and elections, and after this latest (livestreamed) liturgy of American "criminal justice," to recall what really happened, extracting and reconstructing the whole flabbergasting sequence. Last year something massive came hurtling into view and exploded against the surface of daily life in the US. Many are still struggling to grasp what that thing was: its shape and implications, its sudden scale and bitter limits. One thing we know for sure is that it opened with a riot, on the street in Minneapolis where Floyd had cried out "I can't breathe."

THOSE WERE ERIC GARNER'S last words. To hear them repeated, six years later, by another black man slain on camera by police, lent the instant rage and hurt a humiliated futility. The dream of Black Lives Matter now seemed shredded by events. Michael Brown in Ferguson, Freddie Gray in Baltimore—the murders of these young black men launched explosive local uprisings, which were followed (but never matched) by demonstrations across the country. Those were marches, not rebellions; large and passionate, but a degree removed. For the first few days it seemed that Minneapolis would follow suit. A riot in a single city, to be met with the old routine: lament the stubborn "tensions" that rack this "complex" country, then try to pin the violence on notorious "outside agitators." Videos had already surfaced of white militants smashing glass. There were other videos, of course—the ransacked Lake Street Target, brute assaults by the police, clouds of tear gas blotting out entire city blocks—that revealed the robust presence of black people in the street. But fantasy proved irresistible. Was this a plot by anarchists, or the radical right-wing fringe? Tim Walz, the Minnesota governor, announced that 80 percent of the rioters had arrived from out of town. No matter that this was a total falsehood, to be rescinded the following day. In high authoritarian style, the rumors rhymed felicitously with the song sung by the state.

But the destruction of the Third Precinct—this was striking, and truly new. The situation in Minneapolis burst beyond its early outline. On the evening of May 28, the third night of the rebellion, the police were forced to evacuate their own building, trounced on the very territory they had disciplined and patrolled, as they broadcast to the nation their own fear and vulnerability. (Malcolm X, who dreamed of a black revolution that would lift lessons from the French one, would perhaps have smiled at this latter-day Storming of the Bastille.) The retreat was caught on camera and streamed on social media. The infiltrated precinct feasted on by flames, vans pelted with projectiles as they sped out of the parking lot, the sound of shattering windshields mixed with the rebels' howls and cheers.

The event felt like a fulcrum. The whole country seemed to tilt: sacked shopping malls in Los Angeles and pillaged luxury outlets in Atlanta, a siege on New York's SoHo and flaming vehicles from coast to coast. Pictures of Philadelphia and Washington DC showed whole neighborhoods bristling with insurgency, crowds smashed the lordly windows in Chicago's Loop, and rioters set fire to the Market House, where slaves were bought and sold, in Fayetteville, North Carolina, the town where Floyd was born. Not all of this, surely, could be the work of agents provocateurs. Something deeper and more disruptive had breached the surface of social life, conjuring exactly the dreaded image the conspiracy theorists refused to face. This was open black revolt: simultaneous but uncoordinated, a vivid fixture of American history sprung to life with startling speed. One thousand seven hundred US towns and cities—the number was absurd. Within a week, sixty-two thousand National Guardsmen were dispatched to support city forces as they lurched to regain control. But what emerged under the banner of blackness was soon blended with other elements, flinging multiracial crowds against soldiers and police. In living memory, this breadth and volume was virtually unprecedented, apart from the national uprisings sparked by the murder of Martin Luther King Jr.—a name wheeled out, on cue, to bemoan the unruliness of the rebellion.

But "rebellion" and even "uprising" soon fell from widespread use. As spring slid into summer, the preferred term devolved to "protests," a change that marked the last phase in this jagged political sequence. There was constant, fractious overlap between differing attitudes and tactics. At first, battles in big cities outweighed more ordered, placid actions, but the latter soon became the standard (although Seattle and Portland were gripped by an insurrectionist element for months). A controlled but keen exuberance ruled the last months of demonstrations, which were less likely to result in ravaged property or mass arrests. By fall, the marches of the Obama years had in many ways returned but flushed with a new fury—a gift given them by the riots.

We need not fear that word. In fact, it's vital to insist, over the drone of an amnesiac discourse, that last year's spate of protest was *propelled*, made fiercely possible, by massive clashes in the street—not tainted or delegitimized by them, nor assembled from thin air. Those threatened by that fact will work to wipe it from our minds. The first phase of BLM thus made the case—unleashed the anguish—that was acted on last spring, in the flash of confrontation with the shock troops of the law.

Some were more prepared than others. At the start of the New York uprising, I saw a line of baton-swinging officers break through a makeshift barricade; a group of marchers fell back, and were chastised by a young black man who chose to stand his ground. "What are you doing?" he screamed at those retreating. "What did you even come here for?" A few nights later, under citywide curfew and after the trains had been shut down, a friend and I called a cab home in a bid to evade arrest. As we sped along the East River, the driver glanced in the rearview mirror and asked if we'd come from the demonstrations. Yes, we told him carefully, we'd been going out every night. His eyes smiled above his face mask. "You have to find the biggest brick you can," he said, "and then you make it count."

"I AM NOT SAD," Martin Luther King wrote, as cities exploded in the late 1960s, "that black Americans are rebelling; this was not only inevitable but eminently desirable." He was killed on a motel balcony before he could see those words in print. They appear in "A Testament of Hope," an essay often cited as proof of his socialist politics, which grew more rigid and explicit by the time he was taken out. (It happens that "desirable" and "historically inevitable" are key terms in Rosa Luxemburg's account of the mass strike.) King had begun to direct the civil rights movement toward the struggle of black workers; in 1967, he described the National Liberation Front not as a menace but as a legitimate "revolutionary government seeking self-determination" in Vietnam. And he arrived at a rapprochement with what had come to be known as Black Power: his late alliance with Malcolm X posed a brazen challenge to the white power structure that, in the wake of both men's convenient assassinations, pitted them against each other in a facile national myth. Malcolm, the black Muslim, was denounced as a vengeful thug; King is now for many a picture of eloquent docility. But he was hated by the kind of moderate who now invokes him to condemn the riots.

King's nonviolent protest was the fruit of a rigorous spiritual discipline—as well as a tactic, deployed pragmatically, before a scrim of mounting chaos. This was a theory of "direct action." Tension and confrontation were fundamental to the task. By applying unremitting pressure to every facet of civic life, he wished, as he wrote in "Letter from Birmingham Jail," to foment "a situation so crisis-packed that it will inevitably open the door to negotiation." The backdrop to that negotiation was the black rage breaking out in cities across the country; armed resistance groups were forming in black enclaves in the north and west. Here was another "crisis-packed" possibility, so some of the state's concessions to the Baptist reverend may have been clinched by the urban rebels. And by the late 1960s, as King's vision swept beyond mere equality before the law, he came to see revolt as a simple fact of his political moment. Nothing to relish or openly cultivate—or bombastically decry. "The constructive achievement of the decade 1955 to 1965 deceived us," he wrote. "Everyone underestimated the amount of violence and rage Negroes were suppressing and the vast amount of bigotry the white majority was disguising."

This later King has been supplanted by a glimmering hologram of bland obedience, beamed in instantly to vilify anything violent or simply rude. (I saw many demonstrators chide others for taunts and foul language.) Years of peaceful BLM rallies had met with years of elite inertia—but last spring many insisted that "bad" protesters (smashing property) would undo the work of the "good" ones (holding signs), some of whom were so flattered by this divisive strategy by the press that they went to flamboyant lengths to broadcast their own grinning, willing harmlessness. A pageant soon ensued (and fortunately subsided). Officers armed to the teeth marched beside newly minted pacifists; National Guardsmen did the Macarena with the people they were licensed to kill. Nonviolence, once a tool, today glows with the power of a fetish. And, unlike King, many marchers seemed to believe that good manners would be repaid with gentler policing.

They were vigorously disabused of this, as peaceful crowds were bashed, gassed, cuffed, maced, kettled for hours, and driven into by police vans. On May 30 alone, eight people were left partly blinded by rubber bullets. On the first night of the New York rebellion I was nearly struck by an NYPD vehicle barreling down a crowded street; the driver came out and howled at us before bursting into tears. The next week I was arrested at the most orderly demonstration I saw all spring—not a single broken window. After less than an hour marching through the South Bronx, we were choked on all sides by officers who kept us in place until the emergency curfew fell. Then came the attack: cordons of police pressed hard on either side of the trapped crowd and began to wallop anything that moved—many officers clambered onto parked cars to swing truncheons at our skulls. (My friend had worn his bicycle helmet, which within minutes was shattered in half.) The marchers were picked out from the crowd one by one as the police beat their way through the screaming kettle: two officers grabbed my arms and slammed me to the tarmac; a third knelt on my spine and bound my wrists in plastic cuffs. I stayed in that position, arms twisted behind my back, for eight of the seventeen hours I spent in police custody. But from the chaos of that night, one thing burns brightest in my memory: the hush that fell over the crowded cell as the gate swung open for a young white man. Like us, he was still in cuffs. But he'd been beaten worse than anyone else, his head cracked so hard that his red hair was plastered to his skull and his small face blackened with dried blood. With his arms pinned behind his back, he looked like a bird in an oil spill.

As more mayors imposed curfews, suspended food programs, and—in the sadistic instance of Eric Garcetti of Los Angeles—closed Covid-19 testing sites in revenge for the rebellion, the wheedling rhetoric of "nonviolence" implored marchers to submit to official diktat. "Anyone who is a peaceful protester, it's time to go home," Bill de Blasio said on live TV. I suspect that King would be sickened that his legacy was being travestied by the state that terrorized him—and rueful, if unsurprised, that revolt was still flaring in 2020.

But the riots worked. The beast groaned. Despite the many criticisms streaming through the media, the destruction of property struck many as a defensible answer to state violence: *Newsweek*—not known for its anarchist sympathies—reported that a full 54 percent of Americans saw the siege on the police precinct as "justified." The riots were too large and widespread, and expressed too popular a discontent, to be explained away by belting out the familiar anthems of condemnation. One old lament—that looters were destroying their own neighborhoods—seemed especially flimsy this time as, post-Minneapolis, crowds waged war on the (well-insured) commercial districts of the nation's downtowns.

In 2014, the failure to indict Darren Wilson for killing Michael Brown doubled the sense of helpless fury; within days of Floyd's death, Chauvin was charged with murder in the third degree, which as the riot roared along was promptly raised to second. Another third-degree charge was added just before the trial's start at the end of March. But the punishment of particular officers was no longer the thrust of this social movement. (To some demonstrators, it's anathema.) "People are still out protesting," Andrew Cuomo moaned three weeks into the uprising. "You don't need to protest. You won. You won. You accomplished your goal. Society says, you're right. Police need systemic reform." This statement—a lovely mixture of condescension and real fear—sped deftly past the fact that for many "reform" is not the point. They're fighting for abolition: an end to the police.

"ENOUGH," MARIAME KABA, an abolitionist organizer, wrote in mid-June. "We can't reform the police. The only way to diminish police violence is to reduce contact between the public and the police." That this opinion was printed in the *New York Times* announced its debut in the dominant discourse. Here, in the paper of record, was an argument for stripping departments of funding with a view to their full elimination—the chief demand of the rebellion, as the latest round of "police reform" had been a costly, shambling farce. Obama's Task Force on 21st Century Policing, which concluded in 2015, offered recommendations on training, equipment, and department culture, often with the effect of increasing law enforcement spending; indeed, many of these proposals had been adopted in Minneapolis. The blasted carcass of the Third Precinct hinted that the issue runs somewhat deeper. The abolition of police and prisons has always been the ideological engine of BLM, an inheritance of the Black Panthers' Ten Point Program: "We want freedom for all black men held in federal, state, county, and city prisons and jails," reads number eight. This tradition was kept alive by grassroots groups and championed in the academy and public sphere by the scholar-organizers Angela Davis and Ruth Wilson Gilmore.

But even they must have been astonished when, on the thirteenth day of the rebellion, the Minneapolis City Council made an unexpected announcement: it had voted to disband the city's police. The day before the vote, Mayor Jacob Frey had been booed out of a rally for refusing to back the measure. Chants of "Go home,

Jacob!" thrummed the air as he picked his way through the livid crowd. (His embarrassment was, of course, compounded by the fact that the council's vote was veto-proof.) The proposal was for a full-scale dismantling of the Minneapolis police force, to be followed by—something else. But the change may never take place. The effort has already hit a legal roadblock, as the department is protected—and given chilling autonomy—by a city charter from 1920. Faced with the enormity of the consequences, council members walked back their earlier pronouncements and reduced the 2021 police budget by a meager 4.5 percent.

From the start, some abolitionists feared that this attempt could even lead to an insidious sharpening of social control (as when the police in Camden, New Jersey, were disbanded in 2013) or to the city being taken over by the Minnesota State Patrol. Now it's clear that a transformation on the municipal scale will take the continuing mobilization of the people in the streets—as well as a deepening of the conversation about what the police do and are. Scrapping departments isn't enough; neither is closing prisons. Incarceration and policing have become the state's annihilating reflex when confronted with murder and sexual violence, but also homelessness and addiction—the social disintegration that marks those lives consumed by poverty.

Prisons mop up poor people, not bad people. (Last year's decarceration programs—a measure adopted in many, but not enough, jurisdictions as a means to curb the spread of Covid—has yet to be statistically linked to rearrests.) Vital to abolitionist thought is, as a first step, a redistributive mission. The extraordinary amount of money spent on punishment in the US should instead go to preventive and rehabilitation programs—a "nonreformist reform"—but more crucial is an assault, on every level, on the political consensus that's ripped the welfare state to ribbons. This will raise the "social wage" and drive fewer to the desperation simply classified as crime.

But behind even the most sparkling policy initiatives lies the knowledge that a world without police and prisons can only follow from ruthless criticism and transformation of every piece of the social whole. This is a revolutionary project. "Abolition," Gilmore has said, "requires that we change one thing, which is everything." It's this position, which treats the struggles of race and class as historically and strategically linked, that's sparked and revived debates within and beyond the left. The Panthers were armed socialists; Davis was a 1960s militant who's been the Communist Party vice presidential candidate twice. And in *Golden Gulag*, Gilmore's geographical study of the boom in California prisons—her argument is driven in large part by the Marxian conception of "surplus"—her Ten Theses on abolition appear in a chapter titled after Lenin's famous pamphlet "What Is to Be Done?" Somehow *this* is the movement making strides in the United States of America. To the scattered victories of abolitionists toward the tail end of last year—the weakening of police unions, the severance of several law enforcement contracts with universities and public schools, the (token) shrinking of police budgets in a handful of major cities—we might add an ideological one: black radicalism has hacked a path back to the mainstream political scene.

Naturally, the calls to defund police departments have appalled some self-styled sympathizers of the protests; high-ranking Democrats now claim the slogan harmed them in local elections. And commonsense pundits have leapt valiantly into the fracas, citing problems that only a vast, armed, proudly ungovernable, extravagantly subsidized municipal fighting force can solve. It appears not to matter that by nearly every measure US police forces are far from competent (the clearance rate of murder cases across the country is abysmal). In fact, one in thirteen of all murders are committed by police; of those committed by strangers, the proportion is one third. And there's no evident curiosity about the social roots of "crime." Skeptics are of course right to point out the high incidence of murder and assault, but scant effort is made to prevent them or even explain why these violations are so common in the US.

No economy in the "developed world" is as unequal as this one. And no state in human history has thrust so many behind bars. (This is true per capita as well as in raw numbers, as the US accounts for a quarter of the global prison population.) These are linked phenomena: where the state claims to root out roiling chaos and depravity, abolitionists see whole stripes of the population deemed irrelevant to capital—the melancholy underside of a glittering accumulation. That accumulation has twisted nimbly into new and savage forms. In the public mind, the great victims of the neoliberal order are white workers stripped of factory jobs, and castaways from the middle class. But they are not alone.

Those who were already subject to high levels of joblessness and homelessness, who rely on the support of eviscerated public services, and whose rent is currently multiplying in an open bid to banish them, have also been impaled on the rapacity of this new world. They're seen as scrapped, depleted people, darkly troublesome in their superfluity, doomed to rattle through the metropolis until they're hunted by the state. Many of them are black. In reactionary folklore, they all are. "Law and order" policies, tools for disposing of these "surplus" people, were first sold to voters as a way to ward off black rebellion. (Included in that category was the now hallowed civil rights movement.) Now the "informal economy" beckons to those shipwrecked by the real one; cages and police bullets claim the poor and unemployed. Only a steroidal ideology can beat back the glaring fact that the surge in jails, bail, police, prisons—that is, "mass incarceration"—is an expression of this system at its most crashing and advanced. This is a moralism without ethics, an "austerity" of waste: the catastrophic maintenance of a specious urban peace.

That peace is paid for, dearly, in the daily lives of the black poor. For decades every slice of the political class has told a little fable about why this is: absent fathers, the "culture of poverty," a lack of "opportunity," the startling attitudes trumpeted by certain genres of popular music. The right wields these clichés as the weapons they in fact are, while the Democratic center opts to mawkishly rephrase them. Perhaps the blare of sentimentalism can drown out the churn of the machine. Take Mayor Frey's indulgent bawling as he knelt beside Floyd's casket, and the vaudevillian spectacle of Chuck Schumer and Nancy Pelosi striding into the Capitol last June, joined by a clutch of their party colleagues, to introduce the George Floyd Justice in Policing Act of 2020. Each wore an Ashanti kente cloth—a sign of "solidarity" in the florid realm of culture—and proceeded to perform a ritual dreamed up by "peaceful protesters" last spring. The Democrats knelt in silence for eight minutes and forty-six seconds, exactly the length of time Chauvin's knee dug into Floyd's neck. Their gesture echoes Colin Kaepernick but, given the details of Floyd's passing, amounts to a pantomime of his murder.

The Act itself, a second version of which passed in the House in early March 2021, was a rehearsal of the Obama-era reforms. It was also scraped of any acknowledgment of the conditions that made it "necessary"—namely that, measured against whites, black people are vastly poorer and more imperiled. They are nearly twice as likely to be unemployed, twice as likely to go hungry. They're more than twice as likely to be killed by the police, more than three times as likely to be incarcerated, and last year were twice as likely to lose their lives to Covid-19. This is not a coincidence. It follows from the slashing idiosyncrasies of their history as a people, their specific wincing intimacy with the abstractions of "state" and "property." Black people were property. Any abolitionist will remind you that many US police departments grew from slave patrols meant to enforce this, raking the land for runaways and throttling black revolts. From forced labor to endemic joblessness, from hated ballasts of the economy to hated exiles from its present form: this road was paved with bloodshed and contempt enshrined as law. Lynching, segregation, the Great Migration, restrictive covenants, discrimination at work, exclusion from unions, and throughout all this the drumbeat of state violence in the street—the varieties of degradation are enough to make you fling a brick.

It is hard to find new words for this. Radical passion has been gutted, blunted, deflected, suppressed—and frozen into rhetoric, peddled as commodity. In the face of establishment cynicism and the promise of "representation," it can be hard to voice real outrage, and the ache of collective grief. "Each day when you see us black folk upon the dusty land of the farms or upon the hard pavement of the city streets, you usually take us for granted and think you know us," Richard Wright wrote in 1940, "but our history is far stranger than you suspect, and we are not what we seem." Indeed, some of the most celebrated black literature of the last century centers on state terror and rebukes to it, books planted throughout the culture as flags for blackness itself. Every James Baldwin novel but the last hangs on a false conviction or a scene of police abuse. The climax of Ralph Ellison's *Invisible Man* is a riot that streaks through Harlem after officers kill a street vendor. The protagonist can't help but marvel at the chaos that envelops him, the "bursting, tearing movement of people around me, dark figures in a blue glow." Some of the best poems of Gwendolyn Brooks's explicitly militant period—"Boy Breaking Glass," the three-part "Riot" sequence—are angular, late-modernist renderings of an era of black revolt, an era hymned in Amiri Baraka's tribute to the Newark rebellion of 1967. Baraka was beaten and arrested, then thrown into solitary confinement, but his riot poem, "Black People!," rings with euphoria: "Smash the windows daytime, anytime, together, let's smash the window drag the shit from in there. No money down. No time to pay. Just take what you want. The magic dance in the street."

MARTYRS DRIVE THIS MOVEMENT: they are its origin and blazing emblems. But some of the most infamous police murders extend from more quotidian debasements. "Broken windows" theory—cracking down on minor infractions to deter more serious crimes—has drilled an armed state presence deeper into the lives of the urban poor. Eric Garner was harassed repeatedly before his death in 2014; police even took his exhausted fury at this as pretext to throw him to the ground. "I told you the last time," he begs in the video recording as officers close in, "please leave me alone!" Seven years earlier he'd been stopped on the street and told to flatten himself against a police car. According to the federal lawsuit that he later filed against the NYPD, an officer pulled down Garner's pants, groped his genitals, dug his fingers into his rectum, and jeered that he was a paroled felon who should never have been given a job with the city's parks department. The officer "violated my civil rights" for "his personal pleasure," read the suit, which Garner wrote out—by hand—while jailed on Rikers Island.

In Ferguson, Darren Wilson was cleared of all federal civil rights violations after an investigation led by Eric Holder, the head of Obama's justice department. But the findings did expose that the city had been fending off fiscal apocalypse by ticketing black people at outrageous rates. One section, titled "Ferguson Law Enforcement Efforts Are Focused on Generating Revenue," revealed that "issuing three or four charges in one stop is not uncommon in Ferguson. Officers sometimes write six, eight, or, in at least one instance, fourteen citations for a single encounter. Indeed, officers told us that some compete to see who can issue the largest number of citations during a single stop."

Police plundered the black population because at bottom they knew they could. They knew that in the eyes of authority, the black poor are threatening monstrosities but also violable and devalued, available to be pulped. You can stalk them, prod them, punish them; feel free to take whatever you want from them. Those who didn't pay their fines on time in Ferguson were slapped with warrants for their arrest. So when after years of fleecing and abuse, the police slaughtered a teenage boy and left the corpse splayed in the street, the people did what they could: they ripped the city to pieces. Within months the local government declared that all prior warrants for tickets would be annulled. Those people are still impoverished and overwhelmingly endangered; they didn't topple the racial hierarchy or reverse their dispossession. But the events last spring would be unthinkable without the example of Ferguson's poor: under the spotlight of the national media and the fire of the National Guard, they broke open a new phase of struggle when they forced the state to flinch. "Smash the window at night," wrote Baraka, "(these are magic actions)."

Within this rage and mourning, there are layers, contradictions. Breonna Taylor was killed by Louisville, Kentucky, police who bashed down her door in the night and started shooting. They were looking for her ex-boyfriend while scouring the area for undesirables, in advance of a "high dollar" real estate project planned for that section of the city. Taylor's murder took place two months before Floyd's. But his was the one that stirred popular passion, lending further credence to the black feminist claim that, although almost every media-friendly voice in this movement has belonged to a woman (Patrisse Cullors, Alicia Garza, and Opal Tometi founded the Black Lives Matter Network in 2013), victims such as Rekia Boyd and Sandra Bland are tacitly deemed less significant communal losses and thus less worthy of mass grief. The same measure applies to black trans victims such as Tony McDade, who was gunned down last May by Tallahassee police. Though recognition is spreading fast that black trans people face great volumes of targeted violence, the riots were not for him.

Meanwhile the black elite has rarely been so resented by the "community" it claims to champion. Class, a topic scrubbed from much of US political discourse, has swirled into peculiar shapes within black life since the 1960s. Desegregation did little more than lift the legal barrier to the labor market, which meant a ripple—not a revolution—in American arrangements of race and wealth. This new league of professionals has remained so faithful to the Democrats that Biden couldn't help but boast of his seigneurial entitlement to the black vote: "If you have a problem figuring out whether you're for me or for Trump, then you ain't black."

The statement neatly captures the chuckling smugness of his party. Four days later, Floyd was killed. "Black liberal, your time is up," ran the headline in Al Jazeera, as the riots crashed through Minneapolis. Black mayors of big cities—Keisha Bottoms in Atlanta, Muriel Bowser in Washington DC, and (infamously) Chicago's Lori

Lightfoot—were among the most strident voices raised against the rebellion. Writing in the *New York Times*, Keeanga-Yamahtta Taylor offered a biting summary of the past few decades of black Democrats: "Black elected officials have become adept at mobilizing the tropes of black identity without any of its political content." A movement that first tilted gently against party leadership and sought some form of redistribution has since bowed to corporate influence and the edicts of the DNC. All this has been justified by the desire for "black faces in high places." The Congressional Black Caucus and a cluster of black mayors joined the party in embracing finance and austerity as well as "law and order" policies meant to douse the mounting flames.

It's worth lingering here to note that the chief beneficiaries of civil rights legislation were those black people poised to scale the heights of class and meritocracy. (The rest were left to languish as a sociological "problem.") But the path has been a swerving one, lined with prickling little ironies. Many of these people heaved themselves into white-collar employment just as the middle class began its crumble into neoliberal instability and launched their long march through the universities as degrees plummeted in value. A large chunk of this layer grew up within familial earshot of urban poverty and thus carries the vivid memory of what proletarian life actually looks like. Many of them know the pain of visiting family behind bars. So their middle-income existence is pressed up against the so-called underclass—a link to be minimized or insisted on, grateful for or raged against, brandished as cultural birthright or folded shrewdly into sensibility. But never fully severed. They still know the sting of condescension or outright hatred. And though abolition is still a shocking notion, their children are largely raised with blunt distrust of the police. With little wealth to inherit, these families possess far less property than their white counterparts, and even that prosperity seems to vanish with mortifying frequency. "White boys who grew up rich are more likely to remain that way," pronounced a study published in the *Times* in 2018. "Black boys raised at the top are more likely to become poor than stay wealthy in their own adult households."

For huge swaths of black America, Obama was a triumph and realized dream; for the middle class, he was a mirror. The fierce, conflicting aspects of their harrowing evolution were prettily reproduced in his image and political style. His centrist managerialism was cast as a triumph of civil rights; the old injunction to be "respectable" was softened by his much-touted love of rap. His speeches seemed to stream down from a place of unpretentious elevation, so he could lash out at poor black people and expect gratitude for his frankness. Drone strikes, deportations, and fealty to the banks were balanced by the moral prestige of the historical black struggle.

Ferguson ripped a hole in the middle of Obama's second term. He lapsed into ambivalence: though sometimes sonorous about the forces arrayed against young black men, he lambasted the Baltimore uprising as a terror wrought by "thugs." Those sympathetic to Obama saw him as having to placate irreconcilable constituencies—a position he also held as the recession disproportionately affected black families. The period between 2008 and 2016 saw black homeownership decrease at calamitous rates. Negative home equity shot up in the black community when the housing bubble burst and continued to skyrocket for years after it began to decline among whites, all observed from an astral distance by the first black commander in chief. So he was—at best—irrelevant to the fates of those who loved him most. No trill of rhetoric or stirring gesture could stop the tank of financial capital, or shield the fragile fortunes of the new black middle class.

It's that part of the black world—*their* anger, *their* comfort, *their* belated conscription to the harried scramble for the American good life, *their* uncertain place beneath the fluorescent lights of the corporate office—that's become a point of panicked fixation in the aftermath of last year's riots. It was hard not to laugh at the official response to the rebellion, as every brand and elite institution rolled out the same manic public statement, declaring their love for their black employees and allegiance to BLM. But perhaps inevitably that daffy piety became the rule. One outcome of the uprising has been the expansion of a zealous antiracist discourse that remains silent about the street battles that gave it marvelous topicality.

This is not a new phenomenon. The past six years had seen the passions of Ferguson displaced by efforts to give white professionals moral lessons and a smattering of black people prestigious posts. Black professionals, after all, are the crown jewels of the liberal reformist mission: their presence on the campus or conference call performs a shining symbolic task. This is the only sliver of black America to feel the full effects of integration—so the shivering, conflicted existence of this minority within a minority stands as talismanic promise that the wound of history might be healed. In Obama's first public statement after the events in Minneapolis—months before he intervened to break a strike by professional basketball players—he began by quoting an email sent to him by an "African American businessman."

Any sign of this group's ingratitude provokes perplexity and dismay. One of the most sensationalized early episodes from the riots concerned two lawyers in their early thirties who face decades in prison for their alleged actions in New York. One is Pakistani American and the other is black: raised working-class in Brooklyn, he was plucked by a nonprofit organization and spirited away to a bucolic boarding school followed by Princeton, law school, then a budding career as a corporate attorney, only to see this fantastic future evaporate when—for reasons breathlessly speculated on in the national media—he drove his friend around the demonstrations as she pitched Molotov cocktails at police vehicles. This may or may not point to something rustling through the spring, when quite a few young black people placed within this rickety middle class chose to cross the mystic threshold between "respectability" and dignity: they went out to meet the riots.

"WE SHOULD NOT JUST SCREAM," Mike Davis said in May. "We need to start breaking things, quite frankly." But this interview on the podcast *Time to Say Goodbye* appeared a full week before Floyd's death; his comments didn't refer to police murder, but the economic and social catastrophe triggered by the spread of Covid-19. No reckoning with the eruption in late May can elide the role played by the virus. It should come as little surprise that last year the most unequal developed nation racked up just under 20 percent of global deaths from Covid-19. The crisis has brought chaos to the incarcerated population—which, as a result of crowding and neglect, reached an infection rate over five times the national average—and detainees at Rikers Island were forced to dig mass graves for Covid casualties in New York City. Deaths across the country are highest among the nonwhite poor: black and Latino communities were hit especially hard, and several Native American reservations soon became capitals of infection.

The spectacle of governmental fecklessness—right-wing legislators dismissing the likeliness of an outbreak only to quickly reverse their policies as infections soared—reflected an element of popular will. This is the land of the free. The most furious market imperatives throb deep within the soul. It will be hard to forget that the lieutenant governor of Texas insisted with pride that many vulnerable senior citizens, confronted with the prospect that a lockdown might wreck the economy for their grandchildren, would rather die. It was easy to scoff or screech at this, but beneath the boom of right-wing rhetoric, you could make out the faint, metallic whirring of liberal technocratic complicity: the Trump Administration's relief plan, drafted in collaboration with Democratic Senate leader Chuck Schumer, passed with near unanimous bipartisan support.

It was a stopgap, and after decades of neoliberal consensus, perhaps the most one could expect. The Coronavirus Aid, Relief, and Economic Security Act (CARES), followed by dribbles of supplemental legislation, was a forced experiment in social democracy. A single check for $1,200 was supposed to tide people over for months; relief to workers suddenly stripped of income was routed through unemployment insurance and ran out while the virus continued to soar. (A second relief bill proved impossible to pass before the November election.) The historian Robert Brenner has characterized the bill as plutocratic plunder. High earners whose work was uninterrupted by lockdown measures made out quite well, which explains the uptick in national savings and the relative health of the financial markets.

The bill was a corporate bailout of historic proportions, allowing for a galling amount of Federal Reserve money—10 percent of annual GDP—to be handed to the heads of the largest companies, with scandalously little oversight. And what about the entrepreneurs—those mascots of national ideology and great victims of the rebellion? In December the *Times* reported that of the $523 billion disbursed through the Paycheck Protection Program, more than a quarter was awarded to the top 1 percent of applicants—among them corporate law firms and a steakhouse chain owned by CNN founder Ted Turner. As pundits howled last spring at the sickening spectacle of looted storefronts, the vast majority of small businesses were floundering not from riots but from lack of federal support. (Hundreds of businesses received checks for $99 or less.) Across the economic field, a brief period of relief gave way to a still-unfurling disaster. Record numbers are facing eviction, record numbers cannot feed themselves, at least eight million people have fallen into poverty. For months before Floyd's death, the horrors were compounded and combustible.

Black struggle struck the match. The future of that struggle now lies coiled in an enigma: Why, at a point of overlapping crises and hypnotic social freefall, did the killing of a single black man unleash the largest wave of demonstrations this country has ever seen, as well as multiracial revenge on private property and the state? Something more than liberal sympathy was at work here—something more potent and less vaporous, at once rooted in the American past and reflective of recent developments. Slogans notwithstanding, institutions historically justified by the hatred of black people have turned a greedy eye toward other groups. In the US, Native Americans see the highest proportion of people killed by police. Punitive immigration policies have caused prisons and detention centers to swell with Latin American detainees. (The Los Angeles riots of 1992 are remembered as a black uprising, but the majority of those arrested, as well as those charged with arson, were Latinx.) Although black people are still incarcerated at the highest rates by far, abolitionists have long claimed that the state would happily lock up higher numbers of poor whites, as has been proven with brutal flair across the country.

But the fight against police and prisons remains bound up with *black* liberation because one people feels the harshest shocks of economic earthquakes and has served as a kind of vanguard in its subjection to state cruelty. A practice of militancy issued from this historical experience. Clattering with internal disputes and handed down for generations, the real black movement isn't the nursery rhyme recited brightly in the public sphere, but a protracted battle against domination at its most naked and unconstrained—King, on the day he was killed, was to give a sermon called "Why America May Go to Hell." So it's possible that the death of Floyd reverberated so painfully because, under the delirious conditions induced by the pandemic, whole sections of the middle class seemed to walk through the political looking glass. In an instant they were poorer and even more insecure, their noses bluntly rubbed in their disposability to capital. Left without a livelihood by callous fiat in a moment of crisis, they were treated to that peculiar mélange of state control and state neglect—the punitive abandonment that paints the lives of the black poor.

WHAT IS TO BE DONE? (The fraught, irrepressible question comes twisting to the surface.) The paths pursued by Occupy Wall Street and BLM—the twin children of the financial crash—may trace the silhouette of the present challenge. Occupy shot up spontaneously as a brisk political motley—anarchists jostled beside progressives who wanted only to rein in the financial sector. The most lasting legacy of the encampments (which were stormed and at last destroyed by municipal police forces) was the rhetoric of "the 99

percent"—populist, universalist, and by the end of the decade embla-
zoned across both primary campaigns of the social democrat Bernie
Sanders. (The anarchism had been forgotten.) With him "democratic
socialism" entered the mainstream political lexicon.

Last spring, when the black movement came flashing back to
life, it was less legitimate, less "nonviolent," and looked nothing like
the socialists seeking glory at the ballot box. And the riots burst mere
months after Sanders bowed out of the primary, so the two strands
of struggle fell into an enlightening juxtaposition. From Occupy to
Bernie; from BLM to the Floyd rebellion. One rocketed up the ranks
of state, while the other fought its power far more fiercely this time
around; one pinned its hopes on universal programs to be beamed
down from the Oval Office, while the other floods streets under the
sign of a single group. One takes up distribution, the other force,
repression: two functions, in the end, of the selfsame state machine.
But under the particular conditions bequeathed by US history, the
first was coded "white," the second—starkly—black.

Yet the fights are fused and need each other. They form two
spokes on a single wheel: the sociopolitical cataclysm of rising un-
and underemployment. It's no coincidence that the first time the
black movement laid claim to cities since Black Power was amid the
postcrash "jobless recovery"—nor that the riots came hurtling back
as millions were stripped of work last spring. The racist, decades-
long program of mass incarceration accompanied austerity and
stagnant wages, as the incomes of the vulnerable fell even further
into perilous uncertainty. And even the smallest steps on the path
to abolition will rely on Gilmore's call to raise the social wage: a call
being answered, almost exclusively, by a newborn socialist left. Over
two thirds of American voters support this left's main proposal,
Medicare for All—as private health care is a rarefied employee benefit in a time of widening informality. Nothing in recent memory
has fulfilled the socialist hope of politicizing state and city budgets
with the swiftness of the spring rebellion. And we'll never know if
Biden's recent stimulus bill, which constitutes a historic leftward

lurch in fiscal policy, could have been passed without the battles in the street. If this really does foretell a break with neoliberal governance—a somewhat shocking claim repeated in certain quadrants of the left—any honest account of this change will have to feature not just the efforts of progressive legislators, but the rebirth of the black struggle.

But both camps are internally divided and brim with distrust of the other. BLM's most officious, nonprofit element still risks becoming an ornament to philanthropy and public relations; the technical "leaderlessness" of the movement has rendered it malleable by the liberal center. Sanders was savaged loudly, and only sometimes in good faith, for his supposed indifference to US racism—laughable hypocrisy from the Democratic establishment, which he was nevertheless terrible at rebutting. This did not, however, stop him from joining Joe Biden in coming out *against* defunding the police. It's impossible to say what comes next, either for the black movement against state terror or the state-facing redistributive effort, but short of a defeat of capital in a single, stunning stroke, any left that hopes to assemble its flailing forces must find a way to join the two clearest fronts of conflict: on the one hand, build class power by wresting benefits from the state, on the other, slay the beast that eats the dark and poor. Real unity will have to be established by new kinds of action and organization. (It bears repeating that the New Deal, a social democratic reform and nostalgic model for a slew of progressive policymakers—itself riven by racial exclusions—came into being after years of police beating and tear-gassing "disruptive" throngs of the unemployed.) Policy-minded leftists, liberated from their dreams of capturing the executive branch, have now been forced to reckon with the humbling blaze of urban uprising. Socialists must learn from the riots. Legible, polished politics and the smashing fist of black rebellion—they may be linked by the dialectic, which in the famous allegory chains the master to his slave.

"A revolution is not just constant fighting," James Boggs wrote in 1968. Of all of the black radicals whose legacies are now being scoured for lessons, his is among the brightest and most appropriate to this new phase. Born in Alabama in 1919, he spent nearly thirty years working in the Chrysler plant in Detroit, during which he agitated on behalf of black workers and came to see their predicament—their degradation and exclusion; their tenuous, subordinate place in a midcentury union movement slouching toward obsolescence—as the prelude to a wider crisis. Decades before neoliberalism, he knew that postwar growth and high employment would evaporate, and that the working class was changing shape. He knew that the bitterest battles, those with the power to make the most ambitious assault on the order of things, would be waged by those locked out of politics as well as their means of subsistence: this new avant-garde would be molded from the black poor and unemployed.

They were not the majority. But they were the most disruptive and inventive force in the US, vested with the historic capacity to call every facet of social existence into question. Boggs's '60s were spent cultivating organizations that would not only fortify black labor but forge a bond between shop-floor struggle and a fast-inflating sphere of conflict. As the civil rights movement thickened into the militancy of Black Power, he knew that riots—the destruction of property and mass clashes with police—would be a routine feature of a society riven by racial hatred and that refused to feed its poor. The task was not to disavow the smashing clarity in the street but to build forms of collectivity that could outlast the days of rage. There was power in a riot, in its rippling, adaptable passions—power that might even express itself, at some point, by winning seats on city councils (as long as the movement knew not to deify this strategic foothold in the state). Although he split with his mentor C. L. R. James, Boggs held to James's belief that despite the fixation on "equal rights," the vigorous challenge posed by the black movement proved that it was *power*, not the democratic ideal, that was being fought for and forfeited every second in the real world. "Rights are what you make and what you take," he wrote in *The American Revolution: Pages from a Negro Worker's Notebook*, published in 1963—the high noon of civil rights.

The book was bracing. Boggs foresaw an America stripped of manufacturing jobs, its cities bristling with surplus people—disproportionately black people. They were left without stable employment or even the distant hope of it, banished from abundance and desperate to get by: "Being workless, they are also stateless." No organization dared to speak for them. They'd have to organize themselves. From this restless, black-led mass would flow new forms of political practice. He called his fourth chapter "The Outsiders":

> The present workforce is itself a product of the old society and struggling to survive within it. This means that we must look to the outsiders for the most radical—that is, the deepest—thinking as to the changes that are needed. What ideas will they have? They have not yet expressed them clearly, but their target is very clear. It is not any particular company or any particular persons but the government itself. Just how they will approach or penetrate this target I do not know, nor do I know what will happen when they have done what they must do. But I know that the army of outsiders that is growing by leaps and bounds in this country is more of a threat to the present "American way of life" than any foreign power.

LAST YEAR AN ARMY of outsiders, their ranks swollen by the ravages of a freak disease, launched the most widespread spontaneous uprising in the history of the United States. Behind these rigid objective conditions, a few splintered and subjective ones. Something has changed in America; something is still pulsing beneath the carapace of party politics. The rebellion didn't just release a jet of fury but lodged the riot, without apology, in the very rhythm of political life.

Explosion became routine. Summer and fall were studded by local clashes prompted by other murders by police. In June Atlanta rose up again after the killing of Rayshard Brooks: demonstrators obstructed a five-lane highway and burned a Wendy's to the ground. The shooting of Jacob Blake in August set off a citywide revolt in Kenosha, Wisconsin, and yielded the most riveting images of the summer: the packed parking lot of a used car dealership transformed into a shining sea of flames. In response to the murder of Walter Wallace earlier that month, Philadelphians shattered windows just days before the election. But perhaps the most stunning juxtaposition arrived in late September. Less than a week after the death of Ruth Bader Ginsburg sent Democrats into fits of panic, it was announced that the police officers who shot Breonna Taylor would face no charges. While columnists hymned Ginsburg's devotion to gender equality before the law, the people of Louisville inflicted their own feminism on the city: they burst back into the street to avenge their fallen sister.

Soon there will be more riots. The murders of Daunte Wright, Ma'Khia Bryant, Adam Toledo, and Anthony Alvarez are proof of the ongoing horror; the bursts of action in the street mark the arrival of another spring. Again—we shall see. But it's not pat or naive or triumphalist to say that people were changed by the rebellion: they did things they'd never done before, things that no one knew were possible. In late May a Fox News helicopter broadcast footage from Philadelphia that proved the insolence of these new insurgents. As the camera swept up to pan the length of a city street, rioters pushed an empty squad car until it crashed into another. Officers looked on, powerless; within minutes, a whole row of vehicles had been fastidiously destroyed. These weren't "outside agitators," but dauntless outsiders, and there was something marvelous in their comportment, their light, balletic elegance as they slashed tires and popped car hoods to light fires on the engines. They moved with the evident, placid confidence that in that moment, they were winning. The camera zoomed in on one young vandal as he reached his arm through a smashed rear windshield. In an echo of those Antillean slaves who devised the J'Ouvert carnival to mock their masters, he retrieved a blue police cap and placed it rakishly on his head.

I'd seen the footage in May; I cried hard a few months later while watching it again. In an instant it brought back the floating feeling, the roaring weightlessness, of spring. I remembered the elation cut with fear, the shards of unreality and lakes of psychic calm—times when the knowledge rippled invisibly through the sprinting, shouting crowd that the young people of the city had outpaced the armed police. I remembered the first day of the uprising, the sense of being released from the grip of quarantine into the city's three-dimensionality. Here were buildings and swarms of people, thickly present in the stabbing sun.

"What elasticity, what historical initiative, what a capacity for sacrifice in these Parisians!" Marx gasped in a letter when news reached him that the members of the Paris Commune had repelled the imperial army and abolished the police; he said they were "storming heaven." And a version of that thought—a degraded, baffled paraphrase—flashed to mind as I saw the masked children of New York slam their skateboards against police vans and throw themselves at lines of officers packing guns and shields and nightsticks; chanting the name of a dead man while sprinting with hundreds down an avenue, I'd never felt an ecstasy more complicated or a freedom less false. On a plateglass window in SoHo, someone graffitied, simply, "GEORGE!" So many of the faces I saw streaking through spring and summer—lit by burning cars and reflected in broken windows, doing victory laps around sneaker stores and bloodied by batons—belonged to adolescents. Armed only with their psychotic courage, they were running, dancing, singing, smashing, burning, screaming, storming heaven: all rapturous varieties of Baraka's "magic actions." I listened to 19-year-olds talk nonstop throughout the night we spent in jail, as they howled insults at the officers and swapped stories of humiliation by police. It struck me that they were too young to have seen the initial phase of BLM. Though well-acquainted with power and violence, they were tasting "politics" for the first time. Whatever the fate of the movement, I suspect that much of their future thinking will be measured against the feelings that filled the nights of 2020: the vastness and immediacy, the blur and brutal clarity.

Last year the whole world was watching, to quote the '60s slogan. Along with expressions of international solidarity—the marches
in foreign capitals, the Molotov cocktails hurled at US embassies in
Athens and Mexico City, the mural of George Floyd's face covering
a massive wall in Idlib—2020 saw rebellions abroad that cleaved
to local circumstance. Riots broke out in France against Macron's
ban on sharing footage of the police, and for a moment a link was
forged between the gilets jaunes blockades and the migrant rioters
of 2005 who burned the banlieues after the deaths of two teenagers
in Clichy-sous-Bois. But the deepest resonance came in October.
Nigeria—whose economy is over 50 percent informal—saw the sudden resurgence of the movement to abolish its Special Anti-Robbery
Squad (SARS). (It has since been scrapped and virtually reconstituted
under another name.) The unit was ruthless, lawless, feckless; under
the auspices of public safety, officers beat, surveilled, harassed, and
fleeced anyone who fell outside the charmed circle of the elite, such
that many victims came from the tottering but vocal middle class.
One trigger for the demonstrations was a video of a SARS officer
shooting a motorist and driving off in the dead man's Lexus.

The eruption was unreal. Looting on an enormous scale, massive clashes in the street with soldiers and police, official buildings
set on fire, and in Benin, capital of Edo State, demonstrators laid
siege to a correctional facility and sprang prisoners from their cells.
The next day, the police massacred twelve unarmed demonstrators at Lekki Tollgate; a total of thirty-eight civilians were killed by
officers that night. #EndSARS can't be reduced to a postscript of
BLM—it bloomed from the particular chaos of the Nigerian economy and kleptocracy—and the revolt last year in many ways sur-
passed the Floyd rebellion. But the similarity is striking. For much
of the 20th century, revolutionaries argued bitterly over whether the
black movement in America could be compared to African struggles for independence. But now that the "informal proletariat" is
the fastest-growing class on the face of the planet, the fights that
flank the Black Atlantic have never seemed so interlaced. A global

wave of outsiders is crashing on the shores of states. As one wise vandal spray-painted on a wall in Minneapolis: "Welcome back to the world."

The phrase hangs like a banner above the ruptures of 2020—a year that began three months into a civil rebellion in Iraq, which, like its Western torturer, saw the largest uprising in national history. Last spring I was reminded of the demonstration where I first saw windows smashed: I was 20, at the 2012 march against NATO in Chicago, just after the "end" of the Second Gulf War. Among the gathered thousands—scraps of a flouted pacifist left—was a group the others hated for its frank aggression toward the police. Today they're known as antifa; back then the term was "black bloc." At the end of the march, a group of them grappled with armored riot cops, shattering the glass of a fast-food franchise before being cuffed and dragged away. But my clearest memory is of their chant, which I found myself joining. It rang with then-recent outrages—the murder of Oscar Grant, new incursions into Palestine, and the crackdowns in Syntagma Square: *Oakland, Gaza, Greece! Fuck the police!* None of us had ever heard of Ferguson, Missouri.

2021

IN PRAISE OF THE TERRORIST

NICOLÁS MEDINA MORA

Hace veinte años yo era un obrero de la maquila en Tijuana y plane-
aba poner bombas en esas fábricas y en el edificio del PRI frente al
muro que puso Estados Unidos.

—Heriberto Yépez

POET IN TWO LANGUAGES, FIRST-RATE ESSAYIST, SECOND-TIER
novelist, translator, editor, anthologist, video artist, canceled newspaper columnist, Twitter troll, keeper of prolific and ephemeral blogs,
art critic in equal parts brutal and thoughtful, working-class philosopher, theorist of empire, loving cartographer of Tijuana, scholar of
Nahuatl lexicography and the Maya calendar, licensed Gestalt therapist, purveyor of self-help, scourge of the right (and of the portion of
the left that's part of the right without knowing it), the preeminent
expert on American poetry south of the border, the most hated (and
most feared) figure in Mexican letters, a man with many enemies
and ever-fewer friends, a thinker with too many insights, coiner of
neologisms, black-pilled pessimist (or secret optimist?), committed
ethicist, self-serious self-parodist, ironist, trickster, joker, hater, kill-
joy, flamethrower, slinger of shit, Latin America's last avant-gardist,
a victim of his own genius—all these terms apply to Heriberto Yépez,

but if I had to describe him with a single word, I would call him a terrorist. I would mean it as a compliment.

Yépez began publishing early. His first book appeared when he was 26, and by the time he was 30 he had no fewer than seven titles to his name. The prizes and accolades came quickly: Evodio Escalante, a leftist critic, called him one of the two "most powerful literary minds" working in Mexico; Christopher Domínguez Michael, an editor at *Letras Libres*, the right-wing literary magazine founded by acolytes of Octavio Paz, wrote that he was "one of the most protean writers of his generation." This vertiginous ascent culminated in 2011, when Yépez was 37 years old. That year *Milenio*, a widely read Mexico City newspaper that counts many celebrated writers among its contributors, invited Yépez to write a weekly column on any subject that interested him—an important consecration in a country where the opinions of writers are taken seriously even by those who don't read their books.

The problem was that the subject that most interested Yépez was the ethical, political, and intellectual corruption of most other Mexican authors. This would have been fine—there's a long tradition of pugilism in Mexican letters—except that Yépez broke the unspoken rule that requires writers to pick a side: If you are aligned with Paz's reactionary ghost, you don't attack your fellow Pazians; if you are close to the left-leaning Juan Rulfo Foundation, you decline to criticize it; if you write for a given magazine, you refrain from writing negative reviews of your fellow contributors' books. Yépez refused to abide by this etiquette and instead went after anyone who had power, including those who considered him an ally. "I was critical in all directions," he wrote in his final column for *Milenio*, which fired him in 2015, in all likelihood because other contributors complained about his antics. "If I failed to critique someone, I apologize for the oversight."

One could say, anachronistically, that Yépez was *canceled*, but cancelation did nothing to deter him. Consider the open letter he published on his blog in 2017 to protest the induction of Christopher

Domínguez Michael—the same writer who favorably called him "protean"—into Mexico's version of the Collège de France, a lifetime appointment that comes with a large stipend funded by taxpayers:

> I'm not surprised you wound up becoming a bureaucrat-critic, a state-owned opinionator, a subsidized reactionary. That's what you've been from the beginning, in one way or another: You oppose the welfare state that supports the majority while benefiting from the one that pampers the rotten elite to which you belong, and of which you are proud to the point of kitsch, that central feature of your prose. . . . Reading your work is boring; listening to you read it aloud, truly unbearable. Do you even realize the number of times you mentioned Sainte-Beuve [in your acceptance speech]? What makes you think Sainte-Beuve is relevant in 2017? That you take such a writer as a central reference evinces the depth of your ignorance; and the same can be said about your appreciation for conservative and patriarchal critics that have long gone out of fashion, such as Harold Bloom and George Steiner. For you, the literary critic is nothing but a highbrow journalist-reader, an admiring satellite orbiting around gentlemen-writers that became anachronistic in their Nordic countries of origin ages ago. Your dilettante's concept of the critic amounts to an auto-colonized Grand Amateur.*

Yépez has leveled similar vitriol at *Nexos*, the magazine where I work, which he accused of harboring a "neoliberal mafia" that wields all-but-dictatorial power over Mexican literature; at publishing houses ranging from international conglomerates to the state-funded Fondo de Cultura Económica; and at a nearly endless list of writers, including Carlos Fuentes ("You and Paz and your 'successors' applied presidentialism and one-party rule to literature") and Juan Villoro ("You reiterate your cretinous attitude toward people who aren't the

---

* Unless otherwise specified, all citations from Yépez's work appear in my translation. Yépez also writes in English—I'll note when I quote anglophone originals—but as far as I know, only one of his Spanish-language books, *The Empire of Neomemory*, has appeared in translation.

children of intellectuals, politicians, or captains of industry, and who therefore have no choice but to seek out [the help of] people as full of prejudices as yourself").

He has paid the price for his omnidirectional critique: today most of Yépez's many books have gone out of print and are impossible to find. His more recent work has appeared in editions of two or three hundred, often under the auspices of publishing houses so marginal that the term *small press* proves inadequate. Such a fate would be devastating to most authors, especially those who, like Yépez, tasted something like fame before falling from the graces of the gatekeepers. But one gets the sense that Yépez revels in his own marginality; that he cultivates it with the same energy with which lesser artists apply themselves to careerism. Sometimes this insistence on standing apart from the herd becomes a little overstated. In 2014, for instance, he declared that henceforth he would be known as ~~Heriberto Yépez~~, a gesture that he said signaled the end of his authorship.

Is Yépez in on the joke? Is he playing a metaliterary game at our expense? Or does he believe, sincerely, that he has overcome the vanity of the artist to such an extent that he no longer feels ownership over his words? That this is a genuine question, rather than a rhetorical one, is precisely what makes him so interesting: he is, as the poststructuralists might say, an *undecidable*, a locus of ironic ambiguity. If Nietzsche is right when he says that the artist's most important work is their own self, Yépez has created one of the most compelling artworks of contemporary Mexico.

YÉPEZ'S UNDECIDABILITY presents an obstacle for the critic who wishes to attempt a thorough assessment of his literature. Part of this problem is philosophical—isn't reading the so-called body of work of a writer who insists that he is not "an author" a prime example of missing the point?—but another part is practical. When I set out to write about Yépez, I resolved to read his complete works, but after spending several months in Mexico City's legendary secondhand bookstores and trawling the depths of Mercado Libre—Latin America's answer to eBay—I was forced to conclude that I'd never find all or even most of his books. What follows is a brief account of the Yépeziana I did manage to collect, excluding his translations and introductions to others' books. In chronological order:

1. *Todo es otro* [everything is something else]. A collection of essays on "the anticivilizational nature of language," hip-hop, MTV, Paul de Man, Wittgenstein, Heidegger, UFOs, pornography, and the concept of "light" (as in diet soda or superficial literature), among other things. Published by Tierra Adentro (a state-funded press) in Mexico City in 2002.

2. *El matasellos* [the stamp killer, the killer stamp, but also the Spanish term for the rubber stamp with which a postal officer—Yépez is fascinated by mail and all things postal—cancels a postage stamp once a letter has been mailed]. A novel about the mysterious death of a group of obsessive stamp collectors. Published by Editorial Sudamericana (part of Random House) in Mexico City in 2004.

3. *41 clósets* [you can probably figure it out]. A parodic "antinovel" that at times reads like an essay, a collection of aphorisms, or a series of poems, about a queer professor who lives near the US-Mexico border. Also about a well-known historical incident in which forty-one gay men were arrested during an orgy in Mexico City in 1901. Also about literary theory. Published by Conaculta (a government agency), in a small edition, in Tijuana in 2005.

4. *Here Is Tijuana!* [originally in English]. Coauthored with Fiamma Montezemolo and René Peralta, a coffee table book of photographs of Tijuana accompanied by a collage of quotes about the city. Nice to look at. Published by Black Dog (a press I know nothing about) in London in 2006, in part with funds from the Mexican government.

5. *El imperio de la neomemoria* [the empire of neomemory]. A book of "poet's theory" in which Yépez reads the biography of the American poet Charles Olson as a microcosm of American

imperialism. Published by Almadía (a well-regarded midsize press) in Oaxaca in 2007, in an edition of two thousand copies. Much more on it later.

6. *El órgano de la risa* [the laughing organ]. A collection of poems, some better than others, about the embodiment of humor, genetically modified corn, birds, and other subjects. Winner of the 2006 edition of the Raúl Renan National Prize for Experimental Poetry. Published by Aldus (a very small press) in Mexico City in 2008, in part with government funds.

7. *Transnational Battlefield* [originally in English]. A collection of poems, most of them excellent, about the US-Mexico border, Rilke, Wittgenstein (again), Ferlinghetti, Amiri Baraka, Kenneth Goldsmith, and writing in English as a second language. Published by Commune Editions (a small press for communist poets) in Oakland in 2017. Much more on it later.

8. *Mexiconceptual.* A collection of essay-poems, originally published online over the course of a month on a website that was deleted upon the completion of the project, about the political and aesthetic deficiencies of contemporary Mexican conceptual art. Quite good, though the central scatological metaphor—namely, that the "neoliberal museum" "excuses" the artist from serious thought and political commitment, the pun being that, in Mexican Spanish, "excusado" means toilet, which makes "el artista excusado" something like "the toilet artist," i.e., a receptacle for capital's shit—is a little puerile. Published by Satélite (a diminutive press: the book lacks an ISBN), in a handsome, full-color edition of two hundred copies, in "Mexico City, Tijuana, and the Internet" in 2016.

9. *La colonización de la voz* [the colonization of the voice]. A fascinating and impressively erudite meditation on the political and literary implications of early Nahuatl-Spanish dictionaries. Published by Axolotl Editorxs (again without an ISBN), under a Creative Commons license, in "Tijuana, Mexico City, and the Internet" in 2018.

As if all that weren't enough, a good portion of Yépez's work exists (or rather existed) exclusively as internet ephemera: I count at least three blogs, one since-deleted; at least two Twitter accounts, one since-deleted; and a YouTube channel where works of video art commingle with lectures and readings. I am also told, though I have not bothered to confirm it, that at one point Yépez was quite active on Facebook. It is an expansive oeuvre, an iterative one, whose scale is perhaps best captured by Yépez's own 2010 introduction to the first Spanish translation of a series of lectures delivered in English by José Vasconcelos in the late 1920s:

> José Vasconcelos's *Complete Works* . . . do not gather the totality of his books, documents, and loose texts. To come to know Vasconcelos one must track down his polygraphic dispersion, that involuntary self-portrait of the globe-trotting impulsivity which he attributed to mestizos in general. To this day, Vasconcelos remains dismembered.

Vasconcelos was a fascinating and contradictory figure who commissioned the murals of Diego Rivera, single-handedly created Mexico's public education system, and wrote the best autobiography in Mexican literary history—and was also a committed admirer of National Socialism. This makes Yépez's apparent identification with him—elsewhere in the piece he calls Vasconcelos the "first post-national writer" and the first "fronterizo," terms that Yépez often applies to himself—a somewhat scandalous gesture.

But beyond the half-joking attempt to épater le bourgeois, Yépez's voluntary self-portrait in a Vasconcelian mirror suggests that the "dismemberment" of his own body of work is not an accident, but rather the product of a conscious choice to resist definition and interpretation. The term *polygraphic dispersion* describes Yépez's own output as well as or better than Vasconcelos's in at least two senses. First, *polygraphic* could mean "plural, dispersed writings" and refer to the fact that much of Vasconcelos's written production is accessible only to those who go through a great deal of trouble to find it—as indeed is the case with Yépez. Second—and more importantly—the adjective naturally calls to mind a polygraph test and its connotations of deception.

Vasconcelos's *Complete Works* are notorious for including self-censored versions of his books: toward the end of his life, racked with guilt, the writer deleted the passages of his autobiography where he'd discussed his adulterous affairs and other forms of godless behavior, as if by rewriting his account of his life he could rewrite his life itself. The result is that the "definitive" account of Vasconcelos-the-author is not definitive at all. So with Yépez: any edition of his *Complete Works* will be necessarily incomplete. Nobody will ever "come to know" him; he will remain forever undecidable.

WHAT YÉPEZ'S "polygraphic dispersion" means in practice is that some of his most urgent—and morally searing—work is no longer accessible. The better part of his critique of Mexican president Andrés Manuel López Obrador, for example, appeared on a Twitter account he has since deleted. Yépez was one of few people on the left who saw through AMLO's bluster from the beginning. After going through several old hard drives, I could find only a single screenshot documenting his prescient warnings about the trap we were walking into:

> El presidente @lopezobrador_
> es otro proxeneta político

> Eres un perro neoliberal: eres
> un perro neoliberal

> Sabemos cuál es tu verdad
> El nuevo capataz del capital

> Por eso te protege
> Todo perro micro-similar

> El presidente es parte
> importante

del fascismo de tu personalidad

Here's my attempt at a literal translation:

President @lopezobrador_
is another political pimp

You are a neoliberal dog: you are
a neoliberal dog

We know your truth
[You are] the new overseer of capital

That's why every other
micro-similar dog protects you

The president is
an important part
of your personality's fascism

The most interesting aspect of this tweet is the final stanza, with its suggestion that our love for AMLO is the product of a psychological complex that deforms our personalities and makes us *desire* fascism. Yépez is a licensed therapist—he has said in interviews that he saw patients for four years but no longer practices—and his curative methods are harsh: how can we be sure, given the tweet's syntactic ambiguity, that the "neoliberal dog" is AMLO and not the reader? Still, I'm convinced that his goal, even or especially when he hurls insults, is to help us heal from the wounds fascism inflicts on us, particularly when fascism manifests as neoliberalism rather than totalitarianism.

In this sense, and for all his vanguardist bravado, Yépez turns out to be a surprisingly old-fashioned writer. In contrast to most modernist poetics since Baudelaire, he seems to think of literature not as an aesthetic game beyond the realm of morality, but as an *edifying* practice. Consider a few fragments from *Transnational Battlefield,* his English-language book of poems:

1.
What kind of poet
Can you make
    OUT
      OF
    The poet
    You were made
        INTO?

4.
[. . .]
"You must change your life"
Remains
An invitation for
A new science of poetics
To occur, a science
On how writing relates
To particular methodologies
Of life-change
In individuals and groups
Who exchange texts.
[. . .]

13.
Imagining a language
Means imagining a form
Of life
Writes Wittgenstein
Who probably didn't rewrite his life
Enough.

If language games
Only mean
When they make situations
Possible
One question is this:
          What situations are we
          Making possible
          Through our postlanguage
          Games?

Here Yépez reintroduces agency to the closed circuit of historical determinism. We may not be able to change the poet we were made INTO, he suggests, but we can "make" a different poet OUT OF those scant materials. In Rilke's famous line, Yépez finds not only an ethical imperative but also a philosophical anthropology: "You must change your life" implies that you *can* change your life; that you are not condemned to live the life you were given; that you can become someone else, someone new. Part of Yépez's frustration with other writers seems to stem from the fact that so few of them are willing to avail themselves of their capacity for reinvention, preferring instead to persevere in their corrupt ways.

If poetry is the expression of a life-form, writing a truly different poem is a method of radical "life-change." "Man," he tells us in *Battlefield*, echoing Nietzsche, "is / the / greatest / work / of / art / man / has / not / yet / developed / and probably / 'man' / and / 'art' / are / the / obstacles / for / the / work / to / be / done." Perhaps, Yépez suggests, one way to go about remaking ourselves, a possible method to imagine and inhabit new forms of life, is to write a poetry that does without the notions of *man* and *art*—a new kind of literature that strikes through the name of its "author" and thus emancipates not just the text, which can now mean far more than what its writer sought to express, but also the human being formerly known as the "author." (Here we are confronted, again, by Yépez's undecidable ambiguity: much like Nietzsche was at once a megalomaniac and a critic of the notion of "self," Yépez's critique of authorship derives its authority from philosophers who were quite attached to *man* and *art*.)

Yépez takes the "death of the author" not as literary theory but as the starting point for an ethical and political praxis. Rather than inviting us to play around with signifiers, Doctor Yépez's prescription is that we learn to seize the modicum of freedom available to us—which in the context of literature means the liberty to invent new forms, new syntaxes, new vocabularies—and use it to pursue the vita nuova: the new life, the one that comes after we give up authorship and realize that, contrary to what we've been told, we need not remain identical to ourselves. Unlike Pessoa, who was committed to the project of being multiple people at once, synchronically, Yépez seems more interested in diachronic evolution. He appears to want to refute the psychological fatalism endemic to Mexican culture best exemplified by José Alfredo Jiménez's famous ballad:

Nada me han enseñado los años	The years have taught me nothing
Siempre caigo en los mismo errores	I always fall into the same mistakes
Otra vez a brindar con extraños	Once again I toast with strangers
Y a llorar por los mismos dolores	And cry over the same old pains

If you want to get free—if you want to outgrow your inner fascist, if you want to stop hurting yourself and those you love, if you want to be *cured* of the illness that makes you *desire* oppression, the compulsion that leads you to worship neoliberal dogs and reactionary frauds as if they were your personal saviors—you could do worse than trying to embody the central proposition of radical poetics: that "I" is someone else.

BUT WHAT KIND OF POET was Yépez made INTO? The poet was born in Tijuana in 1974 into a working-class family. According to a biographical sketch by the Catalan writer Lolita Bosch included in an anthology of new Mexican writing, Yépez didn't know his father—though he was told that he was an agricultural worker in California—and, in an effort "not to defame him," prefers to go against Mexican custom and use the last name of his mother, whom Bosch describes as a "beautiful light-skinned campesina" who emigrated from rural Michoacán to Baja California. This handful of facts is crucial: as Yépez never tires of pointing out, most people who make a living writing or editing in our star-crossed country are products of the haute bourgeoisie of Mexico City. Being born on the border to a family without a famous last name irrevocably marked Yépez as a noncitizen of the Mexican Republic of Letters. The pride he takes in his own marginality is perhaps survival strategy as much as artistic gesture.

In any case, Yépez's youth featured none of the high-cultural bildung with which aristocratic Mexican families nurture the artistic vocations of their offspring. Instead he spent his formative years as a worker in Tijuana's maquiladoras, light-industry sweatshops that bloomed like poisonous mushrooms in the Mexican borderlands after the passage of NAFTA. This is perhaps why so much of Yépez's critique of the Mexico City literary establishment focuses on money: who gets it, who doesn't, and who decides who belongs in each category. The postrevolutionary Mexican state has historically spent a great deal of money on support for writers, literary magazines, and publishing houses. This largesse has shielded Mexican high culture from the demands of the market and facilitated the emergence of a vibrant literary tradition, but it has also limited the critical impulses of writers and thinkers. Thus the country's most visible intellectuals are often those who align themselves with the faction in power.

AMLO's policy of "Republican Austerity" has dismantled much of the old corporatist cultural apparatus, but even today it's easy to imagine what Mexico City's state-funded literary world must look like from Tijuana, like a game the children of the rich play with other people's money for the benefit of the "rotten elites to which [we] belong, and of which [we] are proud to the point of kitsch, that central feature of [our] prose." Yépez himself has overcome the myriad structural barriers designed to keep artists of his background from receiving state money: he has been a member of the National System of Artists and published many of his books with government funds. (His enemies insist this is naked hypocrisy, but I disagree. Using state money to criticize the state and its scribblers isn't contradictory—it's punk.)

Besides working in the maquiladoras, the young Yépez was for a time a tourist guide for Americans in Tijuana. "One of my first jobs," he told an interviewer for *Asymptote* in 2018, "was to talk to American tourists on the street and bring them down to the dance floor, where they could experience and unsettle their 'desires' (dance, drink, do the after-hours, break racial and cultural barriers)." This experience seems to have been as formative to Yépez as the factory floor, having introduced him to American imperialism in one of its purest forms—the one embodied by the vacationing gringo, that monster in sunglasses and shorts, for whom the colonies are not so much a real place as a psychosexual theme park where those protected by a blue passport and made wealthy by the exchange rate may shut down their superegos and surrender to their ids without fear of consequences.

Yépez's time as a tour guide also confronted him with English. To better understand his complicated, and at times quite painful, relationship to his second language, consider *Voice Exchange Rates*, a work of video art that Yépez made in 2002, when he was 28. The film, available on YouTube, is glitchy and pixelated. At the start we see the Mexican and American flags flicker and flash under the words *SE IRAN AL INFIERNO: THEY'LL WIND UP IN HELL*. The video then cuts to a screen capture from a computer running an old version of Windows: a frame within a frame, a screen within a screen, a metaphorical window that opens to another window. In the center of this mise en abyme we see a clumsily animated skull, the sort of thing an amateur might create with the editing tools available to PC users at the turn of the millennium. Icons from lotería, the strange Mexican blend of bingo and tarot, appear in columns on either side of the skull;

in the background a jagged audiogram suggests infernal flames. The skull begins to speak in English, in the artificial, uncanny cadence of early computerized text-to-speech:

> Hi, my name is Talk It! I am a software program designed to help poetry return to the righteous path of the avant-garde. I am a software program in which you can write and the machine can read for you—can read excellently. . . . I have different aural personalities, one for every type of poet or lyrical voice. I am easy to use and I have ideas on any issue, like Mexican art and why I think America is a melting nuclear plant.

The skull then tells us about its "most faithful client": Heriberto Yépez, "a so-called experimental verbal artist and translator from a border town called Tijuana, the only American city ruled by the Mexican government." Yépez's dream, the skull goes on, "is to turn on his PC and go to sleep, leave a creative writing program running, and wake up the next morning to print the novel or poetry book that the computer wrote for him."

Here we have an early instantiation of Yépez's thinking about authorship: if the poet is indeed a machine that produces language, as the structuralists would have it, why not drop the pretense altogether and let literal machines write for us? The pun *creative writing program* condenses a critique of American literary institutions. The point of an MFA, Yépez tells us, is to transform you into a piece of software, an automaton that produces acceptable—inoffensive, marketable—literature with the same efficiency with which the maquiladoras produce television sets.

Moments later, however, the skull lets us know that Yépez's interest in text-to-speech software also has roots in a far more personal, even *vulnerable*, concern:

> Another reason why Heriberto decided to use me was to have no problems, none at all, speaking English. I have no accent, but

> Heriberto's is strong, and, as everyone knows, having an accent in the US can be a problem. A huge one. So thanks to me, thanks to my great and merciful powers, Heriberto's voice now sounds like an American's, a white male voice. His voice is nearly perfect. Humans should worship a voice like that. A voice like that is better than God.

Underneath the video's formal coldness and parodic humor, what we have is pure pathos: the embarrassment, the shame, the awkwardness that comes from the realization that no matter how well one speaks the language of empire, one will never speak it well enough. If, as the title of the piece suggests, a poet's voice is a form of currency—cultural capital—then an anglophone voice will always be more valuable than one that speaks in Spanish. To speak (or write) in English as a Hispanophone Mexican is thus to trade on the foreign exchange, less a translation of the self than a conversion of pesos into dollars.

Because of his accent, Yépez's anglophone voice will always be counterfeit money: not quite correct, not quite right, incapable of fooling anyone. And still, white Americans (the most "American" Americans, if one understands that the adjective signifies imperial violence) will never reciprocate: few of them will ever learn enough Spanish to order a margarita at the all-inclusive resort, let alone to write poetry in their neighbors' language. This makes sense because, after all, dollars are worth more than pesos. The corollary of the unequal exchange rate is that to be a Mexican writer who works for a US audience is to be constantly reminded of your own colonization: you can't help feeling that you aren't so much an artist as a tour guide. As Yépez asks in a poem from *Battlefield*, where he further develops the metaphor of the bilingual artist as a financial trader: "Don't you realize ♪ / You will / become ♪ / a / cultural / broker? ♪"

The discovery that you have become a salesman of your own culture is disorienting and unpleasant. You feel it in the mouth, which must make an effort to form unfamiliar shapes. The synapses inevitably slow down, making you sound dumber than you know yourself to be. In one of the best poems in *Battlefield*, Yépez describes the "Language Event" that "Happens / (to us)" when "we / ('The Mexicans') / switch into English." How to transform this event into something we make happen to the world? One option, Yépez suggests in *Voice Exchange Rates*, is to mockingly insist that the imperfections of your exophonic English are features rather than bugs. "If there are mistakes of meaning or syntax, technical problems," the skull declares, "just attribute them to the great Western tradition of experimentalism. Call it L=A=N=G=U=A=G=E writing. Or, if you want to appeal to a different American crowd, call it Chicano Spanglish."

But these small acts of rebellion aren't enough. The fact remains that "as a Mexican poet living in an American age, you need to work in English" because, as the skull reminds us, "the next Octavio Paz is going to write like the *New York Times*." It is at this point that the video takes a darker turn that I at one point thought to describe, imitating Yépez's neological prose, as *mexicopessimist*. Instead of the talking skull, the screen-within-the-screen now shows an elongated, egg-like, hairless face with a swastika drawn on the forehead. Around it are four black dildos and drawings of guns. The face speaks:

> Hi, my name is Old Woman. Sometimes I am referred to as Gertrude Stein. I am Talk It!'s most popular voice. I am going to explain to you why I think poets and regular people around the world should switch into English their handling of daily business and transactions.

What to make of the fact that Yépez has drawn a Nazi symbol on a face that he tells us belongs to a Jewish writer? Given Stein's fascist sympathies, one suspects that discomfort is the point. This video, he seems to be telling us, is not a fun guided tour; this is an act of poetic terrorism, literary violence, and it's going to hurt you as much as switching languages hurts him. And then, right when we start to wonder whether we shouldn't close the screen and watch something—*anything*—else, Yépez makes his "Gertrude Stein" speak an extraordinary poem:

Even though this is not my normal Stein-style
My neutral way of doing things
I think
Yes
I think you must change
Yes
Why? Just because
Americans rule the world
The world
Americans rule the world
Rule the world
Rule
Americans rule the world
Rule the world
Rule the world
Rule the world
Rule the world
Why do they rule the world?
Rule the world?
Why do Americans rule?
Why they rule
They rule the world
They rule the world
They rule the world
They rule the world
Americans rule their world
They rule their world
They rule their world
They rule the world
The word
The worm
Americans rule the world
That's why.

The line breaks here are my attempt to capture something of the terrifying, hypnotic rhythm with which the machine speaks the poem in the video, as well as the degree to which Yépez has mastered Stein's stylistic procedures. Here Yépez seems to be challenging us to consider the ways in which American experimental poetry is indissolubly tied to American imperialism. How else to explain that even a tour guide from Tijuana knows—or better, is *expected* to know—*Tender Buttons*, if not by pointing out that Stein's poetry is a central part of a hegemonic culture that imposes itself on all others; that Americans, to quote the poet, rule the word? What would happen if a worker at a maquiladora wrote a poem as nonsensical as "If I Told Him: A Completed Portrait of Picasso"? Would that worker be hailed as a genius, a renewer of language, a founder of an entirely new poetics? Or would the American audience simply assume he didn't speak English?

In one of his columns for *Milenio*, Yépez had this to say about his transition from literal to literary tour guide, from factory worker to cultural terrorist, from one kind of marginality to another:

> I don't know if it was excellent or terrible luck, but the maquila where I worked that year happened to stand across the street from a public university. I applied for admission and I was accepted, and I decided to cross that bridge, which took me out of the assemblage and the cardboardland of eastern Tijuana, where I lived without access to public services and surrounded by drug labs. . . . Sometimes I wonder why I wanted to stop being a maquiloco, that miserable fucker who was so pissed off at every node of the system. . . . Before I was a stinking proletarian; today I am a stinking intellectual.

In other words, Yépez—who holds a doctorate in Spanish from UC Berkeley and now teaches at the University of Baja California—was made INTO a writer who bears the scars of class and nationality, of capitalism and colonialism. He is a poet from Tijuana, that no-man's-land between—*outside*—the Mexican Republic of Letters

and the American Literary Empire; a mongrel, a post-hybrid, a man
who straddles all kinds of borders. An undecidable.

YÉPEZ'S MOST IMPORTANT WORK, *El imperio de la neomemoria,*
was published in 2007 and translated into English six years later
as *The Empire of Neomemory* by Jen Hofer, Christian Nagler, and
Brian Whitener. On the surface, the book is a critical biography of
Charles Olson, a major American poet who developed an influential
theory of "projective verse" in which the spatial placement of words
on the page replaces meter as the poem's unit of "breath." His *Maximus* is one of the few 20th-century American masterpieces that
bear comparison to Ezra Pound's *Cantos* in terms of scale, erudition,
innovation, and sheer linguistic force. That text and others by Olson
served as a generational link between the modernism of William
Carlos Williams and the postmodernism (a term Olson apparently
coined) of the New American Poets, such as Allen Ginsberg, Amiri
Baraka, and Robert Creeley. Incidentally—or not: Yépez argues that
this little excursion holds the key to nothing short of American civilization—in the early 1950s Olson spent six months in the Yucatán
peninsula, where he drank, wrote long and annoying letters to his
friends, and exasperated his Mexican neighbors. It was there that he
also spent some time looking at Maya glyphs in search of a primal
writing that could ground his *'istorin*—Herodotus's word for history
and Olson's term for his own poetry.

Yépez spends a significant part of the book speculating about
Olson's psychosexual development, but the author of *Maximus* is
merely the occasion for *Neomemory.* Over the course of 274 pages,
Yépez writes about, among other subjects, Philip K. Dick's notion
of time, the theory of the author as servant of capital implicit in
Melville's "Bartleby," a wild and somewhat implausible reinterpre-
tation of the Sphinx's riddle in Sophocles, the metaphysical and
political aspects of the phrase *going postal,* the philosophy of Being
and Time expressed in the Indigenous myths of Quetzalcoatl
and Tezcatlipoca, the Maya notion of *kihn* as calendar-made-law,

Borges, Artaud, Joyce, D. H. Lawrence, Lévi-Strauss, Walt Whitman, William Carlos Williams, Walter Benjamin, Marx, Freud, Hegel, Nietzsche, *Casablanca, Total Recall, Eternal Sunshine of the Spotless Mind, The Matrix, The Butterfly Effect*, George W. Bush, al Qaeda, Fredric Jameson, Perry Anderson, and a number of neological concepts—*Oxident, pantopia, neomemory, co-body*—that form a theory of the imperial imagination as sophisticated as those of Edward Said and Frantz Fanon.

This dizzying range of references, typical of Yépez, makes locating the central thesis of *Neomemory* almost impossible. For what it's worth, here's an attempt:

1. At the core of the imperial imagination—the conceptual apparatus with which empire justifies itself and exerts control over the psyches of individuals—there's a notion of time-as-space that seeks to enforce a totalizing vision of reality as a singular universe governed by universal laws, when in truth it is a diversity of different worlds, each abiding by its own rules.

2. Olson's travels in Mexico and the poetics he derives from them are a clear instantiation of this totalizing impulse. By traveling to the "underdeveloped" regions of the empire, Olson believes he's also moving through time, advancing into the past in hopes of collecting the "lost" wisdom of "primitive" peoples, which he hopes, consciously or not, to incorporate into the imperial archive. This is the repository of cultural fragments that imperialist artists remix and recycle in order to control our historical memory.

3. The end product of this process is what Yépez calls *neomemory*, a cinematographic loop of decontextualized images that assimilates all that is foreign to the *Oxident*: the omniphagous West that, like oxidizing rust, slowly eats away at everything it encounters, in the process destroying it.

Yépez's name for this time-as-space, which includes not only all locations but also all times, is *pantopia*, or every-place, or total-place. It is the illusion of a container—better yet: a continent—that can fit everything in existence. Here, then, is a fantasy of the world and its

cultures as an empty, homogeneous extension that empire may conquer and claim as its own; that in truth is already its own, because
empire is nothing other than the illusion of a pantopia transformed
into a political order—it is already everything.

Yépez believes that Olson's "expeditionary" poetics reproduce
this imperialist-militarist vision. In the American's notion of "projective verse," he reads not just "projection" but also "projectile"; in
"composition by field," he finds a battlefield. Olson's poet, Yépez tells
us, is less singer than panzer; his poetry, less verbal music than linguistic blitzkrieg. Like Pound and Williams, Olson wrote incorpora-
tive poetry, collage-texts sewn together from scraps of diverse origin.
His method is juxtaposition, setting images taken from Gilgamesh
and Melville next to one another, placing the Gloucester of the 20th
century and the Yucatán of the Classic Maya on the same plane.
This, for Yépez, is a transparent expression of the empire's pantopian
imagination: by placing cultural artifacts of disparate provenance in
close spatial proximity on the "open field" of the page, Olson's poems
erase the difference between radically dissimilar historical moments,
thus creating neomemories that support the delusion that ancient
Sumer and Tikal were always part of the United States—that the
United States is the sum and culmination of the "human universal."

I worry that in attempting to present a coherent précis of
Yépez's thinking in *Neomemory* I've domesticated a rather wild
and even crazy text. I don't mean this as a reproach. A substantial
part of what makes the book compelling is the sensation that its
narrative voice, like Nietzsche's in *Ecce Homo*, is always teetering
on the edge of lucid madness. This is clearly a performance: unlike
Nietzsche, Yépez is sane and perfectly capable of producing traditional academic writing. But that's not what he's up to in *Neomemory*. Throughout the book he slips in and out of parody and makes
bombastic claims presented with no supporting argument other
than the sheer force of his language. His approach to philosophy is
not the tenured specialist's rigorous, often lifeless concatenation of
logical propositions, but the feral synthesis of the autodidact with a

library card; his psychology and anthropology, like Borges's metaphysics, subgenres of speculative literature; his literary criticism less philology than bibliomancy. Indeed, *Neomemory* is best read not as a scholarly intervention but as a long poem in prose that appropriates the formal devices of Western scholarship to undermine its epistemology.

NEOMEMORY WAS WELL RECEIVED in Mexico, though it didn't make a big splash. In the US, on the other hand, the book provoked surprisingly violent reactions. After the online poetry journal *Jacket2* published a few excerpts from the English translation in May 2013, a handful of American poets, among them Amiri Baraka, Jack Hirschman, Ammiel Alcalay, and Benjamin Hollander, formed a collective—called, rather unoriginally, Il Gruppo—to defend Olson's honor from what they said was Yépez's willful misreading of his life and work. Most of Il Gruppo's statements have disappeared from the internet, but their main complaint, published in *Jacket2* in response to the excerpt, goes as follows:

> If Yépez's thinking on Olson is examined . . . it is clear that at no point does he let the salient facts and relationships of Olson's life get in the way of his theory about Olson as the master poet of empire. . . . Does his "theory" not seem self-evidently backwards when two elder poets, Amiri Baraka and Jack Hirschman, known not only for their clear anti-imperialist politics but for being eyewitnesses to Olson's life and poetry, come forward and find it necessary to critique Yépez's suggestion that Olson and his poetry and prose reflect the impulses of a totalitarian and imperialist servant of empire?

The appeal to authority is flimsy and evinces a disconcerting ignorance of modern literary theory one wouldn't expect from serious writers. What's worse, Il Gruppo's animosity toward Yépez soon began to sound a little imperialist itself. During a reading in Olson's honor in 2013, Baraka had this to say about *Neomemory*: "'In the land of plenty, have / nothing to do with it / take the way of / the lowest / including / your legs, go / contrary, go / sing.' That dude who wrote that book in Mexico, whatever his name is, saying that Olson was an imperialist, he just had to read that passage."

One wonders: Does Baraka truly think that saying in verse that one is aligned with "the lowest" is incompatible with being an (unconscious) agent of empire, or that Yépez was unfamiliar with one of Olson's most famous poems? Were Yépez an American critic, would Baraka have remembered his name?

Part of what makes Il Gruppo's response to *Neomemory* so troubling is that Yépez takes pains to admit that he too is implicated in imperialism—as are, for that matter, all Mexicans. Yépez exerts a great deal of erudite effort to show how the ancient Maya also harbored an imperial conception of time-as-space, albeit a very different one from Olson's. The same, of course, is true for modern Mexico. After the North American colonies of Great Britain became independent, Yépez writes,

> the United States, crazy young thing, represented the bifurcation of the Oxident. . . . The Co-Oxident had been born. Of course, the Mexican Co-Oxident had existed for some time already, though it played the role not of Quixote but of [Sancho Panza]:* the two elements necessary in order for Co-Control to be established. . . . It was only in 1847 [the year of the American invasion of Mexico] that the United States finally developed its essence and body. This genesis, likewise, is altered memory: the United States took form thanks to the rending of Mexico. Since that time, the United States and Mexico are, clandestinely, co-bodies.

Yépez's use of the prefix *co-* serves different functions across his text and is therefore difficult to parse, but in general I take it to mean

---

*   Here the translation has the noun Sánchez where the original has the adjective *sanchezco*— Sancho-like or pertaining to Sancho. Given the context, I suspect this is a misprint: Yépez is clearly referring to Don Quixote's sidekick.

that two entities stand in a supplementary relationship. They sustain, uphold, and define each other; they cannot exist independently; they are locked in a fatal embrace. This does not mean that the two entities are similar, never mind equal: the United States is Quixote, the madman living out his fantasy; Mexico, that madman's faithful (or rather, enabling, *co-dependent*) squire.

The Cervantine analogy is rich. Sancho is the knight's servant, but he's also saner than his master—sane enough, at least, to realize that Don Quixote's aggrandizing notion of himself, and the wild antics with which he acts it out, is grounded in nothing but fantasy. The paradox of the character, what makes him so compelling, is that Sancho nonetheless continues to follow the knight's orders, because without the knight he'd be nothing. So with Mexico and the United States: Mexicans know the Americans are deranged, deluded, dangerous—and yet the fascism of our personality makes us desire our own subjection and continue to obey our imperial masters. The relationship is embarrassing for both sides, which is why everyone involved goes to great lengths to repress it. But if we set aside such self-delusions we'll see that the border is just another Oxidental fantasy. In every sense that matters—the American economy's material dependence on a permanent underclass of migrant laborers stripped of rights and subjected to a regime of police terror; the American imagination's symbolic dependence on a subaltern "other" against which to flatteringly define itself—Mexico is an essential part of the United States. The result, Yépez tells us, is that "all of us are Olson. Each one of us constitutes an avatar of the United States."

Later in the book Yépez holds his project to the same standard as Olson and finds it doesn't pass muster. He tells us that critique itself is just another machine for "the production of a neomemory." One begins to suspect that, in order to free ourselves from empire's iron grip on our societies and psyches, we'd have to destroy our own civilization. But even this seems impossible. The only exit from the labyrinth of neomemory that Yépez can envision is not a revolutionary uprising or a messianic apocalypse, but a slow, gradual decline in which the active force is not a counter-Oxident but the Oxident itself: "When I imagine how to exit the generalized *film-loop*, the only thing I can see in my mind is a bonfire that burns itself out."

Yépez closes *Neomemory* with an unorthodox interpretation of Stephen Hawking's since-retracted "paradox of information"—the notion that not even data can escape the gravitational pull of black holes. Yépez takes this to mean that "the universe forgets"; that the very laws of physics are subject to change, that nothing is permanent, and therefore that freedom exists. "So that I might be Sovereign," Yépez goes on, "we must let go of all General Laws. I know negating the existence of the Universe is absurd but however absurd, I assert it." Here I disagree with the translators. The original reads: "Sé que negar la existencia del Universo es un absurdo; por ser absurdo, lo asevero." Yépez is not saying that he asserts the non-existence of the universe *despite* the absurdity of the proposition, but *because* of it. It's a powerful thought, similar to Kierkegaard's notion of Abraham's faith. But what makes Abraham astounding is that such faith is almost impossible, inhuman. I feel compelled to ask Yépez-the-ethicist: How are those of us who wish to resist empire but lack Abraham's commitment to the absurd supposed to live? What is to be done? Are we meant to wait for the bonfire to burn itself out, for the wreckage of history to be swallowed by a black hole?

UPON FINISHING *NEOMEMORY* it's difficult not to feel fatalistic. This is why I spent a great deal of time trying to get my hands on a copy of *La increíble hazaña de ser mexicano*, "The Incredible Feat of Being Mexican." My friend and fellow reader of Yépez, the filmmaker Santiago Mohar Volkow, once described that book as Yépez's attempt to write a "popular" work of self-help destined to reach a mass readership—a goal not entirely unlike Nietzsche's ill-fated designs for *Zarathustra*. "The joke," Mohar said, "is that it's just as incomprehensible as the rest of his work." Yépez himself has said in interviews that *La increíble hazaña* is a "therapeutic" work, born from his clinical experience, that sought to give Mexicans a practical method for overcoming the psychopathologies of their society.

And yet, though *La increíble hazaña* had a much larger print run than Yépez's other books when it was published in 2010, as of early 2022 it was nowhere to be found. I visited no fewer than twenty bookstores; I inquired with rare book dealers; I polled my friends and acquaintances. Mohar used to have a copy, but the apartment building where he lived collapsed in the 2017 earthquake and Yépez's book, like the rest of his library, was lost in the rubble. This struck me as oddly appropriate: what better emblem for Mexican fatalism than the fact that the only known copy of a critique of Mexican fatalism was destroyed in an earthquake?

After much fretting, I wrote to Yépez to ask if he had a PDF of the book. He replied in uncharacteristically cordial terms and sent me the file, though he also said that he disagreed with my interpretation of his work as *mexicopessimist*. And indeed: *La increíble hazaña* is far more optimistic than *Neomemory*. Consider a passage where Yépez, addressing the reader in the familiar tone of a slightly condescending therapist, anticipates critiques accusing him of writing an excessively sunny and accessible work:

> Do you know what . . . a typical Mexican intellectual . . . would say to me if he read this book? "You've sold out!" . . . And he'd say it because writing a book like this one means betraying the following dogma: "You shall not speak up thinking that things could improve. You may only speak about how everything is going to get worse." And he'd say to me: "You are an idiot, an optimist—the Mexican will never change! Stop fucking around. This is a self-help book!" It'd be useless to remind him that today the wisdom of Lao Tzu, the Buddha, Seneca, or Marcus Aurelius would be classified as self-help and all but certainly dismissed. I bring this up because Mexican intellectuals' mockery of self-help is an extension of a typical feature of Mexican popular culture, which believes—forgive me but it's true—that self-overcoming is impossible.

Yépez opens the book with a discussion of the ways in which pre-Columbian Mexican cultures were "methodologies" for the creation of "a superman." These methodologies, Yépez tells us, were lost in the Conquest, giving rise to "the Mexican": a personality type characterized by an atavistic attachment to the past and contradictory drives to dominate and be dominated. The result is a psychological and political fatalism, reproduced across generations through unhealthy family dynamics, that celebrates defeat and considers success a moral failing. In Yépez's schema, Mexicans who remain beholden to their traditional worldview fear the acute pain of growth—which always implies loss, a metaphorical death. In their effort to avoid it, they take refuge in the chronic suffering of stagnation:

> The old Mexican does not want to forget. . . . The old Mexican sees the world through his wounds. That's why he never lets them close: He believes that without his wounds he'd be blind. Refusing to ignore the past, he ignores the present. . . . The old Mexican is but a set of specific sufferings.

This diagnosis has much in common with Freud's concept of melancholia and Nietzsche's notions of slave morality and the life-denying effects of excessive memory, but also with the sorts of things one hears from motivational speakers. Like all moralists Yépez walks a thin line between insight and banality: *You must change your life* is a fine way to end a sonnet about an archaic torso of Apollo, but it's easy to imagine a Jordan Peterson tract with that title.

What saves *La increíble hazaña* from becoming a tropical cousin of *12 Rules for Life* is that the project is also an intervention in one of Mexican literature's most storied traditions. Yépez's use of the general singular typical of old-fashioned theories of national character—"the Mexican"—suggests that he's writing his version of what we might call the Big Book About What's Wrong With Mexico (BBAWWWM). The most famous example of the genre is Octavio Paz's *The Labyrinth of Solitude,* but there are hundreds more. Ever since Independence, most of Mexico's major writers have at one point or another felt compelled to produce a long essay explaining our country's curse, usually through philosophical speculation and armchair anthropology rather than empirical research or journalistic reporting. Yépez's insistence that he's writing self-help rather than high literature is something of a red herring—and also, I suspect, a secret joke: he dislikes Paz so much that he'd rather be associated with *The Power of Positive Thinking* than with a winner of the Nobel Prize.

But for all his playful disavowals of the great poet's legacy, Yépez's diagnosis of the psychopathologies of Mexican life has much in common with Paz's. Take his interpretation of gender and family relationships. Denied self-fulfillment by men addicted to domination, Yépez tells us, Mexican women devote themselves to their sons with a domineering abnegation that conceals a desire to prevent them from growing into men like the ones who hurt them. This overbearing, infantilizing love in turn causes the sons to develop a guilty conscience that eventually leads them to resent their mothers. But because the profound idealization of the mother is a central characteristic of Mexican culture, men are prevented from admitting that they resent her. Displaced from its original object, their hatred mutates into a generalized misogyny that later in life leads them to punish their wives and girlfriends and deny them self-fulfillment—which restarts the cycle. Consciously or not, Yépez has rewritten the chapter of *The Labyrinth* where Paz describes the archetype of La Chingada: the Mexican Mother as long-suffering Victim-Saint, in equal parts idealized and hated by her children.

The difference between Paz's and Yépez's BBAWWWM—and it is a radical difference—resides not in the diagnosis but in the proposed cure. Against the grain of Paz's nationalism, which celebrates Mexican culture even as it criticizes it, Yépez believes that Mexico's suffering won't end until Mexicans are no longer Mexicans. "The new Mexican," he writes, "will be one that no longer has a fixed definition [or] an identity." Divesting ourselves from our past will hurt a great deal, yes, but the delusion of Mexicanness consists precisely in the fantasy that suffering is preferable to pain.

Here Yépez is once again fighting an uphill battle against the spirit of the times. To say, as Yépez does, that identity is fundamentally "conservative," that "all nationalities are forms of control," is to flirt with heresy. Perhaps being allowed to be the person you were made INTO—a person designed for suffering—isn't what brings about liberation. Perhaps it can only be found by making a new person OUT OF the ruins of your oppression.

Though Yépez is a master of polygraphic ambiguity and a congenital ironist, he can also be disarmingly earnest. Such is the undecidability of Yépez. He is at once an avant-gardist—an enemy of nostalgia, in love with the future—and a revivalist invested in resurrecting a long-lost conception of literature as a means for teaching how to live. It's no wonder he's obsessed with calendars. He's untimely, like Nietzsche, out of joint not just with his country but also with his age. In a time when the thinking left is socialist and collectivist, he's an anarchist and an individualist; in an era when doubt and anxiety are understood to be the marks of intelligence, he's not afraid of confidence and certainty.

For many of us, late imperials beholden to neomemory, *morality* has become a dirty word—almost an antonym of *politics*, anathema to *art*. It's no wonder that Yépez, who's first of all a moralist, has made so many enemies. A terrorist is a true believer, someone with moral convictions so strong that he feels compelled to destroy himself in an attempt to bring justice to the world—or rather, to the many different worlds. "The Universe," Yépez writes in the last line of *Neomemory*, "will never happen." I'm not sure I agree, perhaps because I remain Mexican. Still, I'm glad that somewhere in Tijuana there's a former factory worker willing to plunge headfirst into the absurd to demonstrate that, contrary to all appearances, we are free.

2022

LEAVING ELLSWORTH

NAUSICAA RENNER

JOSEPH WAS BORN AT 7:35 PM ON MAY 28, 2021, IN ELLSWORTH, Maine. They put him on my chest, his limbs splayed on top of me, useless as he cried. He had hair. They put a tiny stretchy cotton hat on his head, which immediately became stained with blood. Jonah said I looked bewildered—the same adjective he had used when I sat down on the couch in our makeshift apartment fifteen days earlier, just home from seeing my mother die. It didn't seem possible she would die until she did. And it didn't seem possible to have a baby until we did. Later, in the quiet overnight while I held my tightly wrapped son, I hallucinated my mom for an instant, sitting on the edge of the recliner, out of the corner of my eye.

Even as a newborn Joseph loved to be outside. We walked him in a stroller around Ellsworth, sometimes intersecting with a flock of young turkeys moving from yard to yard. I laid him on a blanket in the park and showed him things he couldn't yet see. He reacted to the sensation of wind on his face. We took him to Branch Lake, changed his diaper on a picnic table, and dipped his feet in the water. Jonah skipped pebbles from the beach across the surface. I felt confident as a new mother but also worried that there was a part of me that was dead and therefore unavailable to Joseph to use and play with. I felt like a stone that would always sink.

We sat on the porch at my dad's house, with the dog locked up inside, and looked at the clouds and listened for airplanes. Except I still called it "my parents' house." My dad had taken up smoking, his fingers becoming stained yellow with the turmeric derivative he put in the tobacco. He told me he was happy I wasn't angry at him anymore. We had gotten into blowout fights in the weeks before my mom died. When he refused to eat because he thought the food I cooked smelled like "cafeteria food," I told him he was being a baby. He slammed the door. Now he held the baby gingerly and formally. "Joseph, it's your grandfather."

Jonah's siblings came to visit, one by one, and we went for walks at a bird sanctuary on the road toward Bar Harbor. It was hot and sweaty and the air was full of mosquitoes. I paused to watch a friendly black vulture named Gauch, who was very activated by the visitors. You could see right through the nasal passages in his striking bone-gray beak. "This playful personality was separated from his parents while young and bonded with his rehabilitators in New Jersey," the sign in front of his cage read. "Now this highly social bird thinks he is a person and cannot be released to the wild because he would seek human companionship."

I had such a long to-do list. Set my dad up with Instacart. Change the electric bill to my name. Email my mother's death certificate to Quicken Loans. Meet with the estate lawyers. Find a local snowplow to do my dad's driveway this winter. Go to the police station to file a police report about the $2,000 I allegedly racked up at Verizon using the email address nausicaa1990@yahoo.com. Email HR and ask them why I got a paycheck in the mail for $0. Order newborn-size Medela-brand bottle nipples on Amazon. Send a thank-you note to my eighth-grade teacher for sending a children's book and her condolences. Reply to emails. Drive the twenty minutes to my parents' house to check on my dad and pick up the piece of paper he hopefully signed. Pick up any bills from where he leaves them on the top of the dryer in the mudroom. Take out the compost. Wipe up the coffee grounds burned onto the surface of the stove. The coffee grounds conjure a hologram of my mother wiping the surface down with familiar gestures of the sponge.

We took care of everything and made plans to leave. I took pictures of all the pages of my mom's photo album, where she made collages of all our family photos; pictures for my baptism, an infant lying on a white sheet surrounded by rose blooms, now lived next to pictures of baby Joseph in my camera roll. Jonah wanted to make an amateur documentary called *Leaving Ellsworth*, I can't remember why. So much had happened, but we had no plot and nothing in particular we wanted to say. So we shot videos of each other walking or swimming or looking, quiet and reflective. We took a long walk, beyond the hospital, through the Trumpier part of town, and filmed the wide streets on our phones. I took a video from behind the dashboard of our car of Jonah looking one last time at a dramatic bay between Blue Hill and Ellsworth.

When Joseph was two months old, we packed up our Maine apartment to drive back to Maryland, to a house we had barely lived in. Joseph's age became a proxy for how long my mother had been dead.

ONE HOT NIGHT when we were back in Maryland, I wanted to take a walk after dark. I hadn't been outside all day. The baby had gone to bed. The dishwasher was on. Everything was in order. Jonah said he'd stay home, listening in case Joseph cried. It was September, but it was still hot and swampy and loud with the sounds of crickets and cicadas and other mysterious beings. I walked out the back door and dumped the compost in the pile in the backyard, setting down the bowl to pick up on my way back.

People in the neighborhood are opposed to keeping compost in the backyard because, they say, it invites rats. I do it anyway. I have always wanted a compost pile, and now I have a house, so now I can have one. But I had noticed that there were holes appearing in the ground around the plastic column containing the scraps—little pills of mud all piled up. People in the neighborhood want you to use a service instead. They send a lot of emails about it. They also send emails asking how to eradicate the moles digging holes in their lawn. I didn't want to get rid of the compost or the moles. Oh well, I thought to myself, not everyone can think I'm a good person. Some things you can't outsource, some things you have to do yourself. And if they ever confronted me, I would quote Wallace Stevens: "Whoever founded / A state that was free, in the dead of winter, from mice?"

In the poem, the mice all dance on the bronze statue of some human, once great. "It is a hungry dance." It certainly feels that way in the dark, when all the animals come out to eat. I walked out to the street around the side of the house. I could see the silhouettes of bats swooping, eating mosquitoes. Rabbits barely visible were paused on the lawns. They were busy; busy chewing on the edges of human civilization. The air gave the hug of a warm bath. I heard distant laughter following the soft thumps of my chain-smoking neighbors playing cornhole. The sky was stained slightly orange with light from the Beltway, but under the trees it was pitch-black.

My hips felt sore, not from exercising, from not exercising. My joints were still loose from giving birth, my torso sank too far whenever my foot hit the pavement. A bag of bones whose vacuum packaging had been opened.

As I got farther from my house, farther down the rows of houses, I had the feeling it would be possible to wriggle away, to slip through the fingers of who I had become, to turn into a fox or a raccoon, prancing across the neighbors' lawns, caught in high con-trast on their Ring cameras. A line from Steely Dan's "Deacon Blues" played through my head: "I crawl like a viper through these suburban streets." In the city, you feel anonymous because there are so many people and, while you remain yourself inside your own head, your body belongs to the crowd. In the suburbs, anonymity comes from being a carbon copy of everyone else.

My mother never had that anxiety, of being too much like everybody else. Difference was written all over her body. I remember her crying whenever she felt excluded, which was often. Now she was excluded from my son's life, too. It was her I was feeling inside myself, my decaying magnolia bloom, my rotten, shriveled core. It was her I was channeling when I became involved with the miniature dramas of my backyard—she who found it easy to see herself in the fabric of nature and hard to see herself in the fabric of humanity.

Jonah and I watched a science fiction movie not too long ago in which Earth has been deemed uninhabitable. Most people have already left. A daughter and her father, who is a scientist, are two of the few remaining people on Earth. They are trying to grow things, with limited success, because of the polluted air. And they need bees. The signals are mixed; the daughter is not sure if their experiments will succeed. The last shuttle is leaving Earth, and she decides to stay behind. It seems she will live; the air in the city may be starting to heal. Her father, it is revealed, died long ago.

I, too, am stranded. I've chosen to stay behind as the last shuttle leaves Earth. It's the end of the movie, but I still have my whole life ahead of me. And Earth feels more mysterious and frightening than when it was teeming with life, teeming with humans. How many more years of silence and reflection, emptiness and desolation lie ahead? If I was the last person on Earth, would I still get up and make coffee every day? How many more years will my only company be my mother's dead body?

I went back inside, returning myself to myself and to our family and our lamp-lit living room. On the wall hung a framed postcard my mother had sent to my dad in 1988, just before they started dating, from a vacation stay in Okoboji, Iowa. On it she had drawn, in pen, lots of little bugs over a field of prairie grass. "Sssssss, zzzzzzz, buzz," said the insects. "Dear Soren," she had written in her Cubist handwriting. "Summer sounds abound."

> My sister Jane thinks she'd like u. She wants to say hi . . .
> *Hi, I want a ride on your bike. Jane*
> So the lake is cool the nites are cooler and the motor boat is the
>   coolest. See you soon. Judy M.

I RETURNED TO WORK from maternity leave, remotely still. I talked to coworkers on the phone. I tried to be open with everyone about what happened to me. But when you are totally open, other people shrink back. They are not ready to talk about life after the death of a loved one, even if they themselves invite it. People would say to me, "I'm here if you ever want to talk." "If you ever want to talk with someone who's been through it, I'm here. Let me know. I'm around."

Other people talked to me about surviving their parents' deaths, as though welcoming me into a club—"We are scarred people," Jonah's uncle told me; "Mourn furiously," someone else advised.

"Let me know if you ever want the perspective of someone who's a year out," my coworker said. His father had died sometime the previous year. He had offered his wisdom a couple times before—on having a dying parent, on the virtues and difficulties of home hospice care. I hadn't taken him up on it before but then suddenly I did. We had both seen people in unspeakable pain. Perhaps he had come up with some words for it.

"Yeah, tell me! What *is* it like, a year out?" He was taken by surprise. Normally, I could tell, his offer was perfunctory. He wasn't ready to talk about it *now*; he wanted to talk about it at some unspecified point in the future. "Well," he said, pausing to gather himself. Gather, gather, gather. A breath in and then: "Have you ever heard of the ball and the box metaphor?"

"No."

"So there's a ball inside a box." He took it slowly at first and then accelerated. "And on the inside of the box is a button. Every time the button is pressed you feel pain. And just after someone dies, the ball is big, it takes up the whole box, so the button is always being pushed down."

"Uh-huh." I wanted to show him I was listening.

"And as time goes on, the ball gets smaller and it bounces randomly against the sides of the box. So after a month or two it's not always pressing the button. But when it does hit the button, you feel just as much pain as you did right after it happened. And after a year, the ball is a lot smaller."

I wished he had told me a story about his dad instead. I didn't feel closer to him at all. I felt like he was trying to hand me a tool that I didn't need. Like I was trying to decide how to nail this coffin closed but instead of a hammer, he handed me a banana and told me to listen to a TED Talk. The metaphor was his way of containing grief. And maybe I'm just not ready to contain it yet. But I was looking down at this banana like, Is this supposed to help me?

Later, he sent me a tweet, posted in 2017, with a drawn diagram of the ball and the box. "Here's the ball and the box analogy I mentioned," he said. *Mentioned*, I thought, as if he described it in passing. More confirmation that our conversation was marginal.

If I had to make my own analogy, I'd say grieving is like being a lemon that someone has taken a zester to. "Ouch," says the lemon. The lemon's skin is raw. But the air grows a bit more fragrant and life appears fresh and vivid amid the pain.

WE WENT TO A NEIGHBOR'S backyard party on Halloween afternoon. It was chilly, but the children were spread out on a blanket on the lawn: peas in a pod, a cow, a Wookiee, the caterpillar from *The Very Hungry Caterpillar*, a pumpkin with a floppy renaissance cap. There were eleven first-time moms in a three-block radius with kids under a year old. We had a WhatsApp group. We took a group photo of our children, eleven white lumps on a picnic blanket. Did I seem different from them, to them? The old high school anxiety flared up, of wanting to be accepted and wanting to be recognized. Was I a carbon copy of them, too, or did they accept me because we were a crowd?

Joseph, a jack-o'-lantern with a hood, was relentlessly scooching to the edge of the blanket and pulling up grass to shove into his mouth. Jonah sat near him, grabbing him by the waist whenever he got too close to the edge and dragging him backward, unfurling his cold hands and picking blades off them. I thought about apologizing for the bald spots on their lawn, but I didn't.

I talked to one fellow mom who was astounded that Joseph was already crawling. She made me feel embarrassed. "You know this is *really unusual*, right?" I wanted to protect him from her jealous praise. She mentioned that she had to have a good cry when her daughter started eating solids. I knew what she meant. Joseph had a purity about him when he was just drinking breast milk. I could say he was wholly made by me. Feeding him food felt like polluting him. It turned his shit dark and thick. (This morning he ate an entire banana. What?!) Another mom said she cried when her kid slept in a separate room for the first time.

I knew what they meant, but I had never cried about Joseph growing up. I should be sad like that, I thought, about Joseph shedding ways of needing me. Did it mean I wasn't invested enough in my son if I didn't feel his individuation as an amputation? My analyst pointed out that I may find myself feeling happy for Joseph when he goes out into the world and enjoys himself. But it would be so unlike my own childhood that the feeling may be alien to me.

"What's the most surprising thing about becoming a parent?" my husband's friend Mike asked me. We were sitting in a bookstore/record store on a cold fall day in Richmond, Virginia. We had driven down for the day to remind ourselves that we could. "Breastfeeding," I said. I had been looking forward to not being pregnant anymore, to being able to move how I wanted and consume what I wanted. I hadn't realized that birth does not free you, physically, from the baby. He didn't have much to say in response. What about you Jonah? Jonah responded by telling him what he's told everyone: He's surprised parenting isn't hard. Or not as hard as he thought it was going to be.

I have a secret shame when he says this. My boss's wife, who has four kids, recently came up to me at an event after Jonah had told her the same thing. I can't remember her exact words, but she said something to the effect of, "Sorry to criticize your husband but he is being sexist when he says that. It's not hard *for him*." I wasn't sure if she was trying to speak on behalf of me or herself or women everywhere. Oh God, I thought, is she right? I don't think parenting is particularly difficult, either, though I would say it differently. I'd say I've learned parenting isn't complex, it's brute force. It's remaining awake when you're sleep-deprived. I actually find myself wanting it to be more intellectually challenging than it is; I find myself wanting to invent a pedagogy. I want to feel like I'm making *decisions* about how to raise my son. But instinct, which is much wiser than pedagogy, takes over.

I LIVE "IN THE LAND OF turkeys in turkey weather," as Wallace Stevens wrote. There was a giant blow-up turkey set up on a lawn down the block. It wore a pilgrim hat and a checkered bandana and a large red snood hung down its face. It was there last year, too: a comedown from Halloween decorations and a ramp-up to Christmas. Our neighbors' kid liked to touch the turkey, stroking it with her tiny hand. *That's right, Clarissa.* (Pat pat pat.) *Gently. . . . Gently!*

I wondered if I could still hold Joseph's hand long enough to trace it and draw him a hand turkey. His instinct was to grasp, so his hands stayed for much of the day in tiny fists. They had to be unfurled to clean. His palms were always wet and full of fragments of my hair. His other instinct was to wave his arms and smack his hands down. It is delightful to put different things under him to smack—a table, a tray full of food, the rainbow xylophone on the back of the plastic green alligator. Sometimes he would oblige to holding a rattle and waving it around violently. *Gentle, Joseph.*

Children are small but strong. We have to remain just barely stronger than them. Joseph could budge an entire chair from his position on the floor. But if I sat on the chair, it wouldn't go anywhere.

The more meaningful your life is, the less happy it's possible to be. That's what I've been thinking lately. The more you occupy yourself with the Big Stuff—the tragic, the political, Life and Death and Truth—the less whimsical you can be, the less frivolous. Of course, that's not how I felt when my life was simpler. Before I was carrying this weight around. Before my entire life changed. When my life was simple, I craved tragedy. I didn't want happiness, I wanted sadness I could sublimate. I wanted things to happen that would give my life purpose and direction. This is not what my husband would say. He would say, "Duty to others is a relief. Your life should not be your own." His love language is acts of service. Also, he has not yet suffered the death of a parent. Now that my mother is dead and my baby is born I know that hard stuff is actually hard.

My mother-in-law told me that I'm a natural mother. It's a compliment! She wasn't expecting it. She thought I would be anxious about whether I was doing everything right. But *look at me now. The intellectual gets right down on the floor and plays with the baby.* The green plastic alligator was staring up at me from the rug with a frozen and knowing smile, uncanny and immortal. All these baby toys look to me like they could suddenly emerge from suspended animation. "The eyes of an animal when they consider a man are attentive and wary," wrote John Berger. "Man becomes aware of himself returning the look."

IN JANUARY, A DEER sat down in our backyard. We looked at it from our kitchen. This sitting was so awkward, we weren't sure if we had ever seen a deer sit down before. First the front legs buckled, putting its body at a dramatic downward angle—like an accent grave in French—and then the back legs. The deer's belly was rotund. Was she pregnant, or just fat for winter? She looked a little old, a little gray, a little mangy. Her eyes had lines of black around them, like the eyeliner I had decided to wear for no reason, and she sat placidly, not bothered by Joseph's screams from behind the storm door.

It was a cold day but we wanted to get out so we went for a drive. When we got back, the deer was still there. "It's dying," said Jonah. "It's dying?" I said. "Two hours ago you thought it was pregnant!" "It's either pregnant or dying," he confirmed. I tried to google how dying deer act, if they get lethargic, and found some kind of mite was killing scores of deer in Jersey. What would we do if the deer died in our backyard? Call animal control?

Or, we could let it decompose; it was our private property. I heard a radio segment about someone who hauled roadkill to their backyard so that he could observe a particular kind of vulture. I learned that vultures can't actually penetrate the skin on their own; they enter the body through soft spots and wounds. At some point, I looked again. The deer was gone, but I could still see the imprint of its body.

An orange was sitting in a bowl on our dining room table—a symbol of the spirit of life during winter. It had been there for two weeks or more, bright orange in a dark blue bowl. I was too picky to eat it by then. From the outside, you can barely tell when an orange is old. The color was vibrant but it probably already had that faint taste of rot. A hum of decay that persists under everything else, telling slow time like the half-life of grief. It reminds me of the egg on the Passover table of the family I married into: a perfect image of fertility, hard-boiled so its core is yellow and green and dry.

SIGNS OF SPRING only made me remember what came the year before. An enormous bouquet sent to my mother on her sixty-fifth birthday by her semi-estranged sisters, full of guilt and love. Posing for pictures on the porch that day: her stomach swollen with liters of abdominal fluid and mine with a baby. The overexposed and oddly zoomed-in photos she took of me on the lawn, wearing skintight pregnancy leggings that I would frequently pee through. Her leaning on me as we took one pathetic lap down the road and back. How it felt to be too hot in the sunshine and too cold in the shadows.

She felt good, having stopped the chemo, much better than she had felt in the winter. She was able to eat. She wanted spaghetti, she wanted applesauce, she wanted lamb burgers. In the package of ground lamb I brought home, there was a chunk of fat, congealed so that it looked like a small organ embedded in the meat. I threw the piece to the dog and dry heaved into the sink. She didn't eat much of the burger. In her last burst of energy, she bought a ten-pound bag of flour and boiled an entire chicken. She had never boiled a chicken before, that I can remember.

A year later, broth from the boiled chicken was still in the fridge. My father, who has bouts of psychosis, was also reliving the stress of my mom's last weeks; last year, before she died, he believed he was going blind. They vaped a lot of pot together. He tied a scarf around his eyes and stumbled around the house, ending up with a gash across his nose and glass broken all over the floor, which my mom cleaned up. This year, he told me he believed the logical end point of his life was suicide. He stopped eating, and spent a week in the emergency room because the psych wards didn't have beds available. He didn't think he would be able to live on his own forever, but he also didn't want to move out or meet anyone. He couldn't imagine a future, and he didn't have the energy to clean out the fridge. I took it all—the chicken juice with a layer of fat, a pan we'd had since I was a child filled with moldy stew from Christmas, and more broken glass—to the dump.

If people wanted to understand my perspective, I think, they would have to understand how my mother arranged her shelves, how she lined up the mess of knickknacks and stacks of canvases, how she stenciled a line of identical roses around the top of a room. How she arranged objects was also how she arranged the different parts of me—getting angry at me, above all, when I was careless, when I broke special things or lost them. And now, they would have to see her shelves gathering dust, untouched. I got a tattoo of the rose.

IN THE FIFTEEN DAYS before I gave birth, this time last year, I sat, very still, at the plastic folding table in our crummy apartment and did jigsaw puzzles, getting used to the idea that my mother was dead and trying to detect my body preparing to give birth.

No one knows why labor begins. Jonah said that the Talmud explains that God himself controls three things. Most things on Earth are executed by angels—the growing of grass, for instance. But

God holds the keys to when babies are born, when it rains, and the resurrection of the dead.

My mom wasn't buried. There was no coffin. There was a dark-green box made of heavy plastic. Inside there was a plastic bag packed neatly with her ashes and closed with a metal ring. Dyers Bay Crematory, a medallion on the neck of the bag read. The cremation cost $995. We had a small funeral, just me and my dad and Jonah and Joseph and my dad's friend who came across the country to be with him. I carried my mom's ashes down to the cove. The weight of the box felt like the weight of her limbs, which were heavy with swelling in her final months. I used to rub her arms and legs methodically to dispel the lymphatic fluid. Fleetingly, I felt a physical closeness with her—the last I will ever have.

I set the box down on the sloping, brittle seaside grass, opened the bag, and pocketed the medallion. Dyers Bay Crematory—a pun on diers? As in, people who die. My dad took the bag and walked away with it. I followed him. He crouched next to a big boulder on the shore. He dipped his finger gingerly into the bag and tapped his tongue. "Want some?" No, I didn't. Then he put a second pinch of her ashes in a circular hole in the boulder that used to hold the pole for a birdhouse for purple martins. Unceremoniously, he walked out to a rock over the high tide and turned the bag upside down and she fell into the water.

A couple of years ago, I had a dream that I was standing on the bank of a river with my father. The landscape looked like a Thomas Cole painting from *The Course of Empire*: pink and orange light fell across dramatic clouds, and there was a small, white ruin on the top of a steep slope dotted with sheep. It looked like the Parthenon: columns broken off halfway up, a quiet desolation where there were once streams of people. We stood at the bottom of the slope facing the water. There was a canoe in front of us, tethered to the shore, with a woman lying down on the bottom. The woman in the boat did not look like my mother though she probably was. We untethered the boat and pushed it off from the shore, which required some work, as the water pushed it back to us at first. Finally, the canoe was caught by a current and floated downstream. The woman in the canoe stood up and watched us as she floated away. My father asked me, "Did you remember to light the funeral pyre?" I had not remembered to light the funeral pyre.

It felt like I was complicit in sending someone off to die who was not fully dead yet. She used to talk about wanting to be buried and not wanting to be cremated because she was afraid of the fire. She imagined the cremation to be like the fires of hell. But eventually she gave in to my dad's insistence that she be cremated. Why did he insist? I think that if she were dead, he wanted her to be nowhere. Maybe he found graves undignified. Philip Roth wrote in *Patrimony* that one has no interesting thoughts in a graveyard; they reduce even the most interesting of thinkers to existential banality. I always thought how unfathomable it is that each stone on the ground represents someone who was loved. Or, more importantly, hated. It would be interesting, I thought, to know all the stories of hatred that lay around me.

My mother died, my mother was cremated. My mother returneth into dust; the dust is of the ocean; of the ocean is made rain. And why might that rain, whereto she was converted, not fall around me now? God controls when it rains.

Last year, at this time, the first thing I felt when I left my mom's body in the hospital room—when I closed the door on her body and walked past the nurses' station and out to my car and drove my car out of the parking lot and past the hospital window beyond which she lay—the first thing I felt was that we, she and I, had left material life behind. One of her sisters texted me: You are closer to your mother now than you ever were in life. I was floating . . . at the moment of her death she had taken me on a hot-air balloon ride and now we were looking at the Earth together from above as I drove on the stripe of road between Blue Hill and Ellsworth. Eventually Joseph and I would glide back down to Earth and she would just keep rising and spreading out over everything I saw.

It was warm and sunny. The first day of the year when summer's happiness finally seems possible again. She always made note of the moment in the spring when you could throw off your winter jacket and a weight lifted. I had told my mom, in my last monologue to her, that hope was in the air. Joseph, about to be born, was a bud of flower petals blooming, and she was the outside ring of petals, falling off and blowing away.

2023

BABY

BELA SHAYEVICH

THERE IS NO POINT TO ME ANYMORE. MY FAMILY WAS FIRST TO notice.

In Soviet Glenview, the living room has twenty-one clocks in glass domes with spinning pendulums, all showing different times. Grandpa's collection. Binders and pill bottles holding his coins are scattered around a plate of cranberry cake. Nobody touches it.

Grandpa starts in on his line of questioning with the traditional fakely coy giggle.

Had I met anyone "interesting" lately?

Ha.

Overblown, umbrous seascape. Roma growls under the leg of the burgundy leather couch. Enormous burgundy rug blotted in pee pads. Babulya says nothing, stirring her tea.

When am I going to have children?

"When are you going to leave me alone?!"

"Why do you always start yelling! Your dedushka is just asking a question!"

"Stop it! Sasha!"

"I am not yelling! You're the one yelling!"

"You think this is yelling! If I was yelling, the walls would be shaking!"

"Stop! Both of you!"

"Whyyyyyyyyy," Nina whines. "Whyyyyyyyyy."

She is hunched, hovering over the banister. She doesn't dare sit with us at the table or even come down to hide in the corner behind the piano.

"Nina! Vermin! Shut up!"

Nina emits a sound that makes everyone in the house want to kill her, stuffs a handkerchief into the pocket of her tattered house-coat, and shuffles back into her room.

Wish Gleb could see me here—maybe he would yell, too. Gleb must yell, Gleb is crazy. Or he would be, like, engorged with irritation. I hope I hope. But they wouldn't yell at him or in front of him, not until we were family, like if we lived in the basement: our children, the boxes of old-country dish towels, dying geraniums, black mold. Papa, Aunt Nina, my grandma and grandpa, Gleb and me, all together, the natural, communal order. Gleb and Dedushka, Papa and me, all four of us yelling, wow, and in what language.

He would be worshipped.

It is my birthday again.

"How is your brother?"

"I don't know, why don't you ask him?"

You baby, you bitch.

"Listen to how you talk to your dedushka!"

In her cruelest moods, Mama would say I would turn out like Nina. She hands me $300 and doesn't even go off about how much it hurt her how poor and alone I am and how poor and alone I will die. There is no point. Last summer, she had at least said that thinking about me makes her want to kill herself.

LONG AFTER THEY ALL GO TO BED, up on the cramped loft in my childhood bedroom, under the glow-in-the-dark stars, I dream of Gleb. Gleb's basement apartment he's probably squatting, the hideous detritus of a lone, tortured dad. Gleb's legs broken over the arm of the ragged Ikea love seat he now seems three times the size of, naturally awake at three in the morning. His eyes lit up in the dim LED like his Juul, which he longs to take drags from, but shouldn't, it's so expensive, his pods guy has been out of town. Guinea pigs chirruping in their pen on Gleb's white tile floor.

I'd been an only child, too, also an alien. Getting a double—when we were born, we had the same face—created parallel lines. Four hands unspooling a crosshatch of intersections. Trellises, offering up tendrils for recognition, to intertwine. Parallel patterns emerged, made up a network. What if the grid could be integrated all the way up to a concept? The family romance—don't leave me alone in here! "Never stop torturing me," Gleb had pleaded. Do you not realize you're like, my brother?

"What's going on?" I finally broke into our months-long silence.

"What do you mean?"

I'd told him that I didn't want to talk anymore, I'd never expected to in the first place, we'd only spent those forty-eight hours together. He was the one who kept jerking my chain until it triggered an episode. I had said, "We need to stop. At least until I get back from my trip." He said, "I know. Of course you're insane, you're just like me. Pinky swear we will meet again, on our birthdays." And then abruptly stopped talking to me altogether.

"What is the deal?"

"With what."

Idiot.

"I don't know what I have to offer you besides attention. That's what I'm offering."

He had acted so hurt when I told him he was cold, mindfucker, and, on the purely practical level, straight unavailable. He called me cruel, as though he cared. He's not just cold, though: selfish, repressed, (narcissist), insecure, fear-driven, liar, self-pitying, pompous. Losing his frayed, greasy hair, sickening neckbeard, stretch skinny jeans he doesn't even recognize as repulsive. Dating lip-flip Zoomers who call him Daddy. Also: a married girl and her catboy.

All I had wanted was an acknowledgment of the reality.

"Thanks," Gleb replied. "I am all good on attention."

I HAD NOT WANTED HIM. I'd wanted: to finally lay eyes on him, survey the ground we both may have walked. We'd known about one
another for years but had never met. Only a handful of people like
us in this world, we matched on Tinder. One of our mutual friends
told me that his ex-wife had a restraining order against him. I said,
"Sounds passionate."

Tall. Gravel voice. Pedantic and boring, as I'd expected. Prepared to bludgeon me with the details of his bottomless, niche
research project that he would never complete. He made us speak
Russian—insistently, crushing the crust of his dinner panini.

"Why do we have to?"

"Because I speak beautiful, eloquent Russian," he said, straight-
ening up over me.

Then started gushing. Brought up the restraining order himself—how do you say *restraining order* in Russian?—"things happened
that WERE NOT my fault." Revealed that he'd just had a breakdown
so bad, he checked himself into the hospital. His mother had come to
take care of him and then got trapped here because of the war. She
stuffed his freezer with an unbearable quantity of her pelmeni. "I'll
never eat it." Never? I smelled the blood through the shell.

"What do you wanna do now? Wanna go for a walk?"

He led us back to his basement. I didn't care. No sexual tension,
like cardboard. I always hang out with these losers as long as I can
if they are basically tolerable. I will hang out with basically anyone
for as long as I can—what else to do with myself? All of my friends'
babies' bedtimes are six and then everybody is tuckered. Where am I
supposed to be? He didn't want me either.

Would Mama be home?

Drop ceiling, goiter of coats, fluorescent overheads. His kid's
toys all over the floor and his mattress out in the living room since
he had given his mother the bedroom. "Doesn't your mama at least

clean up around here?" Mine would have hired a maid. Papa made Nina. We settled on the outer edges of his love seat.

He launched into the extended mix re: his ex, blamed her for everything. Especially for, as he underlined, blaming him for everything that had ever gone wrong in her life. Ruining his life. Sanguine adult experiences, like in the movies, I could not possibly fathom. Didn't want to hear anything about my glittering geriatric adolescence.

I couldn't make myself leave. Why was I lingering? On our third round on the activities of the CIA Special Activities Division, or SAD, dragging toward 11 PM, no, I had never read Marx, no, I would never.

I always complain that I never meet anyone like me and that's why I'm desperate for it, but that isn't true; it's just that whenever I do, they are deplorable. The problem with people like this is that they are so easy. They never want to be left alone but they need to repulse you: it creates instant intimacy. You can do anything that you want around them, say whatever you please—they'll never care. You don't exist to them. It's real freedom. Or, I don't know, projecting familiar cultural psychopathology, false, but correct in the most typical, painful places, the way we all eat off each other's plates right away—commandeering the butt of my fish without even asking. A longing to reunite in the mausoleum of the communal body, like little zombies: my mouth is your mouth, I'm not a witch, I am you. The problem is I am also insane.

Am I supposed to "recover from" my central characteristic? Am I "unwell"? Am I "supposed to be well"? Is, like, not loving your brother a rule from the Bible?

Ding-dong, knock knock! It's Mama!

He got up to let her in. "Hello, Mama."

She blew down the corridor, tipsy and charmed like a belle in a wood, trailing the smoke of a phantom cig. Freckled and twittering, outlandish but tasteful glasses, black linen dress and a quilted chore jacket. He sees what I see. A proud grin creeps over him. He sees what she sees.

May I sit down with you for a moment? Yes, yes, of course. Let's have some tea. It isn't every day you find somebody like me down here. I went to the kitchen with him to bring cups like a woman.

"Get me a tiny bit of the whiskey? Glebusha?"

"Yes, Mama."

"If somebody will join me?"

Of course I will have some. "Why didn't you offer me any before?"

"I don't drink."

"So? I am your guest."

"I don't know how to pour it."

"What are you talking about? It goes in the glass."

Smiling wide, sweeping aside the mail and receipts that she'd cleared off the chair to lay all the offerings before her. Don't look at me like that, the way that I want you to. I can't resist the urge to modestly dazzle you, pleasure myself with your delight. If only my mama looked at me like that. The way you glance at him now when you can tear your eyes off me—do you always?

"He tells me you translate, too."

Yes, yes, I do. For your most beloved opposition media outlet. Verrrrrry important work.

"All of us do what we can."

Ugh, the war. We never thought it could happen. How it has severed us all and all over again. How it has brought us together, maybe too much in some cases.

He sees us, how we belong. Our wavy red hair, mine, just like hers. I strain to make my Russian more sonorous, fluent, and natural. Yes, it is perfectly natural. I'm a professional. I am faltering. She can tell that I'm trying—my effort, another radiant emblem of my true goodness. His goodness too. I am its avatar now, what she wants me to see when I look at him. Goodness sweats out of his hands, he wipes it off on his jeans; I suck it in through my teeth, she blows it out on her tea. The panini retoasts in his belly, we forget English, our teeth unstraighten, all cataclysms rewind—quick-melting, ecstatic crystal, our little family.

"Well, kids, I better go off to bed," Mama coos.

Two hours later, he was on top of me, crushing my neck, cutting off all my oxygen.

He'd tried to kiss first.

"No!" I ducked. "I don't do that."

"What do you mean?"

"I find patterns of heterosexual engagement inherently violent. You can try whatever you want, but I won't let you."

He understood. Staring me down, he slowly reached for me. I let him come close enough to crack my elbow into his ribs. He grabbed onto my shoulder, squeezing the joint. I tried kicking his shin, he wrestled me down to the floor. He wasn't afraid. I could fight him at full force.

"You have really strong legs."

"No I don't. Are you weak or something? Try harder."

Poor Daddy, he must be so tired. I let him pin me facedown, in a headlock, knee on my spine. I could just die. But I swept for something to kill him with, put baby out of his misery, is that an ice skate?, and smashed it into his thigh. He slipped off, I flipped, but he wrested the skate away, aiming the blade at my neck. You can kiss me now. It had a picture of Mishka on it, the mascot from the 1980 Moscow Olympiad.

Rasping, "Did you get that on eBay?"

"They're mine from when I was little. My mom brought them back for my kid."

Thank you, Mama.

"Did you know that the Mishka float ended up flying into Sparrow Hills where it was eaten by rats?"

"I'm a rat in the hills."

"What do you want?"

"I wanna fuck your mother."

He smacked me. Thank you. I tried to writhe out from under him. He tossed the skate aside and grabbed onto my neck, leaning down over my face. I tried to spit at him.

"This takes a lot of trust."

"What do you mean?"

"What is your safe word?"

"Ai lav yoo."

Vermin.

Twenty-four hours later, still going, now in the Woodpecker Suite, paid for by my class-action settlement money from Facebook for stealing my biometrics, so that his mama wouldn't hear us. ("What could possibly make her happier?" "I know, but I am not used to her.")

"Do it again."

Every time, we locked eyes in a hypnotized terror, our realest selves. Except for the time he strangled me with a rope from behind.

"People will usually fake it."

"Really? What do you mean?"

He showed me what it would be like doing the safe way.

"Nobody ever wants to do it for real."

"Really? Why not?"

Why wouldn't we do it for real when we could do it for real?

"But I don't know if I should see you again," I said after breakfast, once again seething with boredom, somehow again talking about the CIA. "I have so little time left, I shouldn't spend it on someone like you. Although you're actually fun. I am supposed to be trying to have kids."

"I do have experience impregnating people," Gleb said, smirking repugnantly, putting his camera away. "But you don't want my genes."

"As if I don't have the same genes."

And when I told my parents practically everything, wondering if they noticed the marks on my neck, before I realized it was really goodbye forever again—obviously—they were so excited, steely, they begged me—yes, please, hurry up and just have his baby. He is completely awful, you're right, why would you want to be with somebody that terrible (look at yourself), you will break up right away, but we don't need him. Have his baby and hurry. We will do everything, leave it with us, you are free, go be free. We will raise it ourselves. The parents don't matter. Just leave it with us. We do not need you.

ONE MORNING, when I was still waiting to see if he would remanifest, I told them, my younger new friends, about him. We were on ketamine edging down off the molly, curled on deep furniture draped in jade bedsheets. Same color as the cold light coming into the living room through shrouds of ivy. Gray 5 AM, most of my breed, I would guess, arisen to tend to their offspring. Guten Morgen, fellow kids.

"I never wanna have kids, I don't understand how people can do that," Fernanda said, kneeling in front of me. "I don't even know how to be around them."

"Come on."

I am not bitter or immature—maturity, as everybody assures me, is an illusion. I love just everyone. I'm like just everyone else, lonely, I am just on my own path. What an adventure. I comprehend the fullness, the universality of instability, of uncertainty. Yes: it is nothing but true.

"Children are psychedelic."

Fernanda passed me another line on the back of an extremely fine photo book with expensive pictures of mushroom clouds. Like at a prom afterparty at boarding school, somebody's absent parents' smart home, as I imagined—another crime against me.

"Thank you, this is my last one. Then I really will go."

I should have already left, probably long ago. Probably I shouldn't have come. Everyone else was making out, possibly waiting for me to leave, except for Fernanda and Catie. Fernanda backing me deeper into Catie's lap.

"I think the thing is that the oldest child in an immigrant family is always the most fucked up," my revelation. "You lose the most. It fucks your core. Hollows out and perverts any root growth. Permanent damage."

"May I rub your neck?" Catie asked.

They asked for consent for everything.

"They never manage to bridle themselves all the way in, to see a future. So many people I know are like that. Danny, on his second marriage, living in Portugal now. First one in Bolivia. Two extra immigrations. My dad's friend Dima's daughter, who even got like a good PhD, like in STEM, but can't stop moving, changing careers. Refuses to date. It fucks with sex and relationship the most I think."

"Is it OK," Fernanda asked, "if I play with your fingers?"

"The guy I was seeing," I couldn't stop talking about him, I'd only "seen" him that once, "when he was 10, his parents were separating, and they were broke, living with relatives. They told him they were sending him to America for a vacation, to stay with his uncle, but then they wouldn't bring him back. His mother told him she wanted to but couldn't afford to. They thought he was in a better place. He was in like, Arizona, completely cut off, the uncle a total maniac asshole also, of course. He tried to fix it so fast and so hard, as soon as he could, got married real young, had a kid, the whole thing, out of desire to like, tie himself to the mast. Get his family back. Look at him now—sex addict, lives in a basement, pretending to code. Absolute shit wreck. Your life, Fernanda."

"Yeah, but I'm actually the middle child."

Fernanda was half Argentinean with a wealthy white American father. It was her turn to confess. She loosened the neck of her halter top.

"My older sister has Down syndrome, which they didn't know until she was born. They'd only wanted two children, but when she had her, right there in the hospital, my mother swore she would have two more."

She did and then totally lost it. Her husband divorced her and won full custody with all his money and lawyers. Wouldn't let her see her children at all for fifteen years.

"That's why I never want kids."

"Come on. We are too old to be blaming our parents."

I wanted to pull my hands through Fernanda's curls but did not want to ask. She wouldn't kiss me. She wanted me to kiss Catie.

"And then the middle one is scared straight and overcompensates on the assimilation and normativity."

"That's what my younger brother is doing," Fernanda said.

I locked onto her eyes to avoid watching the others, who had begun to undress.

"That's like my cousin Bella. Middle child, has three kids. Nurse in the Israeli army. And she is the only one out of all of us with a job and a family. My cousin Raya, her older sister—so fucked up, married three times, into lifestyle BDSM. She used to put all these pictures up on her Facebook so that our whole family could see her like, being walked around on a leash. Or there was one that was just a close-up of the back of her pussy, captioned like, 'What do you think?'

"My grandma was like, 'There's something up with your cousin.'"

The Parable of the Loneliness of the Cousins.

"But she was always like that! When I was little, there was this funny period when my parents moved to different cities for work and sent me to Israel to live with my grandma and cousins. Raya always had boyfriends over and all of us slept in the same room, so I would always just be there watching them fondle each other, cutting themselves with their ritual knives, licking each other's blood, listening to this Deep Forest tape. One night, she was like, 'Have you ever kissed a girl?' And I was like, 'I'm 9 years old, I have never kissed anyone.'"

That was how this conversation had started! We had been talking about our first kisses!

"And my first kiss with a boy was with my other bad cousin! He was 16 and I was 13. I'd gone to visit him in New York because we had kind of fallen in love on the phone and when we were home alone, he chased me around the apartment, beating me with this toy police baton, holding me down so we could breathe in each other's mouths—"

Catie sighed. I finally got up, gave her a consolation kiss goodbye.

"But my whole thing is, I never read these as like, really sexual. I don't think that's what my cousins were after. They were fucked up. They were so sad. They didn't think I was as bad. I was a little bit younger, a baby—their baby—who loved them, who could truly feel for them. We all lived thousands of miles apart, we'd lost one another as family. I think that we were just trying to make up for that distance."

Putting my shoes on, hand on Fernanda's shoulder.

"It ended up freaking us out, though, for sure. None of us ever spoke again."

Unlatching the door, she leaned into my ear.

"Can we hang out again soon?"

"Was that helpful to you?" I asked, laughing.

2023

WHY IS EVERYTHING SO UGLY?

LISA BORST AND MARK KROTOV

WE LIVE IN UNDENIABLY UGLY TIMES. ARCHITECTURE, INDUSTRIAL design, cinematography, probiotic soda branding—many of the defining features of the visual field aren't sending their best. Despite more advanced manufacturing and design technologies than have existed in human history, our built environment tends overwhelmingly toward the insubstantial, the flat, and the gray, punctuated here and there by the occasional childish squiggle. A drab sublime unites flat-pack furniture and home electronics, municipal infrastructure and commercial graphic design: an ocean of stuff so homogeneous and underthought that the world it has inundated can feel like a digital rendering—of a slightly duller, worse world.

If the Situationists drifted through Paris looking to get defamiliarized, today a scholar of the new ugliness can conduct their research in any contemporary American city—or upzoned American Main Street, or exurban American parking lot, or, if they're really desperate, on the empty avenues of Meta's Horizon Worlds. Our own walk begins across the street from our apartment, where, following the recent demolition of a perfectly serviceable hundred-year-old building, a monument to ugliness has recently besieged the block. Our new neighbor is a classic 5-over-1: retail on the ground floor, topped with several stories of apartments one wouldn't want to be able to afford. The words THE JOSH have been appended to the canopy above the main entrance in a passionless font.

We spent the summer certain that the caution tape–yellow panels on The Josh's south side were insulation, to be eventually supplanted by an actual facade. Alas, in its finished form The Josh really is yellow, and also burgundy, gray, and brown. Each of these colors corresponds to a different material—plastic, concrete, rolled-on brick, an obscure wood-like substance—and the overall effect is of an overactive spreadsheet. Trims, surfaces, and patterns compete for attention with shifty black windows, but there's nothing bedazzling or flamboyant about all this chaos. Somehow the building's plane feels flatter than it is, despite the profusion of arbitrary outcroppings and angular balconies. The lineage isn't Bauhaus so much as a sketch of the Bauhaus that's been xeroxed half a dozen times.

The Josh is aging rapidly for a 5-month-old. There are gaps between the panels, which have a taped-on look to them, and cracks in the concrete. Rust has bloomed on surfaces one would typically imagine to be rustproof. Every time it rains, The Josh gets conspicuously . . . wet. Attempts have been made to classify structures like this one and the ethos behind their appearance: SimCityist, McCentury Modern, fast-casual architecture. We prefer cardboard modernism, in part because The Josh looks like it might turn to pulp at the first sign of a hundred-year flood.

Writing a century ago, H. L. Mencken bemoaned America's "libido for the ugly." There exists, he wrote, a "love of ugliness for its own sake, the lust to make the world intolerable. Its habitat is the United States." However mystical and psychosexual his era's intolerability might have felt in its origins, by the 1940s the explanations were more prosaic. With the wartime rationing of steel and sudden dearth of skilled labor, concrete structural systems quickly gained appeal—as did buildings that could be made piecemeal in a factory, put on a trailer, and nailed together anywhere in the country. And as the postwar baby boom took hold, such buildings were soon in high demand, fulfilling modernism's wildest dreams of standardization with little of the glamour. A few Levittowns later, the promise of salvation-by-mass-production would come to seem elusive: new manufacturing techniques were transforming both the buildings and the builders building them. In *Prisoners of the American Dream*, Mike Davis describes how, in the 1970s, "the adoption of new building technologies involving extensive use of prefabricated structures, like precast concrete, eroded the boundaries of traditional skills and introduced a larger semi-skilled component into the labor force." If it's cheaper to assemble concrete panels than to hire bricklayers, cityscapes will eventually contain fewer bricks.

A construction industry with newly decadent profit margins was ready to spring into action in the 1990s, when—after a violent, decades-long process of urban renewal and white flight—real estate developers, brokers, and local politicians started luring predominantly white homeowners and renters back to the cities they'd abandoned. By the 2000s, infill housing began to crop up in American cities that had for decades been defined by their plentiful surface parking. These residential developments were ugly, but not yet inescapable. Like the fresh-faced presidential candidate with whom it's hard not to associate them (did every wood-and-concrete complex feature a knockoff Shepard Fairey mural, or have we been blinded by the mists of memory?), the buildings spoke to an upwardly mobile, progressive, even post-racial demographic that didn't share its parents' all-consuming fear of city life. Then came the ultimate stop-work order: the 2008 financial crisis.

The urban building boom that picked up in the wake of the Great Recession wasn't a boom at all, at least not by previous booming standards: in the early 2010s, multifamily housing construction was at its lowest in decades. But low interest rates worked in developers' favor, and what had begun as an archipelago of scattered development had coalesced, by the end of the Obama years, into a visual monoculture. At the global scale, supply chains narrowed the range of building materials to a generic minimum (hence The Josh's pileup of imitation teak accents and synthetic stucco antiflourishes). At the local level, increasingly stringent design standards imposed by ever-more-cumbersome community approval processes compelled developers to copy designs that had already been rubber-stamped elsewhere (hence that same fake teak and stucco in identical boxy buildings across the country). The environment this concatenation of forces has produced is at once totalizing and meek—an architecture embarrassed by its barely archi-tected-ness, a building style that cuts corners and then covers them with rainscreen cladding. For all the air these buildings have sucked up in the overstated conflict between YIMBYs (who recognize that new housing is ultimately better than no housing) and NIMBYs (who don't), the unmistakable fact of cardboard modernism is that its build-ings are less ambitious, less humane, and uglier than anyone deserves.

They're also really gray. The Josh's steel railings are gray, and its plastic window sashes are a slightly clashing shade of gray. Inside, the floors are made of gray TimberCore, and the walls are painted an abject post-beige that interior designers call greige but is in fact just gray. Gray suffuses life beyond architecture: television, corporate logos, product packaging, clothes for babies, direct-to-consumer tooth-brushes. What incentives—material, libidinal, or otherwise—could possibly account for all this gray? In 2020, a study by London's Sci-ence Museum Group's Digital Lab used image processing to analyze photographs of consumer objects manufactured between 1800 and the present. They found that things have become less colorful over time, converging on a spectrum between steel and charcoal, as though consumers want their gadgets to resemble the raw materials of the industries that produce them. If *The Man in the Gray Flannel Suit* once offered a warning about conformity, he is now an inspiration, although the outfit has gotten an upgrade. Today he is *The Man in the Gray Bonobos*, or *The Man in the Gray Buck Mason Crew Neck*, or *The Man in the Gray Mack Weldon Sweatpants*—all delivered via gray Amazon van. The imagined color of life under communism, gray has revealed itself to be the actual hue of globalized capital. "The distinct national colors of the imperialist map of the world have merged and blended in the imperial global rainbow," wrote Hardt and Negri. What color does a blended rainbow produce? Greige, evidently.

A LOT OF UGLINESS accretes privately, in the form of household goods, which can make it hard to see—except on the first of the month. Today's perma-class of renters moves more frequently than ever before (inevitably to smaller apartments), and on moving day the sidewalks are transformed into a rich bazaar of objects significant for ugliness studies. We stroll past discarded pottery from wild sip 'n' spin nights; heaps of shrunken fast fashion from SHEIN; dead Strategist-approved houseplants; broken Wirecutter-approved humidifiers; an ergonomic gaming chair; endless Ikea BILLYs, MALMs, LACKs, SKUBBs, BARENs, SLOGGs, JUNQQs, and FGHSKISs. Perhaps this shelf is salvageable—? No, just another mass of peeling veneer and squishy particleboard. On one stoop sits a package from a direct-to-consumer eyewear company, and we briefly fantasize about a pair of glasses that would illuminate, *They Live*–style, the precise number of children involved in manufacturing each of these trashed items, or maybe the acreage of Eastern European old-growth trees.

It occurs to us, strolling past a pair of broken BuzzFeed Shopping–approved AirPods, that the new ugliness has beset us from both above and below. Many of the aesthetic qualities pioneered by low-interest-rate-era construction—genericism, non-ornamentation, shoddy reproducibility—have trickled down into other realms, even as other principles, unleashed concurrently by Apple's slick industrial-design hegemon, have trickled up. In the middle, all that is solid melts into sameness, such that smart home devices resemble the buildings they surveil, which in turn look like the computers on which they were algorithmically engineered, which resemble the desks on which they sit, which, like the sofas at the coworking space around the corner, put the *mid* in *fake midcentury modern*. And all of it is bound by the commandment of planned obsolescence, which decays buildings even as it turns phones into bricks.

Beyond the sidewalk, the street—which is mostly for cars, key technology of the 20th-century assault on the city. Barthes wrote that the 1955 Citroën DS marked a welcome shift in the appearance in cars toward the "homely," meaning that they'd begun to carry the comfortable livability of kitchens and household equipment. Today's automobiles, far from being "the supreme creation of an era," are homely in the other sense of the word. A contemporary mythologist could sort them into either hamsters or monoliths. Hamster cars (the Honda Fit, the Toyota Prius) are undoubtedly ugly, but in a virtuous way. The monolith cars (the Cadillac Escalade, the Infiniti QX80) possess a militaristic cast, as if to get to Costco one must first stop off at the local black site.* No brand has embraced the ethos more than Tesla, with its tanklike Cybertruck. Even Musk's more domesticated offerings feel like they're in the surveillance business: sitting inside a Tesla is not unlike sitting inside a smartphone, while also staring at a giant smartphone.

Dodging huge grilles we walk on, pulled by ugliness toward a gentrified retail strip. Here the violence of the new ugliness comes more fully into focus. The ruling class seized cities and chose to turn them into . . . this? To our right is a place that sells wiggly candles. Past that is a boutique liquor store whose chalkboard sign proclaims, in cheerleader handwriting, that the time is Wine O'Clock, and past that is a Bank of America. Across the street, a row of fast-casual chains, whose names and visual identities insist on modesty and anonymity: Just Salad, Just Food For Dogs, Blank Street Coffee. (This raft of normcore brands finds its opposite in the ghost kitchens down the block, which all for some reason are called things like Fuck Your Little Bitch Burrito.) Up ahead is an axe throwing "experience," and another Bank of America.

Who asked for all of this? Numerous critics—self-hating and otherwise—have argued that the mallification of the American city is the fault of the same millennials for whom all the new construction was built, who couldn't quite bear to abandon the creature comforts of home even as they reurbanized. The story goes that millennials lived, laughed, and loved their way into an unprecedentedly insipid environment, turning once-gritty cities into

---

* See also the increasing dominance of cars with opaque and foreboding matte paint jobs, described by the newsletter Blackbird Spyplane as "putty-lookin' ass whips."

Instagram-friendly dispensaries of baroque ice cream cones that call
back, madeleine-style, to the enfolding warmth of their suburban
childhoods. But the contemporary built environment is not the millennials' legacy; it is their inheritance. They didn't ask for cardboard
modernism—they simply capitulate to its infantilizing aesthetic par-
adigm because there is no alternative. Or if there is an alternative,
it's between an $8 ice cream cone or an $11 ice cream cone (or a $49
ticket to the Museum of Ice Cream).

Our ugliness tour is leading us toward the $11 ice cream cone
zone. On the waterfront, the spatial logic of The Josh persists, only
at four times the cost per square foot. There is less random yellow,
the concrete is glossier, and the view through the precarious glass is
a little more ennobling. Too bad about the build quality. One paradox of the new ugliness is that it flattens the distinction between
the rich, the very rich, the superrich, and the merely fortunate by
ripping them all off in turn. These days housing at the most elite
strata sucks nearly as much as the simply bourgeois kind. According
to a parade of entertaining *New York Times* stories, residents of the
toothpick-like towers on Manhattan's Billionaires' Row complain of
elevator breakdowns, "catastrophic" flooding from poor plumbing,
and "metal partitions [that] groan as buildings sway" in the wind.
Shittiness is a big tent—and the tent is falling apart.

OUR DÉRIVE HAS deposited us near a subway stop. We swipe in with
a trusty MetroCard, soon to be replaced by the privately owned
data-tracking behemoth OMNY, whose neon-on-black logo recalls
the chilly visual identity of another threat to transit, Uber.* But at
least as far as branding goes, OMNY is no uglier than other offenders.
Our train car is covered in ads, all curiously alike despite marketing

* Along with Molly Fischer's 2020 study of the "millennial aesthetic" in *New York*, Jesse Barron's
2016 essay in Real Life remains an authoritative critique of neoliberal start-up semiotics, from
Uber to Seamless. "In 2012, Uber stood alone. Black, sinister, efficient. The logo like devil's
horns. The invisible umlaut. In the place of cuteness, Uber offered a fantasy of minimalist sa-
dism, with the user holding the whip."

a staggering variety of superfluous stuff. How did workplace management systems, body-positive nutritional supplements, bean-forward meal kits, woman-owned sex toys, and woman-owned day-trading services all converge on the same three fonts? Everywhere we look there are little pool noodle–shaped squiggles, and where the squiggles end, there is muted flash photography that makes even otherworldly models look matter-of-fact. With the exception of the food delivery apps, which flaunt their violent takeover of the city in a meaningless word salad designed for shouting about salad—WHEN YOU'RE SO HANGRY, YOU'D TRASH TALK ANY SLOW WALKER BETWEEN YOU AND YOUR BEC, goes one GrubHub ad—the advertising all seems sheepish about being caught in the act of selling something.

But no single ad is as emblematically ugly as the digital screens that have appeared across the city's train cars since 2017. Public transit has pivoted to video, and the function of its new giant iPads mystifies: their purpose is neither civic nor fully commercial. Instead, they're given over to a bewildering set of images for the TikTokified city, the worst of which belong to a marketing campaign called "Moments in Food." We watch, a little nauseated, as the Moments loop by: video tutorials for Homemade Pesto Hack, Homemade Chipotle Chicken Cutlet Hack, Homemade Three-Ingredient Oven-Free Blondie Hack. Why are there no measurements? Would this even seem edible, in the distinctly non-subwaylike atmosphere of an actual kitchen? Like The Josh's synthetic not-quite-surfaces, it all seems gesturally foodlike, a step removed from the real thing. Above us, pesto glistens.

Speaking of moments in food, it's lunchtime. Exiting the train, we pass a food hall, where, again, the theoretical possibility of endless variety manifests as lackluster sameness. Dozens of restaurants' satellite stalls all feature the same signage, the same subway tile backdrop, the same impression of having been shrunk to diorama size and turned into IP. We turn instead to the outdoor dining sheds. After sprouting with uncharacteristic speed in the first chaotic spring of the pandemic, the sheds have performed a sort of guerrilla

Haussmannization of the city—in a good way, clawing back public space from cars. The ugliness they've introduced to the built environment diverges, happily, from the usual kind. Unruly and old-school, the sheds have pissed off deranged community boards and their mouthpieces in the media. "The shanty outside Dumpling Man on St. Marks is unspeakably hideous," declared a recent *New York* article, "its colorless wood fragments hammered together so arbitrarily that you would rather eat in a pile of Lincoln Logs." Yeah—just the way we like it!

Around the corner is a movie theater, one of those places where they bring snacks or cocktails right to your seat. Filmmaking today is supposed to be more powerful than it's ever been, capable of representing everything everywhere all at once. As the world offscreen recedes into sameness, movies can and should look great—but onscreen there is more ugly sameness. The thing we wander into is at first indistinguishable from any other blockbuster of the late green-screen era: only after Ryan Reynolds cocks his signature "terror gun" do we recognize this as *Army Soldier II*, a digitally shot Netflix-financed production based on a TV show based on a comic book. Can a movie be a remake of itself? This is the depleted vibe *Army Soldier II* and its ilk are giving off. The easy recourse to postproduction—"we'll fix it in post"—has resulted in a mise-en-scène so underlit as to be literally invisible. Despite its $275 million budget, the movie looks like it was filmed underwater in a polluted lake. The action scenes are nearly monochromatic, the color palette ranging from Tentative Black to what looks like Apple's proprietary Space Gray. Lighting isn't a lost art, but subsumed in all that murk, we're having trouble finding it.

Two and a half hours in, *Army Soldier II* suddenly becomes a comedy, with Reynolds vamping his way through long, flat takes designed to accommodate his "riffs." Now everything is overlit, as if the gaffers were only available for the second half of the shoot.

Such bad lighting—and such large portions! We exit the movie theater to a bright realization: our films are exactly as overlit as our reality. As our environment has become blander, it has also become more legible—too legible. That's a shame, because many products of the new ugliness could benefit from a little chiaroscuroed ambiguity: if the world has to fill itself up with smart teapots, app-operated vacuum cleaners, and creepily huge menswear, we'd prefer it all to be shrouded in darkness. For thousands of years, this was the principle of illumination that triumphed over all others. Louis XIV's Versailles and Louis the Tavern Owner's tavern had this in common: the recognition that some details are worth keeping hidden. But now blinding illumination is the default condition of every apartment, office, pharmacy, laundromat, print shop, sandwich shop, train station, airport, grocery store, UPS Store, tattoo parlor, bank, and this vape shop we've just walked into.

Surveying a suite of candy-colored bongs, we reflect on the primacy of LEDs. (One of the bongs is bedecked with LEDs.) The shift to cold lighting in recent years was born of urgent environmental necessity, and we accept that climate change requires concessions. We're prepared to make those: we will eat crickets and endorse, if necessary, the blockage of the waterfront park around the corner by a giant seawall. We will even help build the seawall! Change is inevitable. But LEDs can appear in many colors, as demonstrated by our new light-up bong. So why this atomic, lobotomizing white?

Outdoors, the situation is depressingly similar. After New York replaced the sodium-vapor lights in the city's 250,000 streetlamps with shiny new LEDs in 2017, the experience of walking through the city at night transformed, almost . . . overnight. Forgiving, romantic, shadowy orange gave way to cold, all-seeing bluish white. Again environmental concerns necessitate this scale of change, and again we wonder why, when it comes to its light bulbs, New York has chosen to back the blue. Inertia, disinterest, thoughtlessness, yes, but also the promise of increased police vigilance. Still, what is most striking about New York's ominous glow-up is the sense that the city has been estranged from itself: the hyperprecise shadows of every leaf and every branch set against every brick wall deliver a

Hollywood unreality. New York after hours now looks less like it did in Scorsese's *After Hours* and more like an excessive set-bound '60s production. The new ugliness is defined in part by an abandonment of function and form: buildings afraid to look like buildings, cars that look like renderings, restaurants that look like the apps that control them. New York City is a city increasingly in quotation marks, a detailed facsimile of a place.

Gah! Blinded by the intense glare of an LED streetlamp, we bump right into said streetlamp. Fortunately there's an urgent care across the street, still open in the dwindling dusk. We're no doctor—at least not until they start giving out PhDs in walking around—but we can tell that our knee is bleeding. If anything is broken, the CityMD's MD will take care of it. We stumble inside, into the intersection of exploitative private insurance and inadequate public options. Here, like everywhere else, a clash of patterns and surfaces—gray tile, gray bricks, greige wood paneling—enfolds us in a numbing palliative aura. We try to check in at the front, but the iPad doesn't react to the tap of our index finger. Are we a ghost? Is this the afterlife? The lighting is giving gates of heaven, but as with the supertall buildings and their elevators that never work, our problem is technical: the iPad is frozen. Another one is wheeled out and we make our way through a questionnaire. Allergic reactions? None. History of medical litigation? Huh, weird.

Our estimated wait time is three and a half hours, which gives us ample opportunity to reflect on our surroundings. Is there a more contemporary urban form than the urgent care facility? How did the entire world come to look like this nonplace, flimsy and artificial and built unsuccessfully to stave off emergency? Above our heads, the original *Army Soldier* plays on a flatscreen, Ryan Reynolds's leaden features motion-smoothed into alarming definition. Our phone buzzes with a push notification from Zillow: a 0.5-bedroom studio is now available for $4,775 a month in the sub-basement of The Josh. We examine our fellow patients, because nobody else is. The bleeding young man to our left looks to have been the victim of an axe throw gone very wrong. Our neighbor to the right tells us she was hit by a Tesla while e-biking to Roosevelt Island to deliver a single unicorn latte. We overhear someone behind us describe a harrowing food poisoning incident involving a Homemade Chipotle Chicken Cutlet Hack.

In the end we pay $75 for a Band-Aid, two Advils, a Blank Street Coffee gift card, and a branded pen we have no plans to return. After a long day of digital encounters we're asked to sign a paper receipt, and we click the pen. It looks like a pen and works the way a pen ought to work. Our eyes fill with tears at this satisfying tactile experience. Maybe it's just the bruising.

2023

NOT ONE TREE

GRACE GLASS WITH SASHA TYCKO

THE SUN HANGS LOW AND RED LIKE A STOPLIGHT OVER THE CITY. TEN thousand cars idle and litter down Moreland, another interminable avenue, vanishing onward in one-point perspective until the city thins out into strip malls, retail chains, junkyards, and Thank God Tires, where mountains of rubber shimmer in the summer evening heat. It is June 2021, and rush hour in Atlanta, when we drive to the forest for the first time.

The parking lot is half full. A cardboard sign at the trailhead reads LIVING ROOM→ in Magnum Sharpie, so we start up the bike path, where a trail of glow sticks hangs from the trees. A quarter mile later, sky darkening in the distance, the glow sticks veer off to the left down a footpath, which zags through logs and opens onto a clearing in the pines. People with headlamps settle onto blankets, popping cans and passing snacks. A dog in a dog-colored sweater chases a squirrel and stands there panting. There is pizza piled tall on a table. Syncopated crickets. A giggling A/V club pulls a bedsheet taut between two trees, angling a projector powered by a car battery just so.[*]

Princess Mononoke, which we watch tonight reclined on the pine straw, is a parable about humans and nature. An Iron Age town

---

[*] Some names and details have been changed.

is logging an enchanted forest to manufacture muskets. Our prince has been cursed, which is to say chosen, to defend the forest against the destroyers. Will the ancient spirit creatures deep in the woods be able to stop the march of progress? Cigarette smoke swirls in little eddies through the projector beam. The dusk is gone. There are no stars. Fireflies spangle the underbrush. The boars stampede the iron mine, squealing, "We are here to kill humans and save the forest!" The humans on the forest floor around us laugh and cheer.

THIS FOREST IS a squiggly triangle of earth, four miles around, some five hundred acres, lying improbably verdant just outside Atlanta's municipal limits. Bouldercrest and Constitution Roads are the triangle's sides, Key Road its hypotenuse. The surrounding mixed industry indexes the American economy: an Amazon warehouse, a movie studio, a truck repair shop, a church, a tow yard, a dump, a pallet-sorting facility, a city water-treatment plant. Suburbs, mostly black and middle-class, unfurl in all directions. Prison facilities— juvenile, transitional, reentry—pad the perimeter, removed from Constitution Road by checkpoints, black mesh fencing, and tornadoes of barbed wire.

Viewed from above, the forest triangle is bisected once by a flat straight strip clear-cut for power lines and then again by Intrenchment Creek. This skinny, sinuous waterway is a tributary to Georgia's South River and swells with sewage from the upriver city whenever it rains. Intrenchment Creek also marks the property line that splits the forest in two. East of the creek is the 136-acre public-access Intrenchment Creek Park, with a parking lot and bike path and hiking trails through meadows and thickets of loblolly pine, and also a toolshed and miniature tarmac where the Atlanta RC Club flies. West of the creek is the site of the Old Atlanta Prison Farm.

For seventy years, Atlanta forced incarcerated people to work the land here, growing food for the city prison system under conditions of abuse and enslavement both brutal and banal. Since the prison closed quietly in the 1990s, its fields have lain fallow, reforesting slowly. Though it's DeKalb County, this parcel belongs to the neighboring City of Atlanta. It is nevertheless not public property. The driveway to the old prison farm has long been fenced off. The only way in is to scrabble up the berm from Key Road. Or cross the sloping, sandy banks of the creek from the public park and trespass onto no-man's-land.

For years, the South River Forest Coalition lobbied Atlanta to open this land to the public and make it the centerpiece of a mixed-use megaforest: a 3,500-acre patchwork of parks, preserves, cemeteries, landfills, quarries, and golf courses linked through a network of trails crisscrossing the city's southeast suburbs. And in 2017, it seemed like a rare success for grassroots environmental activism when the Department of City Planning adopted the Coalition's idea into their vision for the future of Atlanta. You should see the glossy, gorgeous, four-hundred-page book the city planners published unveiling their plan for a city of affluence, equality, cozy density, affordable transit, and reliable infrastructure for robust public spaces. We no longer thought optimism like this was even possible at the scale of the American metropolis. Even if the dream of the South River Forest had been downsized, the 1,200-acre South River Park was still far from nothing. The book called it "the enduring and irreplaceable green lungs of Atlanta," "our last chance for a massive urban park," and a cornerstone in their vision of environmental justice.

How simple things seemed back then! In 2020, local real estate magnate Ryan Millsap approached the DeKalb County Board of Commissioners with an offer to acquire forty acres of Intrenchment Creek Park in exchange for a nearby plot of denuded dirt. Three years prior, Millsap had founded Blackhall Studios across Constitution Road and now was eager to expand his already giant soundstage complex into a million square feet of movie studio. This is no longer unusual for the Atlanta outskirts. State-level tax breaks have lured the film industry here. Since 2016, Georgia has produced at least as many blockbusters as California. As part of the deal, Millsap promised to landscape the dirt pile into the public-access Michelle Obama Park.

Neighbors had already begun to organize to sue DeKalb County for violating Intrenchment Creek Park's charter when, in April 2021, Atlanta's mayor, Keisha Lance Bottoms, announced a plan of her own. On the other side of the creek, the city would lease 150 acres of the land abandoned by the prison farm to the Atlanta Police Foundation, because the old police academy was falling apart and covered in mold. Cadets were doing their push-ups in the hallways of a community college. The lease would cost the police $10 per year for thirty years. The new training center would cost $90 million to build. But only a third of this would come from public funds, the mayor assured the taxpayers. The rest would be provided by the Atlanta Police Foundation—which is not the Atlanta Police Department, but a "private nonprofit" whose basic function is to raise corporate funds to embellish police powers.

REST IN PEACE RAYSHARD BROOKS still practically gleamed in white spray paint on Krog Street Tunnel. The Atlanta police had killed Brooks during a confrontation in the parking lot of a Wendy's not far from the forest barely two weeks after Minneapolis police killed George Floyd. The nation was still reeling after the upheaval of 2020—and now the mayor of Atlanta wanted not only to give $90 million to the murderers, but to clear-cut a forest to accommodate them. At first we were less indignant than insulted by the project's intersectional stupidity. Hadn't the city just agreed to invest in people's leisure, pleasure, health, and well-being? Instead, the old prison farm would become a new surveillance factory.

In May, some two hundred people showed up to an info night in the Intrenchment Creek Park parking lot. A hand-painted banner fluttered from the struts of the gazebo: DEFEND THE ATLANTA FOREST. There were zines and taglines: STOP COP CITY. NO HOLLYWOOD DYSTOPIA. FUCK THE METAVERSE, SAVE THE REAL WORLD! The orgs were there with maps and graphs. #StoptheSwap detailed the Blackhall–DeKalb deal. The South River Watershed Alliance explained how the forest soaks up stormwater and wondered what would happen to the surrounding suburbs when the hilltop became a parking lot. Save the Old Atlanta Prison Farm narrated a mini-history of the land. Before the city prison farm, it had been a slave plantation.

People mingled, ate vegan barbecue. The cumbia lasted past dark. Half the audience had never been to the forest before, but now wanted to protect or maybe even enjoy it. History has apparently already decided that the movement was started by these organizations—but do you see those young people pacing the parking lot? Ask an anarchist. They all know who painted the banners, who printed the zines, who organized the inaugural info night. Who barbecued the jackfruit, who hauled in the speakers, who gave the movement its slogans and myths and indefatigable energy. Who got neighbors and strangers together to do something more than post about it. Who transformed concerned citizens into forest defenders.

FOR A CITY OF MIRRORED SKYSCRAPERS, of fifteen-lane highways, of five million people and building ever faster, Atlanta is run like a small town, or a bloated feudal palace, royal families overseeing serfs sitting in traffic. For almost a century, a not-so-secret compact has governed the city town council–style, bequeathing positions in the power structure along dynastic lines. The roles at the table are fixed: mayor, city council, Chamber of Commerce, Coca-Cola, the police, the local news, and, uniquely and importantly in Atlanta, miscellaneous magnates of a black business class. The biracial, bipartisan, business-friendly, media-savvy, moderate, managerial tradition the group perfected during the golden age of American capital is called the Atlanta Way.

This coalition steered the city through the tumultuous 20th century, holding things together with the blossoming optimism of economic growth. Desegregation happened in Atlanta unevenly, incompletely, but relatively uneventfully—which does not mean without shocking drama, racist recrimination, or moments of lurid violence. But compared with Montgomery or Memphis, the city was never bloodied in Civil Rights struggle. Even Martin Luther King Jr., its most famous martyr, was assassinated elsewhere. Jim Crow, white flight, gentrification all happened under a top-down, lockstep, synchronized city administration depressurizing the national conflict compromise by compromise: a golf course here, a swimming pool there, neighborhoods blockbusted one at a time.

Since 1974, every mayor has been black. Business boomed and suburbs steamrolled the countryside. Railroading begat logistics and telecommunications: Delta, UPS, IBM, AT&T. Olympic fireworks bedazzled downtown in the '90s, while hip-hop rooted and flourished on the city's south side, and propagated across continents. The airport ballooned into the busiest in the world. Tyler Perry redeveloped a military base into one of the largest movie studios in America. By the 2010s, the general American pattern of white supremacy looked almost upside down in Atlanta.

But in 2020, after a century of technocracy, the City Too Busy to Hate finally cracked. Two days after Rayshard Brooks died, a reporter asked Mayor Bottoms how she felt "as a mother" about Brooks's death. She bit her lip, lamented the killing, ventriloquized Brooks's final thoughts about his daughter's upcoming birthday, announced the creation of a task force, and censured the angry mob who had torched the Wendy's to the ground. (It had existed in a food desert, she said, and "a place where somebody can go and get a salad is now gone.") The police chief resigned. One of the officers involved in the shooting was suspended for investigation. The other cop, who shot four times, was fired and charged with felony murder—a rare indictment, indicative of emergency.

Or was it? In a city so restlessly forward-moving, it's hard to tell sometimes what's truly new and what's business as usual. General Sherman burned the city to the ground, and Atlanta has spent the century and a half since the Civil War reenacting this founding trauma. Its motto is *Resurgens*, its mascot the phoenix, ever resurrecting from the ash heap of history. Every city booster's plan to make Atlanta more modern, international, or cosmopolitan has been carried out by a wrecking crew, enforcing a disorienting amnesia on its residents.

Last year, all charges against the officers were dismissed, and both were reinstated to the department with back pay. Three protesters identified by police on social media from the night the Wendy's burned were arrested and indicted with conspiracy to commit arson. Determined to somersault out of 2020 upright and armored, the city began to stabilize. The solution, as ever: demolish and build. The bulldozers aimed for the forest.

WE SURPRISE OURSELF by coming back to the forest again and again in the summer of 2021, both for scheduled activities and impromptu pleasures. *Princess Mononoke* is only one event on the calendar that first week of action, which is jam-packed to bring as many curious people into the forest as possible. A poetry reading in the living room, a protest downtown, a teach-in in the parking lot. We take a nap in someone's hammock, loblollies dancing overhead in the breeze. Perhaps it is simply a relief to be meeting strangers after a year of social distancing. But we like them, these people coming together to oppose the policification of the planet—and besides, it's also something else, something bracing, immediate, addictive splashing into consciousness, like a rush to the head of a life at last worth living, we realize on the week's final evening at a muddy party on the bank of Intrenchment Creek.

It is a full moon, silvery and damp. A rickety plank spans the creek on tread-worn tires, and feeling brave from the music we teeter over the property line. The woods look the same, but maybe something shifts in us, because we wake up after the week of action to another Atlanta, opening up anew. For the first time in our life, we are interested in plant identification. We check out a field guide from the library and start to notice the mosaic of the life of the world, like the barn owl perched on our neighbor's roof, or the Persian silk tree sunning prettily pink in our neighborhood park, or the different mites and gnats on our porch and the bats that eat them at dusk. "We live in the 'city in a forest,'" says almost every zine we collect this summer—and for the first time we begin to realize this is true and even good.

The forest defenders range from freaky to basically normal. Musicians, carpenters, baristas, bohemians, skaters, punks, special-ed teachers: they are city slickers mostly, all locals. Some are ideologues: socialists, communists, autonomists, a single Young Democrat, defensive until she disappears. Others are artists, utopians, weirdos, unbrainwashed by the world but unhappy with it too. They speak in extremes: police abolition, death cult of capitalism, eat the rich with Veganaise. The forecast of climate apocalypse has given us pretraumatic stress disorder, they smirk, totally serious, with a cheeky, black-pilled grief. Most are white. Many are trans. Almost everyone is between 20 and 35. A Baptist minister invites us to organizing meetings, and, intrigued and flattered and inspired, we start to show up.

Depending on the group, meetings are more or less open, more or less formal. In big and serious meetings, someone volunteers to facilitate, which means keeping track of the stack of hands who want to speak and remaining impassive. Some meetings have timekeepers, some have notetakers. Others are ad hoc: "Shit, what's for dinner tonight?" "Pizza again?" "Is the vegan place still open?" Over the next few months, working groups come together, meeting in the forest, but also in air-conditioned houses. Threads proliferate on Signal. We join a chat for the media team. Our phone buzzes all summer. We mostly only lurk, but find it's fun to brainstorm how to spread the story about Cop City.

The anarchist internet has been on the scoop since the initial info night. It's Going Down has been exulting over sabotaged construction equipment, exalting the black bloc for smashing the windows of the Atlanta Police Foundation headquarters downtown, exhorting readers to take autonomous action against Cop City's corporate sponsors. The photos of burning bulldozers also give us that illicit little thrill, but our angle this summer is gentler. Somehow we want to defibrillate liberals into conscience and action. Not everyone in the media group agrees that the liberal establishment, Democratic machine, or NGO-industrial complex can help us stop Cop City, but we all know that no news is bad news. The problem is that the *Atlanta Journal-Constitution* is owned by major donors to the police foundation, which ensures that the mainstream coverage is bad news, too.

Our group is not very formal. Someone suggests inviting Fred Moten or Ruth Wilson Gilmore or Angela Davis to speak, and we resolve to send an email. The construction companies seem easier to sway than city government. Should we write an open letter? Organize a mass call-in campaign? Get a group together to pay some project manager a personal visit? What about some kind of spectacle? Conversation unspools. The media group starts to look like an action group. "You know those giant dancing tube men? We can get some and paint them into trees, and plug them in outside City Hall when they meet next month, and turn the power on and off so the trees keep falling down."

"One of the figures should be a cop with an axe! He can go up when the trees go down."

"What if instead we do it right outside the mayor's house, first thing in the morning."

"It would be so easy. Go to any car dealership at night." Quickly we realize how willing some of our new friends are to violate the rules of polite society. Once we know where to look, it is obvious there are smaller, tighter-knit, quieter groups planning actions of their own. But the movement is decentralized, which means there are layers of secrecy we don't need to unpeel—and explains why two months later we learn there's been another media group this whole time.

"Just get two people together to do one thing," the forest defenders like to say, "and you are also an organizer." So we do. We don't have many nature skills yet, but we know how to talk about books, so we Photoshop a flyer advertising a book club we want to host in the forest starting in September, to read *Policing the Crisis: Mugging, the State, and Law and Order* by Stuart Hall and four graduate students. We type our event into the shared calendar on defendtheatlantaforest.org. "Meet in the gazebo," we write. "Read the intro and chapter one."

ON A TUESDAY IN EARLY SEPTEMBER, the city council hosts a public meeting over Zoom where Atlantans speak on the record for seventeen hours. At least two-thirds object to the police academy plans. Neighbors hate the snap-crackle-pop of gunshots from the firing range the APF has already built on the property, and just imagine how much louder and more frequent this will be when the police move the whole arsenal over. A public school teacher asks why the police department let their last training center collapse. What are their priorities? DSA members pose the decision as an existential question, not only for Atlanta, but for America. The old ultimatum of socialism or barbarism has been reframed by young organizers as care or cops. They accuse the city council of divesting from public services, sowing poverty and desperation, and then swelling the ranks of the police to keep it under control.

The following day, the city council votes ten to four to approve the lease of the land to the Atlanta Police Foundation anyway. The mayor makes a statement: It "will give us physical space to ensure that our officers and firefighters are receiving 21st-century training, rooted in respect and regard for the communities they serve." We blink past the obvious hypocrisy, drawn instead to that watchword *training*, deceptively neutral, the ostensible justification of a million liberal reforms, because who could argue against training? The police after all are like dogs: best when they obey. But obey what?

On Thursday, the night after the city council vote, a large group has a bonfire in the ruin of the old prison farm. Like forty people, smoking cigarettes and feeling cynical, even if the hard-liners never believed in the power of public testimony anyway. We pass around pieces of paper, write down our hopes and desires and dreams, and throw them in the fire, which helps, even if it's corny, and we are feeling less dispirited, buoyed by solidarity, when around 10 PM two cops walk into the forest. They order the group to disperse, hands on their guns on their hips, obviously terrified, not expecting the group in the woods to be this big or hostile. Raised voices, tense standoff, but reason prevails, and the forest defenders parade from the woods, outnumbering and outflanking the cops, who walk backward, escorting them out. The forest defenders chant: "Cop City will never be built!" "No justice, no peace!" "No forest, no seeds!" "Not one tree!" "Fuck twelve!" "We'll be back!"

The gazebo in the Intrenchment Creek Park parking lot is by now the public forum of the forest, with protest flyers and pamphlets and zines weighed down by rocks on a picnic table, a bulletin board for announcements, surplus granola bars spilling onto the floor, free clothes hanging on a rack or rumpled in the dust, and endless cans of Dr. Priestley's Fizzy Water, the leftover product from some failed start-up people keep carting into the forest from stockpiles all around the city. On the day of our first reading group meeting, we turn up with a thermos of hot cider and a manila folder of photocopies of the first few chapters. We'll meet a few times over the fall, a group of around eight. Not everyone comes prepared every week so we often read whole passages out loud.

Policing the Crisis is about the fundamental transformation of the role of the police in British society during an era marked by economic downturn, immigration, racism, and moral panics about crime. No longer a "peace-keeper" but a "crime-fighter," the new kind of cop cruises into his precinct from the suburbs, technologically enhanced, car-bound, and constantly in touch with central command. "With an emphasis on preparedness, swiftness and mobility, their behavior had something of the military style and philosophy about it," the authors write—in 1978. They're talking about radios.

Our study group makes a list of police technologies that might cause Stuart Hall to un-die if he learned the Atlanta Police Department uses them every day. Georgia law enforcement agencies have more than two dozen mine-resistant ambush-protected vehicles, for example. Also: surveillance cameras, license plate readers, algorithms that predict which people and places are more likely criminal, so police know where to patrol with extra arms and heightened nerves. We learn that the Atlanta police channel surf through the most surveillance devices per capita of any city in the country, 16,000 public and private cameras interlinked through a program called Operation Shield.

We bring printouts to spread on the picnic table: the police foundation website, city press releases, the *Atlanta Journal-Constitution*. Though Atlanta is the eighth-largest metro area in the country, its police foundation is the second largest, smaller only than New York's. Dave Wilkinson, its president and CEO, spent twenty-two years in the Secret Service, was personally responsible for protecting Presidents Clinton and W. Bush, and might be the highest-paid cop in the country. In 2020, he made $407,500 plus five figures in bonuses— more than twice as much as the director of the FBI. Wilkinson lives in a small town outside Atlanta, although, to be fair, three-quarters of city cops live outside city limits too.

We hear the list of major corporations in Atlanta whose executives sit on the board of the APF so often we accidentally memorize it: Delta, Home Depot, McKesson, J. P. Morgan, Wells Fargo, UPS, Chick-fil-A, Equifax, Cushman & Wakefield, Accenture, Georgia Pacific, disappointingly Waffle House, unsurprisingly Coca-Cola— though in October, news breaks that Color Of Change, a national racial justice organization, has successfully pressured Coca-Cola off the APF board. This feels huge! Coca-Cola and Atlanta are conjoined twins, and where one goes, so goes the other. Public pressure is mounting, people keep saying to each other in the forest. We even hear people say they believe that we will win.

TWO YEARS BEFORE the mayor announced the plan for the police training center to the public, the Atlanta Police Foundation posted a video to YouTube taking the viewer on a tour of a digital rendering of their purest vision of the facility. Jungle drums echo over action-trailer strings as the camera swoops and zooms through surface parking, modernist buildings, trees perfectly topiaried. An "institute," an "amphitheater" (folding chairs on a lawn), a "training field" with dark figures in phalanxes. Creepy 3D people jog in place through "green space," on concrete trails flanked by soft grasses the police must plan to plant, because the forest we are coming to know has no such harmless shrubbery.

At the center of the video, and of the APF's marketing campaign, is the "mock city for real-world training." The video gives us one cursory shot of a block with an apartment building, a gas station, and what looks like a nightclub? A synagogue? The streetscape swarms with squad cars, paddy wagons, armored trucks, dozens of officers in bulletproof outfits. What criminal violence or public disorder brought the whole counterinsurgency here? As the camera closes in on the proleptic crime scene, we fade to another shot, where the fire department trains on specialty buildings that catch fire but never burn down.

Images like this—doctored, distorted, ideological—can make it hard to see the forest for your screen. *Princess Mononoke* is not the only fantasy projected onto this forest. Just across Constitution Road, Blackhall Studios speculated, leveraged, and wedged its way to big box office returns: in its four years under Millsap, the studio filmed the fourth *Jumanji*, the eighth *Spider-Man*, the thirty-fifth licensed *Godzilla*, and *Jungle Cruise*, the eleventh movie adapted from a Disneyland theme park ride.

"Atlanta is really hot in the summer, and the light in Georgia is very toppy," the cinematographer of *Jungle Cruise* told a film website. "It was very hard to control. But we had the budget where we could actually do our own sun, make it cloudy or darker if we needed." So Dwayne "The Rock" Johnson, pursued by cartoon conquistadors, quests for the medicine tree as the CGI jungle blossoms with fluorescent lianas. Green screen or "green space"—the glory of creation leaves nothing to chance. And on the far side of the forest, the Atlanta Police Foundation also dreams of total control. Their stage-set city with no shadows will be a laboratory of techniques to menace the metro area. The cops and the celebs each plan to clear-cut the forest for a grid of soundproof boxes, privatized and predictable, where they will drill lines. In the perfect model city, there is action but no crime.

Offscreen, the movie studio and police academy are related through the structure of gentrification. As Hollywood colonizes Atlanta, so too come the techies, New American bistros, luxury condos in low-income neighborhoods, and inevitably cops to clean up the streets, lest the new residents become uncomfy walking past poverty. Their visions are linked at the level of family-friendly fantasy: both condescend to a public desperate and willing to believe in the ongoing triumph of good over evil while they kick back, safely paying for streaming in their houses. There is no death on these screens—only justice. Even inconvenience is merely temporary fuel for plot. If you're interrupted while streaming the comic, supernatural adventure of life, an army is one 911 call away to disappear your neighbors.

In 2021, Millsap sold Blackhall Studios to a hedge fund, which changed its name to Shadowbox Studios and invited other investors on board. Five hundred million dollars later, they were joined by a private equity firm that owns a large stake of the military-industrial division of Motorola—which manufactures the shiny, high-tech, tax-deductible cameras the Atlanta Police Foundation bought for Operation Shield. The arcane structure of the land-swap deal with DeKalb County allows Millsap to still claim to own forty acres of Intrenchment Creek Park, including the parking lot, though it's unclear what he plans to do with it, because he signed a noncompete clause stating he can no longer make movies near the forest. Still, sometimes he hires crews to put up barricades and NO TRESPASSING signs, which makes him an object of pointed hate among the forest defenders, who use his name as a curse word. Ryan Millsap the rapacious, the capitalist, the vampire—Ryan Millsap, always both first and last name, destroying the wild life of the forest to distill it into money. On a metal power box by the train tracks, chunky cursive spray paint reads RYAN MILLSAP IS HUNTING ME FOR SPORT.

THERE'S ANOTHER WEEK of action in October. One morning before decentralized autonomous yoga, we show a colleague the far side of the forest, and follow the trail down to the ruins of the prison farm. We point out the crumbling walls of the cannery, overgrown by greenery. A rusted metal bunk bed twists into vision through the thicket. But is that a tent? We are surprised to find people camping outside the living room. Around the dilapidated barracks, eight or nine people with bleach-dyed tank tops, frazzled bangs, tattoos, and piercings are clumped in little groups with big backpacks, their sun-worn tents scattered through the trees.

This is our first glimpse of the outside agitators. They're nice. They share a bathroom trench and a supply table piled with paracord and batteries and Band-Aids and a cardboard chessboard and stay up late talking about Rojava or ego death or why they went vegan or how to spit-roast a squirrel. They swap stories about running from freight police, make plans to forage food from the dumpster behind Kroger, listen to techno and hardcore from the speakers on their cracked iPhones. At least three have Crass tattoos. Some know one another from Line 3. They are all great at camping: we watch one tie a ridgeline between two trees, unfold a tarp, and all of a sudden there's a dry bright-blue triangle where the group keeps their generator and valuables.

Roaming solo with our camera one morning, we run into Eliza on a walk with two people from out of town. Eliza is a lyric poet and self-inflicted revolutionary, blazing nobly through a world clarified by their confidence. They have spent time among the Zapatistas. It was Eliza's idea to throw our dreams into the bonfire last month, so they might be purified by the flames. They moved to Atlanta in 2019 because it was cheaper than Seattle, and they had friends who had friends here squatting, making music, community gardening, cooking with Food Not Bombs, producing freaky circuses, and interlocking in complicated polycules in a DIY anarchist scene on the east side of the city. We see Eliza in the forest all the time. They wait tables at a Mexican restaurant and bring leftovers to meetings, where they are unfailingly optimistic, eyes on the prize of utopia. We've also seen them whispering a few times with wolf-eyed punks we don't know, and this sighting further confirms that Eliza is close to the center of the decentralization.

We see them before they see us. We wave, and Eliza beams at us, and the outsiders, grainy in the morning mist, clam up immediately. They eye our camera with suspicious contempt. We say, "Hey." Eliza tells them they trust us. So one says, "I'm Meadow." The other says, "Gout."

"Nice knuckle tats," we say, icebreaking. Gout's fingers read WE'VE LOST.

"Thanks." Meadow and Gout are here from Appalachia, where they've been involved in a struggle over a pipeline, and it's nice to be in a different forest, warmer down south, new birds and bugs, but also confusing. Back at the pipeline there are movement elders and formal initiations, and the direct actions there are nonviolent and planned in advance, whereas here in Atlanta . . . the two make eye contact. Gout shrugs. "Anything goes."

The week of action ends more or less without incident, only this time not everyone leaves the forest. A small group settles semi-permanently in the living room, sleeping in tents, cooking on a Coleman burner in a Goodwill pot. We will never see the living room empty again. Chairs appear around the firepit. License plates in the parking lot from Virginia, Michigan, Quebec. STOP COP CITY graffiti goes up around Atlanta.

At the end of October 2021, the Atlanta Police Foundation pledges to heed community input and redesign the training center. They downgrade the "mock city" to a "mock village."

WINTER FALLS. It barely ever snows in Atlanta, but the nights get long and cold. The loblollies stay evergreen, but the oaks lose their leaves, and the shrubby understory dies back to brown and gray. You can see farther in the forest in the winter. It is easier to walk. No snowmelt means the ground is rarely muddy, so everything crunches dry and friable underfoot when we follow the ecologist down the hill from the living room, right at the fork, left at the next, to the mother tree, or grandmother tree, some people say instead, a cherrybark oak ten feet wide at its base and swaying stately up into the thin green canopy.

A forest defender in a long lace dress and combat boots is sweeping the leaves from the clearing with a broom handmade from a branch and spindly twigs and retted forest fiber. She takes care not to disturb the offerings people have started leaving nestled into the mother tree's roots, spilling out onto the brown ground: knitting needles, Buddha candles, jack-o'-lanterns, giant pinecones, some long-dead stag skull, its cranial sutures curling like mountain roads. A magpie flits to the ground to peck at a pineapple in the altar when it thinks she isn't looking. Chipmunks chitter, plump for the winter. A wind rustles the mother tree and more leaves fall.

And yet. The police foundation has recently issued a press release claiming that this land is not a forest at all. The "growth" consigned to be bulldozed, they say, "should not be described as mature." The land is "marked by little tree cover," and is populated by "largely invasive species of plants and trees that have sprouted over a twenty-year period." The ecologist leads us across a skinny, sturdy plywood bridge strapped to empty plastic carboys floating on Intrenchment Creek, so it rises and falls with the tide. He crushes a bulb between his fingers, sniffs it, pokes a stick into the soil, churns up a pool of groundwater. This place, he says, has been disturbed.

This is a technical term. A disturbance is a sudden exogenous shift in a relatively stable ecosystem, as by flood or fire or locust or fleet of angry chain saws. But crops are even more stable than forests, so abandoning agricultural land constitutes yet another disturbance, says the ecologist, gesturing around to the aftermath of the prison farm fields. Disturbance ecologies are wild and weird places.

Imbalanced species compete in volatile dynamics. "How many times has the land been disturbed?" we ask, afraid of the answer.

Most Indigenous agriculture happened closer to the floodplains, the ecologist explains, so the Muscogee likely used these woods for hunting. But the settlers definitely logged. He examines the underside of some leaves. Seems likely the land was in cotton before the boll weevil blight in the 1920s. Then of course there was the prison farm. After which the loblollies colonized the property. They are shading the soil to refresh it, so that stronger trees might grow back later. It is a young forest, diagnoses the ecologist. A promise of a forest in the future.

For now, the ground is covered in Japanese stiltgrass and scraggly privet, which the ecologist pulls up in clumps as we walk down a trail deeper into the woods. It wants a controlled burn, he says, to kill these invasive species so the forest can mature into a healthy adolescence. It is hard for us to imagine controlling a burn; it sounds like controlling a bulldozer. Shouldn't life run wild and free to reproduce as it pleases? The trail meanders down a declivity into a grove, where mossy, weatherworn marble blocks lie scattered in the shade. What is the capital of this Ionic column doing in the forest? The ecologist doesn't know either. We crouch to brush the privet off a complicated carving. Elegantly chiseled into the center is the name VIRGIL.

Huh? Clearly there's still so much about this forest we don't understand. We've heard the Atlanta zoo once buried an elephant here—or was it a gorilla? A giraffe? Is it true that Civil War soldiers shot at one another through these trees? We walk along the bank of a pond, which someone once told us the prison farm wardens flushed with arsenic to delouse the dairy cows. The prisoners who died of arsenic poisoning were buried unmarked in these woods. But where? Nobody seems to have all the answers.

The forest defenders say that white supremacy and settler-colonialism have cursed this place, and the only solution is simple: give the land back. They've started calling the forest *Weelaunee*, after the Muscogee name for the South River—even though the South River does not run through either of the properties at risk. At some point, the name must have gotten mixed up with the civic proposal for the South River Forest, because the forest defenders, and soon the publications quoting them, have all begun to say or imply that this land has been called the Weelaunee Forest since time immemorial. Sometimes *Weelaunee* refers to the territory held stubbornly by the movement against the developers. At other times, it seems boundless, mythical, and much bigger than Atlanta.

We want the documents. We make an appointment at the Atlanta History Center, which means we have to drive to Buckhead, past tacky landscaped mansions and Brian Kemp campaign signs. As we work our way patiently through boxes and folders of pencil-kept files, a narrative starts to take vague shape. It is riddled with inconsistencies, decades-long silences, and is maddening to try to keep straight. Half the official Atlanta historians and land-use consultants confuse the city prison farm with the nearby, similar, but definitely distinct federal prison farm also harrowing the city outskirts. The files in these boxes make references to paperwork at medical and psychiatric facilities whose archives are kept elsewhere. If at all.

THE PRISON FARM was founded in 1922, when the city council rewrote a zoning law in order to build a city prison outside city limits. Free forced prison work solved the problem of the labor shortage at the city dairy farm, which had been founded recently on land Atlanta bought from the Keys of Key Road. The Key family had owned and used this land as a slave plantation since 1827 and been enriched into minor city elites. A census at the outset of the Civil War shows nineteen nameless people as George Key's personal property. We know almost nothing else about this period. The records have disappeared.

In 1939, city council meeting minutes called the prison farm an economic success, and Atlanta resolved to purchase the property on the other side of Intrenchment Creek to expand the promising prison farm beyond the boundaries of the former plantation. In 1953, the *Atlanta Journal* sent a photographer to the prison farm. An image shows five prisoners in the shade of an oak reading the

Atlanta Journal. The men face away, expressions obscure: mixed-race, wearing undershirts, two on a bench, three sprawled in the grass. One takes a nap with a paper on his face. There are no fences in sight.

In 1965, on a tip from a desperate inmate, the *Atlanta Constitution* sent an undercover journalist to report from inside the prison farm. From the bunkhouse, Dick Hebert described drug smuggling, gambling rings, alcoholism, contraband coffee, bribery, bedbugs, boredom, and terrible food. He cut kudzu on the side of the highway. The other prisoners wandered away unsupervised to recycle glass bottles into pocket change for booze and returned to the chain gang, Hebert was astonished to report, because there would still be a bed and more booze at the prison farm tomorrow. He did not see or mention the farm work.

Four years later, the prisoners went on strike. In May 1969, they stopped work over the food, the indignity of being forced to work for free as office lackeys for the Atlanta Police Department, and the same old catch-and-release cycle: dropped off uptown late at night with nowhere to go and rearrested in the morning for sleeping outside. In July, they went on strike again. Bill Swann, an ex-mechanic who had been in and out of the prison dozens of times within the past year, spoke to the *Atlanta Constitution* on behalf of the strike. "This is a peaceful, nonviolent protest. But I ain't saying there aren't some who want to tear things up. I've been walking around from bunk to bunk to try to keep things like that from happening."

Eight years later, the downtown central library was demolished. Andrew Carnegie had donated the building to the city out of Gilded Age beneficence, but the homegrown capital of the New South no longer needed philanthropists patronizing from the North. To clear the block for a brutalist box, the marble facade of the neoclassical library was dismantled stone by chiseled stone. VIRGIL ended up dumped on the prison farm site alongside HOMER, AESOP, DANTE, POE, MILTON, thousands of tires, mounds of household garbage, and other hazardous material the city didn't know what to do with.

The prison was already shrinking, on its way to an inevitable closure. After federal court–ordered desegregation, after years of prisoner strikes against recrudescent conditions, after round after round of reforms implemented at great cost—new dormitories, better meals, new infirmary, new fences—the farm hit diminishing returns. Mechanical agriculture consolidated in the distance, and even prison slavery couldn't compete. Throughout the 1980s, the farm was scaled back down to dairy and livestock—250 cows, 300 hogs, 145 prisoners—and abandoned field by field.

Another group of newspaper photos in the second half of the decade shows black men hosing down a concrete cell of piglets, staring out a blurry window, and exiting an empty classroom. On the board in white chalk is a crowd of naked torsos, ambiguously gendered, ambiguously human, a skeleton hand hovering, a field of cartoon jugs of liquor labeled XXX receding into the distance, and a micro-manifesto:

DYING

FOR

A

DRINK

??

How is it possible no city documents commemorate exactly when the prison farm closed? Sometime in the early 1990s it was open, and then it wasn't. The silence makes us shudder. In our less materialist moments, we can sense some telluric, demonic force, older even than money, seething through the archive. The plantation, the prison farm, the police academy: it sounds like a history of America. Is this not one symmetry too many to be a simple coincidence?

AND THE PINES REGREW over the prison farm. With them came pecan, persimmon, muscadine, yarrow, vetch, privet, greenbrier, sorghum, hackberry, dewberry, wood fern, Bradford pear, honeysuckle, iris, so many mushrooms, tufted titmice, white-tailed deer, little turtles, rat snakes, butterflies, woodpeckers, wrens, and earthworms squirming through the loamy soil. Some of these plants never left but grew back. Others grew here anew. The vetch and sorghum were likely planted by the prison farm, holding on now to the fledgling forest in its afterlife.

Time passed. Intrenchment Creek Park was founded in 2004, underwritten by the charitable foundation of Arthur M. Blank, a Home Depot cofounder and the owner of the Atlanta Falcons. The prison farm site stayed off-limits, though only on paper. Soon its mongrel ecosystem also harbored mountain bikers, RC pilots, teenage lovers, the homeless, joggers, dog walkers, bird-watchers, and amateur archaeologists seeking respite, pleasure, and adventure away from traffic and taxes. Every few years the prison farm ruins would spontaneously combust. In 2009, the fire department scolded homeless squatters. In 2014, when it happened again, the perplexed fire chief said to the local news, "I don't know how much more you can burn an old prison down between the walls and the bars." In 2017, an enormous tire fire took eighteen hours to put out. You could see it from planes taking off and landing at the world's busiest airport just across town.

THE FIRST FOUR ARRESTS take place in January 2022. Instagram said the event would be "fun and friendly": breakfast, banner-making, kids, for some reason a march through the woods. OK. We follow the crowd. On the west side of the creek, the protesters play telephone in between chants. "Misdemeanor trespassing," someone turns around and says to us intently. "Pass it on." So we turn around and say it the same way to the next person in line.

Neon-vested workers appear through the trees, drilling into the ground—taking soil samples? Suddenly there's shouting at the front, a line of masked people surrounding the workers, and then, from nowhere, cops surrounding the march, a warning on a megaphone—a kettle in the trees! Now everyone's shouting. We look around for eye contact with our friends, and just as suddenly the line breaks and people scatter in all directions. Fugitively, ridiculously, we fly through the foliage, cursing our hi-vis purple coat, until we crash through the brush out onto Key Road and into the suburbs beyond, slowing our breath and our gait, nothing to see, another pedestrian on an innocent walk. A knight in a shining station wagon glides up the street. "Do you need an evac?" Blue lights flash as we wheel past the parking lot. A hooded figure is being led out of the forest in handcuffs.

Instagram roils with outrage, told-you-so, and recommitment. As winter thaws, new people keep coming to the woods to check out the hubbub firsthand—and to live deliberately, in self-sufficient solidarity against the state and its forces of plunder. Soon, half of the people in the forest are trans. It is less white but only slightly. Crustpunks and oogles take the freight train into town and say things like "DIY HRT." Forest names are by now common practice, both for security purposes, because who knows who might be listening, and out of a common sensibility slightly more serious than play. By spring, there's a new cast of characters in Weelaunee: Blackbird, Dandelion, Hawthorn, Shotgun, Squirtle, Gumption, Wish, living on dumpstered or bulk-bought food, tentatively cosplaying the other possible world. Someone calls it Season Two. We watch one teenager recruit another to the unfolding miracle, the invasion of an alternative into reality. "Life in the forest is awesome!" she shouts, barefoot in the mud. "No rent, no parents!" Once the first treehouse goes up, it's only a matter of time before the whole forest is building treehouses.

They work mostly in teams of three: two above, harnessed, nimble, feet in the crotches of branches, one below, tying tools to the end of a rope to be hoisted plumb up into the canopy. It is hard to see unless you're right underneath, because the forest defenders have also settled on a uniform: camouflage and balaclavas, like tropical guerrillas. Online, this is widely interpreted as a signifier of the movement's militancy. But when we ask Eliza, they tell us it's primarily an anonymity measure, because people are camped on the far side of the creek, which is technically trespassing. This is the same reason the anarchists turn off their phones and leave them in a bag a hundred feet away before meetings, even if all they need to meet about is whether the floor joist of this treehouse should be a catwalk or a traverse.

In April we meet Magnolia, in their characteristically sensible tank top and ponytail and glasses, who is building a kitchen in the woods. Magnolia is a practical person. Patient and gentle and modest until you get in the way of their work, at which point you get pulled aside for a meeting about how we can work together better. Instagram has advertised another week of action—the third and biggest yet. All hands are on deck. Everyone knows someone coming from out of town, and no one knows how many people to expect. We invite an anarchish friend from Philadelphia to sleep on our couch, and not two hours later, someone we forgot from college texts to say they invited themselves from online and are planning to show up with an even stranger stranger.

Magnolia moved directly from college to the forest. They have been cooking in the living room for months, mostly basic sustenance to keep the campers happy, but also for big events, which are happening increasingly often as the movement agglomerates allies. Even more than the police, Magnolia knows, the enemy is hunger. Back in November 2021, when a Muscogee delegation came to do a stomp dance—the first ceremonial return to this land since walking the Trail of Tears, we heard—the forest cooks made mashed potatoes and nine vegan pies and wild rice with black Weelaunee walnuts, and stew from a frozen roadkill deer, which took too long to thaw, so Magnolia had to hack it into pieces with a pickax. "How long has it been since these trees heard our language?" asked the Mekko to nodding allies. After the ceremony, the Muscogee dancers turned out to have already eaten, so the forest defenders ate venison like kings all week.

But the week of action slated for mid-May 2022 is bigger than even Magnolia can handle. They call up a traveling trio of cooks they met at a land defense struggle out west a year earlier, movement

veterans who have catered all the major environmental activist summits since the '90s, and ask them to help. Now it is merely a matter
of building a kitchen to make the lunch ladies proud. Magnolia and
their partner choose a spot five minutes from the living room, close
but far enough away, and borrow and bargain and reroute donations
toward coolers and ten-gallon pots, propane and burners, cutting
boards, can openers, a five-hundred-foot hose. Various infrastruc-
turalists lift milk crates from the streets, scavenge metal shelves and
armchairs from the junkyard, dig poop trenches, cut the privet and
kudzu back to widen the path to the living room. Someone rigs up
a camouflage tarp over the kitchen so you can't see it from above or
even thirty feet away. During the work, someone else names the new
kitchen Space Camp, and it sticks.

On the first morning of the week of action, Eliza wakes in the
living room to clamor and panic. "Cops in the forest!" They unzip
the tent, strangely calm, and listen to the ambient gossip. A bulldozer
has just barged into the forest and the activists are already cursing out Ryan Millsap. By instinct or hive mind, campers swarmed
the machine throwing rocks, and Eliza arrives during a cinematic
standoff in the RC field, yellow machine alone against giant blue
sky. Every inch the bulldozer gains is met with a rain of rocks. Four
cop cars arrive with sirens and the officers stand on either side of
the bulldozer, preparing to pepper spray, when from the trees some
thirty people in camouflage emerge and march in a line on the cops,
chanting "Move back! Move back!" as if they are the cops! The squad
cars peel away in fear and the bulldozer lumbers back, rocks pinging
off its back grille. The forest defenders exult as the camo bloc deli-
quesces into the trees.

SOMEONE HAS BUILT a suspension bridge across Intrenchment
Creek, a genuinely beautiful piece of engineering, strong and springy,
made from supple softwood and steel wire. There's a big camp in
the living room, but also many small camps all over the forest, and
though there's a difference in activist cultures on either side of

the property line—public/trespassing, hippie/anarchist, peaceful/
militant—people use the bridge to bounce across the creek all week,
so many that there's a line built up on both sides. Waiting to go see
the treehouses, a nearby forest defender in a balaclava suddenly feels
woozy. Philadelphia rushes over, says I got you, opens their backpack,
pulls out a Gatorade, energy bars, Advil. "CVS was giving stuff away
today for free."

So much else happens this week: art builds, movie screenings,
public marches, Shabbat dinner, a foraging walk for a wild psychedelic mushroom only found in North Georgia, a puppet show in
which Joe Biden is incarcerated in Plato's cave. An upside-down
black sedan appears overnight in the entrance to the power line cut.
A delegation comes from Standing Rock carrying a sacred fire. The
forest defenders pledge not to let it extinguish, and spend the week
taking shifts tending the fire in a clearing between the kitchen and
the living room, singing corny country on the guitar and organizing
expeditions to gather firewood. We spend two afternoons this week
chopping cabbage and stirring onions downhill in the kitchen for
the rolling buffet of rice and vegan beans and low-FODMAP slaw.
Insiders and newcomers wander in and out, washing their hands in
these magic hydraulic sinks someone's contrapted out of two plastic buckets and a foot pump, drying dishes with donated T-shirts
because we ran out of rags on day three, mashing chickpeas with the
bottom of a mason jar, sweat glistening down spines, adjusting salt
until everything's too salty, making the same lewd joke about Mayor
Dickens succeeding Mayor Bottoms.

By now the Atlanta Police Foundation has announced the
training center is on track to open in fall 2023. For months, forest
defenders have been targeting Reeves Young, the Atlanta-based lead
contractor, flooding phone lines by day and sabotaging construction
equipment by night until the company backs out. During the week
of action, activists march on the Atlanta headquarters of the new
contractor, Brasfield & Gorrie, and vandalize their offices: graffiti,
broken windows, splashes of red paint to symbolize the carnage. It's

$80,000 worth of damage, says Fox 5. The next day, other activists march through East Atlanta Village led by a delegation of preschoolers. Later in the week, yet another group marches through the city carrying branches from the forest like a punk production of *Macbeth*. The cops surround this group in a park, tackling activists indiscriminately, spraining someone's wrist, squeezing zip cuffs way too tight, and arresting twelve people on charges that all get dropped.

Magnolia initially calculated needing seven hundred gallons of water to last the week of action, but we watch them watch the water flow unexpectedly fast out of the giant plastic tanks at Space Camp, increasingly nervous, until someone else approaches the kitchen with the same concern. This person and Magnolia and whoever's nearby and interested turn off their phones and have a meeting to organize an infrastructure to run water through the woods. They designate a zone in the parking lot where campers can leave empty carboys to be filled up at people's houses and visitors can drop off water to be hauled back to the kitchen. More than anything, Magnolia loves this task: no meetings, no conflict, no speaking, no thinking even, you just strap a jug to your back and walk through the woods.

They call this "the unfathomable bliss of being a cog in someone else's machine." For all the talk about autonomy, sometimes you want to be of use. Is this what's so enlivening about the week of action? We are happy to see our friends, of course, but it's something more, and they sense it too, a subtle reorientation of our body to other people, to abstractions like work and time. We chat while we work with young strangers, exchange biographies and motives and meanings. They mostly say they came to the forest to learn from militant struggle at the crossroads of racism, ecocide, and the forces of social control, and then laugh when we say that we're here because we love the logistics.

But it's true. For a few transcendent instants this week we feel like a gnat in a swarm, a spontaneous, collaborative choreography unfolding around us. Again we are exhilarated by the rush of—it's not exactly solidarity, but something even stranger and more miraculous, closer to goodwill. There is no money in the forest. People share what they have and borrow what they don't. Something clicks about gender and number: everyone in the forest presumes without asking that others are all they/them, because assembling here is something like a we/us, which feels both lost and found, long forgotten and newly, mawkishly recovered.

Which is of course not to say it's all a happy trippy orgy. We notice ourself developing little resentments toward the militants in camo sitting all day by the bonfire and gloating about smashing up windows while never seeming to cook or haul or clean or help make camp. But Eliza reminds us that everyone has strengths and needs, even us. This is in fact a sign, they say, of a healthy ecology of tactics. For every militant crowing about the next direct action, a pacifist making them possible through indirect activity.

The people who came go home. Two days after the week of action ends, the police raid the forest encampment. They slash and trample tens of thousands of dollars' worth of tents and generators and kitchen supplies, stomp out the sacred fire, cut down the suspension bridge, topple six treehouses. Eight people are arrested on charges ranging from "criminal trespass" to "obstructing law enforcement." The Atlanta Police Department releases a video of a flaming object flying from a tree. Our mom calls to make sure we're safe. "Aren't you concerned about . . . law enforcement?" she wheedles, all concern. The term sounds so neutral and alien, it hardly registers what she means.

The next day, Unicorn Riot releases an audio file of radio banter among a police unit participating in the raid. One says *Molotov cocktail*. The next says *deadly force encounter*, meaning *we are authorized to shoot to kill.*

"Is this the uh protest against Cop City?"

"Sure is. They're mad about a forest that they've never been to."

"They probably never even knew about the forest until now too. Man that sounds like a uhhh uh scene out of *Mad Max*."

"I don't think they actually care about the forest at all. I think it's just all about being anti-police."

"That is a uh great movie by the way, right? Really good movie."

"I was about to ask if you, uh, if you'd watched that flick before."

"Believe it or not, I actually watched it when we were all on that detail at the mayor's mom's house. Watched it out there on my phone."

EARLY SUMMER, 2022. On Instagram, a gallery of graffiti under highways across the country: STOP COP CITY and DEFEND ATL FOREST in Portland, Pittsburgh, New Orleans, New York, Kansas City, Tallahassee. In places like Highland, Indiana, and Erie, Pennsylvania, people smash plate glass windows at Banks of America, Wells Fargos, and the offices of Atlas, a national technology consultancy and Brasfield & Gorrie subcontractor.

Undaunted, committed, hardheaded, the forest defenders move back into the woods. Treehouses keep appearing as if the forest is a fairy-tale Levittown. They build outposts deep into APF territory, but also in the border zone by the creek, in sturdy old oaks not at risk from either Cop City or Ryan Millsap. Is this strategic? Some activists also start spiking trees, a tactic straight out of the Earth First! playbook, which involves hammering long metal rods into tree trunks at random and then posting signs all over the forest that say something like, "Don't log here or your chain saw will blow up," in English and Spanish.

One Friday morning in mid-July DeKalb County police officers accompany a construction crew to the parking lot, where they put up concrete barricades. Did Millsap the Rapacious ask them to do this? The county recently issued a stop-work order against him after the incident with the bulldozer. Is this legal? Does it matter? The lawsuit over the land-swap deal is ongoing and nobody knows whether the park is actually open, but the law seems less important now anyway than who is in the forest and with what force. Antlike, activists quickly lift the thousand-pound things out of the way and paint them bright colors to prepare for the fourth week of action, upcoming already. A new sign at the trailhead announces yet another name, Atlanta echoing Berkeley echoing the Cultural Revolution: WEELAUNEE PEOPLE'S PARK.

On the Saturday morning of the week of action, Millsap sends a man in an excavator to tear down the gazebo. Its bucket collides with the roof. The people inside throw what they can. Hummus sandwiches splatter across the windshield. Dr. Priestley's Fizzy Water bursts on the treads like a thousand clowns' seltzer sprinklers. The ungainly machine trudges off. The work crew leaves behind a year-old Dodge Ram. By the end of the week of action, it has been husked by flames and washed by rain and covered in symbols: the squiggly arrow for squatters' rights, the trans circle sprouting with pluses and arrows, the uppercase Ⓐ and lowercase @, the Black Power fist, here and there a HA HA, cartoon cats, hearts, cop cars on fire, and a million graffiti flowers.

The permanent camp in the forest continues unbidden into the fall, with the constant help of a network of Atlantans hauling in water, hauling out trash, coordinating essential services with forest defenders over Signal. New, very young people arrive constantly from all over the country, some from Canada and France and Italy, because they heard on Instagram that the forest is a bulwark against the creep of fascism and it needs bodies. They spend all day hanging out at the living room campfire writing poems, eating Nutter Butters, and strumming on mandolins.

One September afternoon we are delivering ice to the forest and ask a Signal thread for help hauling it into camp. A new upright piano sits in the dented gazebo. We start up the bike path, ice dripping down our shoulder, when out of the woods walks Tortuguita carrying a cooler, smiling in the sunlight. It is hot. Big dinosaur clouds overhead. Tortuguita is jazzed, chatty, petite, as graceful as you can be carrying a cooler. We carry it together, one person per handle, and chat on our way into camp. Tortuguita just returned from a two-day intensive wilderness medic training program. They had dropped out of pre-med in Aruba. Do you still want to be a doctor? we ask. "Hell nah," Tortuguita says, insouciant. "You have to cut out some of your empathy to be a doctor."

A group of reinforcements comes from Albuquerque to help build infrastructure, a couple at a time, every few weeks, like little needful drops from a pipette of know-how. They build a new kitchen in the parking lot with a rainwater catchment system for the dishes and plant a vegetable garden behind it, which they fertilize with composted leftovers. Winter is coming, they say, doing math for a week to determine where the hothouse should be, at what angle its roof will trap the most sunlight, efficiently distributing tasks. They steal nails from Home Depot, ask a group of party kids from New York to pay for two-by-fours, put together a frame in a day, make a slanted roof out of corrugated plastic and walls out of shipping pallets. They stuff insulation in the gaps of the pallets and shellac to the shack a skin of political signs—Warnock, Abrams, Williams, Kemp, mostly upside-down—plucked at night from the Moreland Avenue median.

This month we also meet Pandabear, who is building a tree-house alone. Radicalized by videos of vegan street activists and bored of bouncing around upstart farming communes in the Northeast, Pandabear used his stimulus money to buy backpacking gear and walked alone down the Appalachian Trail almost directly to the forest this spring. He is gawky in an endearing way, wears camo everything: balaclava, gloves, even olive-khaki boots. He is not a skilled carpenter, but is borrowing tools and learning to build plank by scrapyard plank. He recruits us to hold a piece of particleboard in place sometimes when we pass by his construction site, in the shade of a beautiful oak on flat ground near the creek.

Temperatures drop, slowly then quickly. There are deer all over the woods this fall, more deer this year than last, which moonier forest defenders interpret as a sign of nature's boundless abundance, overflowing with life, affirming their mission, though the deer leap away whenever humans approach. Magnolia finds two black rat snakes and names them Anti-Freeze and Slinky. Despite the new kitchen, the campers are hungry and quarreling. Eliza starts to have to act like a camp counselor, encouraging the teenagers to take some initiative and clean up after themselves. The Albuquerque builders brigade says it more bluntly: Use your autonomy or die.

Winter descends upon a discontented living room. New young people show up alone and act reckless: graffiti nearby suburbs, throw cinder blocks at passing traffic, slash the tires of the Al Jazeera rental car. Things get paranoid, almost nihilistic. Just as the governor invokes outside agitators, the forest defenders murmur about agents provocateurs, and you can tell who went to college by how they pronounce it. Pandabear must have miscalculated, because when he tries to pulley his platform up into the tree, something doesn't fit. He gives up for a week or so, but daunted by winter, comes back to his woodpile and says OK it will be a hut.   •

In early December 2022, a construction project near the forest burns down in a mysterious fire. The police have no evidence linking the forest defenders to this fire, but they raid the camp in retaliation, arresting five—this time, for the first time, on felony charges of domestic terrorism. The district attorney cites a law rewritten in 2017, after the white supremacist massacre at Emanuel African Methodist Episcopal Church in Charleston, when the Georgia legislature redefined domestic terrorism as any criminal act that "is intended or reasonably likely to ~~injure~~ cause serious bodily harm or kill ~~not less than ten individuals~~ any individual or group of individuals or to disable or destroy critical infrastructure."

War on terror tactics have become Georgia jurisprudence. The statute defines critical infrastructure as "public or private systems, functions, or assets, whether physical or virtual, vital to the security, governance, public health and safety, economy, or morale of this state." Stuart Hall et al. echo prophetic through the treetops: "The state has won the right, and indeed inherited the duty, to move swiftly, to stamp fast and hard, to listen in, discreetly survey, saturate and swamp, charge or hold without charge, act on suspicion, hustle and shoulder, to keep society on the straight and narrow. Liberalism, that last backstop against arbitrary power, is in retreat. It is suspended. The times are exceptional. The crisis is real." Pandabear watches from the branches of his oak, breathing as quietly as possible, as the police destroy his hut with heavy machinery down below.

The forest defenders flee. Some go back home to Knoxville or Houston. Others crash on the couch or floor of a house in the suburbs some benefactor of the movement has rented for a year. Just before Christmas, contractors hired by Millsap return to the parking lot. They jackhammer everything to smithereens: the parking lot, the trailhead, the bike path all the way up to the line where Millsap's fiefdom apparently ends. The next day they start to fell trees, including one with a treehouse. A week too late, DeKalb County issues another stop-work order, this time for removing trees without a permit.

It is New Year's again already when gingerly the defenders move back into the forest.

IT IS JANUARY 18, 2023, and dense with morning fog. The Atlanta Police Department, DeKalb County Sheriff's Office, Georgia State Patrol, Georgia Bureau of Investigation, and Federal Bureau of Investigation conduct a joint "clearing operation" in the Weelaunee Forest.

Pandabear hears shots, so many shots, from up in the branches of his oak by the creek. This time, the police sweeping the forest spot him through the withered leaves. There's a standoff for what feels like hours. Pandabear sends videos out on Signal threads. We are home, glued to the screen, whiplashed with rumors—did someone die?—all alone, when the police start shooting pepper balls into the canopy and he stops responding to texts.

Eliza is pulling into the parking lot at work when they get the call from their partner. They enter the restaurant sobbing and their managers understand. They drive to someone's house, where twenty forest defenders sit in the dark, scrolling, vacant faces glowing, silent as conversations all trail off into nothingness, taking constant smoke breaks outside where months-long grudges disappear without words.

Signal doesn't know who it is either when the stories start to spread across our timeline: "First Environmental Activist Killed by Police in America." This first day, the news's only source is the GBI. No one wants to go to the forest, so there's a vigil in Little Five Points instead, where the forest defenders, dwarfed by the enormity of the city, cry, block traffic, chant into megaphones, and huddle to keep candles lit in the rain, wondering who it was, crowdsourcing information and winnowing the list down to a few forest names. A half-hearted riot dissipates before they've even smashed a window. We feel hollow to watch it. We won't feel anything until tomorrow when the media releases Tortuguita's legal name, and even then, we don't know who that is until someone posts a photo on Instagram.

The GBI says Tortuguita shot first but doesn't have or won't release the bodycam footage to prove it. An independent autopsy later says Tortuguita was seated on the ground with their hands up. They were on the public park side of the forest, not even trespassing. Fifty-seven bullet wounds. Is this a mass shooting? The exonerating injuries perforate their palms like stigmata.

By the time *Democracy Now!* picks up the story, Pandabear is in the intake room at DeKalb County jail. His clothes reek of pepper ball and the officers can't stop coughing. When he finally takes a shower, the water reactivates the chemical, scorching and pouring down his body.

TURNS OUT DEATH is what it takes to break the national news. Almost even more confusing than the loss of Tortuguita is the sudden attention it brings to the movement. Congresswoman Cori Bush tweets about the killing. A professor and former president of Emory University steps down from the board of the Atlanta Police Foundation under pressure from faculty and students. Morehouse and Spelman College professors and students sign public letters to Stop Cop City. We scroll and scroll as these bastions of the Atlanta elite founder at the force of the news. National racial and social justice groups demand the resignation of Mayor Dickens, who says nothing, only breaking his public silence the following week to condemn "violence" and "property destruction" when the forest defenders regroup to take vengeance on the city.

Is the Atlanta Way finally falling apart? Does it matter? The latest round of photos of burning cop cruisers feels less exhilarating than mechanical: you strike, we strike back, you always strike back harder. The damage only ever gets worse. How many more of these cycles can we withstand? A secret, selfish thought starts to whisper through the solidarity. Do we care enough to die?

Tortuguita's parents and brother fly to Atlanta to meet the forest defenders in an Airbnb. Their mom brings childhood photos from Panama. Eliza sits there sifting through the pictures and a life starts to take shape in time. Tortuguita had been vague to them, one of hundreds of comrades in the forest, but comradeship is impersonal. Whereas there now is tiny 2D Tortuguita cheesing for the camera at Disney World. Grief hits Eliza like a bulldozer: slowly, unstoppably, inevitably, then all at once. They shake, suppressing sobs on the couch. Tortuguita's mom comes over to comfort Eliza, holds their hand, wiping away tears and sitting up straight, somehow, impossibly, composed. "Thank you for being there with my Manny," she tells Eliza. "He was—they was—they is—my hero."

Pandabear is charged with criminal trespassing and domestic terrorism. He is the only one of the seven forest defenders arrested that day to be denied bail. At least his cellmate is chill. While his dietary form is processing, he trades packs of commissary ramen for whole trays of food with the guys in his pod, and then individual items from their trays to make himself vegan feasts. He hoards apples in his cell, works out, plays chess, talks to his mom on the pay phone every day. It is almost a relief to spend so much time away from the internet. He receives more than a hundred postcards from comrades around the country. The dietary form finally processes and procures him vegan meals until the jail hires a new food service provider that serves all the inmates baloney and cheese.

Pandabear's cellmate's head is bashed into the cell wall one morning. That afternoon, the cellmate is moved to another pod. Pandabear plays chess with the assailant. He mostly loses. He reads crime novels, how-to-garden books, and a biography of Fryderyk Chopin. His eczema flares up. He submits a medical form. The nurse gives him a vision test and suggests he submit a dietary form. The lawyer from the Atlanta Solidarity Fund appeals the charges three times, and eventually Pandabear is granted bond. After thirty-seven days in DeKalb County jail, he is released into a crowd of forest defenders waiting in the parking lot with fruit and vegan snacks and water and Gatorade and sweaters and a ride to wherever he wants, and music or silence as Pandabear prefers.

We're not there. We needed to get out. Impulsively we bought a ticket to Vermont, to move in with a friend we hadn't seen in years. For a month, Signal vibrates in the background: vandalism, arrests, domestic terrorism charges. Organizers prepone the fifth week of action to ride the momentum of the media and call in reinforcements sooner rather than later. It is hard to pay attention from Vermont. The world is blanketed in thirty inches of snow, white and almost noiseless. Different owls coo here in the long nights. Come back, Magnolia texts. We leave them on read. We are having sleeping problems, dreaming of privet grabbing at our ankles, Philadelphia in uniform, being frog-marched by giant spiders toward an acrid lake.

Reluctantly, full of dread, we buy another ticket to Atlanta.

SOMETIMES IT SEEMS LIKE an evil gray cube has hijacked the planet and multiplied into jail cells and condos and cubicles and tofu and Ikea and shipping containers and parking lots and tombs. Like industrial civilization is a religion organized around worshiping the cube, digging ever deeper quarries, building ever drabber monuments, coordinating unfathomable oceans of more-than-human energy to produce and profuse and proliferate cubes to put the bodies in. We get it: the cube's cool smoothness, its reassuring regularity. The

jungle it steamrolled and conquered is barbarous, malarial, obstrep-
erous, twisting in the wind.

We stay overnight in New York, which feels like Cop City
already. Military men in bulletproof pants march in formation
through Penn Station, intimidating weary people waiting for trains:
no benches, no sitting on the floor. The TSA beeps our belongings.
We shuffle along an endless line to fly from one concrete desolation
to another, fart carbon into the ozone, and return to our cruel city to
defend the damaged landscape we've been doomed to love.

We take off into the morning. Manhattan grubs greedily
into the sky. Container ships queue up out into the ocean, minuscule
on the roof of the gleaming deep. Babylon sprawls: Philadelphia, Baltimore, DC. The view from the air turns industry into entomology.
We watch aloof, above, transfixed, as out the window something
almost glorious rusts and crumbles into landfill, and colorless cube
metastasizes over green world.

"In prison, time is The Enemy," wrote Dick Hebert, the undercover journalist, of the day he spent entirely indoors at the Atlanta
prison farm. "It is slow-footed. It wants filling, and many of its prisoners find sleep the only recourse." Is this also what happens, we
wonder idly, tracing the curve of the sky with our finger, when the
world outside becomes prison? Is our *Jungle Cruise* society, are their
Mad Max fantasies, is our Disney world the collective dream of a
culture of inmates?

This is, after all, the ultimate effect of the police. They knit
together the prison and military into one inescapable complex. They
stalk and corral and control the poor, confine them to suffocating
ghettos, convert whole cities into open-air prisons, and stand at
attention at borders, real and imaginary, with ever greater guns. It is
so clear above the mid-Atlantic. The military has become the police,
the police mimic the movies, the movies are all for children, and the
children have no future. Time, The Enemy, drags everlastingly on.
Can we, how do we, how dare we wish to abolish history?

We look to the forest as we descend upon Atlanta. Wispy ghosts
of smoke plume lazily into the sky.

OUR PHONE BLOWS UP when we land. It is Monday, March 6,
midafternoon, already the fifth week of action. A thousand notifi-
cations on Signal. Words puncture the screen out of context: raid,
DT charges, jail support, see you? Philadelphia has driven back to
Atlanta and is waiting at arrivals, their hatchback full of strangers
buzzing with wiry energy, sleepless, eager, cross-talking, correcting
one another, embellishing—and laughing like manic seagulls now
that the danger has passed.

Our head throbs as we piece together what's happening. Yesterday, a hundred forest defenders dressed in camo swarmed the
Cop City construction site, overwhelmed the police, tipped trailers
over, set excavators on fire, broke materials, stole tools, shattered
glass, sprayed paint, and shot fireworks at the backpedaling police.
Two hours later, the cops retaliated, raiding the music festival on
the other side of the forest, arresting twenty-three indiscriminately,
citing evidence like muddy shoes as proof of terrorist conspiracy.

But the week of action is still on, and already people are
regrouping in the forest. We're not ready to go back. Our roommates
are sheltering people evicted from the forest. The dryer hums and
thumps all night. We dither all morning as updates ping. Jail support says a legal observer from the Southern Poverty Law Center
was arrested. Anarchists send hyperlinks to AliExpress to buy those
green laser pointers that can interfere with helicopter vision. Philadelphia, impatient and excited, goes back to the forest for lunch and
says they'll text us with a vibe check. We dither all afternoon, afraid
of the worst, which has already happened. And yet. It's calm here,
Philadelphia texts eventually. Come back.

Fine. We will go to the forest to do the dishes, we decide, and
no more. This round we are militant peaceniks, reactionaries on
the question of violence. To indicate our dissidence with the guerrillas wearing camo we put on an old tie-dye T-shirt. We dust the

pollen off our car and drive back to the forest. We're surprised to be disappointed that the gazebo is still crumpled upside-down at the entrance to the parking lot like a dead cockroach. We didn't realize until now we were hoping someone would have removed it. But who?

We walk down the remnants of the bike path and turn down the footpath into a living room burbling with people. We overhear a Southern accent say, "Reorganize this area for dinner," and instantly, involuntarily become critical infrastructure. Peanut butter goes next to jelly. Yerba maté and hibiscus leaves in a box we decide is for tea. Oat and almond milk and sugars sort themselves. We establish a fruit zone with a basket in the corner. "Have you also worked in kitchens?" we ask our helpmate after we establish a rhythm.

"Since I was like twelve."

"We're Quail," we say, feeling lightheaded, almost off-balance.

"No shit. My friends just today renamed me Pheasant. Because I also go by Pleasant. Ta-da," they trill, admiring the table as someone spills honey all over the napkins.

Dinner comes, hauled in through the trees by a team of masked punks wearing camo and khaki. Beans and rice and slaw again, almost painfully classic. A crowd is gathering around the living room fire for Purim, but we are too underadjusted, and have just noticed the dish pit anyway, and can't imagine being festive while things still look like this.

"We do dishes here in the living room now? Not in the kitchen?" A bearded man shrugs over a muddy tub.

"Is there dish soap?"

He points to a crushed plastic water bottle lying slimy on the pine bed. Trichinosis! we think. Botulism! "What happened?"

"Cops yesterday."

"Attacked the dish pit?"

He shrugs again and doesn't respond to our follow-up questions either. We start down the path to Space Camp, but remember it was wasted last November in the raid. So we make a new dish pit, drag trash bags together, designate a recycling bucket with our Sharpie,

518   NOT ONE TREE

and listen as the crowd tells the Purim story, calling and responding, heads nodding in uncanny synchrony to the tale of sexy Esther,
whose pussy snapped so hard she brought down a king.

HELPLESSLY, AS IF MARIONETTED, we come back every day. Food Not
Bombs throws a potluck in the parking lot, where a Muscogee elder
visiting from Tennessee tells a story about a dream they had in which
Tortuguita came to them and came close to them and said nothing
and they knew they were OK and they were going to be OK and we
are going to be OK. People cry and hug and hold hands. We run out
of vegan burritos. Magnolia tells us the kitchen is off-site this week,
which comes with added logistics but less chance of being destroyed
in a raid. Can we drive food to the forest?

Maybe tomorrow after the protest downtown. Buildings in
every historical style stand crisp against cloudless sky. College students vape between classes. The city has sent every black cop on the
force to supervise this march, at least as many cops as protesters,
and way more guns. The march-and-chant crowd downtown is older
and less white than the campers in the forest. The Atlanta police,
Fulton County sheriffs, Georgia State University police, and Georgia
State Patrol chaperone our protest down the sidewalk, past empty
parking garages and mute office towers. The march gets split by a red
traffic hand, and, surrounded by light infantry, someone says, "Don't
jaywalk or we'll be charged with domestic terrorism." If that is not a
forest, we think, this is not a city.

Machine guns, muscular dogs, bulletproofing, zip ties ready
to cuff, college cops on ridiculous Segways surround us, so many
they stop traffic. The cops look bored and banal, sip coffee, check
their steps on their Apple watches. One shows another his new tattoo, a cross with wings on his forearm. We chant past hundreds of
surveillance cameras, feeling helplessly exposed. It is stressful and
sweaty under our balaclava. A construction crew has stopped work
to scratch their helmets and watch us pass, except for the one black
worker livestreaming, smiling, neon in the sun. Black women yell at

the cops on megaphones: "Y'all look dumb as dirt!" Cop cars prowl alongside the protest, blaring messages from their sirens citing some legal code we're breaking, all numbers, which we can't hear anyway over the crowd.

Philadelphia convinces us to sleep in the forest. People sing campfire songs until someone yells at them to shut up already, it's 3 AM, and if I have to hear one more verse about a shrimp in the sea. Breakfast comes from the off-site kitchen around nine-thirty every morning, and there are announcements around ten: events, activities, projects, advisories, what else is on your mind. Reporters walk in and around the forest this week and are met with everything from indifference to hostility. *Le Monde*, the *LA Times*, the *New York Post*. One affinity group is dressed in black and crouched in the underbrush and ready to throw rocks at CNN when a movement boomer trips over them and talks them sagely out of it.

The boomer makes an announcement at breakfast: "Remember, the media is not our enemy. The media is a tool. Just make sure to only speak in sound bites, so they can't twist your words out of your mouth. You are in control. Take as long as you need to answer their questions. They will cut the dead air. And your answer doesn't even need to match their question. Even if they ask like 'What do you have to say about the anarchists shitting in the woods?' Just take a deep breath and tell them: 'The police are the real terrorists!'" Campers laugh into their porridge. People volunteer to help rainproof camp, keep watch with burner phones at strategic forest entrances, hang banners, cook chili in the middle of everyone else's work. Someone gives a report-back from the jail vigil yesterday: a big group went over to make noise outside DeKalb County jail and the prisoners inside went crazy, lighting papers on fire, dropping them out the windows. Two cops used their nightsticks to beat the fire out of a burning bush.

Tortuguita's mom shows up in the forest and scatters their ashes on the ground around their tent, which has been left undisturbed since January, rainwater pooling through the bullet holes. Banners with Tortuguita's name are raised and reposted on Instagram at an occupied dam in France, at a tree sit in Germany, in the central square of Exarcheia in Athens. Anarchist farmers from Louisiana and Indiana have organized the first annual Weelaunee Food Autonomy Festival this weekend and have brought literally thousands of fruit trees they need the camp's help planting. The plan is to garden this land into a food forest. The Albuquerque builders have put up a pavilion in the parking lot where the gazebo used to be, and we stand under it for an hour and give out hundreds of saplings to middle-aged women.

Returning, head ringing, from a DIY show at No Tomorrow, we aim in the dark through the forest toward Philadelphia's tent. Thunder rumbles long and low out there somewhere, preparing. Is that a banjo? Cicadas, harmonicas, laughter, a quiet constant rustle like TV static, and quickly, cutting in front of us, a broad bald man in an orange jumpsuit speedwalks shoulders-first into a bush, which waves closed behind him and melts into the scenery. A bonfire flickers off to the left, casting darting shadows. Have the trails changed around since yesterday already?

But it's this way, uphill, toward where the bike path loops back— we catch ourself an inch short of walking face-first into a spider suspended between two trees. And there, on the far side of the spider-web, wavering in the uneven firelight frame rate, is that . . .? Two men in blue work a long curved saw back and forth at double speed. They look like Civil War soldiers. We blink. No men. It's empty and dark. A crushed can of Dr. Priestley's glints on the pine straw.

"Hello?" we call. The canopy begins to patter with rain, and nearby people make scurrying sounds, gathering their things. A silhouette in tattered rags rushes by. Paper figures flit in the distance. Philadelphia's tent should not be so far up this slope. And why is the air so heavy and hot? It's only March.

We retrace our steps, speeding up, down the soft forest floor. Conquistadors and vampires cackle through the shadowscape. VIRGIL gambols past in stony toga. The treetops bend down to block our every step and misstep. And this wet wind! We whirl around into a man in gray button-ups polishing a leather boot on a tree stump. Grizzled, scarred, ginger-bearded in the moonlight, looking unhurried up from his hands, those eyes so black, and the sound disappears like we're far underwater, and we stare at the soldier and realize the Civil War never ended, and was maybe ten thousand years old already, because neither Union nor Confederacy was on the side of the trees.

A motorcycle saws down Bouldercrest. We rub our eyes hard like in a cartoon, and there is the path in the rain, and down the path the living room, dry under a bright-blue trapezoidal tarp someone must have slung up today while we weren't looking. Teenagers stir a pot over the fire. A medic in a tie-dye dashiki applies a Band-Aid to the bare foot of someone in camouflage pants. Pop country croons from a quiet speaker. Someone tells a joke and everyone laughs. And here is Magnolia all of a sudden asking are we OK? Do we want a hot chocolate? Freight trains clank in the distance. The tarp clicks with rain, letting up already. "You shoulda seen the Kroger dumpsters today," says Magnolia. "Can you believe they let this stuff go to waste?"

TWO MONDAYS LATER, the CEO of DeKalb County declares Intrenchment Creek Park officially closed. Work crews guarded by police put up more barricades overnight. This time the police don't leave. The following week, people repost footage shot from a civilian drone of workers clear-cutting the prison farm site. Not one tree, but eighty-five acres of green matchsticks topple in rippling waves. The destruction site smells like sap and gas when we drive past. We go to a meeting in a nearby park. No one there knows what to do either. A helicopter flies overhead, and the anarchists instinctively flee to the trees. We brainstorm halfheartedly for over an hour and resolve to announce another week of action on Instagram anyway.

This month, Atlanta Police Foundation meeting minutes get released through open records requests, which show them somehow strapped for cash, despite millions in constant corporate infusions.

They are considering reaching out to Shadowbox for funding in exchange for filming rights on the training grounds. These same leaked meeting minutes also confirm that, when it comes to their pledge to replace lost trees, the APF still has no idea what they're talking about:

4. Tree Recompense
    a. Need to understand this project's commitments
        i. Planting 100 hardwood trees for every specimen tree
            1. Site has 3 specimen trees and there are 3 additional trees that will be impacted due to the required pedestrian walkway
        ii. Plant 1 specimen tree for any invasive species tree that is removed
            1. Need to define invasive species tree

IT IS MAY. Dogwood, magnolia, wisteria, honeysuckle season, everything colorful and fragrant, the city abloom like in *Jungle Cruise*. Three people are arrested for wheatpasting posters that list the names of the six Georgia State Patrolmen who killed Tortuguita. Felony intimidation of law enforcement and misdemeanor stalking. One early morning, three bail-fund organizers are swarmed by a SWAT team at home. Felony money laundering and charity fraud. The city council meets again to decide whether to approve the $31 million in public funds for the police academy, which suddenly looks more like $67 million when they explain an obscure provision in the original agreement that would give the Police Foundation another $1.2 million of taxpayer money per year for thirty years.

Hundreds of people come to speak at this meeting: lawyers, neighbors, black and white, community organizers, old Democratic women, militants from the forest dressed up in business casual. Long lines out the building down the block. Chants resonate through the linoleum atrium, loud and unified enough to almost make you believe in democracy, even if the city council meeting begins two hours late today, and the bailiffs pass around a clipboard with far fewer spaces to sign up to speak than there are people in line. The police forbid the people waiting to speak from eating and drinking. The speeches last fourteen hours, dignified and gracious and civil, and overwhelmingly against Cop City. At five in the morning, the city council votes to approve the funding anyway. The assembled public jeers as the council members file out of the chamber. The sun is already rising when everyone goes home.

Forty-two disillusioned idealists still await trial in state courts on cruel and spurious criminal charges of domestic terrorism. But the lawyers are picking up where the militants left off. (Evidence, Eliza echoes in our head, of a healthy ecology of tactics.) Labor organizers file paperwork with the Atlanta Planning Advisory Board to put the police academy's construction to a citywide referendum, the first in Atlanta's history—and the board capitulates. Activists have sixty days to gather seventy thousand signatures in favor of repealing the lease. But City Hall stalls. Canvassers are already collecting signatures when a municipal clerk invalidates their petition on account of being incorrectly formatted, and forces them to start over.

And hope and despair keep doing their dance. The Friday before Juneteenth, when referendum organizers show up to the clerk's office to pick up some paperwork, they find it closed four hours early, their signature-gathering window squeezed three days tighter. But in July, a federal judge overturns the city council's constraints, extends the deadline by another month, and allows nonresidents of Atlanta to canvass, too. The training center, after all, would be outside city limits. The DeKalb County DA recuses her office from prosecuting the Cop City cases, implying that the evidence doesn't stand. But this decision shunts the cases to the state-level DA, who is a bulldog of the hard-right Georgia governor.

The sixth week of action is small and quiet. The forest is ringed by police, so all the speeches and ceremonies and cookouts take place in Brownwood Park nearby. Everyone misses the forest's sprawling secrecy. The instant the first forest defender drives a tent stake into the playground, thirty cops in military fatigues and bulletproof vests and balaclavas materialize from the trees to issue a "friendly reminder" that the park closes at eleven.

But when a group gathers later in the week to chant and wave signs and play music outside the home of a project manager at Atlas, the construction technology subcontractor, the exasperated man comes out of his house and tells the forest defenders to go away, they already got what they want, the company broke the contract. "Then we won?" you can hear someone ask on video. "Sweet!" "Why?" "Because you guys are fucking nightmares and you broke all our fucking windows. So thank you." The forest defenders clap, confused behind the camera. "Protest works!" "That's great! I'm glad. We'll leave you alone."

The South River Watershed Alliance files another lawsuit against the Atlanta Police Foundation and the city, this time over pollution projected from the construction site. Bernice King, daughter of Martin Luther King Jr. and CEO of the King Center, publishes another open letter, still ambivalent about Cop City, but bravely in favor of the citywide vote. The Democratic National Committee selects Chicago instead of Atlanta as the site of the 2024 Convention, and local liberal politicians diplomatically bemoan the attention they won't get. The petition passes one hundred thousand signatures, and city officials announce their plan to scrutinize every line with signature-matching technology known to suppress votes.

Francis Ford Coppola finally wraps *Megalopolis* just south of Atlanta. *Jungle Cruise 2* will start shooting after Emily Blunt finishes a biopic of the first female Pinkerton. Ryan Millsap, apparently eternally impervious to irony, plans to inaugurate a new streaming service for action-adventure content: an underrepresented genre, he believes, showcasing American values "like self-reliance, self-determination, self-defense, and a ruggedly independent ability to survive and thrive." The lawsuit over the forty rubbled acres of Intrenchment Creek Park is still ongoing, and under a gag order—but you should hear some of the rumors we've heard swirling out of the courtroom.

Undergraduates occupy the quad at Emory University under a giant STOP COP CITY banner, screenprinting T-shirts and tote bags, and there is Magnolia, teaching a college student how to dice an onion. Some kid plays "The Times They Are A-Changin'" on an acoustic guitar, which makes us wonder if they ever will. Pandabear is home in Ohio with his parents, gardening, reading, waiting to see what will happen. Eliza finally quits their job at the Mexican restaurant, free at last to go rock climbing in Nevada to clear their head. They send us photos of desert sunsets like jigsaw-puzzle paintings. We call them, and they say they are already running out of money, but who isn't? We are in a moment of doubt again and need them to tell us about winning.

"Winning?" they ask. "Nothing more happens. The forest gets to stay the way it is. Well, no, that's not true. We clean up Intrenchment Creek to the point where we can swim in it. Shut down capitalism. Let the fruit trees we've planted grow into mature trees so we can eat of their fruit. We plant more food in the forest. Have it be a fully open public space abundant with coexistence, life of many species. We stop Cop City everywhere. Destroy all the surveillance cameras in the whole city. Abolish the police. Free all the prisoners."

"All the prisoners?"

"Mhm. Practice conflict resolution. Meet our neighbors. Plant more trees. Protect the trees that are already alive from English ivy and wisteria and other vines choking the life out of the old big trees."

"What if that's part of coexistence?"

"It is, but so is us protecting the trees."

"Why do the trees matter so much?"

Eliza pauses, thoughtful. "Because they're beautiful."

2023

ACKNOWLEDGMENTS

Special thanks to those who served on *n+1*'s editorial board between 2014 and 2024: Richard Beck, Carla Blumenkranz, Lisa Borst, Ari M. Brostoff, Laura Cremer, Moira Donegan, Tess Edmonson, Clare Fentress, Keith Gessen, Mark Greif, Elizabeth Gumport, Chad Harbach, Jane Hu, Emma Janaskie, Juliet Kleber, Benjamin Kunkel, Nicole Lipman, Rachel Ossip, Charles Petersen, Nausicaa Renner, Sarah Resnick, Elias Rodriques, Marco Roth, Namara Smith, Colin Vanderburg, and Emily Wang. Extra special thanks to Dani Oliver and Alan Dean, and to Dan O. Williams and Emily Votruba for sticking with us through the decades.

OUR CONTRIBUTORS

Alyssa Battistoni is a professor of political theory at Barnard College. Her book *Free Gifts: Capitalism and the Politics of Nature* is forthcoming from Princeton University Press in 2025.

Richard Beck is a senior writer at *n+1*. He is the author of *Homeland: The War on Terror in American Life* (2024) and *We Believe the Children: A Moral Panic in the 1980s* (2015).

Lisa Borst has been co-editor-in-chief of *n+1* since 2024.

Ari M. Brostoff is the author of *Missing Time* (n+1 Books) and a member of Writers Against the War on Gaza.

Andrea Long Chu is the author of *Females* and a critic at *New York* magazine. She received the Pulitzer Prize in Criticism in 2023.

Grace Glass is a pseudonym.

A. S. Hamrah is a writer, film critic, and documentary film producer, and the author of *The Earth Dies Streaming: Film Writing, 2002–2018* (n+1 Books).

Tobi Haslett has written about art, film, and literature for *n+1*, *Harper's*, and elsewhere.

Mark Krotov has been co-editor-in-chief of *n+1* since 2020.

Dawn Lundy Martin, poet and essayist, is Distinguished Writer in Residence at Bard College. She's the author of five books of poems and the forthcoming memoir *When a Person Goes Missing*, from Pantheon Books.

Jesse McCarthy is a professor of English and African & African American studies at Harvard University. His book *Who Will Pay Reparations on My Soul?* won the Whiting Award for Nonfiction in 2022.

Nicolás Medina Mora is a senior editor at *Revista Nexos*, a magazine of culture and politics published in Mexico City. His first novel, *América del Norte*, was published in May 2024.

Christina Nichol is the author of the novel *Waiting for the Electricity*. She teaches environmental studies at Sonoma State University and creative writing to high school students.

Francesco Pacifico is the author of five novels, including *The Boss*, which is forthcoming from McNally Editions in 2025.

Nausicaa Renner is a writer and a contributing editor at *n+1*.

Sarah Resnick is a writer living in New York. Her fiction has been awarded a Pushcart Prize and her nonfiction selected for *The Best American Essays*.

Nikil Saval is a Pennsylvania state senator and a former co-editor-in-chief of *n+1*.

Elizabeth Schambelan is a writer and editor living in New York. Her first book is forthcoming from Farrar, Straus and Giroux.

Bela Shayevich is a writer and translator from the Russian.

Christine Smallwood is the author of the novel *The Life of the Mind* and the nonfiction book *La Captive*.

Anthony Veasna So (1992–2020) was the author of the collections *Afterparties* and *Songs on Endless Repeat*.

Dayna Tortorici has been co-editor-in-chief of *n+1* since 2014.

Tony Tulathimutte is the author of *Private Citizens* and *Rejection*.

Sasha Tycko is an artist and anthropologist. She is completing a PhD in anthropology at Emory University in Atlanta.

Anna Wiener lives in San Francisco and is a contributing writer to the *New Yorker*. Her first book, *Uncanny Valley*, was published in 2020.

Gabriel Winant teaches history at the University of Chicago. His first book, *The Next Shift: The Fall of Industry and the Rise of Health Care in Rust Belt America*, was published in 2021.